Britain in Numbers

For Marjolaine and Roch, who prove that love cannot be measured

Britain in Numbers

Simon Briscoe

POLITICO'S

First published in Great Britain 2005
by Politico's Publishing, an imprint of
Methuen Publishing Limited
215 Vauxhall Bridge Road
London SW1V 1EJ

A catalogue record for this book is available from the British Library.

ISBN 1 84275 130 1
Printed and bound in Great Britain by St Edmundsbury Press, Suffolk

Contents

Introduction

This book uses statistics to paint a picture of Britain at the start of 2005. There has been an explosion of data yet despite seeing more and more figures being published every year, people are often no clearer about the important trends in our society. Political debate suffers, a democratic deficit opens up, and voters are left feeling disenfranchised. This is a shame, as the availability of good statistics, like any key facts, is of immense interest and value. Everyone feels on firmer ground if they have some compelling figures to support their case.

Statistics do not have a good reputation. Most people find them boring or are suspicious. "Lies, damned lies and statistics", they say, often justifiably so. Perhaps "Lies, damned lies, statistics, and politicians using statistics" would be a more suitable updated version.

Yet despite the problems, it is becoming increasingly hard for anyone interested in politics and public policy to avoid statistics. Statistics are only one of many sources of information relevant to policy making and sources of information are only one set of factors influencing policy, but it is hard to see many policies being launched and widely accepted if they fly in the face of statistical evidence.

This book presents figures from a wide variety of (mainly government) sources covering all the themes at the heart of the national political debate. Are taxes rising? Where is Britain on the asylum seekers league table? How fast are school standards improving? Read on for the answers. The book aims to pick out data that give meaningful messages. It sets out as good a version of the statistical truth as can be found anywhere and will be a useful and straightforward reference source. Importantly in an election year, it will help judge what real impact the Labour government's policies have had on the country. The book highlights some clear successes and failures.

But the book does more than set out the figures. It explains why the statistics used in political debate and the media are often not what they might first seem to be. It highlights the gaps in our knowledge where no figures are available and tricks used by politicians and others to show their policies in the best light. It also looks at the political interference in government statistics. Britain is not a dictatorship and the Cabinet does not sit around inventing numbers to launch on an unsuspecting population. But at a time when the importance of data is increasing due to target setting and the needs of evidence-based policy, statistics are subjected to too much political involvement, given they are a basic building block of democracy.

In a democratic society, the objectivity and openness of official statistics should be beyond reproach. Like all democratic ideals, this one is only imperfectly realised in the UK and many other Western democracies. The British government has only very rarely been accused of "fiddling the figures" and there are only a few examples of "gross misconduct".

The more general problem relates to less explicit "manipulation". The fear of manipulation, which is real and widespread, is simply a consequence of the fact that successive governments have felt it necessary to control the statistical service rather than allow it to be independent.Governments have always controlled the supply of statistics for fear of what widely available and impartial data might reveal.

In practice, government manipulation is subtle. It normally takes the form of a selective use of statistics – the government, like any other user of statistics, will try to camouflage reality if it is unfavourable – meddling with the timing and content of publications and determining, with little regard for outsiders, the priorities of a poorly funded statistical service. The over-egged presentation of statistics and the daily television and radio arguments between politicians about the interpretation of figures – coupled with some naivety and occasional ignorance of the facts – adds to the public's air of scepticism. The situation is compounded in some areas, notably that of health statistics, by a lack of data that many would view as shocking given the NHS budget will soon be £100 billion a year.

Good statistics could play a vital role in helping to rescue politics and the democratic process from the distrust and apathy that is currently dragging it down. But governments tend to be happy with the status quo as it gives them more power over the data – and thus the media and public opinion. The governing party, backed up by the resources of the executive, has little interest in having a level playing field when it comes to data availability. Why should they spend precious resources giving help to their opponents and exposing their own policies to scrutiny? But perhaps, we the taxpayers would be happy for better data – £1 per person each year would represent a 50% budget increase for the ONS. It is mainly left to the opposition parties to argue the cause. While the government is not directly responsible for many of the problems we have with official data, it is culpable of not putting in every effort to resolve those problems it could do something about.

Despite the adverse publicity that data often gets, Britain benefits from a rich supply of numbers. Many of them are of good quality. But as the civil service has become more politicised, the ancient art of bending the statistics has moved to a higher level. The crying shame is that with a little more honesty and a very little money, Britain could be really well served by its statistics – and be among the best in the world. Yet the publication of so many quantified targets means that the government has an incentive to keep its hands on the data that will judge their performance.

The statistics in this book are tasty snippets designed to encourage the reader to find out what is going on in the country. It will be a useful tool for anyone who does not trust a politician or journalist quoting statistics – surveys regularly show that government ministers and journalists are among the least trusted in our society.

The days of reliance on dull government compendia of data churned out belatedly and in a very dry fashion are thankfully gone. This book is full of sources – virtually all on the internet – for those looking for more detail and up to date information. Of course, while figures are valuable, they can be pressed too far and they cannot explain all of the relationships in an increasingly complex world. Even so, they paint a vivid picture of the state of Britain in 2005.

The statistics in the book reveal an exciting diversity and variety of life experiences. The country has a very complex make up which is at times shocking and yet invigorating. The book also highlights a number of trends that the government has kept quiet about.

This book would not have been possible a decade ago – the nation has never been measured quite as extensively as now. We have never before had the computing power to allow us to collect and analyse these numbers. And the internet makes them readily available and generally they are free. But the vast majority of the statistics churned out by government are of little use as no one knows where to find them – people are left looking for needles in haystacks. Often there are difficulties and frustrations in trying

"The statistician keeps his fingers on the pulse of humanity, and gives the necessary warning when things are not as they should be",
attributed to Adolphe Quetelet, 19th-century Belgian social statistician

"The right to information has become one of the most fundamental rights of the 20th-century citizen. In a society where information and the media play a considerable part, statisticians' actions help safeguard a fundamental human liberty,"
Lionel Jospin, former French Prime Minister

to find the right figures. Coupled with the fear that many people have about handling data, it has become easy for politicians to skew the presentation of figures, adding to our mistrust.

When the London Statistical Society was founded in the mid 19th century, one rule of conduct was to "exclude all opinions". Similarly, the ONS now aims to publish its figures in a neutral and objective way. This book is written in the same spirit but with an eye to pointing out any misleading impressions that might have been given by the way the government presents figures. In any case, as anyone reading the book will discover, interesting numbers inevitably give rise to interesting debate and strong feelings.

Pioneering French statisticians were among those who believed that counting things could abolish politics altogether and usher in a reign of facts. It wasn't true then, and it isn't true now but, as this book reveals, part of the current political debate is superfluous due to its weak factual foundations. It is a sensible target for the country to have robust, accessible, trusted and reliable figures on the key issues of the day within a decade. At that point political debate will be able to be focused towards those areas where it would be more valuable.

The book starts with a summary of the sort of problems encountered when dealing with official statistics data. That is followed by a chapter on government-set targets, which have become so important in the last few years, a brief history of official data and another setting out some thoughts on the politics of government statistics. The heart of the book follows with detailed data – and descriptions of the data – on a wide range of social and economic issues. The subjects chosen are important, topical, controversial and in the public eye. A glossary of statistical terms is at the end of the book.

Most of the data presented in this book are for full years. Corresponding figures are sometimes available on a monthly or quarterly basis. Generally we have shown data over the latest 10-year period, to set the government's performance in some context, though in some cases where data has not existed for that length of time we have had to show a shorter period. Where there is an opportunity and good reason we have shown a longer run of data.

Inevitably it is impossible to show all of the data relevant to each subject covered. We hope that the references given – many pointing to free resources on the internet – will be useful for those wanting to delve deeper into any topic. Much of the data used in this book comes from government sources but, perhaps surprisingly, there are many key areas of policy and of interest to voters and the media, where official figures are not available. In some cases the gaps have been plugged by think tanks, trade bodies, academics, local authorities and charities, thereby shedding some light on these important areas. The state of Britain is set in an international context where appropriate and possible, though international comparisons of data often give rise to major or insoluble statistical issues.

The book's publication cycle means that some of the data included will have been revised or updated by the time it is read. This unavoidable weakness is not a major problem as the trends of a decade will not have been reversed by a single piece of data. Indeed, if one lesson is important, it is that one new data point does mean a new trend has been established! Figures are presented in rounded terms for the sake of simplification, to isolate genuine trends and avoid any accusations of spurious accuracy.

We are now entering a new era so far as data is concerned. Every year more figures are published and they have become more important in the political debate, mainly through the setting of targets. This new world of data overload is unappealing to some but if you know where to go – and this book sets out the sources – and you are forewarned about risks in the figures, the new world is empowering. In any case, the statisticians are here and will not be going away.

Well over a hundred people have contributed facts, leads, explanations and inspiration during the writing of this book and I want to thank them all. As some did so on the grounds of anonymity, I feel it is only fair to name none. I thank the *Financial Times* for allowing me the opportunity to write this book and for all the help my colleagues have given, directly and indirectly. At Politico's, I am indebted to Sean Magee, who has shown so much interest and enthusiasm, and Emma Musgrave, whose extraordinary industry kept the project on schedule. John Schwartz has done a magnificent job in pulling the book together. I would like to thank Ray Thomas for the inspiration he has given me. And nothing would have been possible without the help and support of my wonderful parents and my dear, incomparable wife, Laure.

Readers are encouraged to send any comments, errors and omissions, or suggestions for future editions of this book, to:
britaininnumbers@simonbriscoe.com

"We cannot, with our own eyes and ears, perceive more than a minute sample of human affairs, even in our own country – and a very unrandom sample at that. So we rely on statistics in order to build and maintain our own model of the world. The data that are available mould our perceptions."
Dudley Seers, *The political economy of nationalism*

Did you know that ... ?

- Over one million cars are registered to disabled people
- The wealthiest 1% of adults own nearly one quarter of the wealth
- There are three abortions for every ten births
- Half the births in London are to mothers born out of the UK
- Over one billion passenger journeys were made on British railways in 2003/04
- More black people go to prison each year than to a British university
- 30% of Britain's children live in poverty and half of these live in single-parent families – only one in ten lived in poverty 15 years ago
- Half of the country's households have less than £1,500 in savings and half of those have nothing
- Around three out of four asylum seekers are refused asylum and only about one in six of those are recorded as leaving the country
- 100,000 English children have a teenage mother
- The nation produces enough solid waste to fill the Albert Hall every hour
- Over 1,000 people a year are injured as a result of "the troubles" in Northern Ireland
- One quarter of new prisoners are under 21 years of age
- Nearly 2000 new cases of sexually transmitted infections are diagnosed each day
- There are more children with special educational needs than there are attending private schools
- The UK has more credit cards in issue than any other European country
- The UK is near the top of the international league table for the number of under 13s who have been drunk
- British residents travel 750 billion kilometres in Britain each year – the equivalent of 200,000 journeys to the moon
- Three in ten people in the UK would be living in poverty – with Ireland, the highest rate in the EU – were it not for social benefits
- School children play truant for over 10 million half school days a year
- One in four children have seen their parents separate
- 22% of men and women are obese

- The poorest fifth of the population earns only one 40th of the income
- One in five 11–15 year olds took drugs last year
- One in 17 households has at least one vegetarian
- Nearly one in five people have parking restrictions outside their home
- Each person spends on average one hour a day travelling
- Male incomes peak at the age of 40 to 44 and have fallen by over one third by retirement
- There are fewer primary school teachers now than in 1997
- Alcohol misuse accounts for one in 26 NHS bed days and the loss of 17 million working days each year
- The rate of imprisonment for blacks is just over one per one hundred
- The pop ulation is taking on debt at the rate of £1 million every four minutes
- Three million adults do not have a bank or building society current account
- 3% of households are burgled each year and 10% of car owners experience vehicle theft
- The tax we pay to government each year is the equivalent of paying every penny we earn up to the end of May
- Complaints about train services are at a record low
- Workers in Britain clock up 900 million hours of work each week
- 600 jobs in manufacturing are lost each day
- In some local authorities, one in five working age men are receiving sickness benefits
- Nearly four out of every ten over 16 year olds are not in the labour market
- The UK equity market is one of the worst performing in developed countries since 1997
- Just how low the nutritional standards of school meals are
- Women are the victims of less than one in five instances of stranger violence
- Britain accounts for 40% of Europe's £500 billion credit market
- Next year's public sector spending on health will be in the upper half of comparable countries while private sector spending on health will be among the lowest

- Robbery is four times more common in urban areas than rural
- The incomes of the top fifth are roughly 15 times those of the lowest fifth but after taxes and benefits, they are only four times larger
- Sales of organic food have quadrupled since 1997
- At every age group except 16–24 year olds, more people move from urban to rural than vice versa – and four times as many move from the town to countryside than from north of the country to the south
- Since 1997, tobacco prices have risen by over 50% and clothing prices have fallen by 20%
- There are four motoring offences a year for every ten vehicles
- Homes are sold on average every 14 years
- The NHS is the world's third largest employer – after the Chinese army and the Indian Railways

Some trends the government does not highlight

Rich and poor
- The number of working age adults and pensioners in poverty is unchanged under Labour
- There has been next to no change in income distribution for a decade – the rich stay rich and the poor stay poor
- One million extra people compared with 1996/97 have inadequate pension provision
- The high proportion of the population depending on state benefits
- The number of homeless up since 1997
- The declining proportion of rural housing in the public sector
- The number of inactive working age people at record levels

Education
- The exaggeration of school standards improvements
- Rising truancy rate
- Fewer children are walking to school
- Record number of children at private schools

- The increased number of pupils per teacher in primary and secondary schools
- There are more children at grammar school than in 1997

Economic change
- Personal debt at record highs
- Government borrowing rising
- Mortgages are the largest ever
- Tax receipts as a share of the economy rising
- Public expenditure as a share of national output rising
- Council tax bills at record levels
- Poor equity and bond market returns
- Public sector debt is the highest since records began – in nominal terms
- Interest rate differentials with other countries are rising
- A deteriorating trade deficit
- Lack of private sector investment
- Falling international competitiveness
- Rising taxes on petrol
- Personal bankruptcies up

The cult of the car
- The number of households with a car and the number of cars per household are rising
- Motoring offences are on the up
- Deaths on the roads involving alcohol are becoming more common
- Roadside breath tests for drivers become less frequent
- Parking tickets are becoming more common
- More cars on our streets – up by 4½ million since 1997
- Travelling greater distances in Britain every year
- Fewer young people are taking the driving test
- The rising number of abandoned, untaxed or unregistered cars
- The number killed in police car chases is rising

Health, sickness and disability
- Rising numbers on sickness and disability benefits
- More people signed off work from stress and other mental disorders
- The declining trend in the number of hospital beds
- The increased prevalence of sexually transmitted diseases and HIVl
- Deaths of motorcyclists increasing
- People killed at work
- Child immunisation rates falling
- Poor diets
- We are walking less and driving more
- Abortions on the increase
- The number of homeless in temporary accommodation
- The increase in the homicide rate is among the highest in the world

The changing nation
- Immigration, and not natural change from births and deaths, is the main driver of population change
- The number with internet access has stabilised
- Immigration and people granted British citizenship are rising
- Non-expulsion of illegal immigrants
- Record level of inmates in prison
- Rising fear of crime
- The rise in the number of violent offences recorded by the police
- Petrol stations in the countryside replacing village shops
- Declining birth rate
- Births outside marriage on the up
- Record levels of household waste
- The number of civil servants rising
- The number of manufacturing workers falling
- The rise in alcohol and tobacco consumption with health, crime and family consequences
- More animals being used in scientific experiments

The state of Britain's statistics

There is no one single problem with the nation's statistics – we face a complicated cocktail of issues. Many problems could be resolved, but a culture change in government and the executive is required. We were promised a big clean-up of data after the 1997 election following the pledge to introduce an independent statistical service. But it is very slow in coming and its implementation is half-hearted. While there are many success stories of new and better statistics, the controlling instinct of government and a few highlighted problems with the statistics tarnish the good work and undermine public confidence, not only in the data but in the whole process of government.

The low level of public trust of government figures is in turn part of the wider problem of the general mistrust on the part of many people of all government information. But how great is the problem? Perhaps curiously given statisticians are so keen on surveys and collecting data, there is little hard evidence about what the public thinks of the numbers they are fed by the government. One survey, however, carried out in 2004 presented a far from rosy picture. It showed that the majority of people believe that official figures are changed to support particular arguments, are politically influenced in their production and that mistakes are suppressed. (see box overleaf for details)

The frustrating experience of the user trying to track down the appropriate figure for their needs is made all the worse by the apparently unshakeable confidence of most of the producers that they are doing a brilliant job. To quote the opening lines of the 2004 year book from Eurostat, the Luxembourg-based statistical office of the EU, "Eurostat is the synonym for the high-quality information service providing statistical data about, and for, the European Union. Using our data means having a finger on the pulse of current developments in Europe: we report the background figures and facts needed to understand these developments."

This was the introduction to a yearbook published in October 2004 when the latest data related to 2002 – hardly "on the pulse of current developments" – and famously had a map of Europe on the front cover that

Who trusts the figures?

Some figures about trust were collected and published by the Office for National Statistics in 2004 as part of its effort to improve confidence and trust in official data. They are trying to improve public confidence by demonstrating that their figures are produced to the best professional standards and are free from political interference – the brand "National Statistics" was established in 2000 as part of that drive. The ONS sees the survey as the start of the process as there was previously very little hard information about the level of trust. (source: www.statistics.gov.uk)

Respondents to the survey were asked to score their level of trust in six different data sets – for road casualties, exam passes, unemployment, burglaries, council performance and hospital waiting lists. The most trusted were road casualties as people felt they were easy to measure and that there was little advantage to be gained by the government in manipulating them. Hospital waiting list figures were the least trusted on the grounds of personal experience, having read "something bad" about the figures and not trusting the health department's presentation of the data.

Exam passes figures were thought to be accurate "but alone they do not tell the whole story". The unemployment and domestic burglaries figures were below average trust as they were deemed hard to measure and in the case of unemployment, there was the concern about the "politicians use and presentation of the figures". Six out ten people did not think that the government "uses official figures honestly" when talking about its policies, compared to one in seven who did feel that they were presented honestly. Six out of ten also thought there was political interference in their production compared to two out ten who did not. Seven out of ten thought mistakes were covered up. The main concern is about integrity rather than quality – slightly more people thought the figures were generally accurate than not.

The survey suggested that the scope for the statisticians to improve trust might be limited as those who have little faith in the numbers also have little faith in government institutions. Younger and older age groups were the more trusting. The survey also found that the word "statistics" was deemed "intimidating" by people, so the survey used the more acceptable "figures". And the Office for National Statistics – the source of many of the key statistics – had been heard of by only half of the respondents to the survey. The survey results, along with a survey of opinion formers and some research from other countries, was worked up into a report on public confidence and published in February 2005.

omitted Wales. It hardly inspires confidence. The ONS also engaged in similar overselling with regard to the 2001 population census – and yet a year after the release of the first data, revisions were being made to the estimates of the population of several areas including Manchester and London. Statisticians would earn more credit over time if they highlighted the limitations of the data, which most people could understand, instead of claiming too much for their outputs that sometimes have rather doubtful qualities.

The examples in this book will show how perceptions of our world and particular areas of government policy can be twisted by these problems. The remainder of this chapter summarises the many and varied types of problems with data. It is unclear how much of our current predicament is rooted in conspiracy and how much in cock-up. We will probably never know and, arguably, it does not matter. What is needed is parliament, government and the statisticians to work together for the common good. If ministers and statisticians spoke less about the "form filling burden" and more about the many uses of good data, it would be a start. As Len Cook, National Statistician, has said, investment is required in what he sees as an essential public infrastructure for the sake of the nation.

Britain's statistical infrastructure is improving and there are promising signs on the horizon that we will have better data in the years ahead. But it is also hard to know what our prevailing system should be judged against and how we can measure progress. It is clear that our ministers and the government's statisticians have some way to go if they are to be the whiter than white public servants we would all like. There seems to be little sense that the government is collecting data – from us! – about us for our collective benefit. Statisticians in most departments need to think more seriously about how users and potential users might want to access the figures.

One external benchmark is the set of basic principles for national statistical systems which has been set out by the United Nations. While mainly

Fundamental principles of statistics

At the end of the 1980s the countries of Central Europe began to change from centrally planned economies to market-oriented democracies. A few years later the Soviet Union was dissolved. Among the many changes that these developments generated was the need for complete transformation of the national statistical systems. Part of this transformation process was about redefining the role of official statistics, as well as making it clear to governments and other users of statistics that a good system of official statistics must meet certain general criteria. In order to get this message across, and to assist heads of national statistical offices to defend the position of their institutes, the Fundamental Principles of Official Statistics were developed by the UN, the world's highest statistical authority in 1994. (source: http://unstats.un.org)

There were several themes that drove the work of the Statistical Commission of the UN:

- that official statistical information is an essential basis for development in the economic, demographic, social and environmental fields and for mutual knowledge and trade among the states and peoples of the world
- that the essential trust of the public in official statistical information depends to a large extent on respect for the fundamental values and principles which are the basis of any society which seeks to understand itself and to respect the rights of its members, and
- that the quality of official statistics, and thus the quality of the information available to the government, the economy and the public, depends largely on the cooperation of citizens, enterprises, and other respondents in providing appropriate and reliable data needed for necessary statistical compilations and on the cooperation between users and producers of statistics in order to meet users' needs.

The ten principles are:

- Official statistics provide an indispensable element in the information system of a democratic society, serving the government, the economy and the public with data about the economic, demographic, social and environmental situation. To this end, official statistics that meet the test of practical utility are to be compiled and made available on an impartial basis by official statistical agencies to honour citizens' entitlement to public information.

- To retain trust in official statistics, the statistical agencies need to decide according to strictly professional considerations, including scientific principles and professional ethics, on the methods and procedures for the collection, processing, storage and presentation of statistical data.
- To facilitate a correct interpretation of the data, the statistical agencies are to present information according to scientific standards on the sources, methods and procedures of the statistics.
- The statistical agencies are entitled to comment on erroneous interpretation and misuse of statistics.
- Data for statistical purposes may be drawn from all types of sources, be they statistical surveys or administrative records. Statistical agencies are to choose the source with regard to quality, timeliness, costs and the burden on respondents.
- Individual data collected by statistical agencies for statistical compilation, whether they refer to natural or legal persons, are to be strictly confidential and used exclusively for statistical purposes.
- The laws, regulations and measures under which the statistical systems operate are to be made public.
- Coordination among statistical agencies within countries is essential to achieve consistency and efficiency in the statistical system.
- The use by statistical agencies in each country of international concepts, classifications and methods promotes the consistency and efficiency of statistical systems at all official levels.
- Bilateral and multilateral cooperation in statistics contributes to the improvement of systems of official statistics in all countries.

designed for emerging and developing countries, it helps to identify some areas of weakness with the UK system which falls foul of at least half of their ten principles. (see box.)

As the power of figures becomes more apparent and widely appreciated, demand for trustworthy, fairly presented data grows. "Spin" is less acceptable than just a few years ago. Opposition politicians now, as was the case with

Labour in the mid-1990s, are calling for greater openness on data, so with every change of government some incremental progress can be expected to be made. As more people become aware of the – still voluntary – codes of practice that do exist, the more blatant bad practices become fewer. In this sense, the Statistics Commission, an independent watchdog with a remit to "ensure that official statistics are trustworthy and responsive to public needs", has made a valuable contribution since it was launched in 2000.

No one can object to government using data to highlight its successes but it must do so fairly. It should not take advantage of weaknesses in the data to allow false impressions to be picked up and it must make available the data it has at its disposal to allow others to analyse the progress of policy for themselves. A more level playing field is required.

Twenty data issues have been isolated:

The mentality of deception

Politicians are probably more prone than people in many other walks of life to engage in a certain amount of deception or sleight of hand. The very nature of the combative, adversarial political process will push many of the players to – and occasionally beyond – what are seen by society as acceptable limits of behaviour. There is perhaps no better example than the political play in the run-up to and in the aftermath of the war in Iraq, revealed so fully in the Hutton and Butler reports. Statistics, which have become an important component of the political debate, are in their own way subjected to the same pressures and processes.

We do not need to look far for a good illustration of the art. The Labour Party's own website contains one of the most perfect examples of statistical manipulation, showing how close such dark skills are to the heart of power. The web site presents an Orwellian database which appears to show that the government has been successful in improving all aspects of the lives of everyone in Britain everywhere during its period in office. The data set is a fascinating lesson in the modern use of newly available data and demonstrates how sophisticated the manipulators are. (see box for details)

The precise definition of data matters

Concepts that seem simple and straightforward rarely are. A good example for understanding this is to ask how many people are attending a seminar.

continued on page 10

"Things can only get better" – a case study in data manipulation

This song was the theme tune for the Labour Party in the 1997 general election. A kind interpretation of this choice of music would be that it simply reflected the Labour Party's enthusiasm to do a good job. From a statistical point of view, however, the definition of "a good job" led to the presentation of a remarkable database showing that the government had been successful in improving all aspects of the lives of everyone in Britain everywhere, all of the time.

The evidence is drawn directly from the statistics on "What Labour's done in your constituency" made available on the Labour party web site. (At the time of the 2001 election, the website was www.labourparty.org. It is now www.labour.org.uk and the data can be found by clicking on "making life better" and then "in your area".) In essence, the methods that Labour adopted meant that a picture of general, but modest and variable, social improvement was transformed into a picture of universal improvement. The web site contains thousands upon thousands of apparently relevant performance indicators, every one of which the party can claim illustrates the success of its policies. In fact the database is the result of a certain amount of sleight of hand designed to provide a somewhat distorted picture of the local geography of Britain. (source: "A good place to bury bad news? Hiding the detail in the geography on the Labour Party's web site", *Political Quarterly* 73, 2002)

In the months leading up to the 2001 general election the Labour Party's web site included certain statistical indicators for each of the 641 parliamentary constituencies in England, Wales and Scotland. The constituency profiles were designed to indicate how conditions have improved in each local area after four years of Labour. If they had not improved, then the data being shown was changed, to make them improve. The profiles of each constituency were arranged in several categories – for example, economic stability, families and children, pensioners, schools standards, crime and rebuilding the NHS – and each category contained a number of indicators, up to 28 in total. For example, under the crime category, data included the increase in police force numbers and the percentage fall in crime since 1997.

It is extremely unlikely that the many thousands of indicators improved for all constituencies. However, the Labour Party reported the figures in such a way as to make it appear that they did. For example, if an indicator had not improved for the default, common timescale than the timescale was changed for that constituency to one in which conditions had improved. Indicators are also reported on different spatial scales – if conditions had not improved at the constituency level, for example, then a larger scale – such as the region – was deployed at which things had improved.

In the case of crime figures, for example, one third of constituencies had indicators given in terms of averages for the whole of England and Wales, not by police force area, if those constituencies were in areas where crime had increased. Crime fell in England and Wales overall, but in only two thirds of police force areas. Thus, on this web site, crime had fallen under Labour everywhere and police numbers had similarly risen everywhere, even though to show this both the spatial and temporal scale had to be altered to ensure universal improvement.

The figures for the number of people receiving unemployment benefit are reported in nearly every case at the constituency level. The exceptions (at the time of the 2001 election) were a small number of constituencies such as Bosworth and Stoke-on-Trent South, where the figure for the region was published, as unemployment in those constituencies had risen. Similarly, the figures for hospital waiting lists were health authority specific for all constituencies (as constituency level data do not exist) but the data were based on two alternative time periods: the decrease in waiting lists was reported since either 1997 or 1998 depending on which provided the better picture. The figures showing the increase in nurses employed in the NHS were generally presented at health authority level. But for nearly one third of the constituencies in England, the numbers were presented by region (a larger spatial unit). Between 1997 and 2001, the number of nurses increased across all regions but not across all health authorities within some of them.

Some geographical statistics are only available at scales above that of the constituency and Labour should not be criticised for reporting these at higher scales. For instance, literacy estimates are only available for whole local education authorities so it is right that Labour reports that at that scale. But when figures are reported at a mix of scales in such a way as to produce a better picture – or where they could be produced at a lower scale and have not been – there is a clear accusation of manipulation.

In the case of a few indicators – such as the average decrease in mortgage payments and the increase in average school spending per pupil – figures were reported only at the national scale for every constituency. In some cases the Labour Party could have done more with the data to further their cause. For example, taking no account of variations in the size of mortgages by constituency or the number of households with a mortgage in each constituency makes the use of this national average of little value in most local settings. Had the figure been broken down, Labour might well have found that the greatest benefit had been in seats where they needed most extra votes – typical New Labour areas where house prices were generally higher and where a higher proportion of the population has a mortgage.

Any election candidates, party agents, activists or voters logging on for information for their constituency was not aware of the sleight of hand that had taken place. They would merely download the "sanitised" data for that constituency and were bound to get "good news". Bad news was not censored but rather manipulated through changing scales to translate it into good news. Nothing presented on the Labour Party web site is untrue in the strict sense of the word. It is just that the way in which the statistics have been put together – mixing and matching years and areas to present the best possible picture of improvement – is disingenuous overall. Once such practices start, where do they stop?

It seems unlikely that the manipulation of a few figures in a few places is a sustainable strategy for long-term reporting of political achievements. At some point mortgage rates will rise – do you then remove those statistics from the web site or continue to compare but with different dates? What happens when unemployment is not continuing to fall in most places most of the time? The steps required to make it appear that every constituency had seen an improvement in every indicator will become more convoluted overtime. Perhaps there would be a greater level of trust if the party could have admitted that just one thing, in one place, at one time had not got better – 15,000 to 20,000 indicators all getting better is just too hard to believe.

For the number of chairs required it is the maximum number present at any one time, for catering it is the number wanting to eat, for reporting it will be all those who show up, for accounting it may include no-shows who still get billed. All responses are perfectly legitimate but all can give a different number! It is important that all users know what lies behind the figures they use and it is vital that the producers make it clear what the data really are and where they come from. One analogy is the labeling of food – supermarkets cannot be held responsible for what consumers do with their food but they can be expected to ensure that it is edible and properly labeled.

This problem is very real for many statistics describing our society as few aspects of it are black and white. Someone's height is unambiguous but his or her employment status will often be quite unclear. "Unemployment" seems simple and most people have a sense of what it means, but when you ask for an unemployment statistic, life gets trickier. Do you want a figure for the number of people claiming unemployment benefit or the number of working age adults who are not working – or perhaps the proportion of those who are actively seeking work? And how active does the work seeking have to be to count and what about someone doing a few hours casual work a week who wants to work full-time? How many hours of work in a week counts as employment? The International Labour Office, which sets these definitions, thinks that one hour of work makes someone employed but many school children doing some babysitting would hardly see themselves as employed. Do you count people on government training schemes, and what about those caring for a relative or doing voluntary work? Does someone who is off work this week but starting a new job next week count as unemployed or employed? Users need to be guided.

It is a fact of life that the perfect data set for any given situation often does not exist so it is necessary to make do with something less than perfect. This inevitably means that users are forever engaged in a process of compromise, as a result of which the unaware can draw misleading conclusions. For example, the figures for the number of people coming to local authorities asking for accommodation double up – inadequately – as an estimate of homelessness.

The difficulties of international comparisons

The problems encountered when making comparisons between statistics within one country are magnified when comparing figures between countries. Statistics, which on the face of it, seem to be identical, often turn out to be quite different. For example, consumer price indices (even in Europe where comparisons are made using a so-called harmonised index of consumer prices) include different products, relate to different time periods, have different sample sizes and structures etc. As administrative systems are invariably different in different countries, data derived from them, such as recorded crime figures, will nearly always be on a different basis. Even data from specifically constructed questionnaires can elicit different responses in different countries. Employment surveys, for example, have to struggle with a different view of what constitutes work in different countries where family and business structures can be very different.

The nature of data from administrative systems

Often data come from surveys (or censuses) conducted by government but in an increasing number of areas figures are being produced as a by-product of administrative systems which are now available on a greater scale and far more accurate than a few years ago. Data from administrative systems have several potential advantages: they are cheap to produce with a reduced compliance burden for people and business, available for small areas, can be produced more frequently and in a more timely fashion, and may be linked to other databases. Also, subject to certain quality issues, they can be more accurate.

But the figures come with a different range of problems and caveats than statistics derived from surveys: categorisations used in administrations are rarely the ones desired for a wider statistical use, there could be less "richness" of data (such as class, income or ethnicity), and it is impossible to make definitive statements about accuracy in the absence of statistical confidence intervals that can be derived from survey data. Sometimes administrative systems are not comprehensive – a database of tax payers will not be representative of society at large as it will exclude non-tax payers, for example. The making of data linkages between databases is

Using administrative systems to define social states is not new – in the second half of the 1800s, the poor or the numbers in "pauperism", were defined as those receiving assistance through the application of the Poor Law

attractive in theory but often constrained in practice, as legislation may be needed. There is also real public anxiety about the use of administrative data.

Some people worry that the influence of the administrative data will be negative in the sense that its structure tends to confirm existing world views and existing policies. Accordingly, in the face of the greater use of administrative data, users – and the producers – must ensure that neutral data is also produced so that the public's view of the world does not become too based on the structure of the machinery of government. The section on health data offers up perfect examples – there is a difference between measuring how people interact with and benefit from health professionals and measuring the through put of the NHS. And only the latter is readily available.

The New Deal gives us a very good example. The government is very keen to remind us at every opportunity that the scheme for young people has effectively eradicated long-term youth unemployment. But armed with a clearer understanding of what the New Deal actually requires of young people and how long-term unemployment is defined, leads to the conclusion that the official figures have next to no value. In effect, the terms and conditions of the New Deal have been skilfully crafted in such a way that the scheme has effectively made it impossible for a person under 25 to be long-term unemployed. Hence, so far as the record book shows, the problem of long-term youth unemployment has disappeared under Labour. This could be a statistical deception on a par with the Conservative tweaking of the unemployment numbers in the 1980s.

The shift to resource accounting in the late 1990s means that detailed public expenditure data from prior to the switch are not comparable to the current figures.

Deliberate distortion of administrative data

As management systems of public sector bodies become increasingly computerised and sophisticated, more of the data that falls out of such systems is being brought into the public domain and used in the target setting and monitoring process. The chapter on targets lists many examples where the desire of public servants to meet targets has led to a certain degree of corruption of this administrative data. Some of the examples which have come to light include the removal of wheels from hospital trolleys – to convert a trolley into a bed – so that an increased proportion of patients can be admitted earlier and certain practices to reduce hospital waiting lists and improve the response times of ambulances. It is important to think who is collecting the data and what they might have to gain by distorting it. Is any such action centrally controlled or is it just the result of the initiative of people in local areas making subtle changes for fear of what might happen if their department is at the bottom of a league table?

The problem is not new. For many years unemployment was defined as the number of people receiving unemployment benefits but changes, especially in the 1980s, to the eligibility rules reduced the number on benefits, thereby corrupting the figures as a measure of unemployment. During the 1990s, an estimate of unemployment from the Labour Force Survey became more readily available and, as the surveys were conducted more frequently and the results published more swiftly, it became the preferred measure. The LFS has flaws but it is not corrupted by administrative whim.

Shifting targets

It becomes very difficult to have faith in the system of target monitoring established by the government if the targets are frequently shifting. One of the fundamental weaknesses of the target regime when it was launched in earnest in 1998 was that no data was available to set the benchmark for a number of the targets and to monitor progress being made. As time has passed, plenty of targets have been abandoned and many others have changed in their precise definition, with a knock-on effect on the availability or otherwise of trustworthy data for the monitoring process.

The subtle change in a target from a mean to a median, for example, would not be noticed by most people, but when it is noticed, there is a suspicion that the minister is up to no good. The government's target for a reduction in childhood poverty is one example. Originally childhood poverty related to the number of children living in households where the income was less than 60% of the mean earnings in the economy. This shifted to become median earnings including housing costs, and then excluding them. A recent report suggested that a more holistic basket of indicators would be used to measure poverty going forward. Does such shifting do the system any good?

At the latest count the Office for National Statistics says that only roughly one third of targets are monitored against figures which have met the National Statistics quality benchmark. Ministers can hardly be surprised if the public is confused or cynical when they are launching initiatives when they know there is no quality, audited data to judge whether it has been a success. The pledges set out by Labour in February 2005 in advance of the general election were so broad and bland as to be unmeasurable.

There is also much shifting of definitions going on for data which are not formal targets. Chancellors now present public expenditure as a proportion of GDP at market prices rather than factor cost as it delivers a lower figure. Gordon Brown now presents the tax burden as a proportion of national income on what he calls a "net" basis. This includes a number of "accounting adjustments", notably tax credits that have risen sharply under his chancellorship. Statisticians, both in the UK and international bodies, treat tax credits as public expenditure, like other social benefits, and not, as the Treasury, as negative taxation. The impact of the Chancellor's decision is to show a flatter path for the tax burden since the introduction of tax credits in 1998.

The system of targeting has not only increased pressure on the public servants responsible for delivering services, it has also increased pressure on ministers. Several have said quite explicitly that they are happy to be judged by whether a target is met or not. There have been several resignations where the failure to hit targets has played a part, but in other cases ministers have ignored the original pledge, willingly changing the target, or hoped that a reshuffle would come along before the date on which some important target was due to be delivered.

Political control of National Statistics

While the individual number crunchers in government are widely seen as impartial and scrupulous in their honesty and attention to detail, that does not mean that the eventual fruits of their efforts are not politically influenced. Statisticians working in the Office for National Statistics, the powerhouse of the British statistical system, have day to day freedoms to do the best job possible, yet the organisation reports to the Chancellor and depends on his goodwill for funding. This link might distort the priorities of the senior statisticians and the work programme of the office. The threat is perceived to have increased in recent years with the arrival of three senior Treasury civil servants at the ONS.

The close links between the Treasury and increasingly the Bank of England have tended to mean that the ONS has focused particularly on improving economic rather than social data in the last decade or more. It also means that the Treasury is unique among government departments at being able to get work done that it requires. The last couple of years have seen two good examples: the Allsopp report into the data needs of regional policy making and the Atkinson review of the measurement of public sector output both came on the ONS with little warning. The origin of the Allsopp review was clear – Treasury command. That is not to say it was not worth doing – it is a valuable and high quality piece of work but it is not one that the ONS was expecting to do.

The story on Atkinson and public sector productivity is much less clear. In the summer of 2004, after months of political and public comment that the large injections of spending into the health service did not seem to be delivering extra outputs visible in the main data aggregates, the Office for National Statistics published out of the blue new figures for health service output. These had the effect of doubling the rise in health sector output over the previous six years. It seemed strange to many observers that there was so little forewarning about such a large change when normally much smaller changes are thoroughly publicised. While it was perfectly clear that improvements in measurement were required, the management of them and the political nature of change was suspicious. A few months before, there were rumours that Len Cook had been called in to see the Prime Minister and Chancellor to explain why the national accounts apparently failed to take account of the public funds that been injected.

The new data were said to be linked to the Atkinson report but work on them must have been done in parallel and probably started before – the first, interim Atkinson report was published after the new data. The main point is that both pieces of work required plenty of effort within the ONS that was not foreseen in its published work programmes. This inevitably means that other work that was planned has not been done. Again this was good example of the lack of medium term planning and coordination of all the much needed work in the field of government statistics.

Norway – an example of statisticians' freedom from politicians
The Norwegian statistical office publishes at least one statistical report on a political issue such as the economy, poverty, migration, education and the environment, every day in the run up to each election. In contrast, the ONS is not allowed to publish anything except standard releases whose publication date had been previously announced. According to Norway's chief statistician, the statistics series was set up because of the belief "that official statistics can contribute to election debates as they are based on sound facts" and "democracy works best when there is agreement on some basic facts about society". The Norwegians say that public debate should be about goals and the measures required to achieve them and not about statistical foundations. The chief statisticians says, "If our statistics are not useful when people are making their most crucial decisions as citizens, when are they?" (source: *Significance*, the magazine of the Royal Statistical Society, June 2004)

There is also a concern that it is ministers who decide which statistics should be classified as "National Statistics". Most people would expect that this branding, which is meant to be some mark of quality, would only apply to data that statisticians had checked as reaching some appropriate standard. But no, it is ministers who choose whether each pieced of data from their departments should be a National Statistic or not.

The Chancellor has also – bizarrely – decided to retain control over the key inflation figures, the retail prices index, which are not a National Statistic. The Treasury's argument for doing so is essentially that they are too important – as they are used to uprate pensions, social benefits and many savings products each year – to be left to the statisticians! Most people would take the opposite view, that the more important the figure is the less appropriate it is for politicians to be controlling it. There is no evidence whatsoever that the Chancellor or his Treasury officials in any way get involved with the production of the figures from month-to-month. But when there are changes to the methodology, such as the introduction of hedonics, a new way of measuring quality change, in early 2004, many people feel that the statisticians need total independence to ensure that they choose the best route statistically. This change, which had the happy consequence of reducing the inflation rate thereby saving the Treasury millions of pounds a year in payments (for index-linked benefits and savings products) and taxes (by up rating allowances by less), was also released without warning. (See the inflation chapter (44) for further details.)

The chain of political control in the Treasury is somewhat obscure. The Chancellor is formally the minister responsible but he seems to delegate responsibility to either the Financial or Economic Secretary (two of his junior ministers). Sadly, as the people in these posts change so frequently – there has been nearly one minister a year since 1997 – they do not have too long to become acquainted with the subject matter.

There is no measure of quality

It is almost impossible for any user of official data to know how good quality the figures really are. There is in principle the basic distinction between those figures classified as "National Statistics" and those that are not. But the distinction is far from perfect – there are many reasons other than quality that can explain why a figure is not part of National Statistics, and likewise there are some National Statistics that are of more doubtful quality than others. There was a hope before National Statistics was established that it would be a more rigorous quality benchmark than it has turned out to be.

There are examples in the book of important data being of a very low standard. Perhaps the most damning of reports was that from the Pensions Commission in October 2004. It said that some of the data had "exceptionally severe" problems and "significant" problems, The problems are now being addressed but it seems that it always takes a crisis to get any improvement.

At the better end of the spectrum of figures pumped out by the public sector are those among the best in the world. At the other extreme, figures cobbled together from a management system, without any recognised quality checking, and without the involvement of a statistician, can be press released by the government department and enter the public arena. It is a shame that many of the figures used by the government in key areas – such as health – are of questionable quality that cannot be verified.

There is even a question mark over the quality checking process of data labelled National Statistics. Each department's web site sets out the

Data quality

Not all data are of the same quality. Accordingly, it is appropriate to give greater weight to trends reported in data of higher quality. The key points to look for are features such as the size of the survey, revisions policy, timeliness and seasonal adjustment. Data from a small survey, which are subject to large revision and fail to adjust for seasonal factors, for example, will generally be less reliable, and will certainly be less keenly followed if they are published some months after the relevant time period. Regarding the collection of data, it is interesting to know which items were collected and how. How were the data coded and classified? How were they tabulated and analysed? Is data available that has not been published? What was not collected and why? Have definitions or collection methods recently changed?

There are many examples of how improvements in data quality have led to increased attention being paid to the numbers. The Labour Force Survey, for example, was annual and published nearly two years in arrears at the start of the 1990s. Now it is published quarterly soon after the end of the reference period and accordingly receives much more attention.

Unfortunately it is becoming harder to get good statistics, just as more importance is being attached to them. The main reasons for this include deregulation of economic activity; the desire to minimise the burden of form filling on companies and organisations; economic and financial innovation (making it harder to measure activity); the expansion of e-commerce; increased international trade; and the blurring of the boundary between public and private sectors. All of these developments cast doubts over the meaning, accuracy and worth of some of the related indicators, but perhaps most important is the increasing reluctance of people to fill in forms. As the response rate of surveys falls, their accuracy especially with regard to minority or hard to count groups becomes increasingly debatable.

There are, nonetheless, some benefits from technical change and modernisation for statisticians. They are, for example, likely to have increased access to the ever-expanding number of databases, containing all sorts of information.

programme of quality reviews which, over a period of five years, are meant to cover all data so branded. As National Statistics was established in 2000, all data falling under its umbrella should have been reviewed by this year. Yet it is clear from a glance at the web sites that large chunks of the data have not yet been reviewed and are unlikely to be in the years ahead. The National Statistics annual report admits that only about half of the planned 120 reviews, in turn covering only part of the statistical output, will be conducted in the first five years. Most people, most of the time, will simply have to take the figures at face value and hope that they are of sufficient quality for the purpose required.

Poor quality data is accepted

It seems that ministers and senior officials in many policy departments are happy to carry on with poor quality data. After all, new data might make their lives harder – and in any case is unlikely to come on stream during their tenure at a department. One example concerns the fall in recorded unemployment and the rise in numbers on sickness benefits. Many external researchers say that there is an element of "hidden unemployment" in the rise in numbers on benefits but the government strongly denies it without making the effort to get appropriate data to analyse the situation. Indeed, the relevant chapter in the book quotes from a draft civil service report on the topic that was never released, presumably because of the conclusion it drew.

The example of the apparent "grade inflation" in the Key Stage (KS1, 2 and 3) exam results is a case in point. A later chapter explains that some studies have suggested that between one-third and two-thirds of the improvement seen in recent years is illusory. But the issue has not been tackled as it suits everyone's case – parents, teachers, unions, ministers – to see "improving standards". It might not be in the best interests of the children but they don't have a voice. There are systems for measuring quality change, such as having a bank of standard questions from which a selection can be made each year, that would give a better measure over time. Similarly, some schools seem over willing to "authorise" pupil absence which means that the unauthorised rate of absence – truancy – is kept low in the statistics.

The failure of the Treasury and ONS to publish timely public expenditure forecasts and data on a consistent basis so that they can be compared

Two conflicting statistics

The government machine does not help itself. There are many instances itemised in the book – from the use of childcare to the number of second homes, for example – where the government statistics machine produces two estimates, from different sources, of ostensibly the same variable. More could be done to explain the differences which might be quite valid but look daft to a non-expert who simply wants a number. It is no wonder that journalists and others choose the measure that suits!

is a frustration. And ministers are unwilling to measure the scale of the illegal or non-observed part of the economy as it is a controversial area – if everyone knew how large it was there might be demands for government action.

Leaking and spinning

Leaking and spinning are among the oldest forms of government manipulation even if it has come to the fore under the current government with the "burying bad news" saga after September 2001 and the subsequent Phillis review of government communications. Statistics are leaked and spun like any other piece of information.

But it is made easier for ministers and their senior officials as they have access to data up to three days prior to its release. They say they need this pre-release access in order to be well briefed when the data are released so that they can respond to any questions they might be asked. Unfortunately some ministers and officials occasionally find the temptation to leak the data irresistible. The 2004 annual report of the Statistics Commission listed a number of instances during the previous year when it appeared that the data had been leaked and expressed its dissatisfaction with the practice. Both the commission and the National Statistician would like to see an end to pre-release access but they are powerless to bring this about unless ministers agree.

Leaking is rare and generally very subtle in its form. Press releases and statistical compendia are not photocopied and widely dispatched around all news outlets! Normally someone in a government department – a press officer or special adviser – will have a quiet word with a favoured journalist

How are the data released?

In the UK most of the important indicators are released by means of press notices and most are published on the internet (www.statistics.gov.uk). A calendar of forward release dates covering most of the data is also regularly published. Most people never see these press notices, and have to rely on the incomplete and selective versions of them which are released on wire services, internet, radio and television, and in the next day's newspapers. Others buy the information in a variety of government statistical publications. In the early 1990s, there was a considerable tightening of the security surrounding the release of official data and most are now published at 9:30am. The strict embargo is meant to ensure that no one gets an unfair advantage, in the financial markets in particular, by seeing the information early. A small number of people (mainly government ministers and senior officials – the list is available from the ONS) see the data a day or two prior to its release. Accordingly, although information from official economic releases seldom leaks out of Whitehall in advance, there remain a small number of instances each year when ministers are suspected of leaking, usually with the desire to soften the blow of bad news, or data are released by accident. Statements from the government often accompany the release of the important data. These "political" press releases are meant to be distinct from the "neutral" statistical releases, but are often confused in the eyes and minds of readers.

attached to a prestigious radio or television programme or newspaper. The advantage to the government of leaking a few key numbers is clear as it allows them to set the news agenda by selecting carefully the numbers and the story to go with it.

In September 2004, for example, a morning radio programme ran a feature about the use of animals in scientific testing. As explained in the programme, the figures for the number of animals involved in scientific tests were to rise when published later in the day in contrast to the fall that the government had promised. The department was able to get the government's excuses and explanation in early, setting the agenda for the story. The National Statistician says he follows up every suspected case of leaking (though the investigations are not published) – and the Statistics

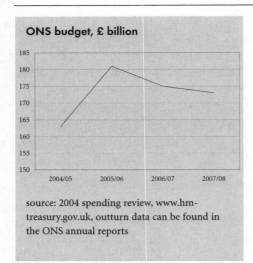

ONS budget, £ billion

185
180
175
170
165
160
155
150

2004/05   2005/06   2006/07   2007/08

source: 2004 spending review, www.hm-treasury.gov.uk, outturn data can be found in the ONS annual reports

Commission has followed some too – but no department has ever admitted the practice and by its nature it is almost impossible to prove even if the evidence is compelling. Sometimes the leak might be accidental but it would not be possible if there was no early access. Many other countries give their ministers no, or much shorter periods of, access.

Funding constraints

Funding constraints and political control are inextricably linked. When government wants to move rapidly it can, regardless of the existing pressures government statisticians find themselves under. A recent example is the politically important Allsopp Review, which was carried out very swiftly and the many and complex recommendations look set to be funded by the Treasury.

In contrast, where government decides it does not want to move quickly it effectively grinds to a halt. For example, on the issue of animals used in scientific tests, most people would like to know either how many animals die in the testing process or what their suffering is. The current data – and only available data – show instead the number of animals in the latest year that have been used for animal experiments for the first time. Pressure groups have been dissatisfied with the existing data for many years but it was only under pressure from a House of Lords committee report that the Home Office announced a review of the statistics. The review was announced in the summer of 2003 and yet by early 2005 there was still no response. If there was a real desire within government to have proper data surely the recommendations would have been produced more quickly and they too would have been funded.

The haphazard nature of the funding process is evident from the fact that in periods of general austerity there can be funding for pet projects in some departments. Even when the CSO was being starved in the 1980s, some new projects in other departments went ahead. Priorities can be slow to change too – the detail of information gathered by the EU on agriculture in relation to the negligible amount information about the service sector shows how it is still working in a previous generation.

The funding of the government statistics machine is far from transparent. Figures for the ONS budget are available after each two-yearly Treasury spending review (the latest was in summer of 2004, www.hm-treasury.gov.uk). Planned spending figures for the other half of the statistical machine, working in government departments, are not separately identified and are therefore unknown. Outturn data for spending in other departments on some aspects of National Statistics are presented in the "National Statistics" annual report. Adjustments to any totals as a result of management consultant reviews or new government-led initiatives are never spelt out clearly.

Presentation of data

A politician, like anyone else, naturally presents data in the best possible light. The ONS philosophy is different – they aim for a presentation that is neutral and objective. Generally the ONS is fine but many people would expect civil servants presenting statistical releases in other departments to be more frank in their presentation.

Sadly this rarely seems to be so, making it important for users to be aware of all the normal "tricks of the trade" such as presenting data in crude numbers, as percentages, or rates of one sort or another, so that they look more dramatic or less dramatic as required. On the issue of health service staffing we might expect the government to choose the headcount or full time equivalent measure according to which is showing the best trend but both measures should be available for all to access.

Trends in data over time can also be made to look more favourable by choosing an appropriate starting point for a comparison being made. None of this is untoward but sometimes the claims made stretch the reality a little too far. And as a large proportion of the population has a low-level of practical numeracy, the electorate is a soft target for a skilful presenter of data.

The charts below show the power of skilful presentation. The first two are lifted directly from goverment publications and give a strong impression of falling hospital waiting lists and policy success in England. The third chart suggests the improvement has been more modest, even though the very long waits have been eradicated. The fourth chart, plotting data over a 15-year period, shows that the apparently dramatic changes over the last few years do little more than return the waiting lists to where they were a decade ago.

Users must feel happy that a statistic is plausible – it has been said that a statistic that shocks is probably wrong. But asking questions such as: where the data came from, who produced it, why they produced it, and what is their agenda, are useful habits.

An impressive number?
The government might say that only around 1% of secondary school sessions are missed without authorisation. The opposition might say that 150 million school sessions are missed in schools each year. Both are true. Presentation matters.

1. 6-month inpatient waits

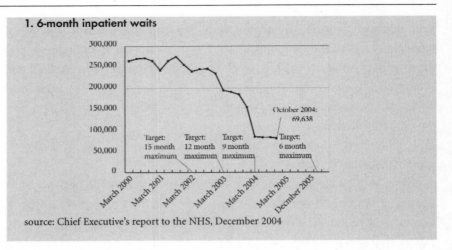

source: Chief Executive's report to the NHS, December 2004

2. Total inpatient waiting list from 2002

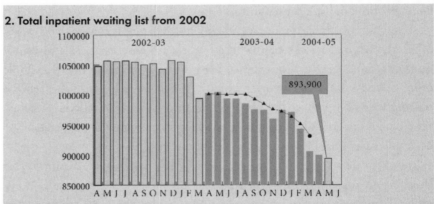

source: Department of Health, Prime Minster's press conference, "Delivery Update 2004", July 2004

3. Total inpatient waiting list from 1999

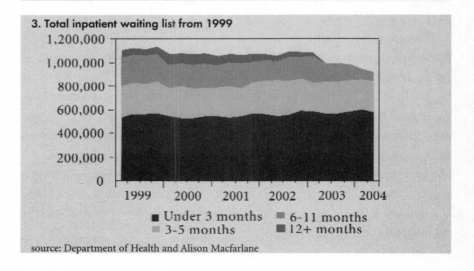

source: Department of Health and Alison Macfarlane

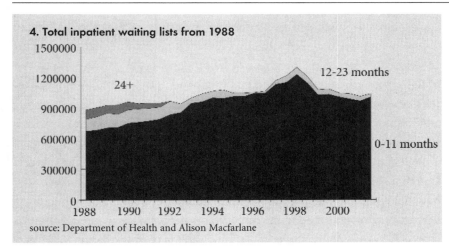

4. Total inpatient waiting lists from 1988

source: Department of Health and Alison Macfarlane

Most politicians love quoting figures. It suggests they have grasped the detail of policy and they come over hard-nosed and unanswerable. But their use of numbers is often counterproductive. As the old saying goes, politicians use the figures for "support rather than illumination".

Certain patterns in the use of statistics and targets become evident between different ministries and branches of government. Some appear to be relatively naive and unsophisticated, while others appear to be fully aware of the advantages of manipulation. Frank Field, a minister in the first term of the Labour government, spoke for many when he said in a television interview in 2004 that "what most people dislike about new Labour is the dissembling of truth".

Trebling up?

Sometimes presentation is plain exaggerated – presumably with the intention of influencing opinions. In the public spending review of 1998, the Chancellor announced that spending on education, for example, would be rising by £19 billion. Close examination of the figures showed that what he meant was that the level would be rising by £3 billion in the coming year and additional amounts of £3 billion and £4 billion in the two following years. The sum of these three increases – £3 billion, £6 billion and £10 billion – being £19 billion. This unusual way of presenting public expenditure increases – which did not represent particularly high real terms increases going forward compared to the past – probably contributed to the setting of (too) high expectations that voters had of improvements in public service.

Lumpy data

Many series are naturally lumpy from time period to time period. The deaths of cockle harvesters in Morcombe Bay has affected the figures for deaths at work and the allocation of most of the Shipman murders to one year are examples of how blips must be understood and discounted.

Lloyd George is said to have remarked during the First World War that his civil servants kept three sets of casualty figures, one to delude the Cabinet, one to delude the public and one to delude themselves. Has much changed?

The most sophisticated user of data – reflecting in part the data-heavy nature of his ministry – is the Chancellor. He is more prone than many of his colleagues to blackening the image of his predecessors by the selective choice of data and a crude representation of past trends. He sometimes exaggerates the negative impact of external forces for weaknesses in the British economy and has rarely acknowledged that other countries have had a greater success in terms of, say, faster growth of output, exports, or employment.

Politicians rarely lie but their sound bites effectively convey the impression that something is when it isn't. We might be told that personal tax rates have not risen but that does not mean that most people are not paying more personal tax or that the total tax burden on people has not risen. Britain is currently experiencing a period of historically very low inflation and long-term interest rates, but we will have to wait a long time for the government to give us an honest assessment of how much is due to their policies, global influences or the policies of their predecessors. Has a minister ever launched the latest data showing a rise in employment and said it is in line with the trend in other industrialised countries? No! Good figures are always due to their intervention.

Some of the Chancellor's claims are over-egged. A good example is the claim – now converted into an election street poster – that it is 200 years since the UK last had a 12-year sustained period of growth. Unfortunately, anyone looking at annual data will find the period is somewhat less than two hundred years. There was a fifteen-year period from 1959 when the annual figures showed no fall. But the claim is based on quarterly data and there were some quarters in the 1960s when output did not grow. Did the quarterly falls matter? Probably not. No one recalls the Swinging Sixties grinding to a halt due what the Chancellor would probably call a "bust" but was probably just a single quarter's statistical blip in the days when data were less smoothed and massaged than they are now.

Some questionable presentations of data are simply a result of tradition rather than anything more sinister. One example is the presentation of the number of prisoners as a percentage of the population in the country. This presentation puts England pretty much at the top of international league tables – and at the top within the EU. It has created the impression that the country has "too many prisoners". But, if the prisoner numbers were presented as a ratio of the number of crimes committed, England would fall well below the half way mark in the EU. The Home Office offers no rationale for its presentation other than "that is how it has always been done" – even if it is not the most enlightening.

There are also some examples of information which is presented confusingly, probably just because no one has taken the effort to present it more clearly. One example would be the figures for life expectancy. An English baby boy could be expected to live to either 76 or 83 depending on whether expectancy is measured on a period basis or a cohort basis. In an era where we are being expected to take responsibility for financial arrangements later in life, the gap between the two is large. But we get little guidance from the government as to which is the most appropriate measure.

Misrepresentation and falsification

Thankfully, outright lying rarely happens – or at least we very rarely spot it. One example was exposed early in 2005, when it was revealed that the government published charts creating a distorted impression of employment in the Department of Health by exaggerating the increase in the number of staff over the past three years.

In 2004's annual publication of the National Health Service workforce figures, reporting 2003 data, about 60,000 health workers were dropped from the previous years' figures. As a result, the published bar chart appeared to show a steeper rise in employment than had actually occurred, supporting the government's assertion that the extra resources pouring into the health service were being reflected in higher staffing.

The chart was described by independent statisticians as one of the most blatant misrepresentations of data seen in a government publication and yet the department said it stood by "the validity of the presentation of the figures in the report", adding that "the graphs are a representation and not for research purposes or academics". It said anyone with a serious interest in the numbers would not look for them in the chart, which was designed just for "casual readers". It added that no one had complained about the chart since publication and complaints about it were "petty". (source: *Financial Times*, 5 January 2005)

One leading statistician was quoted as saying it was "preposterous to present charts when you can't trust the figures", adding the document "fails to match the basic expectations on presentation" that would be hoped for.

Several other concerns were voiced about the presentation of data in the document. Notably, the claim that managers numbered only 35,000, about 3 per cent of the workforce, was viewed as dubious. Many bureaucrats it seems are put into other categories, such as the 72,200 working in "hotel, property and estates", 92,300 working in "central functions" and 88,000 non-medically qualified people working in GP practices. The figure also excluded the record-keepers and secretaries among the 360,700 offering support to clinical staff. The Conservative health spokesman said he expected the government to present "a full and rounded picture" of the health service given the importance of health in the forthcoming election.

Some misrepresentations are in forms that look as if they could be the result of an incompetent error. Ministers were asked in parliament to provide the data that supported the statement that, "The average performance of the top 24% of pupils in comprehensive schools is slightly higher than in grammar schools." To "prove" the point, data was given showing the GCSE performance of all grammar school children against the performance of the top 25% of 15-year olds in comprehensives (assuming that in areas where there is selection, roughly one-quarter on average will be selected). As 100% of the top comprehensive school pupils achieved 5-plus grade A–C passes compared to 96% of grammar school children, they felt the case was proven. But the difference might have arisen simply because a few grammar school pupils were sick on the day of the exam and failed it – any sick counterparts in comprehensives would not be among the top 25%! It is also likely that a small number of those selected for grammars at age 11 turned out not be so bright or had difficulties that damaged their exam performance, but these people would also not be counting among the top comprehensive people. The two figures are not comparing like with like.

Sometimes the misrepresentation is more innocent. A transport department document of vehicle licensing statistics has an estimate of the number of unlicensed cars of 34 million compared to the 26 million that are licensed! This striking statistic – suggesting probably the greatest case of mass law-breaking in the country – is in fact far less interesting. The so-called unlicensed vehicles are simply those that are still on government records as not having been scrapped when, of course, most will have long been destroyed one way or another.

Ministerial meddling

At least half of government statisticians – and many of those producing important data – work away from the ONS and therefore report more directly to ministers. How can they ever be seen as independent? After all, their careers depend on pleasing their bosses. In the increasingly wide-spread culture of "for us or against us" and the reduced impartiality of civil servants, it is hard to imagine that ministers would reward statisticians if the statisticians told them that some claim they want to make is unjustified or that some figures the statisticians have produced should be released despite the fact that they show that the minister's favourite policy has not been successful as he would like to think. It would take a brave person to speak out as isolation would almost certainly follow.

The consequence of this is increasingly pervasive year on year. One striking example concerns presentation of unemployment rates for Parliamentary constituencies. For many years, the only source of constituency unemployment rates had been figures produced by the House of Commons library. But in the late 1990s the ONS under pressure from several government departments, started publishing a competing figure.

The two figures gave very different impressions – the rate for Birmingham Ladywood was at the time nearly 18% on the House of Commons measure and just 4% on the ONS figure. Both measures used the same numerator, namely the number of constituency residents claiming unemployment benefit, but different denominators. The House of Commons figure used the economically active resident population while the ONS used the number of jobs in the constituency. The difference between the two numbers is greatest in inner city areas where net in commuting boosts the denominator, reducing the percentage of unemployment.

The rationale for the publication of the rate – which should in any case have been a ratio as the numerator is not a subset of the denominator – was never fully spelt out. We do not know whether pressure for its publication from the then Department of Education and Employment and the Treasury played a part. No doubt ministers were delighted that the new figures showed the unemployment rate in the fifteen worst unemployment black spots – all coincidentally Labour seats! – fall by an average of three percentage points. It also supported the policy view that unemployment was not concentrated in certain areas. After widespread complaints the ONS withdrew the figures from publication.

It is certainly true that many more cases of apparent ministerial meddling seem to happen in the major policy departments, such as health, education, work and pensions, and the Home Office, than to data published by the ONS. One of the fundamental reasons why the ONS was established was to ensure that there would be greater separation of those involved in the construction and reporting of statistics from those managing the policies and programmes judged by the same statistics. Such separation rarely occurs in the main ministries of state. Trusting them to produce impartial data has been likened to giving an alcoholic the keys to a pub.

Non-existent data

As this book will show, many questions that people would like answered remain unanswered because the right data do not exist. The reasons for any piece of data not existing are generally unknown. Sometimes the explanation might be for "political reasons". There is a vicious circle that means that if no data exist, no minister has responsibility for it, if there is no responsibility there is no funding and no political will to start collecting it. If there is no data, there will be less substance to any debate on the associated issue and it will generally be lower down the list of priorities. That often suits ministers who are busy dealing with what is already on their plates. Outsiders can ask government to start collecting data but are unlikely to succeed as there is no open, transparent mechanism for planning such changes. In contrast, if a major department like the Treasury clicks its finger, new data will be found.

Privatisation

The widespread privatisation of public sector services and involvement of private sector companies in contracted out services has damaged the availability of statistics. The arrival of compulsory competitive tendering in the 1980s led to the demise of surveys, and the resulting figures. The data on waste disposal were lost until a new survey was created in the mid 1990s. We no longer know how many traffic wardens there are as local authorities can now employ their own rather than use police service. The lack of relevant information has also undermined the control and accountability of public money to the public at large.

Figures we don't have

There is generally no information whatsoever for the items on the list below. In some cases unaudited private sector data are available or there have been one-off estimates made by government or others. Such one-off estimates can be hard to find – they might be in replies to Parliamentary questions or in reports by research institutions – and the quality of the figures can be hard to judge. In other cases we might think the data exist but we use proxies.

- Election results data and official turnout data
- Adequate data to know if the NHS is being run properly or delivering value for money
- The gap between men and women's pay for the same jobs
- Information on the medical performance of the private healthcare sector
- The number of illegal immigrants living in the country
- Adequate information on pensions and savings
- How long people are waiting for hospital treatment from the date of their GP referral
- How many of the 270,000 people in jobs on pay below the minimum wage represent non-compliance with the legislation
- Consumption of genetically modified or organic food
- The countries that foreign national residents in Britain come from
- The extent and value of the black economy
- Inflation figures for household types such as pensioners and single parent families
- How many people have secured permanent jobs as a result of the New Deal
- How many drivers are uninsured and cars untaxed
- Effective literacy and numeracy rate
- The activity of the voluntary sector
- The causes of road accidents
- The size of the "fridge mountain"
- The number of cars running of alternative fuels
- Animals killed in scientific experimentation

- Data about hunting
- The number of journeys we make on motorways
- Deaths from MRSA
- The number of "tax dodgers" and "benefit scroungers"
- The number of redundancies
- The prevalence of sexual activity and rape
- The number of missing children
- The number of children having vaccinations outside the NHS
- Use – and effectiveness – of alternative therapies
- Accurate figures for homelessness
- The number of children educated at home
- Sufficiently accurate estimates of the country's population
- "Social exclusion"
- Timely public sector finance data consistent with the Treasury's forecasts
- Accurate and timely figures for public sector spending and employment
- Regional inflation figures – indeed, data for regions and local authorities are only available in rare cases
- The number of people in the UK on student visas not attending a course
- Emigration, immigration and country of residence for Britons overseas
- Sufficiently common definitions across countries to allow meaningful international comparisons
- The number of absconded criminals
- Quality of life or degree of happiness
- The number of closed-circuit television screens in public places

Often, it seems to an outsider, that the government just does not care about presenting data. The health service is a case in point. It seems extraordinary that there is apparently so much information in the NHS, and so many complaints about form filling, and yet so few statistics are available. The explanation for this is unclear but probably not unrelated to complex politics in the health service between its constituent parts and two decades of failed information systems which have not delivered results. The

Reasons for disappearing data
- A change in a survey question
- Change in the nature of publications – book to web based
- Equivalent data collected from a new source
- Diminishing data quality
- Data no longer meets a need
- Cost/burden of collection no longer justified
- Risk of disclosure of personal/corporate information
- Change to administrative systems
- Changes in nature of economy or life, e.g. components dropped from the RPI as people stop buying the product or from the breakdown of manufacturing as a component shrinks
- Dropped form NS branding but still published by a department
- Responsibility shifting for departments

End of the National Debt?

The Bank of England announced in November 2003 that it would cease publication of figures for the National Debt. It was reported to be £448,006,333,974 at the end of March 2003. The justification was that there are better measures. (source: www.bankofengland.co.uk and www.crnd.gov.uk)

promise of such systems being up and running reduced the focus on the provision of traditional statistics. It is clear that outsiders cannot judge the NHS performance – but can ministers? Figures from the National Statistics annual report suggest that, very roughly, one penny is spent on statistics in the health department for every £5,000 or so spent on services. A rapidly expanding private sector company would spend proportionately much more on ascertaining the success of its efforts.

Sometimes the lack of data is because it is hard to collect. Part of the reason for there being no data on the number of illegal immigrants in the country, the scale of the black economy or most other illegal activities, is the technical issues. The increasing use of the private sector in the provision of public services also ensures that a range of data is not publicly available as the companies claim that it is commercially confidential.

The statisticians sometimes seem slow to produce new data when they had freedom to do so. The computer and software services sector during its boom in the late 1990s is good example. Even though there are a number of problems in measuring the IT sector – it is dominated by hard-to-measure small firms, it was growing very rapidly, much of the growth occurs in firms which are not classified to the IT sector, there is no standard classification system for such companies, and the value and volume adjustments are virtually impossible as technology is changing so rapidly – the tech boom came and went without any new data specific to the sector being produced. This meant that statements about the impact of the e-economy in the late 1990s and early 2000s were made without the appropriate statistical foundation.

Even where a particular move by the statisticians has been successful the practice does not readily spread to other parts of the organisation. There was a clear success with the decision to publish a range of inflation numbers in part to diffuse the debate that raged in the 1980s about whether mortgage interest should be in the measure. The publication of a range of measures means some have it included and others do not, so users can choose accordingly. The practice could have spread to other areas such as unemployment where there is some dissatisfaction with the existing measures. This would mean that users would no longer have to cobble together their own variants of the total – a far less satisfactory outcome.

Statistics withdrawn

From time to time data are withdrawn in a high profile manner – average earnings, regional GDP and pensions figures are examples from the recent past. Typically this will be after an error has been found. Sometimes they are removed because "taste" or political will changes. School league tables used to be published across Britain but the Scots decided to stop doing so. This seems strange since ministers still want school standards to improve but are denying the public the chance of seeing how their school is performing.

More often than not, however, figures are removed from the public domain much more quietly. No announcement is made and one day, when looking for a table or a breakdown of published figures, they are no longer available. Often there is an innocent explanation but sometimes political motives are suspected if, say, someone had written a critical report based on the data. An annual article published in the ONS publication Economic Trends showing the tax and social security burdens compared to other leading countries has not appeared since March 1999, when the latest year referred to the Conservative government.

The "Annual report on GSS survey activity" does in theory say when most, if not all, changes to surveys are approved. Beyond that there seems

The Japanese introduced a "Statistics day" in 1973, to coincide with the centenary of the collection of modern statistics. Its purpose is to provide the public with a deeper understanding of the importance of statistics. Should Britain follow suit?

to be little tracking of lost data within government. The National Statistics annual report lists data no longer qualifying as NS, but no full list of "cut" figures is available. A new concern – that of disclosure control – has appeared more aggressively on the scene in recent years. The statiticians are understandably keen not to reveal any one person in the detailed tables they publish. As a result, they will suppress detailed information. In the census results, for example, all data cells with one or two people in were converted to zero or three. This has made many tabulations less useful than in the past.

While data might have quietly disappeared in the past, new mechanisms are now in place – in theory – to ensure that a proper internal process and, if appropriate, external consultation takes place. Sometimes data are still available but not in such a user-friendly format. They might no longer be published but are available if anyone asks. Many users feel that the removal of data should be market tested, say by making a statement in a press release, before they are chopped.

The downgrading of statisticians

As ministers have become much more accountable in terms of their performance and outcomes, the statisticians who produce the data have paradoxically become less important as part of their roles have been taken away by ministers' special advisers and press officers, as well as other professionals such as economists, social scientists and operational researchers. As explained in a brief history of official statistics, the number of senior statisticians in government has dropped from well over 100 thirty years ago to about 80 now. The irritation for the statisticians is that it is often their data that is presented to ministers by the social scientists or economists – who are higher up the ministerial "food chain" – and they will be given the resources for the further work!

Revisions, updates, improvements and corrections

As data become more important and more widely used it is inevitable that the producers and their product are put under closer scrutiny. The ONS and other government departments have come under some criticism in the last two or three years for some high-profile problems with the data, including a small number of instances where data has been withdrawn.

Some of the criticism has been fair, but by no means all of it. Some of the revisions have reflected the upgrading of obsolete legacy systems and it seems unreasonable to criticise the statisticians making this progress.

At the same time the statisticians are grappling with the erosion of long-standing understandings of the nature of society and economic processes that underpin laws, relationships and business processes across the world. As the scale, diversity and dynamism of the economic base, demography and culture of the UK change rapidly, the abilities of the statisticians to get decent data are severely tested. Unfortunately all the resulting problems with data have led to a greater loss of confidence in the government statistics machine and the quality of the numbers it producers.

It seems that language and communication is also part of the problem – if people knew the problems and understood the work of the statisticians, there would not be the same level of criticism in most cases. One proposal – attributed to Professor Adrian Smith of Queen Mary College, part of London University, and a past president of the Royal Statistical Society – is for statisticians to adopt more accurate terminology. He proposes that the word "revision" no longer be used, and be replaced by updates (for normal revisions due to better data), improvements (for methodological changes) and correction (for errors).

Innovation is a difficult area for statisticians. It is right that definitions for indicators change over time and nearly always such changes are for the better – as new, improved sources make the estimates more accurate. But such changes have not always been advertised in advance, thoroughly signalled when they occur or properly explained after the event. Changes can also be made too frequently to the annoyance of users.

There is also the suspicion that some of the recent innovations from the government statistics machine have not been properly tested and fully resourced. It could also be that too much focus on what might be called the science and systems of statistics has meant that some of the basic, more mundane surveying and clerical duties have been neglected giving rise to errors in the data.

It is not uncommon for the systems used to collect the data to change and when this happens, the statistics usually experience a step change that is disruptive for analysis. There are three main reasons why change can occur:

- The rules and regulations of an administrative system can be changed.
- Statisticians can make changes to purpose made surveys in order to improve data quality. Such changes are usually made with good intent but can nonetheless be damaging.
- The government itself can also redefine indicators to suit its cause. Unemployment, monetary aggregates and public sector borrowing are examples of statistics that have been changed for political or policy reasons.

The act of counting makes things worse

Statistics can start to show a rising trend after there has been a panic about the variable being measured. Sometimes figures only start to be collected or broken down into certain categories when an issue has been highlighted. Examples might be the reporting to police of racially inspired attacks (for example, the number of racist attacks reported to the Metropolitan Police increased several fold in the year after the death of Stephen Lawrence), the number of rapes, or sex attacks on children (when more are reported after a wave of publicity). Some of the rise in occurrence of the "hospital super-bugs", such as MRSA, is thought to be due to more people looking for it and testing for it. This is a common problem across the public health field where diagnostic tests have improved, allowing complaints such as autism and skin cancer to be detected much more readily than in the past. It can some-times seem that a problem did not exist before the data were collected.

Geography

The nation's statistical framework has always been somewhat fragmented but since 1997 ministers in Westminster and the devolved administrations have allowed the devolution agenda to damage the national coherence of data, despite a concordat in the devolution legislation designed to prevent the problem. Indeed it seems they often thought the point of devolution was to be different and so cause damage.

The 2001 population census, the most fundamental of statistics, was so fragmented that very few outputs are available for the UK as a whole. The failure of the four countries to agree on a set of questions for the popula-tion census is extraordinary when we hear so much about "joined up government". If the statisticians could not reach agreement among them-selves, ministers let the nations down by not stepping in to ensure that the data was available for the UK. There are times when genuine policy differences, such as the provision of free care for the elderly in Scotland, mean there is a need for different data but such differences are few and far between. Common data are needed too, precisely to help evaluate the impact of different policies.

Where possible, figures in this book relate to the United Kingdom. Sadly – and confusingly – only in a minority of cases is data for the whole of the UK readily available. Often we have to make do with data relating to Great Britain, England and Wales together and sometimes for England on its own. Some government studies even present data for the odd entity of England, Wales and Northern Ireland! The reports are even poorly described – the British Crime Survey does not cover Britain.

Many observers are curious to know how some of the data submitted to international bodies, purporting to be UK data, are derived.

It is impossible to find!

The difficulty of working with statistics is compounded by one other "fact of life" – the numbers are hard to find. I did not know where to find all of the data in this book when I started on the project, but I did expect the officials in government departments to know. It has been quite revealing how low the knowledge levels about statistics are in some government departments. Few officials use the internet to get data – they have internal sources – so are unaware of the day-to-day trouble that users have.

Different departments have different ways of presenting data. Some are free, others are not. Some are only in books, others are in databases. Most are on line but many are not. Some have customer service units to help while others positively discourage contact with users. Some encourage communication with the statisticians producing the numbers, others forbid it. Some statistics are found on websites under "statistics" while others will be under "research", "publications" or the relevant subject area. There are some exceptional examples of good presentation but they are never department-wide and are outweighed by the bad examples. Communication skills are low and very little thought seems to be given by the producers as to who might need the data and in what form different users might want it.

Although the advent of the internet means greater access to more data for more people, it also makes it easier for statisticians to change data and drop series. It is also harder for researchers to see an "audit trail" of how an esitmate has changed over time.

The bottom line

All statistics are created through people's actions. Someone has to decide what to count and how to count it, peole do the counting and interpret the result. So keep asking, "Who created the statistic?", "How was it created?" and "Why was it created?".

Further reading

David Boyle, *The tyranny of numbers*, HarperCollins, 2000

Alain Desrosieres, *The politics of large numbers*, Harvard, 1998

Simon Briscoe, *Interpreting the economy*, Penguin, 2000

Daniel Dorling and Stephen Simpson, *Statistics in society*, 1999

Len Cook, "Some thoughts on official statistics in public life in Britain", speech at City University, November 2004

ONS and National Statistics annual reports, www.statistics.gov.uk

Joel Best, *Damned lies and statistics*, UCP, 2001

Targets, targets everywhere

The measurement culture has become an increasingly important feature of public services over the last 10 or 15 years as more and more organisations began to have data that could be used as the basis for measurement. Targets were given a kick start and increased political importance by the Labour government in 1997 with its five key election pledges, notably on hospital waiting lists and the New Deal, and became especially important in 1998 following the comprehensive spending review and the original publication of public service agreements. Both the 2004 Budget and spending review emphasised the government's continued enthusiasm for them.

Labour's five election pledges in 1997

The manifesto said, "We have promised only what we know we can deliver" and included five pledges as "the first steps towards a better Britain".

1. Cut class sizes to 30 or under for 5, 6 and 7 year olds by using money from the assisted places scheme
2. Fast track punishment for persistent young offenders by halving the time from arrest to sentencing
3. Cut hospital waiting lists by treating an extra 100,000 patients as a first step by releasing £100 million saved from NHS red tape
4. Get 250,000 under-25 year olds off benefit and into work by using money from a windfall levy on the privatized utilities
5. No rise in income tax rates, cut VAT on heating to 5% and inflation and interest rates as low as possible.

Most people agree that performance indicators have managerial, democratic and research value. Organisations need to have a means of measuring their own performance internally (often between people or groups doing the same job) and in comparison (as an organisation) with others in order to learn and develop. Taxpayers and users of public services have a right to know how well their services are being delivered and who is accountable for them. And there is a genuine research role in discovering "what works".

Despite the general support for the government's use of public service targets and performance tables many people have serious reservations about how they have been used in practice. There are allegations of cheating, perverse consequences and distortions in pursuit of targets, along with unfair pressure on professionals. League tables and ranking lists are often seen as untrustworthy and misleading. The increase in accountability and transparency which targets in theory bring, and should be invaluable, has been marred by insufficient heed being given to the risks of over interpretation in the presence of large, often inadequately reported uncertainty.

As the Royal Statistical Society said, "Good performance monitoring is productive for all concerned but done badly, it can be very costly, ineffective, harmful and destructive." (source: "Performance monitoring in the public services", Journal of the Royal Statistical Society, A-167, 2004) A working party report from the RSS offered practical solutions for resolving critical issues in target setting and in the design, analysis and reporting of performance indicators, against which current and future performance monitoring of the public services could be judged. (source: "Performance indicators: good, bad, and ugly", RSS, 2003)

The government set out its own aspirations for the targets. It said they should provide a clear statement of what the government is trying to achieve, a clear sense of direction and ambition, a focus on delivering results, a basis for what is and is not working, and better accountability. In the eyes of the government, an effective target would be one that was SMART – specific, measurable, achievable, relevant and timed. (source: "Public services for the future: modernisation, reform, accountability", Cm 4181, 1998.) Laudable as these aims are, in many cases there has been a failure to connect between the politicians at the centre setting the targets, the employees on the front-line whose job it is to deliver them and the wider community of interested parties.

Research produced by the Liberal Democrats in 2000 claimed that the government's targets were SMART in another sense: secretive, manipulative, arrogant, repetitive and trivial. The targets were deemed:

- **secretive** due to the lack of independent scrutiny of performance, and poor communication which sometimes meant that either central government, or the agents, or those on the ground delivering services, did not know what the target was.

The 25 target setting terms

There is a complex and imprecise language of target setting. Further down the target setting pyramid you go, the greater the proliferation of terms and the scope for confusion as to what are, or are not, targets. The terms included: aims, objectives, goals, challenges, performance tests, performance measures, key performance indicators, strategic priorities, performance targets, key targets, policy targets, efficiency targets, intermediate targets, overriding targets, milestones, milestones targets, future policy milestones, intermediate milestones, intermediate outputs, measures of success, indicators of success, service standards, specific actions, purposes, drivers.

(source: "From the sublime to the ridiculous: a critique of government target setting", Liberal Democrat Research Unit, March 2000)

The Treasury's own targets

The Liberal Democrat research was particularly critical of the initial targets set by the Treasury for itself. It claimed that 26 out of the 32 key targets were meaningless as they: were achieved before the date when they were set, relate to trends which are already well-established, are inappropriate as the Treasury is the sole judge of its own success, do not relate to the objectives set, are a statement of government policy rather than performance, and would not be able to be checked against performance data before the following comprehensive spending review was decided.

(source: "From the sublime to the ridiculous: a critique of government target setting", Liberal Democrat Research Unit, March 2000)

- **manipulative** because they diverted attention towards the future and away from present failings, they encourage ministers to "recruit" service providers to become cheerleaders to government, requiring them to provide some success stories, and they tempt service providers to cheat.
- **arrogant** because it is a top-down process that is Treasury-driven, targets "severely constrain" the ability of service providers to respond to local needs, there is increased micromanagement, and, when problems arise with the targets, ministers are keen to ridicule their own targets or explain failure away rather than open up government and render it more accountable.
- **repetitive** because some targets overlap, conflict, or point service providers in opposing directions, others restate government policy or replicate existing outcomes.
- **trivial** in that success in meeting trivial targets is used to mask failure in more important ones.

The paper was also critical of targets as they: focus attention on the aspects of public services towards which resources may be directed and away from others where spending constraints may be tighter, give an inflated appearance of action and "modernisation", often carry deadlines beyond the likely date of the next general election rendering accountability difficult, and are "tailor-made for control-freakery". (source: "From the sublime to the ridiculous: a critique of government target setting", Liberal Democrat Research Unit, March 2000)

Targets can be categorized in three broad ways. The most important group is public service agreements made between the Treasury and government departments. Beyond that are targets announced by the Prime Minister, other ministers or heads of non departmental bodies, or those included in white papers and other reports. Finally, there are targets which were set by Labour in opposition or come out of party conferences or other political events. The government said in March 1999 that it had set 350 policy targets and 175 efficiency targets. The Liberal Democrat research found many more – 8,600 – and that did not to include any set for the Scottish, Welsh or Northern Ireland offices, the regional development agency, and most of the Best Value targets set for local authorities. In the extreme, if the targets set centrally for education that are applicable to individual schools, teachers and pupils, are included the number of targets would run into millions. In response to this growth in the number of targets, the Treasury made further cuts in 2003 (in the pre-budget report), notably the demise of the (over 500) service delivery agreements and a reduction in the number of PSAs.

The Public Administration Committee made a number of recommendations in its report. (source: "On target? Government by measurement", fifth report, July 2003, HC 62-1) These included ensuring greater local autonomy to construct more meaningful and relevant targets, making sure they are as few as possible and focus on key outcomes, widening the targets' consultation process to involve professionals and service users, and reforming the way in which targets are set to move away from the simplistic hit or miss approach. The committee also called for common reporting standards on targets and an independent assessment by the National Audit Office of whether, and how far, targets have been met. These hopes along with the committee's desire to see a more mature political debate about the measurement culture based on a better understanding of targets as tools to improve performance have yet to be fulfilled.

Problems with targets

There are several failings:

1. Failure to provide a clear sense of direction and a clear message to staff

Targets can never be substitutes for a proper and clearly expressed strategy and set of priorities – they can be good servants but are poor masters. Targets should drop out of the business plan and not the other way round. Local people need to feel the centrally imposed targets reflect sensible aspirations if they are not to be counterproductive. Professionals need to feel ownership of the targets – they have often expressed concern that targets fail to take account of their special expertise and judgment. Many have felt undermined by targets with the late 1990s obsession with cutting hospital waiting lists frequently cited by doctors, who say they distorted priorities for medical treatments, as the most damaging example.

People involved with service delivery at the local level often say there are too many targets. When there are too many, the management of them creates so much bureaucracy for the staff that they become distracting. The

---

Sublime and ridiculous targets

"Improving the quality of life for everyone"

"abolish child poverty within 20 years"

"offer everyone the opportunity of a decent home"

Reduce "the number of reams of photocopier paper used by 300 over three years" – National Maritime Museum

"Maintain the percentage of people saying they 'eat as much meat as ever'" – Meat and Livestock Commission

To "seek sponsorship for an outreach programme in 1999–2000" – Royal Armouries, Leedss

"Increased the number of inquiries about astronomy answered from 10,000 to 11,000 by 2001" – Royal Observatory Greenwich

(Source: "From the sublime to the ridiculous: a critique of government target setting", Liberal Democrat Research Unit, March 2000)

Inputs, outputs and outcomes

The setting of targets helps to shift attention from the classic concerns of inputs such as money and personnel to outputs and outcomes. Outputs are goods and services delivered to individuals, households, businesses and communities, for example, patients having operations or students passing exams. Outcomes are conditions in society, like the number of ex prisoners getting jobs after release, patients being successfully treated, or children being able to read. In successive spending rounds, an increasing proportion of the targets has addressed outcomes, as opposed to inputs or outputs.

The number of public service agreements set by the Treasury has fallen in successive spending rounds. There were 600 set in 35 areas of government in 1998, 160 for 18 main departments in 2000, 130 for 20 departments in 2002, and down to 110 in 2004

NHS Confederation has complained that there has been a "considerable increase in often uncoordinated requests" for data, the relevance of the data requested is unclear, there has been some duplication in requests, little feed back on the use of the data, an often weak link between clinical practice and data requested and many of the returns require data that are not computer generated. (source: "Smarter reporting", NHS Confederation, December 2003)

Another problem is the tendency for central government sometimes to appear to pluck targets out of the air in support of the latest initiative. Such targets tend not to command respect or credibility. The aim to reduce school truancies by 10% by 2004 compared to 2002 is relevant and highly desirable but the target figure was seen as quite arbitrary – 5% or 20% would have had just as much (or little) rationale.

It is also usually inept, said the RSS report, to set extreme value targets, such as "no patient shall wait in accident and emergency for more than four hours" because as soon as one patient has waited more than four hours, the target is forgone and seen as irrelevant to staff. Typically, avoiding extremes consumes disproportionate resources for an organisation. It would have been far wiser to have the target as "95% of patients will wait in accident and emergency for under four hours" but it was presumably not deemed as politically desirable. Politicians generally prefer the black and white of success and failure, which is unsuited to such real life activities.

2. Failure to focus on delivering results

Even if the government is achieving the majority of the PSA targets it has set itself that does not mean that results are also being delivered. There are clearly documented cases where the measurement ceases to be a means to an end and becomes the end in itself – more effort is being directed into ensuring that the figures produced have hit the targets than to improving services.

Another danger with the measurement culture is that excessive attention is given to what can easily be measured at the expense of what is difficult or impossible to measure quantitatively even though this may be fundamental to the service provided. The quality of patient care or the time devoted by a teacher to a difficult child's needs is not easily measured.

What makes a good performance indicator?

- Indicators should be directly relevant to the primary objective or be an adequate proxy measure.
- Definitions need to be precise but practicable.
- Indicators and definitions should be consistent over time.
- They should obviate rather than create perverse behaviours.
- Indicators should be straightforward to interpret, avoiding ambiguity about whether the performance being monitored has improved or deteriorated.
- Certain statistical requirements should be met when surveys are being used.
- Indicators should be produced with appropriate frequency, disaggregation and timeliness to support performance management.
- Indicators should conform to international standards if these exist.
- Their collection should not impose an undue burden – in terms of cost or staff – on those providing the information.
- The cost of collection and processing should be commensurate with the likely information again.

(source: "Performance indicators: good, bad, and ugly", RSS, 2003)

The measurement culture also has the potential to threaten standards of service delivery. There is evidence that targets for ambulance response time were jeopardising the effective delivery of services and with it clinical outcomes. The national targets for ambulances require them to respond to incidents defined as life threatening emergencies within a certain number of minutes. There has been no uniform standard of measurement of ambulance response times within the many ambulance services. The clock starts at different times – the time the call was made, was answered, classified to a particular grade of emergency, dispatch of the ambulance, or the ambulance leaving – which may vary by several minutes. Similarly the classification of what is a life threatening emergency differs between ambulance services and ranges from less than 10% of all emergencies to about 50%. These differences in measurement of starting points and definition of a 'life threatening emergency' cast doubt on the usefulness of their targets.

One particular management response to the targets had the potential to deliver perverse consequences and undermine professionalism. As the measurement of response allows the clock to stop when a qualified responder arrives on the scene, ambulance services have developed single paramedic fast response capabilities and lay first responders to help achieve response times. It is questionable whether such individuals are properly trained or equipped to meet the range of emergency conditions to which they are sent but they help to hit the targets.

Hospital consultants have explained that the waiting time targets for new outpatient appointments at their hospitals have been achieved by canceling and delaying follow up appointments for existing patients often with damaging consequences for those patients whose treatments had not been completed.

The government stresses the benefit of targets as a way to make different services pull together to deliver results for the public. In some cases, however, cross boundary and trans-departmental targets were not fostering a more joined up approach to service delivery but were simply incompatible. For example, the more the police met their targets for closing the "justice gap" by putting people in prison, the more difficult it became for the prison service to meet its own targets on overcrowding and re-offending. Similarly it is difficult for any department to achieve its targets if it is reliant on other departments or agencies with other targets to contribute towards meeting its targets.

It has also been said that the sheer number of targets coupled with the government's sensitivity to short-term criticism has discouraged initiative, risk taking, longer-term thinking and a willingness to learn from mistakes.

3. Falsification

A more direct threat to the public service ethos is the deliberate falsification of information and failure to follow proper procedures, amounting at times to cheating. Inevitably such cases are usually hard to detect and prove but the phenomenon exists. In 2003 there was a well-publicised case of a primary school head teacher who, anxious to avoid a low league table placing, helped his pupils to cheat on SATs tests. In the NHS, some accident and emergency units have appeared to be prone to creative accounting. Targets for accident and emergency maximum waiting times were being circumvented by imaginative fixes where trolleys either had their wheels removed or were redesignated as "beds on wheels" and corridors and treatment rooms were redesignated as "pre-admission units", according to the British Medical Association, the Royal College of Nursing and the Patients Association.

The Consumers' Association has highlighted near corrupt practices in ambulance services. In some cases, ambulance trusts reported reaching patients in the near impossible time of less than one minute. Paramedics have also talked of calls being reclassified once the ambulance has arrived at the scene, so that any late category A call may be reclassified as category B in order to meet the category A performance target. There have even been instances of pressure being exerted on paramedics to achieve the response time targets by altering records.

Evidence of deliberate manipulation of figures has come to light in other parts of the NHS, perhaps most notoriously the case of hospital in patient waiting lists – which comprise the people who have been referred by a GP to a hospital consultant and, having seen the consultant, are waiting for the start of the treatment. The figures for hospital waiting lists were vital for the government as the promise to reduce waiting lists by 100,000 was a key pledge of Labour in the 1997 election. The lists have indeed got shorter since 1997 but only in part – probably in large part, but we cannot be certain – to people being treated more quickly.

The 2001, the National Audit Office reported on the inappropriate adjustment of waiting lists by nine NHS trusts. (source: National Audit Office, "Inpatient and outpatient waiting in the NHS", HC 221 and HC 452, 2001) The adjustments reduced the apparent numbers of patients on waiting lists, affected thousands of patients' records and resulted in delayed treatments for some.

Waiting lists were also shortened by a process of so–called "cleaning", where staff have been employed to telephone people who have been on the waiting list for some time to find those who have either moved away or died and can then be removed from the list. Another way to shorten the lists is to slow the rate at which people get onto them. This can be done by increasing the length of time it takes to see the initial hospital consultant from the time of referral by a GP. This phenomenon led to the creation of new data – essentially the length of time to get on the waiting list for the waiting list! More recently, a new "hidden waiting list" has come to light. These are people who have seen the consultant but have not yet been referred for treatment as they wait for further tests or a second opinion. Such people are on neither of the current waiting lists and it is hoped that new data will become available covering the length of time from GP to treatment. Waiting lists have undoubtedly fallen but it is not clear what proportion of the fall is "genuine".

4. Failures in reporting and monitoring

The NAO has noted the absence of either centrally accepted standards for reporting performance or of any general audit requirements for validation of results reported. Many of the NAO's value for money reports have examined departments' performance measurement systems or validated performance data. The NAO reported that, in over 80% of such first-time validations, they found that the organisation had materially misstated their achievements or had failed to disclose potentially material weaknesses with their data. In over 70% of validations there were material inaccuracies in performance data used to track progress against one or more key targets.

According to the NAO the reason for these problems was a lack of attention to, or expertise in, performance measurement and reporting techniques. But the absence of any routine external validation of the measures meant that there was no discipline of reporting and no routine independent review of the quality of information. There has been little central guidance on how such reporting should be carried out but this situation jeopardises the credibility of the whole policy of government by measurement.

Difficulties in monitoring and reporting have also sometimes been the result of poorly thought out targets. The Statistics Commission has pointed out that in some policy areas targets have been set without consideration of the practicalities of monitoring and what data already exist. (source: Statistics Commission memorandum to the PAC, 2003) Target setting without baseline information runs the risk that targets are set at levels which are either unrealistic or undemanding or which may be difficult to monitor effectively. In the absence of good baseline information, the inevitable arguments about whether such targets have actually been met are liable to undermine public confidence in government.

Many people feel that performance targets need to be independently validated if they are to be credible. At the moment, all such assessments are based on departments' own judgments of how well they have performed against their targets. While the National Audit Office has started external validation of data systems feeding into performance reporting, this falls well short of independent external validation of the actual judgments about whether targets have been met or not – and the justification for the regular year to year tweaking of targets and the data used to monitor them. The credibility of departmental annual reports will be undermined without external validation.

Arguing about percentages

It is no surprise, therefore, that it is difficult to have a sensible discussion about whether targets have been met. The Public Administration Committee analysed the first set of PSA targets published as part of the 1998 comprehensive spending review. Their research found that 221 of the 366 performance targets – some 60% – were judged as met. In contrast, a comparatively small number of targets – just under 10% – were not met. Relatively high percentages – 25% – were recorded for the number of targets when no judgment could be made of whether they had been met or not, since there was either a lack of data on their achievement or there was simply no final reporting at all on their achievement. Excluding the results for the small departments and the crosscutting targets, some 67% of the remaining 249 were deemed to have been met.

In 2002, when this assessment was first made the government claimed that nearly nine out of ten – 87% – of the 1998 targets had been met while the Conservative opposition claimed that 38% had not been met. At one level both parties were correct. The government's percentage counted only the main departments' targets, targets partially met as well as those fully met, those with a deadline of 2002 or sooner, and only those where performance information was available. Hence the 87% figure for targets met was heavily qualified, something not always made clear.

Similarly, the Conservatives' claim that the government had failed to meet 38% of its targets was also arguably over-inflated since it included some targets which cannot properly be considered "not met". The subtle distinction between "not assessed as met" and "assessed as not met" is something which is likely to be missed by most observers. It is clear that independent verification by a credible external source – or a group in government such as independent statisticians – would help to dispel the current confusion about the number of targets that have been achieved.

Institutions can appear out of line with others in rank orderings based on performance indicators for various reasons other than their true performance, one of which is poor quality of data. For example, in one piece of research based on official data, the university given the title "the worst university" in 1997 found itself in that position because of incorrect data. It had accidentally included 267 students who had enrolled on a single year course as students on the traditional three year course. Naturally their progression rates to a second year course were very low – about 11% – compared to the national average of 77% for those on three year courses. But the incorrect inclusion of these students in the aggregates caused the averages for that institution to plummet. (source: "Performance indicators in UK higher education", Journal of the Royal Statistical Society, A-167, 2004)

If the creation of league tables leads to institutions producing more accurate data than that must be a good thing so long as the punishment for making a mistake in submitted data is not too great. The people producing the league tables should, of course, pay particular attention to the data checking processes they employ. Data used to produce rankings have been found to have very basic errors, for example, percentages adding up to a total distant from 100, or illogical date sequences (patients apparently dying prior to receiving the treatment).

5. Confused accountability

A major cause of confusion over accountability is that the centre often does not have a strong enough sense of the importance of the structure of service delivery. Although the Westminster system tries to centralise the responsibility for the performance of all public services, the delivery of services is dispersed and often devolved. Departments do not have their hands on the management of programs – they supervise policies for which ministers answer to Parliament, while others deliver them.

A decade and more of structural reforms in public administration has increased the complexity of what is in effect multi-layered government. At the top is a layer of Whitehall departments, in the middle is a set of institutions such as local authorities and health bodies supervising the delivery of public services, who are working with others, often contractors, who are organising the manpower, and at the bottom are individuals who meet the public when they go to a school, the surgery or a library. This complex geography has a profound effect on accountability and motivation and means there are fundamental problems with the accountability of any target that is set centrally without proper reference to those on the front line.

As long as targets are being met, the centre and local providers can happily claim ownership and credit. However, missed targets may well lead to acrimonious dispute about where the blame rests. The setting of impossible targets is a recipe for the growth of blame culture.

6. A lack of clarity about what the government is trying to achieve and risks to equity

There is no guarantee that a reliance on national targets will promote greater equity. A national target can be met in more than one way and some of them promote greater equity that others. For example, a 10% improvement in services can be achieved if all providers improve equally. It can also be achieved if some units do disproportionately well while others regress. If top performers improve most, the gap in the available service quality will widen between citizens in different parts of the country.

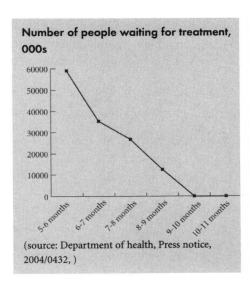

Number of people waiting for treatment, 000s

(source: Department of health, Press notice, 2004/0432,)

The hospital waiting time figures provide a very clear example of the establishment of a target that affects treatment. The length of time that people had been waiting used to tail off steadily but that changed when the government said that it does not want anyone to wait more than nine months for treatment. The impact is clearly visible in the latest data – at the end of the October 2004, 27,000 were waiting between 7 and 8 months, 12,000 were waiting between 8 and 9 months and only 14 were waiting 9 to 10 months. Most people get seen within a few months but, for those waiting for longer, it would seem that clinical need does not determine which people get seen quite so much as the need not to fail on the target.

7. The problems with league tables and other simplistic measures

There is a danger that any achievement short of 100% success is classified as failure. Simplistic approaches of this kind, with political and media charges about failure to meet fully the targets, can be profoundly demoralising to schools, teachers, police officers and hospital staff who have worked hard to achieve progress in the face of local difficulties. Crude league tables and star ratings can be particularly misleading and demotivating, as they can make everybody except the "league champions" look and feel like failures.

Crude ratings tend to take no account of the particular features of local communities which can go a long way in explaining the different performance of areas. For example, it might be expected that the school exam success in English for a London Borough such as Tower Hamlets, where two thirds of the population is Bangladeshi, might well be lower than the national average even if the efforts of the teachers and pupils are above average. Even so there have been press reports that ministers had seriously considered using such "naïve" information to help decide on the fate of head teachers.

Targets are meant to be stretching and so it ought to be acceptable that not all targets can be hit so long as everyone can see what progress is being made towards them. It could also be thought unhelpful to sharpen targets progressively by requiring that next year's performance is better than "the better of current target and current performance".

League tables also usually fail to take account of uncertainties due to the quality and variability of the data. For many purely statistical reasons the performance of a hospital's surgeons or a school's pupils will fluctuate from year to year. A surgical team's one-year mortality after cardiac artery bypass surgery should not be judged on whether "the number of deaths within the one-year divided by the number of cardiac artery bypass operations performed is less than target. Rather, it is better to judge that team's performance on whether an appropriate estimation interval (or range) for that one-year mortality after cardiac artery bypass surgery includes the outturn – and a view should be taken over several years to allow for quite natural peaks and troughs due to the erratic nature of the data.

This can further be illustrated with an example relating to an exercise to judge the quality of British universities. Using a number of criteria, researchers ranked 165 universities from best to worst. However, due to the different sample sizes of students from each university the true "quality score" allocated to each institution will be in a range around the precise (say, best guess or central) figure used in ranking exercise.

When these ranges are plotted on a graph it becomes clear that the likely difference between many universities is not as great as the gap in the ranking would suggest. The ranges show that only 30 of the 165 universities were 95% likely to have had a quality score that was below zero (seen as the average score) and 44 were likely to be above zero. In one extreme case the quality range for the university appearing ninth on the ranking list overlaps with the institution appearing 110th. Yet, despite there being no statistically significant difference between these two universities, their relative rankings on a crude league table would give very different impressions to the casual reader. (source: "Performance indicators in UK higher education", Journal of the Royal Statistical Society, A-167, 2004)

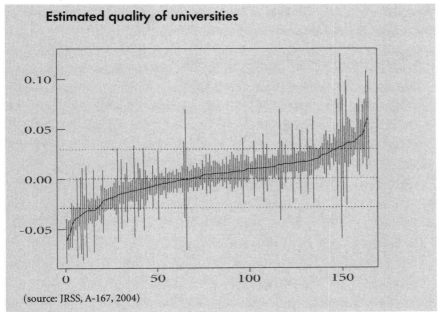

Estimated quality of universities

(source: JRSS, A-167, 2004)

Another example of the unreliability of league table rankings is found in a study of graduate labour market outcomes. Information on the post-university employment status of university leavers is obtained from responses to a survey sent by each institution to a target population of individuals in its leaving cohort. The target population comprises all home domiciled students obtaining an undergraduate level qualification and who studied full-time. Despite a reasonable response rate to the survey the probability of a response from a student is unlikely to be a random event, rather it is likely to be correlated with the individual's performance at university and with their post-university labour market outcomes. The study calculated the median and the 95% confidence interval for the ranking position of each university.

As the chart shows there is considerable uncertainty in the ranking positions of the universities. Although a small number of universities at the extremes of the ranking have small confidence intervals, most other universities have very wide overlapping confidence intervals indicating considerable uncertainty in the rankings derived. The confidence interval for the 20th ranked university for males overlaps with all those which are ranked as high as sixth and as low as 62nd of the 101 universities included in the study. It is clear that it would be misleading to publish league tables of universities – without the confidence intervals even though that is what normally is done – as we can have little inferential confidence in the rankings. (source: "Higher education outcomes", Journal of the Royal Statistical Society, A-167, 2004)

Post university employment outcomes

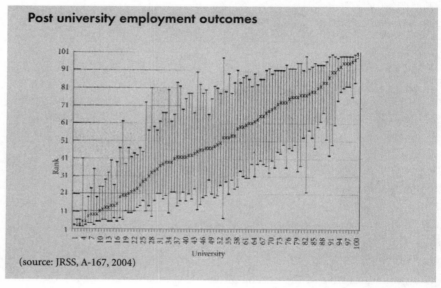

(source: JRSS, A-167, 2004)

"Star ratings show you how well an NHS organisation is performing. The star ratings give you an overview of how good the Trust's service is to its patients - how well it is run and whether it is performing well on important factors like reducing treatment waiting times." The large majority of trusts received two or three stars and only a small minority, just over 5%, received no stars

Any conclusions that might be drawn from any ranking based on these data also suffer from weaknesses in the "First destination" survey. First, rather than carrying out a survey of first destination in the months after leaving university, a suitable period of time, perhaps three years, should be left before conducting the survey. Second, the survey should include dropouts as well as graduates to obtain information about the post-higher education experiences of all students. Third, information is needed about salary levels, training received, and additional qualifications acquired. Information about each graduate's educational and social background would also be useful.

League tables are best avoided if there is no measurement of ranking uncertainty included. Star ratings – essentially presenting a series of categories or leagues rather than a straight ranking in one league table – are generally deemed preferable but they also need to explain the uncertainty involved in the categorisation.

The star ratings system for hospitals (first published in 2001, it graded each of the hospital trusts as having zero, one, two or three stars) has suffered particular criticism. The star ratings, derived by adding up around 20 separate ratings, are influential because they are used to determine access to a performance fund worth hundreds of millions of pounds a year and the extent of the hospitals' autonomy. Apart from any distortion to organisational systems which might not be conducive to patient care, due to the need to achieve high star ratings, it is quite possible that due to statistical uncertainty a hospital graded as two stars could genuinely be a one or three. Such uncertainty would rarely, if ever, be pointed out and would not be taken account of in the central government assessment process. Sometimes the league table and divisions approach are merged: for example, in the presentation of school results in some newspapers.

Many practitioners have advocated the use of so-called funnel plots, which can identify outliers, in preference to league tables. If the primary focus of the presentation of performance indicators is to identify "extreme" units, then funnel plots may be preferable. For example, the relevant question may not be what absolute rank should an institution have, but rather whether the lowest ranked institutions in the set examined are, in fact, worse than the others or worse than the worst are expected to be. The chart presents a funnel plot of emergency readmission rates for stroke patients plotted against the number of stroke patients treated per year. Divergent hospitals stand out but the ranking of the remainder is not implied.

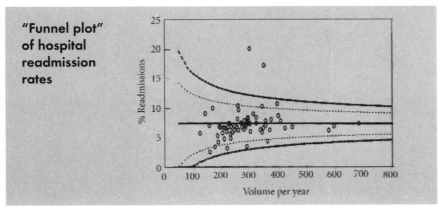

"Funnel plot" of hospital readmission rates

If there are several or many performance indicators available for analysis, and amalgamation into a single summary figure can be avoided, information can be illustrated by means of a so-called "spider web", sometimes known as star plots. The advantage of this presentation is that it precludes overemphasis and distortion often inherent in single measures. The example here is designed to show the disparity in health equality between a rural area of southern England – Wiltshire – and one in the north – Northumberland.

The indicators collected were ordered in such a way that high numbers represented a good situation. When this was translated onto the spider diagram that meant that the nearer the score was to the outer rim, roughly the greater the amount of space filled on the diagram, the better the health situation. Each indicator was scaled in reference to scores across all groups being compared –in other words all the local authorities in England. A score of zero is given to the local authority with the lowest score on that item and one – on the outside the circle – to the local authority with the highest score. All the other local authorities would be placed on that scale depending on where they lay on the range between the minimum and maximum score. Some sixteen indicators, allocated to five broad groups, show that in most cases the rural area is the more healthy. The same methodology could be used for one area over time, to show how its services are changing.

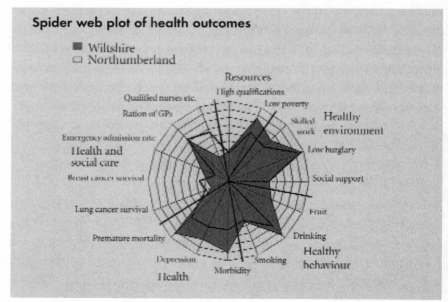

Spider web plot of health outcomes

The measurement culture adapts

There would be less confusion if there was greater clarity about what the publication of performance data is for and therefore the form it should take. Is it to enable citizens to choose? Or to spur providers to do better? Or to offer reassurance about the spending of public money? Or to provide the basis for either the grant of greater freedoms or the imposition of greater controls? There can, of course, be more than one purpose, but in each case it is important to be clear what these purposes are and therefore what is the most appropriate form of publication of performance information.

There is no doubt that the management culture has been adapting fast during the 1990s and is continuing to adapt. The number of PSAs has been reduced since they were first introduced in 1998 and more targets are now outcome or output related. Some key targets have been changed (for example the switch between waiting list numbers to waiting times in health) or abandoned as unhelpful or unrealistic (examples can be found in the fields of drugs and traffic congestion). Some targets have become less rigid and more aspirational. There is also a greater emphasis from the centre on consultation. The publication of the pan-government FABRIC report in 2001 provides guidance to government departments on setting targets. The report stressed the importance of reliable data and recommended the use of National Statistics where appropriate, on the grounds that these data are more likely to meet the expected standards in terms of transparency, quality and integrity. But the framework is only a guide and its existence is by no means widely known, nor its guidance incorporated systematically into departmental practice. Probably only a third of PSAs are monitored using data classified as National Statistics.

We are still some way from having better and more intelligent comparisons. Effective benchmarking would see service providers being compared with other providers working in a similar environment or with similar groups of clients or users. A hospital that specialises in treating heart conditions should compare its performance with the performance of other heart hospitals. A school with a high proportion of free school meal pupils (i.e. those from low income households) or a high proportion of children whose first language is not English is best compared with a group of others facing similar challenges. The effective manager can use such information to ask staff to explain what it is that might be making life difficult for them and what can be done to put it right.

There has been a call for the provision of measures of progress that can give a more rounded and accurate picture of how schools, hospitals and other public services are performing – in direct contrast to the 1990s' fashion for "naming and shaming". Such measures would be much closer to what most people want from public services. People probably do not care whether targets are being hit, they want to know that services are improving. The more targets can be related to trends or "progress" by service providers, the more they can be meaningful – and there is every chance that that might be the case as data become available over a longer run of years. Data about targets used to be very hard to find. But the latest figures relating to the major public service agreements can now be found on the Treasury web site.

So long as the acceptance of shortcomings by the centre continues to be matched by an acceptance among professionals that government by measurement is here to stay, it seems likely that a sensible set of targets and a sufficiency of analysis will in future be possible. Meanwhile the breadth and range of figures in this book present one assessment of progress and change in society.

Additional reading:
2004 Budget
2004 Spending review, along with the PSA White Paper published at the
    same time
"Measuring government performance", Conference proceedings, Statistics
    Users' Council, November 2003
"Choosing the right FABRIC", a framework for performance information, ,
    March 2001
Audit Commission, "Targets in the public sector", September 2003

The birth of government figures

Concerns about the adequacy and purpose of statistics are nothing new. The word statistics derives from the word state, reflecting the origin of the first data collections, and points to a purpose that had nothing to do with informing the general population. The earliest civilisations had censuses to inform rulers about the manpower available for warring – and the ability to pay for such escapades.

The Domesday Book from 1086, the earliest survey of England's population still in existence, was commissioned by William the Conqueror after his invasion of 1066, though due to his death, it was never completed. Primitive surveys of land and people are in the tradition of a "Prince's mirror", intended to instruct the king and show him the reflection of his grandeur in the form of his kingdom. It is not hard to see today's ministers using their department's statistics to proclaim the success of their policies! As time passed, "statistics" came to mean a collection of pieces of information, quantified and periodic, intended for state administrators.

It was in the 16th century that important stages of the statistical process were born that led to more regular data: keeping written records, scrutinising and assembling them according to a predetermined grid, and interpreting them. Keeping written records of baptisms, marriages and burials is linked to a concern with determining a person's identity, to judicial and administrative ends. This was the basic act of all statistical work implying definite, identified and stable communities. Such records became obligatory in England in 1538 and later on lists were made public, for example, announcements of burials were posted during epidemics.

In the 17th century, a set of techniques originated in England for processing and calculating basic data – and the term political arithmetic was first used. Early pioneers were individuals such as Graunt, Petty and Davenant. William Petty, who published his studies of life expectancy in London in 1661, has been described as a "reformer who saw the collection of facts as an indispensable preliminary to practical and effective reform".

In tune with the practice of his and our times, he would typically collect data that would support the reforms which he desired.

Yet there continued to be resistance to more formal collection of data by the state. In 1753, a plan to take a census of the population was violently denounced by the Whig party has "utterly ruining the last freedoms of the English people", mirroring concerns today about a population register! The first census took place in Britain in 1801 but a number of other European countries were able to benefit from their first censuses in the half-century before that.

Even in the 19th century, when more statistics were collected by the state, they were not intended to inform civil society or an autonomous public opinion. A survey conducted on behalf of a parliamentary enquiry into the employment of children in mines in 1840 was not to be released but saw the light of day only after a copy had been leaked. Similarly, in 1929, the then Chancellor stopped the publication of the first official set of national accounts supposedly on the grounds that they showed a decline in the share of income going to workers.

Accordingly, a private tradition emerged of social description. Accounts of journeys, analyses of specific places, compilations of documents and data, and so forth were produced by local scholars, learned men, doctors and others. Men, such as Booth, Engels, Farr and Rowntree, and women such as Florence Nightingale, were driven by the new philosophy of the Enlightenment and were often grouped into societies and reform clubs, which debated and formulated the dominant themes of the time. They studied social and economic variables in the context of industrial and urban growth and their dramatic consequences. The statistics often led to legislation intended to treat the problems connected to this growth: poverty, public health, and unemployment. Their work was the start of the era when data really began to influence public life and was a key foundation for the statistical procedures that were to follow.

Their work revolutionised how public policy would be advocated and shaped the accountability of those who could influence it. People who collected data became a strong force in the context of a limited role for the state in the redistribution of wealth. Over time the state became more active in the collection of information as it struggled to understand the impact of the industrial revolution on people's lives. One person is quoted as saying at the time that, "A more general diffusion of accurate knowledge regarding the state of public affairs would tend to check the excitement and party spirit which has often been created by misrepresentation or exaggeration, and has produced an annoyance to government, and at least a temporary disaffection of the public mind". The same comment could be made now about some areas of public debate in the media even though there has been enormous improvement in the availability of statistics.

It was a time of considerable social discovery through the use of newly available data. In the early 19th century, for example, the general perception was that Liverpool was a healthy city and that it was its good health that accounted for the rapid growth in population it experienced. But when figures for infant mortality in the large industrial cities were published, it became clear that Liverpool was an extremely unhealthy place to live – a place where half the children died before the age of six.

Then, as now, official figures failed to answer the many questions that people asked. In the mid-19th century there was considerable concern over the number of prostitutes in London but there were no government figures setting out the scale of the problem. Henry Mayhew, a well-known observer of London life, estimated the number at 80,000. The *Lancet* in 1857 came up with the much larger figure of one woman in 60. Nobody knew then and nobody knows now.

The momentum of development accelerated in the 20th century when statisticians such as Rowntree, Bowley and Fisher established the scientific basis for sampling, through the capacity for statistical inference through randomisation. This new phase with increasing government involvement saw the extension of data collection nationally and internationally using common standards – and the first appearance of data that now forms the bedrock of our knowledge base. Sampling allowed all forms of business and households to be measured and as the century progressed more and more data were collected.

There has always been a genuine debate as to what should be counted. An early attempt by French kings to measure national wealth counted only agriculture. Adam Smith started to include industry and factories but even he excluded entertainment, government spending and lawyers because they were "unproductive of any value". It was only around a hundred years ago at the time of Keynes that the service sector was included in national output for the first time. Activities without a price such as work done in the home or bringing up children are still excluded. It used to be said – and it is still true – that when a man marries his housekeeper the value of GDP goes down.

A legitimate debate still rumbles on about the definition of investment. Building a new factory clearly counts as investment and yet education – arguably at least as important – does not. Some ministers seem at times to refer to almost any public expenditure as investment. But what about the use of natural resources? A country that chopped down and sold all its trees or sold its oil reserves would be seen in the national accounts to be richer when selling these resources. But would that "economic growth" be seen as valuable over the medium term when the resource was depleted? Counting the flow of money – currently the focus of our economic accounts – is no easy matter but it is much easier than counting rather more illusive aspects of progress that most people would want for their society.

Ever since figures were first collected, there have been statistical problems. Any set of figures will have its reliability and usefulness limited by factors such as: the difficulty in measuring the precise concept that the statistics aim to reflect, the limitations of methodology at the time, and practical constraints such as respondent load and cost that prevent what is theoretically possible being done. Government manipulation, inadequate funding and public misunderstanding are also key problems – as they always have been.

Measuring the so-called "feel good factor" and trying to understand why people often seem to be so stressed, angry and unhappy, despite their increasing wealth, is proving far more elusive. The index of economic growth – gross domestic product, recently renamed gross value added – is estimated and published in great detail at high cost and dominates over all other statistics. Meanwhile measures of privacy, happiness, cleanliness, peace, quality of life and so on that might be considered just as important do not exist. Such concepts are hard to define and near impossible to measure.

But, despite the many problems mentioned in this book, some progress is being made. So called satellite accounts, to run along side the main measures, are being set up by the ONS on subjects such as the environment and work in the home. And since 1999, the Department for the environment, food and rural affairs has made a statistical attempt to measure quality of life. It listed a number of headline indicators and dozens of sub indicators, including measures of property quality and river cleanliness. Although these could not be aggregated into one single measure for the whole country, most people would agree that if the majority of these indicators were moving in the right direction, the country would be a better place in which to live. (source: www.sustainable-development.gov.uk)

The politics of official statistics – history and prospects

The publication of statistics is one of the government's tasks and many fear that it could use its monopoly in this field as a political advantage by distorting, postponing and suppressing figures that put its own performance in an unfavourable light. It could exaggerate, leak in advance, and publicise figures that seem to be to its credit. While the worst fears are rarely manifested, the reliability of official statistics used in political debate has become a political issue.

Despite rare cases of outright 'fiddling', the history of official statistics in Britain has been far from golden. To put it simply, three phases can be identified in the post-war period. The first period, up to the end of the 1970s, was a time of optimism as more and more statistics were published even though by today's standards they were pretty basic. The second period, lasting much of the 1980s, saw political enthusiasm for data evaporate, especially at the highest levels in central government. As the 1990s progressed, and certainly by the end of the decade, confidence steadily and slowly grew, not least because of the prospect of greater independence, and that bodes well for the future.

Post-war optimism

The first major landmark was when the then Prime Minister, Winston Churchill, established the Central Statistical Office in 1941, under its first director, Harry Campion. The statisticians were brought in as part of the war effort but such was their success, they became a permanent feature. He was succeeded by Professor Claus Moser, who presided over a major expansion of official statistics, particularly in other government departments. This reflected the support for statistics of Harold Wilson, who became Prime Minister in 1964, and it followed the recommendations of the now-defunct Parliamentary Estimates Committee in 1966.

Their main recommendations were: the creation of the Business Statistics Office to collect data from businesses; the establishment of the Office of Population Censuses and Surveys to collect information from individuals and households; an enhanced role for the CSO in managing statistics across government; and the development of the Government Statistical Service (GSS), an inter-departmental network of statisticians. With this backing, the government statistics machine grew dramatically in the 1960s and 1970s, producing more and better information. It is interesting to note that this pivotal moment was inspired by a parliamentary committee and not ministers or the government of the day. As with the current reforms, the pressure for change largely comes from outside the government of the day.

The 'cuts' of the 1980s

A far less glorious era descended in 1980, when the then Government's approach to official statistics underwent a substantial change. In that year, there was a review of government statistical services under the auspices of Sir Derek Rayner (his team also reviewed other areas of government). On statistics, his main task was to economise on their cost and reduce the compliance burden on the private sector. It was a blow to the democratic concept of statistics as a public good rather than a political tool.

The Rayner Report said, "The primary duty of the CSO is to serve central government requirements … we have found the Office too heavily committed to serving the public at large". The review was part of a wider initiative of the Thatcher government to cut back on bureaucracy across the public sector. It raised questions about the need for a number of the social surveys, the extent of quality checking (criticising the "fulsome and perfectionist attention to technical detail"!), the value of research and the rising demands of the European Community. It sought to find private sector players to plug gaps, cut subsidies to publications (forcing up the prices) and introduced the "value for money" remit for the director.

There is nothing wrong in principle with such reviews but in the prevailing climate there were vigorous reductions in statistical resources and activity. The staffing and administrative costs of official statistics were cut by about one quarter over five years, with the CSO's funding falling by one-third. Within the limits imposed by the Rayner cuts, and the primary responsibility to ministers, government statisticians made some effort to serve the public interest, but the quality of service suffered. In part this was because the plan for rationalisation failed to recognise the importance of official statistics as key, commonly accepted contextual information about the demography, culture, economy and place of peoples in the UK – the common knowledge we all share by knowing what we are like and who we are.

For nearly the first fifty years of its life, the CSO was a department in the Cabinet Office. It was technically responsible to the Prime Minister, although in practice it worked closely with the Treasury, and indeed the CSO shared the same building as the Treasury (until the mid-1990s). In the late 1980s, the CSO had a modest remit. It was, for example, directly responsible for publishing less than half the key macroeconomic press releases. The other departments that published key indicators in press notice form, because they were responsible for collecting data, included the Treasury, the Bank of England, the Department of Trade and Industry and the Department of Employment – and the CSO had little influence over them.

New dawn for official statistics

The new era for National Statistics dates from 1988 when a number of pressures came to a head. The trigger for change was the Treasury and Civil Service Committee of the House of Commons which, in its report on that year's budget, recommended that an investigation into improving reliability of economic statistics be carried out. The Committee noted a number of weaknesses, such as the discrepancies between the measures of GDP and the large balancing items and revisions, which had led to the problems encountered in interpreting the state of the economy in the mid-to late 1980s. In particular, economic policy was found to have been too expansionary, because the government did not know how rapidly GDP was growing in the mid-1980s. That economic boom (and subsequently the 'bust' of the late 1980s and early 1990s) was blamed in good part on the incorrect policy pursued as a result of poor statistics giving a wrong impression. A price was truly paid for the Rayner cuts.

There was, however, a broader undercurrent of criticism of government statistics during the 1980s. The government had been repeatedly accused of suppressing, abolishing, delaying and manipulating data for its own political ends. In 1989, a television documentary investigation into the integrity of official statistics reported ten examples of interference with official data from many sectors including unemployment, poverty, the census, privatisations and the health service.

The programme included an interview with the late Sir John Boreham who had been the director of the CSO until 1985. He said, "There is a frontier zone in which the Government's desire to show that it is doing well, and the statistical service's desire to be objective and neutral, leads to constant skirmishing. Usually, ministers had an interest in making sure that what was published did not do them a great deal of harm." He had said (in an article in *Statistical News* in 1985), "Where necessary we should try, by logic and diplomacy, to persuade colleagues and ministers of the risks of losing public confidence they would run if they suppressed, delayed or misused our statistics, or selected figures to satisfy their social, economic or political viewpoint."

In June 1988, the government announced an efficiency scrutiny into the improvements that could be made to government economic statistics. In November 1988, a review team concluded its study and the government published a report entitled "Government Economic Statistics". It made a number of recommendations, many of which were implemented. The CSO was established as an enlarged department in July 1989, incorporating the Business Statistics Office (previously part of the Department of Trade and Industry), and assuming responsibility for the RPI and the Family Expenditure Survey. It was also set up as a separate department under the Chancellor of the Exchequer rather than as part of the Cabinet Office. A number of further initiatives were subsequently announced, notably the launch of the CSO as an executive agency, though it remained a government department, headed at Permanent Secretary level.

The then Chancellor explained that there were two main aims in launching the CSO as an executive agency. First, he said that "it put the focus on the quality of service provided to customers, inside and outside government." Indeed, the CSO was allowed to "consider requests to collect a wider range of data than that needed for the conduct of government business." Second, he took the opportunity to set out "publicly the arrangements to ensure the integrity and validity of UK official statistics." It was made clear that "ministers will ensure the freedom of the director to maintain and to demonstrate the integrity of the output". These comments were backed up by detailed aims, objectives and targets. The move was designed to increase public confidence in the statistical output.

The Treasury said it needed data on a regular basis that are comprehensive in coverage; accurate; timely; coherent; not subject to large revision or bias; and consistent with other information. The framework document set out targets in respect of all these features and it required the director to report to ministers annually, summarising the extent to which targets had been met and what action was being taken, where necessary, to remedy the situation. There was some extra cash as part of the initiative and the document suggested that the Treasury would view any further requests for additional resources favourably. Although substantial additional resources were never forthcoming the rhetoric was very different from that associated with the 'Rayner doctrine' in the 1980s.

The 1993 White Paper on open government, part of the Citizen's Charter initiative, further spelt out the need for readily available data and included social as well as economic statistics. The CSO devised and launched a mission statement in 1993. The overall aim was to ensure that CSO statistics are used, "because our efforts are not worthwhile, however laudable they may be, unless decision-making, research or debate is influenced". The four key principles were communication with others, respecting providers of data, professionalism and integrity, and valuing staff. Progress indeed, even if the new framework left many unanswered questions.

It is always dangerous to be complacent about government statistics. *The View From No. 11*, the biography from Nigel Lawson, Chancellor from 1983 to 1989, gave some insights into how politicians feel about statistics. It shows that improvements in statistics must be delivered – and not just spoken about – and institutionalised, as they can easily be lost. In full awareness of the issues, the Royal Statistical Society, for instance, in 1991 called for greater centralisation and control of statistics; an enhancement of methodological work; a National Statistical Commission; and a UK Statistics Act. The set-up achieved by the mid-1990s went a good part of the way towards the ideal envisaged by the RSS, but it clearly fell short.

The improvements in the 1990s continue

The initiatives of the early 1990s provided a platform for the CSO to encourage developments across the GSS. There were four areas in which the then head of the GSS, Bill McLennan, sought to make progress: co-ordinate the statistical work with Europe, provide up-to-date information on statistical sources, develop a code of practice and investigate the overall efficiency and effectiveness of the GSS. (Indeed, the appointment of

McLennan, an Australian statistician, was widely viewed as radical, and was in itself probably a sign of willingness to change.)

It was from these investigations into the gaps in official statistics and a perception that the fragmented nature of the statistical service reduced the potential for integration and coherence in statistics, that the case for the creation of a new Office for National Statistics, combining the Central Statistical Office and the Office of Population Censuses and Surveys (OPCS), was born. The driving force for the proposals – in 1995 – was to meet a widely perceived need for greater coherence and compatibility in government statistics, to improve the setting of statistical priorities, to improve presentation and to achieve easier public access.

Coincidentally, the Employment Department was abolished around this time and responsibility for labour market statistics was transferred to the CSO. This transfer was widely welcomed as it fitted neatly with the proposed agency's agenda better to integrate social and economic statistics. Labour market statistics are, of course, important to both economic and social conditions. In addition, there had always been suspicions about the political motives of the Employment Department's statisticians, not least on account of the damage to the reputation of official statistics caused by the many changes to the definition of unemployment.

Dr Tim Holt, who had been appointed head of the CSO and Head of the Government Statistical Service in July 1995, became the first director of and launched the Office for National Statistics at the end of March 1996. The framework document for the launch was issued with a forward by Kenneth Clarke, the then Chancellor of the Exchequer, to whom the Director would report.

It is clear that compared to the dark days at the end of the 1980s, much had changed for the better and more improvements were promised. The 1990s were, however, a time of rapid change in information provision and dissemination and government statisticians were finding the pace hard to keep up with. During this period, private sector companies became increasingly involved in the collection and dissemination of their own and official data. Most notably, the collection of the data for the RPI was put out to tender. Demands and expectations from users were nonetheless growing exponentially and many economic activities were becoming harder to measure. Against a background of constant reorganisation and staffing difficulties – and, despite the rhetoric, continuing budget restraint – it was difficult for the ONS to fulfil its potential.

New Labour, New Statistics?

In May 1997 the new Labour Government was elected. Its manifesto committed it to a comprehensive programme of constitutional reform as part of developing a new relationship between government and citizens based on openness and trust. One element was the commitment to an independent national statistical service.

Accordingly, in February 1998 the then Economic Secretary to the Treasury launched a Green Paper ('Statistics: a matter of trust'). The key aims of the Green Paper were widely welcomed even if there was some criticism of the content itself which was seen as shallow. There were warnings that parliamentary time for legislation would be hard to find and that the government would have to look closely at the likely costs of any change. All of this hinted at modest change relative to the expectations that had built up. In opposition, Labour had been a vocal supporter for improvements in official statistics. It began to appear that, once in government, the enthusiasm was waning, perhaps offering further evidence of Ministers' desire to exert control over statistics.

The submission from the RSS (May 1998) set out a number of principles which it felt ought to guide the deliberations:

- The establishment and maintenance of a set of National Statistics, the scope and content of which reflected public interest and continue to respond to needs over time. The independence and integrity would be assured by adopting the highest professional standards.
- There should be a cultural shift among those producing and using statistics, to include among other things an increased focus on the usefulness of outputs.
- The scope of National Statistics should include all statistics of public interest at the national, regional and local levels, regardless of the agency that produces them.
- A UK statistician should be appointed to have the ultimate professional authority for defining and auditing the accuracy, relevance and integrity of the statistics.
- A National Statistical Commission should be established to protect and

promote the quality of National Statistics. It should be independent of any single producer and of political interference.

- An Act of Parliament should establish the powers, duties and rights of the UK statistician and of the Commission.
- A system of quality and fitness for purpose self-certification, subject to audit by the UK statistician, means that only limited changes to statistical structures within government and agencies would be necessary.

The Government's proposals, in the form of a White Paper, were not published in 1998 as expected. Instead, the Economic Secretary announced (in July 1998) an efficiency scrutiny by external management consultants to cover the whole of the ONS's operations. Its report was published in February 1999. The study envisaged a streamlining of activities and more private sector partnerships to allow the ONS to direct its professional resources to those areas – statistics and customer relations – where it has the largest contribution to make. It envisaged a drop of about 1,000 in ONS staffing from the prevailing level of 3,300. While many of these posts could be transferred to the private sector, it said, a number would be lost. It was estimated by the consultants that efficiency savings of £20 million a year, roughly 16 per cent of budget, could be achieved within several years. There was some scepticism as to whether the savings were achievable – and indeed about the Treasury's motivation for launching the review in the first place – but some the general principles of the report were accepted.

Independently, the House of Commons Treasury Committee announced in May 1998 that it had established a sub-committee to scrutinise the departments and agencies for which the Chancellor is responsible. In view of the government proposals to change the framework governing official statistics, set out in the Green Paper, the sub-committee decided that the ONS would be the subject of the first inquiry. The sub-committee published a critical report in December 1998, including twenty-two recommendations. The report did not want to pre-empt the consultation on the new framework but did identify criteria which it said the new arrangements would need to satisfy.

These exercises on their own were probably sufficient to delay the publication of the White Paper, but an additional factor – the suspension of the average earnings index in November 1998 due to concerns over the

Senior statisticians in government

	1975	2004
grade 1 (perm secretary)	1	1
grade 2	5	0
grade 3	19	9
grade 4	0	6
grade 5 (chief statistician)	82	65

source: ONS

Eroding statistical expertise

Throughout the period of the last 30 years there has been a steady chipping away at the number of senior statisticians in government service. In 1975 there were twenty-five statisticians at Under Secretary level (grade 3) or above compared to just ten now. Given this has happened at the time when the statistical outputs have increased dramatically, the fall in senior staff raises questions about the integrity and quality of the outputs in some departments. The role of the government statistician has developed through the increased complexity of sources and measurement methods, the application of richer data bases, and heightened expectations from customers. But the status of statisticians within departments has probably been eroded by the increased number of political advisers, press officers, economists and social scientists.

quality of a new methodology – implied further delay. The Treasury launched a review of the earnings series which subsequently reported in March 1999.

The government's White Paper "Building trust in statistics", was eventually published in October 1999. The Economic Secretary, launching the White Paper, said "Enhancing the quality and integrity of official statistics is at the heart of our new proposals". The proposal to create a Statistics Commission which "will be independent of both ministers and the producers of statistics" to "help ensure that official statistics are trustworthy and responsive to public needs", was widely welcomed.

There was, however, some concern expressed by the statistics community, including the Royal Statistical Society. First, the proposed scope of National Statistics was very narrow, with only the outputs of the Office for National Statistics being automatically included. In future, ministers would determine the scope, rather than statistics being selected if they were important or if they met some quality threshold. Second, the Treasury did not intend to enshrine the changes in legislation. Accordingly, it would be open to future governments to alter the arrangements on a whim or water them down over time. The Treasury promised a more detailed document, the Framework for National Statistics, by the end of 1999 – it was eventually published in April 2000.

The importance of statistical legislation

Len Cook, National Statistician, says the essential arguments for statistical legislation rest firstly on the fact that the huge impact of the decisions taken on the basis of official statistics justifies the authority to make the response to many statistical surveys compulsory, in particular business surveys and the ten-yearly population census. Secondly, to provide a check on this authority to obtain information, the official statistician has three obligations to safeguard integrity which are fundamental to trust in the official statistical system: to protect the confidentiality of individual respondents, ensure impartiality in the presentation of all results and to demonstrate objectivity and methods.

More specifically, he has listed 12 reasons why he feels statistics legislation is important for Britain:

- to carry out surveys that need very high response rates in order to be confident of their reliability
- to protect statistical records from being used for any other purpose
- to distinguish official statistical surveys from the great plethora of information gathering that goes on in households and business
- to recognise that records of public and business transactions are able to be valuable, and sometimes unique, statistical sources
- to ensure the validity of published statistics, by a high level of confrontation, more increasingly at a micro data level
- to ensure that official statistics are of sufficient quality that the whole community is represented by them
- to embrace in the definition of official statistics, not only statistical measures and statistical sources, but also micro data access, methodology and practice
- to define the conditions under which official surveys can form the resource base for research in the community
- to enable all government records to be used for official statistics, subject to requirements to protect confidentiality
- to manage the respondent load from official surveys
- to allow the national statistical office to be a special place to match records that are unable to be joined for operational purposes
- to ensure that confidentiality of survey respondents is protected,

particularly in respect to a population register, the business directory, a national address register and the national geographic referencing system

source: "Some thoughts on official statistics in public life in Britain", Len Cook speech at the City University, November 2004

The Statistics Commission set out its arguments in favour of legislation in their report published in May 2004. (source: www.statscom.org.uk)

The Statistics Commission was duly established in June 2000 and the new structure with it but in many respects little changed "on the ground" for users of data. There was new branding and high expectations. The ONS has published a stronger code of practice (in September 2002, with a preface by the prime minister) and lots of supporting protocols. There has been progress in statistical outputs in recent years but many of these, such as the neighbourhood statistics initiative (giving data for communities) and the increased availability of information on the internet, would have happened regardless of any changes in the governance of statistics. Yet, the demands being made on the ONS from international organisations, the British government, the devolved administrations and a range of other users, continued to expand regardless of any changes in governance.

The programme of "quality reviews" of data (to be conducted by departments), promised for every dataset every five years, as part of the new framework has, however, been slow to take off, leaving a large backlog. In part this has been due to other initiatives coming along: the Allsopp review of regional statistics, set in motion by the Treasury, reported in 2004, the review of population estimates after the failures of the 2001 census, and the Atkinson review of public sector measurement which reported in January 2005.

The Commission also got off to a slow start but when its second chairman, Professor David Rhind, along with the second chief executive, Richard Alldritt, took over in 2003, more impact was seen. It has since produced many useful publications – published on its website and summarised in its annual reports – including a proposal for statistics legislation.

One of the themes of this decade – and a phase that is only now being exploited – is the integration of measurement with government and business process allowing the mass monitoring of transactions, events and attributes. This produces more timely data and gives a far greater immediacy to the analysis – and allows one series to be linked with other outputs. This has led to a new issue arsing, namely the politics of information access, ownership and use. Discussion about the possibility of a population register – something that all statisticians should be in favour of given the possible data that might flow from it – has served to highlight the fact that British official statistics are much less founded on the administrative records, such as tax returns, held by other government departments, than almost all comparable countries.

But there is hope that progress can be made on this front – although it is unclear how rapidly, if at all, the National Statistician will gain access to the administrative records. The government spending reviews of 2002 and 2004 have allocated to the ONS sufficient funds for a major transformation of the processes, methods and practices behind the official statistics it produces. The investment is long overdue and will remove the risks inherent in a system which is heavily based on a legacy of fragmented and often obsolete processes. Unfortunately for users, the upgrading of the methodology across the ONS will lead to larger than normal revisions in some data as each series is in turn brought up to standard.

The government needs this progress just as non-government users desire it. Government operations and policy have also changed becoming much more linked to personal information rather than being dependent on universal programmes and benefits – a shift from macro to micro policies. Neither this policy shift nor the public service agreement targets that the government has set itself reflecting the subjects that ministers think they should be judged on, could have existed in the same form just a few years ago as they depend on the new data sources. Cheap and widely available computer processing has democratised statistics too, allowing anyone with a computer to engage in analysis of the raw data.

In this state of constant evolution, if not revolution, the structures never seem to have time to bed in. An announcement was made in September 2004 that, as part of the Treasury's plan to relocate civil servants out of London, a large part of the ONS would be moving, mostly to boost its existing office in Newport. The Statistics Commission has produced, as it was required to by the Treasury, a proposal for legislation to underpin the independence of the government statistics machine. At the time of writing, the Treasury's response was still awaited. Len Cook, the Kiwi head of the ONS and first National Statistician, has announced that he will not be seeking a renewal of his contract and will be leaving in the summer of 2005. There are suspicions that his job will be split up when a successor is sought. And the Conservatives published an ambitious proposal for a much tougher framework for statistics in December 2004. It looks like 2005 will be another year of change.

Key websites:

www.statistics.gov.uk – to find the framework documents, code of practice, NS annual report, information about the ONS and work programmes

www.statscom.org.uk – the Statistics Commission

www.rss.org.uk – for responses to the evolving structure of official statistics

www.hm-treasury.gov.uk – the Treasury is the department responsible for national statistics

The statistics

Section 1 • Birth and death

The cliche of a family with 2.4 children is now just an historical relic from the 1960s. In 2003 the total fertility rate in the UK was 1.71 children per woman. This was a slight increase from the record low of 1.63 in 2001, with the rate in 2000 and 2002 being at similar levels. During the 1960s 'baby boom' the TFR peaked in 1964 at 2.95 children per woman, but the rate has been between 1.6 and 1.9 for the last 30 years. An average family size of just under 2.1 children per woman is needed for the population in the longer term to replace itself if mortality rates are constant and there is no net migration.

As well as falling fertility rates, changing fertility patterns in the UK over the last 30 years or so have also been characterised by rising mean age at first birth and higher levels of childlessness. In 2003, the mean age of women having their first birth was 26.9 years, a rise of 3.2 years from 1971. The average age of the mother for childbirth is now just under 30 years old. The highest fertility rate remains amongst women aged 25 to 29, at 96 live births per thousand women. In recent years the rate for women in their thirties and forties has been rising while that for younger women has been falling. The fertility rate is 20% higher in the west Midlands (the region with the highest rate) compared to Scotland (the region with the lowest rate).

Throughout the twentieth century there were large fluctuations in the number of births in the UK. Sharp peaks in the number of births occurred after both world wars. The largest annual number of births during the twentieth century occurred in 1920, when there were 1,127,000 births. In the 1960s there was a more sustained 'baby boom', with births rising to a peak of 1,015,000 in 1964. This was followed by a rapid decline in the numbers in the 1970s, reaching a low of 657,000 in 1977. The large numbers of women resulting from the 1960s 'baby boom' contributed to a small rise in the number of births in the late 1980s and early 1990s. In 2003 there were 695,500 births in the UK, an increase of 26,800 on the year.

The proportion of live births outside marriage has increased since the early 1980s to 41% in 2003. The proportion varies considerably across the

Around one in five women currently reaching the end of their fertile life is childless, compared to one in ten women born in the mid-1940s

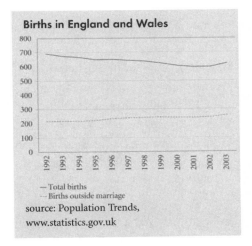

Births in England and Wales

— Total births
-- Births outside marriage

source: Population Trends, www.statistics.gov.uk

Total Fertility Rate
The TFR is the sum of the age specific fertility rates expressed per woman and is useful as it removes the effect of different age distributions over time. It can be interpreted as the average number of children per woman that would be born to a group of women if current age specific patterns of fertility persisted throughout their childbearing life.

19% of UK births in 2003 – and 47% of the births in London – were to mothers born outside the UK despite only 8% of the whole population being born outside the UK

What's in a name

In 2004 Jack celebrated its tenth year as the most popular name in the UK for baby boys. Joshua, Thomas, James and Daniel join Jack in the top five. The top five is unchanged since 2002, reflecting a consistency with which parents select boys' names. Emily occupied the top spot on the girls' list for the second year running. Chloe – top for six years until 2003, fell to number five, behind Ellie, Jessica and Sophie.

Nearly 800 women over the age of 85 die each year for every girl who dies between the age of five and nine

country, from over half in the north east and Wales to just over one third in Northern Ireland, London and the south east. The proportion also varies considerably by the age of mother – over 90% of births to teenagers occurred outside marriage in 2003 compared to just over a third for mothers in their late twenties. Nearly two thirds of births registered outside marriage were registered jointly by parents living in the same address, with the remainder being sole registrations, including only the mother's details.

Sole registration of births is a strong indication of entry into lone parenthood although in one in twelve cases the mother is cohabiting with the father and in some others there is known contact with the father. Women who have made a sole registration are more likely to have started their families at an earlier age, have had larger families and more likely to come from a lower social class. Women born in the Caribbean or West Africa are more likely to have a sole registered birth while those born in India, Pakistan and Bangladesh are less likely than average to have a sole registered birth. (source: Population Trends 117, www.statistics.gov.uk) The trends in registration might change from 2005, when it becomes possible for unmarried fathers to give birth registration information separately.

In 2003, just over 9,000 women gave birth to twins, 127 to triplets and three to quadruplets. The multiple maternity rate was just under 15 maternities with multiple births per thousand women giving birth. The 2003 figure was down slightly on the previous year, but the trend over the last decade has been for an increase in the number of multiple births. Married women in their late thirties were most likely to have multiple births. (source: Population Trends 118, ONS)

In 2003, 612,000 deaths were registered in the UK. For the first half of the twentieth century there was no strong trend in the number of deaths although there was noticeable annual fluctuation. The peak number of deaths in the UK during the twentieth century (715,200 deaths) occurred in 1918, at the time of an influenza pandemic. From the 1950s the number of deaths rose slightly and annual fluctuations were smaller. Deaths reached a peak of 676,000 in 1979 and then started to fall, continuing to date. However, deaths are projected to increase as generations born in the 1960s reach the end of their life span.

The first year of life is far less dangerous now than it used to be, but the death rate is still higher than in the person's next 30 years. One baby from every 570 live births in 2003 died. The death rate then falls and is the lowest for children between the ages of five and nine. The rate then starts to rise, especially so for young men so that by their early twenties, more than three young men die for every young woman. The rate becomes more even between the sexes in the older age groups but men are more likely to die than women at every age. For men in the over 85 category, the death rate rises sharply to nearly one in five every year.

In 2001, there were 136,000 new widows and 67,000 new widowers. These numbers are on a gently declining trend reflecting the decreasing popularity of marriage. 160 people were widowed under the age of 25.

The Scots have by far the highest death rate of any UK region. Measured by the standardised mortality ratio – the ratio of observed deaths to those expected by applying a standard death rate to the region – Scotland tops the league at 114 compared to the UK average of 100. The east, south east and south west are the lowest at between 90 and 92.

The driver of mortality decline changed over the twentieth century, from reductions in infant, child and young adult mortality to improvements in old age mortality. Infant mortality accounted for 25% of deaths in 1901, but had fallen to 4% of deaths by the middle of the last century and less than 1% now. Deaths at age 75 and over comprised only 12% of all deaths at the beginning of the last century, rising to 39% in 1951 and 65% in 2001.

The number of deaths reported to coroners was a record high in 2003, at 211,000. The long-term upward trend in the number of deaths reported to coroners probably reflects the growing use of deputising services by GPs, in which cases the doctor attending at or after death cannot legally give a medical certificate showing the cause of death. The percentage of registered deaths reported to coroners has risen to 39%, from 33% a decade ago. Post-mortem examinations were carried out in 57% of the cases reported to coroners and an inquest was held in 13% of cases. The most common verdict returned at an inquest was death by accident or misadventure (40% of all verdicts), followed by natural causes (20%), suicides (13%), and open verdicts (11%). (source: "Deaths reported to coroners", England and Wales 2003, June 2004, Home Office)

100 years ago, over half of deaths occurred under age 45, but by 2001, 96 per cent of deaths occurred at ages 45 and over.

Death rates by age, deaths each year per thousand people of that age

	men	women
Under one year	5.7	4.9
1-4	0.2	0.2
5-9	0.1	0.1
10-14	0.1	0.1
15-19	0.5	0.2
20-24	1.0	0.3
25-34	0.9	0.4
45-54	3.8	2.5
55-64	9.6	5.9
65-74	26.3	16.7
75-84	72.8	51.3
85+	190.4	165.8

source: Population Trends, www.statistics.gov.uk, England and Wales

Just under 1,000 children aged between one and nine died in 2003, compared to 354,000 people aged 75 and over, in England and Wales

Section 2 • **Population and censuses**

The UK population, mid-2003

	Headcount	%
UK	59,553,700	100%
England	49,855,700	83.7%
Scotland	5,057,400	8.5%
Wales	2,938,000	4.9%
Northern Ireland	1,702,600	2.9%

source: Population Trends, www.statistics.gov.uk

The UK's population

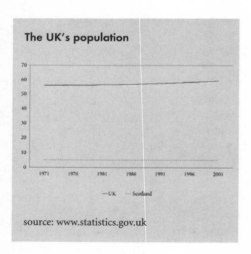

source: www.statistics.gov.uk

In mid-2003 the UK was home to 59.6 million people. The average age was 38.4 years, an increase on 1971 when it was 34.1 years. In mid-2003 one in five people in the UK were aged under 16 and one in six people were aged 65 or over.

The UK has a growing population. The UK population increased by 6.5% in the last 30 years or so, from 55.9 million in mid 1971. Growth has been faster in more recent years, reflecting the rise in immigration – indeed, immigration has contributed more than double the growth from natural change in each of the last four years. Between 1991 and 2003, the population grew by an annual rate of 0.3% . It grew by 232,100 people – a record for recent years – in the year to mid 2003, growth of 0.4%

The UK also has an ageing population. This is the result of declines both in fertility rates and in the mortality rate. This has led to a declining proportion of the population aged under 16 and an increasing proportion aged 65 and over. The population pyramid showing the population in 2003 illustrates clearly the impact of wars on the country's population. The sharp increase in the population aged 84 and 85 reflects the end of hostilities in 1918. The relative shortage of 62 and 63 year olds reflects the outbreak of the Second World War just as the large number of 55 and 56 year olds reflects the end of the war. Britain's "baby boom" is seen in the bulge in the numbers now in their late thirties and early forties who were born in the prosperous and fertile 1960s. Though these patterns are quite marked, many other countries have much more marked shadows from wars. (From the www.statistics.gov.uk website, click on the "Census2001" icon to see subject profiles of the country or profile of individual local authorities.)

In every year since 1901, with the exception of 1976, there were more births than deaths in the UK, hence the population has grown due to natural change. Until the second half of the 1990s, this natural increase was the main driver of population growth. Since the late 1990s, there has still been natural increase but net international migration into the UK from abroad has been an increasingly important factor in population change.

Not all parts of the UK are sharing equally in this population growth. Scotland, notably, has had a declining population for several decades, having fallen from 5.24 million in the early 1970s to 5.06 million in 2003. Both Wales and Northern Ireland have had an increasing population in recent years but their combined population has risen by less than 100,000 in the last decade. England, in contrast, has seen its population rise by nearly 1¾ million in the last decade. Over half of that rise has occurred in London and the south east, at a time when the population in the north east and north west has been falling. The age distribution of the population is reasonably uniform across the country with the exception of London, where there are proportionately few retired people (14%), and the south west where the proportion of retired people is high (22%).

Across the European Union, countries are experiencing a wide range of different population trends. Some countries such as Estonia, Latvia, Hungary and Poland, have seen population decreases in recent years. Most countries are, however, growing, but without inward migration some major countries such as Italy and Germany, would also have seen population falls.

UK population change, 000s

Change in the year to mid 2002/03

Population at the start of the period	59,322
Live births	682
Deaths	605
Natural change	77
Migration	155
Population at end of the period	59,554

source: Population Trends, www.statistics.gov.uk

Population: by gender and age, mid-2003

source: www.statistics.gov.uk

Population trends in selected European countries, millions

A. natural change over the decade
B. migration
C. population in 2003

	A	B	C
EU25	+3.0	+7.4	454.6
Germany	-0.9	2.5	82.5
Spain	+0.3	+2.2	41.6
France	+2.1	+0.2	59.6
Italy	-0.2	+0.6	57.3
Latvia	-0.1	-0.1	2.3
UK	+0.9	+0.8	59.3

source: Population Trends 118, www.statistics.gov.uk

Household composition		
	Millions	%
One person	7.39	30.2
Married couple	8.98	36.7
Cohabiting couple	1.97	8.0
Lone parent	2.37	9.7
Other	3.77	15.4

Source: www.stastistics.gov.uk, as at April 2001

Population figures – important but problematic

Population statistics are a fundamental output for any national statistics organisation because they provide essential information about the country's people. The estimates are also at the heart of the statistical system because they are the core information without which it is impossible to contextualise other information – figures are, for example, often given as a proportion of the whole population or some age group. The problem is that the population is getting harder to count as populations become more fluid and mobile, as more factors influence population change and there is an increasing unwillingness on the part of many people to be counted.

One question that needs to be addressed is what population should be counted. Traditionally the measure has been the resident population, but the increased population mobility and more complex living arrangements mean that a concept of usual residence is becoming less clear. There are significant numbers of people who no longer regard themselves as being associated with a single place of residence. The link between people and dwellings has weakened, which has a huge significance for the data collection exercises that have been based on the traditional premise that such one-to-one association exists. People can now more easily belong to more than one household, live in more than one dwelling and therefore be part of more than one community. The relationships often now span national boundaries as more people spend time living in different countries.

In the past, migrants were mainly people who moved to settle in a new land, but they now form a much more diverse group including economic migrants and their dependants, refugees and asylum seekers. Globalisation has led to much greater short-term and long-term mobility. There is a need to understand better the extent of such population movement – people can change country for seasonal work, to undertake short contracts, to study, or for retirement and the spell in each country could be from a few months to a few years, and one-off or periodic.

Population statistics are used for a multitude of diverse purposes, including allocation of funding, planning service provision, developing and monitoring policy and monitoring trends – consequently no single population definition will meet users' needs. The range of different population bases which could be useful include: population in households, population in institutions, de facto population, daytime population, the working population or the population for whom specific services are provided. (source: Population Trends 118, www.statistics.gov.uk)

Population is an important indicator for any country and the subject of periodic political debate. In 2004, the Italian government proposed that the EU changes the way it calculates member states' population from the number of people living in the country to citizenship. Germany's 2002 population of 82 million includes 7.3 million "foreigners" who cannot vote. Yet curiously, people who cannot vote in their country of abode are having their "votes" used by that country in the EU where the new system of qualified majority voting requires 62% of the EU's population to vote in favour.

The UK breaks up

There were three censuses conducted in the UK in April 2001 – for England and Wales, Scotland and Northern Ireland. The differences between them, in terms of questions asked, processing and publication, were greater than ever before. The sad end result for users is that only one basic book of results was published for the UK. For most data it is necessary to go to three separate web sites to get information – that is, if it exists in all three censuses.

In the last decade, only Spain and France have seen a larger population increase than the UK.

At the heart of population measurement in the UK is the decennial population census. Demographic methods using information on births, deaths and migration are used to estimate the population in the intervening years. It was clear from the 2001 Census (and with hindsight from the 1991 Census), that this approach is increasingly inadequate. The Office for National Statistics has embarked on a major research exercise to ensure that population counts going forward will be on firmer foundations. As the figures on births and deaths are relatively robust, attention needs to be focused on estimating the existing population and the migration flows.

A number of countries use population registers of various forms either in place of or to heavily supplement censuses, and such a possibility might be open to the UK in the years ahead. It could be effective if used with administrative records and an address register which is under development. Other countries choose to use rolling surveys around the country rather than one national census on one day every ten years.

English Regional Populations, 2003	
	Millions
North East	2.5
North West	6.8
Yorkshire	5.0
East Midlands	4.3
West Midlands	5.3
East	5.5
London	7.4
South East	8.1
South West	5.0

source: Population Trends, ONS

A million missing men?

When the figures from the 2001 Census were published in the autumn of 2002, there was an immediate suspicion among experts that the recorded population was too low. The census figure was 1.1 million below the latest estimate for the population in 2001. In particular, it seemed that the number of young men between the age of 15 and 35 was too low.

Several local authorities found that their population had dropped by a sizeable amount – 15 authorities saw their population "fall" by at least 7% "overnight". Westminster, which saw a fall of nearly one quarter from 245,000 to 181,000, lobbied aggressively to have its figure revised since such a large fall would lead to large cuts in its funding from central government.

By July 2003, following a meeting on the census at the Royal Statistical Society, and a parliamentary committee report calling for "clear leadership and drive at the top of the ONS to restore confidence", and just before the ONS was due to publish mid-year estimates of population, it was announced that the census figures would in effect be by-passed to allow higher population figures to be published.

In September 2003, a year after the first results were published, the ONS tacitly admitted the error by adding nearly 200,000 people, mainly young men, to its mid-year estimates of population. As most of the additions were to the population of London, it implied that the census failed to count one in six young men in the capital. The census figures themselves were never revised, leaving the so-called "one number census" figure of 58,789,194 some way below the 2001 mid-year estimate of 59,113,000 – it is even below the latest published estimate of the mid-year population estimate for 2000.

In November 2003, 22,000 people were added to the population of Manchester, following the 5,000 that were added as part of the more general exercise in September, in total adding 7% to its population, recouping much of the 10½% gap opened up by the census results. Finally, in July 2004, the ONS made a long-awaited adjustment to the population of Westminster. The addition of 17,000 people was part of a package announcing increases to 15 local authorities. The ONS admitted that there were some areas where enumerators had not done their job properly. Indeed, there were reports of entire blocks of flats being left off the count in Westminster.

Traditionally there is considerable interest in specific categories in the population such as minority ethnic groups, those with certain religious affiliations and carers. Had any of these special interest groups been mis-estimated to the extent that young men were, there would have been a national outcry. Young men, however, is not a category that anyone particularly cares about.

Indeed, it could be argued that it is in the interests of government to have fewer such people counted. For example, the government's target to have 50% of young people going to university instantly became a little more achievable. The reduction in young people recorded as being in the country meant that the number currently in tertiary education equated to 43% of the target group rather than the 41% reported on the basis of the earlier figure.

The ONS is planning a mini census for 2007 and the next 10 year census in 2011 but has yet to say how it plans to count the young men. They said most had emigrated but it is widely suspected that they failed to count a large proportion of them. Reasons for young men not filling in the forms are many: no sense of civic duty, moving often between homes, and many being foreign and feeling it did not apply to them. It is also possible that many are cohabiting with women who are drawing single parent allowances and felt the benefit might be under threat if it was known that they lived there.

The fiasco – with the non form filling described as the biggest case of civil diobedience in the last decade – was the subject of a BBC radio four documentary called, *Where have all the young men gone?* broadcast on January 2nd 2005.

Notwithstanding the difficulties of enumeration in certain areas (particularly the inner cities) and certain types of people (young men and the very elderly), the census is an incredibly rich source of data. One major development for the 2001 census was the availability of local area data. This is readily and freely available on the internet and gives full census information for very small geographic areas, roughly a hundred or so households. (source: click on the "neighbourhood" section of www.statistics.gov.uk) Information is available on a large range of demographic indicators such as age, sex, marital status and ethnicity, but also for occupation, social class, industry of job, living arrangements, country of birth, health, qualifications, and various features of accommodation.

Section 3 • Marriage, cohabitation and divorce

Most people in England and Wales, nearly 31 million out of 52 million (roughly 60%) live in a married couple family. Around 6½ million people live alone, a slightly smaller number live in lone parent families and 5½ million live in a cohabiting couple family. Some 3½ million people live in a household with others or a communal establishment. (source: Census 2001, ONS)

The number of marriages in 2003 was fractionally higher than the year before, but more data will be needed before the end of the long-term downward trend can be called. The proportion of marriages that are civil ceremonies has risen every year in the last decade, reaching 68%. Since 1995, it has been possible to have civil weddings in approved premises, as opposed to registry offices, and such ceremonies now account for just over one quarter of the total. Roughly three fifths of marriages are the first marriage for both parties. Nearly 5% of divorced people remarry each year.

Around 1% of women aged under 19 – 12,000 in 2003 – are married. The married proportion then rises sharply with age, so that 10% are married by their mid-twenties and one third by the age of 30. Over a half are married by their mid-thirties and two thirds by the mid-forties. The proportion of women married at a young age used to be much higher – in the early 1970s over 10% were married by 19 and 60% by the age of 24.

The average length of a first cohabitation is 40 months. The average length of a second cohabitation is 32 months. One quarter of all cohabitations have lasted five years or more, yet 60% last less than three years.

In 2003, the number of divorces granted in the UK increased by 3.7% to 166,700, from 160,700 in 2002. This is the highest number since 1997, and the third successive annual increase. It is still 7% less than the peak of 180,000 in 1993. (source: www.statistics.gov.uk) The peak age for divorce is between 25 and 29, with over three divorces being granted each year per hundred married couples. The rate is just a little lower for all couples between the ages of 16 and 44 but tumbles to one third of that for those aged 45 or over.

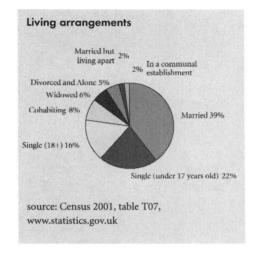

Living arrangements

Married but living apart 2%
In a communal establishment 2%
Divorced and Alone 5%
Widowed 6%
Cohabiting 8%
Single (18+) 16%
Married 39%
Single (under 17 years old) 22%

source: Census 2001, table T07, www.statistics.gov.uk

Six out of ten households in rural areas comprise of a married couple compared to fewer than one in four in inner London

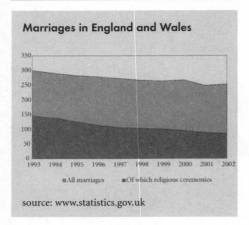

Marriages in England and Wales

source: www.statistics.gov.uk

Nearly 70% of divorces in England and Wales were granted to the wife. The most frequent fact on which divorce was granted to a woman was the "unreasonable behaviour" of her husband, while for a man it was separation for two years with consent. Of those getting divorced, one quarter of the men and one third of the women were aged under 35. Demographic factors associated with an increased risk of subsequent divorce include marrying at a younger than average age, having a pre-marital birth, and having previously been divorced. While the number of petitions filed for divorce and the number of divorces follow the same trend over time, the two figures will be different in any given period. (source: Population Trends 117, www.statistics.gov.uk)

There were 84,000 couples divorced in 2003 who had children aged under 16. The number of children so affected was 154,000 in 2003, the highest number for some years, meaning that one million children aged under 16 see their parents divorced after six or seven years.

One quarter of those getting divorced have been married for less than five years and one fifth for over 20 years – the median duration of marriages for which a divorce is granted is 11 years

The decade divorce took off

In 1961, there were 27,200 divorces in Great Britain, which by 1969 had doubled to 55,600. The number of divorces then doubled again by 1972, to 124,600 in Great Britain. This latter increase was partly a 'one-off' effect of the Divorce Reform Act 1969 in England and Wales, which came into effect in 1971. In England and Wales, 69% of divorces in 2003 were to couples where both parties were in their first marriage. Over the last ten years the average age at divorce in England and Wales has risen from 39 to 42 years for men, and from 36 to 40 years for women – partly reflecting the rise in age at marriage.

The mean age of divorce is at a record high – 42 for men and 40 for women

Section 4 • Population change and life expectancy

Population projections have become interesting in the last couple of years as migration is now a larger component of change than natural growth from births and deaths. In 2004, for example, migration is forecast to add 130,000 to the population while natural change adds 106,000. The projections for migration are far more uncertain than for natural change.

The Government Actuary has, since 1954, produced the official national population projections for the United Kingdom and its constituent countries. The projections are produced at the request of the Registrars General of England & Wales, Scotland and Northern Ireland. The assumptions on which they are based are agreed in consultation with the statistical offices of the four countries. The primary purpose of the projections is to provide an estimate of future population which is used as a common framework for national planning in different fields.

Population projections are produced for the United Kingdom and constituent countries by age and sex. These projections are normally prepared every second year. Additionally, however, an interim set of 2003-based national projections was published on 30 September 2004 to reflect the publication of the latest 10-yearly population census results. The main focus of the projections is on the first 25 years currently up to 2028. Longer-term projections to the year 2043 for individual countries, and to 2073 for the United Kingdom and Great Britain only, are also available. GAD also produces population projections by marital status for England and Wales. (source: www.gad.gov.uk) The population of the UK is expected to rise from 60.0 million in 2004 to 62.4 million in the next decade.

The GAD also publishes life expectancy tables by country and sex. The Pensions Commission report was the latest to highlight the two different definitions of life expectancy used in published figures. It refers to the "cohort life expectancy" as the "correct" figure. This gives, say, a 65 year old in 2004 what it calls the "best" estimate of how long he or she will live incorporating a range of assumptions about future trends – strictly speaking, it is worked out using age-specific mortality rates which allow for known or

39 is the age at which a man in England is on average over half way through his life – as his life expectancy drops below his age. For English women the cross over age is 41. Using the cohort figures, which adjust for improvements taking place in society a man currently in his forties passes the half way point at 42. The halfway point for a boy born in 2004 is 43 years due to life improvements expected over the coming years

Life expectancy for English males is 76½ on a period basis but over 83 on a cohort basis.

projected changes in mortality in later years. The "period life expectancy", in contrast, is the measure of life expectancy assuming that the person experiences the age-specific mortality rates that each age group is currently experiencing. For example, period life expectancy at age 65 in 2000 would be worked out using the mortality rate for age 65 in 2000, for age 66 in 2000, for age 67 in 2000, and so on. Cohort life expectancy at age 65 in 2000 would be worked out using the mortality rate for age 65 in 2000, for age 66 in 2001, for age 67 in 2002, and so on. (source: www.pensionscommission.orguk) The choice of definition does make a difference – at the age of 60, the period basis points to 20 years of life and the cohort method to 23.

The problem with the period version is that it underestimates true life expectancy if expectancy is on an upward trend – as people born in successive generations benefit from better health care, diet, working and living conditions and so forth. Unfortunately, partly because period life expectancy figures are easier to produce and (supposedly) to understand, they are the most commonly used in government publications and press reports.

The commission recommended that official publications where possible use the cohort approach when describing current and future trends in longevity. But doing so will require assumptions to be made about the future which are very hard to make at the moment. Death rates have been declining for 150 years but that does not mean that they will continue to do

Population projections and life expectancy, UK

	2003 –2004	2004 –2005	2005 –2006	2006 –2007	2007 –2008	2008 –2009	2009 –2010	2010 –2011	2011 –2012	2012 –2013
Population at start	59,554	59,787	60,024	60,254	60,481	60,707	60,934	61,166	61,401	61,640
Births	706	703	692	684	680	679	681	683	686	689
Deaths	603	597	592	588	584	582	579	578	577	577
Natural change (births - deaths)	104	106	100	97	96	98	102	105	108	111
Migration	130	130	130	130	130	130	130	130	130	130
Total change	234	236	230	227	226	228	232	235	238	241
Population at end	59,787	60,024	60,254	60,481	60,707	60,934	61,166	61,401	61,640	61,881
EOLB Males	76.4	76.6	76.9	77.2	77.4	77.6	77.9	78.1	78.3	78.5
Females	80.7	81.0	81.2	81.4	81.6	81.8	82.0	82.2	82.4	82.5

source: www.gad.gov.uk

2003-based, components of change (mid-year to mid-year) and expectation of life at birth based on the mortality rates for the year, thousands

so. There is no reason why the rise in childhood obesity in developed countries, for example, in the last decade might not deliver unusual patterns of death as, but probably not to the same extent, as Aids has in less developed countries (where it has become common for children to die before their parents).

A person's life expectancy increases with each year that they live – as they have avoided death in that year. A new born male in England can be expected to live – on a period basis – for just over 76 years according to the latest figures. While a 40-year old can expect to live for a further 38 years – to the age of 78. Similarly, a 60-year old has just over 20 years of expected life and an 80-year old has 7 years.

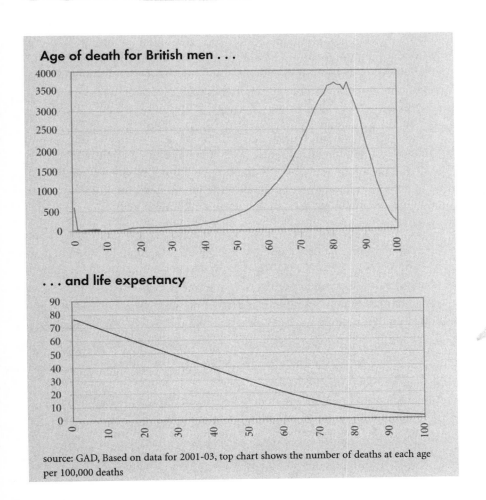

Age of death for British men . . .

. . . and life expectancy

source: GAD, Based on data for 2001-03, top chart shows the number of deaths at each age per 100,000 deaths

Section 5 • Migration and asylum

Immigration is now a bigger driver of population change than births and deaths

Poor data?

"Whilst there is much emerging research on migrants and refugees in the UK and Europe, much is based on small scale studies, often oriented to individual migrant groups in particular places."

"Little attention has been paid to how those who migrate experience changing economic, social and policy contexts over time."

"There is no doubt that there are significant gaps in available datasets on asylum and other international migrants in the UK."

source: Sussex Centre for Migration Research, Working Paper No 14, www.sussex.ac.uk

The figures for migration and asylum are not what would be wanted in an ideal world when such a sensitive topic is so high up the political agenda. Fears and prejudice can breed in the absence of a clear government policy and accurate and reliable data. There are gaps in the data and a too heavy reliance on administrative data and poor quality surveys measuring the flows across the borders which often do not answer the questions that people want answered. Without data on the extent of illegal immigration – no official figures exist for the number of illegal immigrants – despite such studies being conducted in a number of other countries, it is impossible to know the scale of the problem and the success that the government is having tackling it.

Immigration has risen up the political priority list due to the large recent changes in the size and nature of UK international migration and its contribution to overall population change. Indeed in the space of a decade, net international migration has grown from near zero to contributing three-quarters of the growth of the UK population in 2001. In terms of absolute numbers, in 1992 the 268,000 immigrants arriving and 281,000 emigrants leaving were already substantial in relation to the other components of population change, consisting of 781,000 births and 634,000 deaths. By 2001, however, 480,000 immigrants arrived in a year that saw only 669,000 births, while emigrants numbered 308,000 in a year that saw 602,000 deaths.

So how many people are entering the UK each year as migrants? It is hard to say. Around 91 million people were recorded entering Britain and Ireland during 2003, of which 64 million (some 70%) were British citizens. Very few of these passengers are stopped at the point of entry, indeed in 2003 only 38,000 were refused entry and subsequently removed from the country. This figure was down on the 50,000 in 2002 but broadly in line with the two years prior to that.

Some 12.2 million arrivals (13% of the total) were not British or European nationals – most were visitors (7.5 million, 8.3%), people returning from a temporary absence abroad such as a holiday (2.8 million, 3.1%) or passengers in transit (1.1 million, 1.3%). The remaining 730,000

Why do we need migration data?

International migration statistics are required to fulfil the most funda-mental need of a country – the monitoring of changes in its basic demo-graphic characteristics: its size, geographic distribution and composition by age and gender. For this purpose, annual immigration and emigration at the level of constituent country and government region and local authority, are required. Statistics on the size, composition and duration of stay of immigrants and emigrants are required to address additional key user needs, such as government and business planning at both the national and local levels and informing policy on the migration of non-citizens subject to immigration control. Statistics on both demographic and work-force-related attributes of migrants are desirable, as are figures on persons subject to immigration control including their legal status with regard to residence and work. Comparability wherever possible of migrant defini-tions between data sources and between statistical outputs is needed by researchers for analysis.

Arrivals in 2003

Students	319,000
Dependents and children	185,000
Work permit holders	119,000
Working holidaymakers	47,000
Spouse or fiancè	31,000
Au pairs	15,000

source: www.homeoffice.gov.uk

visitors (just under 1%) includes students (319,000), work permit holders, au pairs (15,000), people with UK ancestry, and also those admitted as a spouse or fiancé(e), those accepted for settlement on arrival, and others given leave to enter for a variety of reasons, including asylum seekers. (source: "Control of immigration, statistics UK", Home Office statistical bulletin, August 2004) Around 9,000 husbands and 19,000 wives were admitted in 2003 for a probationary year prior to settlement.

There are two main sources of information about immigrants: the inter-national passenger survey – which was designed to count the number of tourists – and statistics which are a by-product of the immigration control process. In the case of the latter, this means that changes in many of the series can reflect legal and administrative factors such as changes in the legislation or resources available to process cases. There are some other sources that can be used to cross-check the plausibility of the numbers, such as the ten-yearly population census and the Labour Force Survey.

The latest census, carried out in 2001, was in many respects very high quality, but one of its weakest links was the count of transient people,

Overseas students

The government has been criticised for handing out student visas too readily, amid evidence that some visas were given to people who claimed to have places on non-exis-tant courses at fictitious colleges. The number of overseas student visas – 319,000 – seems high compared to 540,00 awards (of which 280,000 were undergraduate degrees) made by British universities in 2004.

Bogus Marriages

The government claimed that there were around 1,700 suspicious marriages in 2003, double the number in 2001. Leaked internal memos from the Home Office said "there could be around 15,000 sham marriages each year".

What is a migrant?

A migrant is defined by the international passenger survey as someone who intends to stay in the country for more than a year and is foreign born. Migrants include students, those employed on work permits, EU citizens with freedom of movement and those coming to the UK for family reunion. They also include forced migrants such as asylum seekers and refugees. Refugees and asylum seekers are migrants but the large majority of migrants are not refugees and asylum seekers. (source: "Migration and employment", Working Brief 150, www.cesi.org.uk)

notably foreign nationals in inner-city areas, with the result that those figures are very unreliable. The results "highlighted substantial differences between net immigration as estimated indirectly from inter-censal population change and net immigration as estimated directly from survey and administrative sources in the years between the censuses. A considerable amount of user concern about National Statistics on international migration was consequently related to recognition of their increasingly crucial role for the quality of inter-censal population estimates", according to the ONS. As a result of the weaknesses in both these sources, the ONS carried out a quality review of its migration figures. (source: "International migration statistics", National Statistics quality review no 23, 2003)

The quality review showed that the British system for measuring immigration by means of a port survey was unusual – indeed Britain was the only large country relying on such a system. Most other countries use one, or a combination of, population registers, border controls (such as passport scanning) or household surveys designed at least in part for the purpose. The review came up with nineteen recommendations over five broad categories: development and better use of existing surveys, the use of existing administrative data (such as NHS records), the development of longitudinal data sets and improved social and economic analysis, improved methodology for combining data from different sources, and active consideration of new possible data sources such as population registers and electronic recording of arrival in the country and departure. While some improvements in the quality of the data can be expected in the next year or two, it is likely to be a decade or so before truly trustworthy figures are

What is the International Passenger Survey?

The IPS is a continuous voluntary sample survey of all international passengers. Until 1999 it excluded travellers to and from the Irish Republic. About 1 in 500 travellers (0.2%) are interviewed, and asked various questions including whether they intend to stay in the UK – or leave – for at least 12 months. If they do, they are considered to be immigrants or emigrants, according to the United Nations' definition. About 1% of the 260,000 interviewees in 1999 were intending migrants which means that the statistics from the IPS are based on 'grossing up' these 2,600 migrant interviews.

Those counted as immigrants will include all those entering with work permits, or intending to work, for 12 months or more, students on long courses, spouses, fiancé(e)s, children and other dependents. Asylum claimants who declare at the port of entry are not included. Those who intend to claim asylum after entry are not included either, because if they enter legally it is usually on short-term pretexts. Not all answers will be accurate or truthful – if you are entering illegally you are unlikely to tell someone carrying out a survey! – and intentions may change. Estimates tend to fluctuate for inevitable statistical reasons, as they are based on a relatively small sample size. This applies particularly to estimates of net migration, which is the difference between two large estimated numbers.

Despite its drawbacks there is currently no other suitable source for estimating the demographic effect of international migration on the UK. Estimates based on the IPS are therefore used for population and household projection. However, to be useful for these purposes the basic IPS estimates have to be corrected for the large number of people who now enter the UK on short-term pretexts and who then acquire long-term rights to residence by claiming asylum or by marriage. These 'visitor switchers' and also those who claim asylum on arrival must be included in the total of immigrants for demographic purposes. Corrections must also be made for movements between the UK and Irish Republic. The effect of these corrections has been to increase the net international migration to the UK since 1982 by up to 50,000 persons per year. Thus in 1998, the original IPS estimate of net inflow was 133,000; the corrected one 178,000. Only the 'corrected' estimates were published in 1999 (net inflow 182,000). (source:www.migrationwatchuk.com)

Only one in five women in Britain from Bangladesh and Pakistan work compared to over three-quarters of those from Australia and the Philippines.

available – and that will depend on the development of new systems such as a population register or scanning of passports at entry points.

The net inflow due to immigration has increased over the last decade and is now forecast by government (The Government Actuaries Department, www.gad.gov.uk) to stabilise at approximately 130,000 each year – the highest forecast ever. The immigration assumption would rise to 145,000 to year if failed asylum seekers and their dependants were included. (source: www.migrationwatchuk.org)

The five countries with the largest number of working age "migrants" in the UK are India, Ireland, Pakistan, Germany and Bangladesh – but these figures come from the Labour Force Survey question about country of birth, as opposed to nationality. Accordingly, the figure for Germany will give an inflated indication of how many Germans are in the country as it will include many people born to British servicemen while serving in that country. The top ten countries account for about half of the working age population in Britain that was not born in the UK.

The male employment rates for the leading migrant countries vary considerably – from around 90% for Australia and France to below 70% for Ireland, Pakistan, Jamaica and Bangladesh, compared to a rate of just over

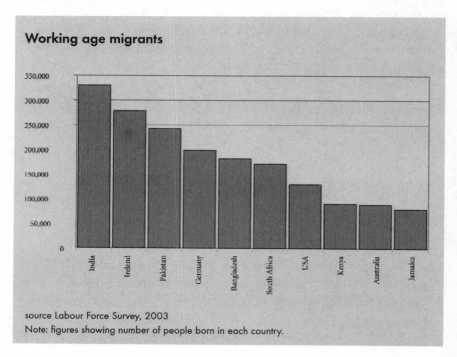

Working age migrants

source Labour Force Survey, 2003
Note: figures showing number of people born in each country.

80% for the UK as a whole. The female employment rates are much more variable with those born in Pakistan and Bangladesh below 20%, while those born in Australia, South Africa and the Philippines are all over 75%. (source: "The benefits of migration", Working Brief 152, www.cesi.org.uk) Migrants account for about 8% of Britain's working age population.

The administrative data we have to make do with have a number of weaknesses, (source: "Asylum and migration – a review of Home Office statistics", National Audit Office, May 2004), including:

- There is a weakness in the system for referrals of illegal immigrants that means Home Office data is incomplete. When illegal immigrants are arrested but then not detained by the police, they may be referred to the nearest Home Office unit where they can make their applications for asylum but the suspicion is that many do not make an application and disappear once more from view.

- Non nationals currently in a British prison are missing from the aggregate figures.

- Figures for one year might well relate to actions taken in another year.

- In the first half of 2002, a new database was implemented by the Immigration and Nationality Department to record case information which has led to a number of data quality and consistency issues.

Data users want greater comparability of migration definitions and more immigration-related variables in survey, census and administrative data sources. This would enable the reconciliation of estimates across sources, the reconciliation of migrant stocks and flows, evaluation of social and economic impacts of migration, and estimation of the approximate number and characteristics of persons entering the UK illegally or whose length of stay or employment activity extend beyond those authorised under their conditions of entry or stay.

The number of asylum seekers rose sharply during the second half of the 1990s, nearly trebling from 1996 to peak at 84,000 in 2002. These figures exclude dependents. The bulk of the increase was accounted for by people applying in country as opposed to at the time of arrival at port, suggesting that they arrived under false pretences or entered the country illegally.

A relatively small proportion of asylum seekers – less than one in seven in the last eight years – is granted asylum. A similar proportion is granted

Immigration - Myth or fact
"Britain takes only 2% of the world's refugees (Refugee Council)". Well, yes, if you include all the refugees in Asia and Africa. A better comparison is the number of asylum seekers coming to Britain compared to the number coming to Europe in a particular year. UNHCR figures for 2002 show that approximately 23% of asylum seekers arriving in Europe (and 29% of those coming to the EU) came to Britain. Beware of figures presenting immigration as a ratio per thousand inhabitants or in terms of population density.

The number of asylum seekers in Britain increased twentyfold between 1988 and 2002 and trebled between 1996 and 2002.

Number of applications for asylum

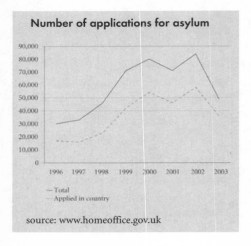

— Total
- Applied in country

source: www.homeoffice.gov.uk

Where do asylum seekers come from?

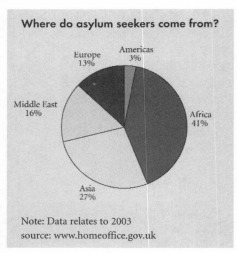

Note: Data relates to 2003
source: www.homeoffice.gov.uk

exceptional leave to remain, humanitarian protection or discretionary leave. This means that typically around three out of four asylum seekers were refused asylum. The percentages in each category are volatile from year to year but have shown a broadly flat trend from 1996 to 2003.

What is asylum?

The criteria for recognition as a refugee, and hence the granting of asylum, are set out in the 1951 United Nations Convention and in a 1967 protocol. It defines a refugee has person who "owing to a well founded fear of being persecuted for reasons of race, religion, nationality, membership of a particular social group or political opinion, is outside the country of his nationality and unable or, owing to such fear, is unwilling to avail himself of the protection of that country; or who, not having a nationality and being outside the country of his former habitual residence is unable or, owing to such fear, is unwilling to return to it".

Anyone refused asylum has the option of appealing against the decision. In this respect there was a marked change in 1999. Prior to that year fewer than 10% of the appeals were allowed, but since then over 20% – and of the larger number – have been allowed.

The weakness of the asylum system is that few of those who are refused asylum are thought to leave the country. In the four years from 2000, the recorded number of removals and voluntary departures is only about one in six of the number refused asylum. Even then, a National Audit Office report found that in a number of cases where the Home Office have claimed to remove a failed asylum seeker from the country, there was no evidence to confirm that this had happened.

There are signs that the asylum system had tightened up by 2003. The number of people granted asylum, at 4,300, was the lowest since 1997, and the number granted other forms of leave to remain, at 7,500, was the lowest since 1999. The refusal rate at 83%, was the highest since the current data format began. The proportion of applicants who were refused asylum or any other leave to stay or withdrew their applications, rose from 58% in 2001 to 60% in 2002 and 72% in 2003. The number of asylum applications outstanding at the end of 2003 was 24,000, the lowest for a decade.

The nationalities accounting for most applicants in 2003 were Somali, Iraqi, Chinese, Zimbabwean and Iranians, together accounting for 38% of the total. Compared with 2002, large falls occurred in the number of applications from nationals of Iraq, Afghanistan and Zimbabwe. More than four out of five principal applicants in 2003 were aged under 35 years old and just 3% were aged over 50. Seven out of ten principal applicants in 2003 were male. (source: "Asylum statistics UK 2003", Home Office, August 2004)

The government is not obliged to provide an asylum seeker with support – subsistence or accommodation – if the person did not make the claim as soon as "reasonably practicable" after arrival in the UK. The exceptions include families with children and those who can show they would suffer treatment contrary to human rights agreements if they returned home. In 2003, two thirds of asylum cases were refused support on the grounds that the claim was not made as soon as reasonably practicable. Just over a quarter were exempt on the grounds of it being a family application or to avoid a breach of human rights. At the end of 2003, just over 80,000 asylum seekers including dependents were in receipt of government support, including nearly 50,000 receiving accommodation. Unfortunately these figures could give a misleading impression as many thousands of asylum seekers are looked after by other organisations. In addition, local councils care for several thousand unaccompanied children.

The UK had by far the highest number of asylum applicants of any EU country in 2002 but the fall back in applications in 2003 meant that France, UK and Germany were all roughly the same, and with a larger number of applicants than any other country. (On the basis of the figures published by the Home Office, France received the most asylum applications followed by the UK. In figures supplied by Eurostat, the UK received more asylum seekers in 2003, some 61,000 compared to 52,000 in France and 51,000 in Germany. The figures from UNHCR – www.unhcr.ch – are different again. Apart from the difficulties in obtaining data, the figures often mean different things in different countries due to different definitions, legal terms and practices.) When the relative size of domestic populations is taken into account, the UK falls to the middle of the European countries'

One in three refugees is unemployed – they commonly face barriers including poor English, lack of networks and poor qualifications.

There could be up to 250,000 failed asylum seekers in Britain, equivalent to a town the size of Brighton

In the context of the 10 million refugees worldwide, western Europe's migration problems are modest

Who is covered by immigration statistics?

Home Office Immigration statistics relate to people who are subject to immigration control under Immigration Acts, that is people who do not have the right of abode in the UK. British citizens, those Commonwealth citizens who also have the right of abode, citizens of the Republic of Ireland and nationals from other European Economic Area countries are not included. EEA nationals may apply for settlement but are not obliged to do so. Since 2002, Swiss nationals enjoy the same rights as EEA nationals and their family members.

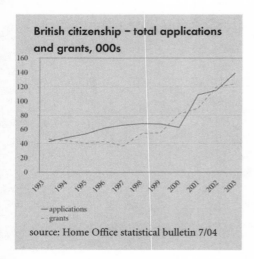

British citizenship – total applications and grants, 000s

— applications
- grants

source: Home Office statistical bulletin 7/04

league table in terms of asylum seekers per head of population.

The number of people becoming UK citizens has more than trebled since 1997, reaching 124,000 in 2003. The rise reflects the increase in the number of people granted "settlement" in the UK, excluding European Economic Area nationals, which has risen very sharply in the last six years. Having been fairly stable at between 50,000 and 60,000 during the 1980s and much of the 1990s, the figure rose sharply from 1997 to reach nearly 140,000 in 2003. While the number of asylum related grants has eased in recent years – to 21,000 in 2003 – the number of employment related grants and family grants has continued to rise. Although it is quite possible that a good number of the family grants relate to asylum seekers who have been granted settlement deciding to bring their family to the country. Rather worryingly, the mysterious categories of "other" and "category unknown" have both risen quite sharply from under 5,000 in 1999 to over 23,000, one in six, of the total. (source: "Persons granted British Citizenship, UK, 2003", Home Office, www.homeoffice.gov.uk/rds, May 2004)

Some of the rise in the number of settlements reflects a change of policy in 1998 that abolished the qualifying period for those recognised as refugees and given asylum. In addition many people who applied for asylum in the early nineties and were still awaiting a decision were granted settlement in 1999 in an attempt to reduce the asylum backlog. The Home Office describes the settlement figures as "the main available measure of longer term immigration of persons subject to immigration control".

Is illegal immigration a drain on the health service?

The claim is often made, but we do not know as no figures exist. In 2002/03 around 5 million people registered with a GP. Yet, as the NHS admits, there is no effective check on entitlement. Entitlement is based on the concept of "ordinarily resident", which is somewhat obscure: "Ordinarily resident is someone who is living lawfully in the United Kingdom, voluntarily and for settled purposes as part of the regular order of their life for the time being, with an identifiable purpose for their residence here which has a sufficient degree of continuity to be properly described as settled".

It is hard to see how a receptionist at a general practice can be expected to interpret such language. They do usually ask for proof of address but this is not the same thing as "ordinarily resident". A further requirement is that an application to join the GP's list can only be refused if there are reasonable grounds for doing so which "do not relate to the applicant's race, gender, social class, age, religion, sexual orientation, appearance, disability or medical condition". As NHS guidance says, "As the regulations stand this means that a practice has the discretion to offer NHS treatment to all people – UK residents and overseas visitors from any country."

Exclusion from a GPs list is quite unlikely – they are already facing a rising number of complaints and increasing litigation against them – as to refuse to treat a non-eligible patient based on a few brief words at the reception desk would be unwise. Should the prospective patient subsequently prove to have a serious condition which would have been deemed "emergency" or "immediately necessary treatment", the GP might have to face complaints of professional malpractice. (source: www.migrationwatchuk.org)

The cost of treating "health tourists" in the NHS who are not entitled has been estimated at £200 million by the government but could be up to ten times higher

Half of Britain's non-white population was born in the country - Mohammed was the country's 20th most popular name in 2004, its highest ranking ever

GB population by ethnicity

	000s	%
British	45,534	87.5
Irish	642	1.2
Other white	1,345	2.6
Asian and Asian British	2,273	4.4
Black and black British	1,140	2.2
Mixed	661	1.3
Chinese	227	0.4
Other ethnic group	220	0.4

source: Census 2001, ONS, www.statistics.gov.uk

GB population by religion

	000s	%
Christian	41,015	71.8
No religion declared	13,030	22.8
Muslim	1,589	2.8
Hindu	558	1.0
Sikh	336	0.6
Jewish	267	0.5
Buddhist	149	0.3
Other religion	159	0.3

source: ONS, www.statistics.gov.uk

Section 6 • Religion and ethnicity

In an increasingly multicultural world, it becomes harder to segregate people by ethnicity and race. Indeed some countries have decided not to collect such figures on the grounds that either they can be divisive or they become meaningless in areas where the population is increasingly mixed. In the UK, figures exist for ethnicity, religion and place of birth, and taken together they give a reasonable indication of the make-up of the population.

Of the 52 million people in England and Wales recorded in the 2001 census, 45½ million declared their ethnicity as British and 47½ million (over 91%) as white. Asian and Asian British is the largest ethnic group with 2¼ million people. The black and black British group – broadly equally divided between black Caribbean and black African – comprised just over one million (some 2% of the population of England and Wales).

The so-called ethnic minorities still remain a minority – even among those aged under 16, 87% are categorised as white. In some areas the ethnic minorities have become a majority – the London boroughs of Brent and Newham both recorded a white population of under 50% in the 2001 census. Even so the vast majority of British local authorities – and especially those away from inner city areas – remain virtually entirely white. Indeed, even in some entire regions, including the northeast, Wales and the South West, over 19 out of 20 people are white British. In Scotland, only 2%, one in 50, are not white and less than 1% in Cornwall.

It is really only in parts of London where people of very different backgrounds live side by side. Even then each ethnic community tends to gather in a certain part of the capital. For example, 19% of the residents of Brent are Indian compared with less than 2% in neighbouring Hammersmith and Fulham. Likewise, while 12% of the population of both Lambeth and Lewisham is black Caribbean, the figure is only 2% in neighbouring Bromley. Just over 1% of England's population describes itself as of mixed ethnic background – a proportion rising to only 2% in London.

Christianity is overwhelmingly the main religion in Great Britain – the 41 million Christians recorded in the 2001 Census, make up almost three quarters of the population. This group included the Church of England,

Church of Scotland, Church in Wales, Catholic, Protestant and all other Christian denominations. People with no religion formed the second largest group, comprising 15% of the population (and half as many again chose not to state their religion).

About one in 20 of the population belonged to a non-Christian religious denomination. Muslims were the largest of these religious groups with the 1.6 million Muslims living in Britain, comprising just 3% of the total population, yet over half (52%) of the non-Christian religious population. Muslims comprised 8% of London's population and 4% in both Yorkshire and the Humber and the West Midlands. Hindus were the second largest non-Christian religious group. There were over half a million Hindus, just over a third of a million Sikhs, and just over a quarter of a million Jewish people, constituting 0.5% of the total population and 9% of the non-Christian religious group.

Rather than select one of the specified religions offered on the 2001 Census form, many people chose to write in their own religion. Some of these religions were reassigned to one of the main religions offered, but in England and Wales, 151,000 people belonged to religious groups which did not fall into any of the main religions. The largest of these were Spiritualists (32,000) and Pagans (31,000), followed by Jain (15,000), Wicca (7,000), Rastafarian (5,000), Bahà'ì (5,000) and Zoroastrian (4,000). The religion question was the only voluntary question in the 2001 census and 8% of people chose not to state their religion. The census gave no indication of "religiosity", the degree of religious involvement, as opposed to religious identification.

Around 8% – some 4.9 million people – in the UK were born overseas. The geographic spread of the countries of origin is very wide. The largest group – around one million – were born in South Asia, essentially the Indian subcontinent, a further 800,000 were born in Africa, and another half million were born in Ireland. Around 730,000, 1.2% of the British population, were born in the European Union (excluding Ireland).

These figures probably over estimate the number of legal "foreigners" living in Britain, as they include all the children born to British people while they were living outside the UK. The figures for the number of births in Germany is particularly high, for example, well over double the number for France or Italy, reflecting the presence in that country of the British armed forces. (source: Population Trends, summer 2004, ONS, www.statistics.gov.uk)

There is one Muslim for every 250 Christians among those aged over 75 – the ratio is one to 13 for the under 15s

The distribution of non-Christian religions, 2001

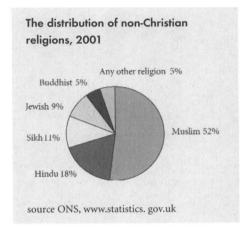

Buddhist 5%
Any other religion 5%
Jewish 9%
Sikh 11%
Muslim 52%
Hindu 18%

source ONS, www.statistics. gov.uk

Return of the Jedi?
390,000 people used the freedom to write in your own religion in the census to choose Jedi, the "noble order of protectors" from the *Star Wars* films. Had the response been listed with the main faiths, it would have come fourth, above Sikhism and Judaism. It shows how responses to a survey – in this case promoted by a student campaign – can affect survey results.

Section 7 • Childcare

Trend in childcare use for couple families,

source: FRS survey, DWP working paper number 16, 2005

The government set out a "National Childcare Strategy" in the Green Paper "Meeting the Childcare Challenge" in 1998. The aim is to "ensure good quality, affordable childcare for children aged 0 to 14 in every neighbourhood, including both formal childcare and support for informal arrangements, by: raising the quality of care, making childcare more affordable and making childcare more accessible by increasing places and improving information."

This initiative is part of a wider plan for children. The "Every child matters" Green Paper was published for consultation in September 2003. In March 2004, the Government published "Every child matters: next steps". The new Children Act 2004 provides the legal framework for the programme of reform. And finally, the Government's ten year strategy for early years and childcare, "Choice for Parents, the Best Start for Children", was published in the Pre Budget Report in December 2004. (source: www.everychildmatters.gov.uk, www.hm-treasury.gov.uk and www.surestart.gov.uk)

Despite the commitment to better childcare being on the table for some years, it is only recently that research has been undertaken to form an accurate assessment of the extent of childcare currently used. There are four government surveys which collect information on childcare use in different ways. Who the questions are asked of, how the questions and preamble are phrased, what time point is referred to, and what options are on the showcard of childcare types, are all different between surveys. The result is that, in some respects, the surveys give very different results – hardly the firmest

Some facts about children
- Three out of ten children live in poverty
- A quarter of children have experienced the separation of their parents
- 1.4 million, 17%, of school children have special educational needs
- There are around half a million disabled children in England
- Over 60,000 children are in care
- 26,000 children are on child protection registers
- One in five 11 to 15-year-olds had taken drugs in the last year

of foundations for policy formation or monitoring. (source: "Childcare use and mother's employment: a review of British data sources", DWP working paper number 16, 2005, www.ifs.org.uk)

The proportions of families using child minders or nannies is reasonably similar across the data sets, but there can be large differences in the proportion using centre-based care, out-of-school clubs and relatives. There seems to be a particular problem in the surveys collecting accurate information about the early pre-school years. Because of the large differences in the proportion of children recorded as using childcare across the three surveys, however, the implied average expenditure for those using childcare varies markedly.

Around half of non-working mothers use some form of childcare, compared with 60 to 70% of the couple families with a working mother and 70 to 80% for working lone parent families. Childcare use among families with working mothers falls as the age of child increases. For children in couple families, there is a pronounced drop in the use of childcare at age five when starting school, suggesting that it is easier for parents in couples to organise work around school hours. A lot of families with working mothers use only a little childcare: for children using childcare, the hours distribution has a mode of roughly ten hours per week for children in lone parent families and five hours a week for children in couple families.

There is a worrying difference in the trend in overall childcare use: the Family Resources Survey shows childcare use to be on a downward trend, but the Families and Children Study and the Labour Force Survey, which cover shorter time periods, show a flat or rising trend.

Childcare use – uncertain data

Family with two children using childcare

A: lowest percentage recorded in one of the four surveys
B: highest percentage

	A	B
Lone parent	49%	82%
Couple families	41%	72%
Couple families use of a relative	19%	29%
Couple families use of child minder	64%	80%

source: DWP working paper number 16, 2005, selected aspects of the survey

Section 8 • Schools

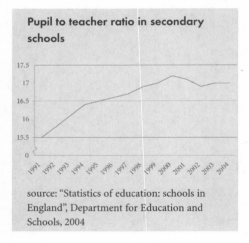

Secondary school teachers, 000s

source: "Statistics of education: schools in England", Department for Education and Schools, 2004

Pupil to teacher ratio in secondary schools

source: "Statistics of education: schools in England", Department for Education and Schools, 2004

45% of pupils in inner London do not have English as their first language compared to 2% in the south west – the national average is 9%

For all the talk of "education, education, education", the pupil to teacher ratio in secondary schools is currently higher than it was in 1997. Having averaged around a ratio of 16 in the decade before 1997, it has averaged around 17 in the period since, and stands at exactly 17 in 2004. The rise in the ratio has occured despite the number of teachers in secondary schools rising from the low point in 1994. The failure of the ratio to fall despite the extra resources is explained by the rise in the number of children. At the most recent low point, in 1991, there were 2.9 million children in secondary schools this has risen steadily every year since to reach just over 3.3 million by 2004.

The impact of demographics can be dramatic. The number of primary school pupils rose steadily through the late 1980s and 1990s to peak at 4.1 million in 1999. Since then the number has declined, dipping below 4 million in 2004. This means that fewer teachers are employed in primary schools in 2004 than was the case in 1997, and yet the pupil teacher ratio has fallen. The pupil to teacher ratio in 2004 was slightly above the most recent low point of 2002 and had returned to the level of 1994. In the decade up to 1993 the ratio averaged just over 22. (source: "Statistics of education: schools in England", Department for Education and Schools, 2004)

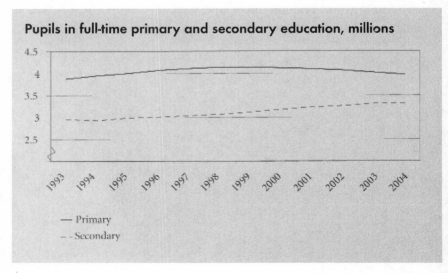

Pupils in full-time primary and secondary education, millions

— Primary
-- Secondary

The number of children attending independent schools has risen every year since 1996, and is at a record high of 586,000 in 2004. The pupil teacher ratio stood at 9.4 in 2004. There were about 70,000 children at boarding school in 2004. (source: www.boarding.org.uk)

The average class size in maintained (in other words run by the state) secondary schools is just under 22 pupils – yet some 11,000 classes, about 8% of the total, have 31 or more pupils and just one teacher. The average class size rose to 21 in 1993 and has been broadly stable since. Nearly 11% of children in secondary schools are entitled to free school meals (on account of coming from a low income household). The percentage varies from 31% in inner London to 6% in the southeast of England. About 10,000 pupils – about one in 800 – are permanently excluded from school.

Nearly 600,000 school children are classified as having a special educational need. Nearly a half of these children have learning difficulties, just over one fifth have behavioural, emotional and social difficulties, and one in ten have a speech, language or other communication need. About 5% – some 30,000 children – are classified as having an autistic spectrum disorder. There are a number of limitations with the SEN data not least because many children have a number of needs, professionals from

Special educational needs and free school meals by ethnic group, %

	SEN pupils	Pupils eligible for free school meals
White British	16	12
Indian	10	12
Pakistani	20	37
Bangladeshi	17	55
Black Caribbean	25	27
Black African	19	37
Chinese	9	10
Gypsy and traveller	48	52
All pupils	16	14

source: "Statistics of education: schools in England", Department for Education and Schools, 2004, table shows only a selection of ethnic categories.

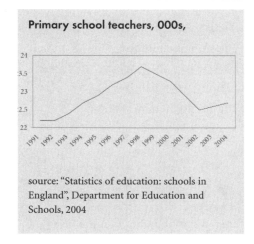

Primary school teachers, 000s,

source: "Statistics of education: schools in England", Department for Education and Schools, 2004

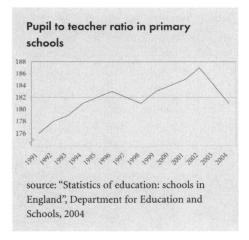

Pupil to teacher ratio in primary schools

source: "Statistics of education: schools in England", Department for Education and Schools, 2004

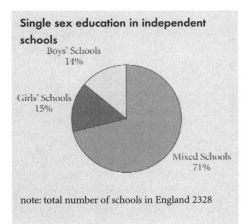

Single sex education in independent schools

Boys' Schools 14%

Girls' Schools 15%

Mixed Schools 71%

note: total number of schools in England 2328

There are nearly 600,000 children attending private schools – the same number of children with special educational needs

There are 151,00 grammar school pupils, 4.6% of all pupils. This is up on the 112,000 3.8%, figure in 1993. The 162 schools have grown to meet increased demand

different fields may classify children differently, parental background can affect the diagnosis, and variations in policies and funding practices between local authorities can affect the classification.

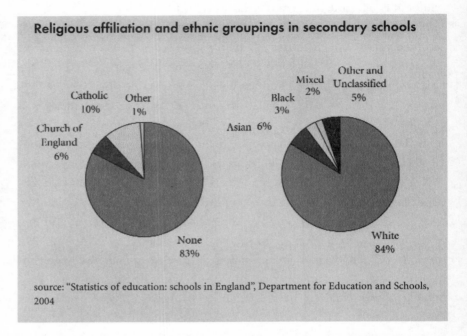

Religious affiliation and ethnic groupings in secondary schools

Catholic 10%
Other 1%
Church of England 6%
None 83%

Black 3%
Mixed 2%
Other and Unclassified 5%
Asian 6%
White 84%

source: "Statistics of education: schools in England", Department for Education and Schools, 2004

Teacher turnover and wastage
One in eight teachers changes job each year and one in twelve resigns. Turnover is correlated inversely with exam results, poverty of the catchment area and special needs demands. Leavers were disproportionately the young or the old, approaching retirement. (source: "Teacher Turnover, wastage and destinations", www.dfes.gov.uk)

Section 9 • School standards

Each year the Department for Education and Skills publishes the results of the National Curriculum assessments of children at various stages in the school career. There are Key Stages 1, 2 and 3, to test children (who are typically) at ages 9, 11 and 13. Children are tested in the spring – recently in May – and the results are published in the late summer – typically August (with typically modest revisions to the data coming later in the year and again in the following year).

Children are allocated to bands (1 to 5 for KS2, for example, with 5 being the best) according to their performance. As Level 4 is deemed to be the required standard, results for schools, education authorities and the country as a whole are often viewed in terms of the percentage of candidates passing at level 4 or above. This is not ideal as a figure for the percentage of children passing at level 4 or above says nothing about the standards being achieved at the top or bottom end of the range. There has been talk, for example, of a long "tail" in some subjects, where a significant group will have achieved very low scores.

Beyond that there are issues about the monitoring and grading which are more serious. As the DfES says, "Proportions are decided entirely by how pupils' attainments measure up to the standards of the National Curriculum" and not by any quotas for each level or "underlying assumptions about the proportion of pupils who should be at any particular level". The results feed into the "Achievement and Attainment Tables", the much-debated league tables, published later in the year.

The government has set itself two public service agreement (PSA) targets for the achievement of 11-year olds at KS2:

- By 2006, 85% of 11-year olds achieve level 4 or above in English and maths, with the level being sustained to 2008, and
- By 2008, the proportion of schools in which fewer than 65% of pupils achieve level 4 or above is reduced by 40%.

The achievement of the first of these targets will be hard. The proportions of children getting level 4 or above in English and maths has been similar in recent years, with both seeing a rise from under 50% in 1995 to over 70%

in 2000 at which point both have plateaued – English was at 77% in 2004 and maths at 74%.

The department has dropped an earlier target, reaffirmed as recently as 2002, which proved to be too ambitious, to have 35% of pupils reaching level 5 separately in English and maths by 2004 (the provisional figures for 2004 pointed to 27% and 31% respectively). The target to reduce to zero the number of education authorities where fewer than 78% of pupils achieve level 4 or above in English and maths was also dropped. In fact 84 of the 150 authorities failed the English grade and 122 – 81% – failed the maths target. (source: www.dfes.gov.uk)

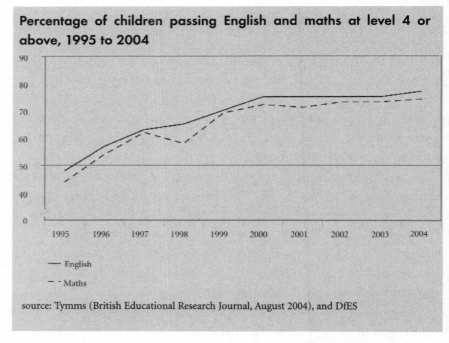

Percentage of children passing English and maths at level 4 or above, 1995 to 2004

source: Tymms (British Educational Research Journal, August 2004), and DfES

Despite the dropping of the targets and unlikelihood of meeting the current ones, the rise in standards in the late 1990s led to some strong claims being made. An article by Michael Barber, then head of the standards and effectiveness unit at the then Department for Education and Employment, in "School effectiveness and school improvement" (source: Vol 12, no 2, 2001) was one example. He said he would show that the experience in England means, "We know how to create successful education systems". In the context of literacy and numeracy at age 11, he said that "Already it has become clear that the pace of change in education does not need to be glacial, contrary to the assertions of researchers over many years. Proven policies, driven vigorously, well implemented and genuinely sustained can bring rapid progress, measurable in student outcomes."

While there is universal agreement that primary school standards have risen the scale of the improvement is debateable. One academic study was clear that standards are not rising as fast as the official figures claim. The research by Professor Peter Tymms, director of the Curriculum Evaluation and Management Centre at Durham University, calls into question the value of the government's targets for literacy and numeracy and accordingly questions whether the policies on primary education were working. (source: British Educational Research Journal, August 2004.)

The research said the bulk of the improvement reported in the statutory tests reflected a "slackness in statistical procedures" for setting the pass mark and teachers coaching children in how to take the exams, rather than pupils actually getting cleverer. While children's literacy and numeracy skills have improved between 1995 and 2000, he estimated that the real improvement was just over one-third and about two thirds of that claimed, in English and maths respectively.

The official English test results showed the number of 11-year-olds meeting the literacy standards expected for a child of that age had risen from 48% in 1995 to 75% in 2000. For mathematics, the statutory test scores suggest an improvement in numeracy from 44% to 72%. Prof Tymms estimated that the true figures for 2000 were just 58% and 64% respectively. The conclusions follow an assessment of several sources of information, independent studies and individual tests.

The steady upward drift in results ended when the Qualifications and Curriculum Authority tightened its procedures in 2000/01, he said, highlighting the suspicion of statistical problems. The Statistics Commission, the government watchdog, said it was "actively investigating the issues" and was due to produce a report on the topic.

There is no suggestion that the figures are being deliberately massaged, but as one statistician said, the upward drift had been "caused by a combination of wishful thinking on the part of the authorities and a lack of statistical rigour". It is clear that it suits everyone involved to have gentle upward drift.

International comparisons

The TIMSS study compared the performance of year 5 and year 9 pupils in maths and science. Taking both subjects and both levels, England's performance was about one third of the way down the league table of the 25 participating countries. (Data related to 2003.)

Data failure

The failure of the ONS and DfES to get adequate data meant that the UK was the only one of the 40 OECD's countries not to appear in the important PISA study in 2004.

Exam pass targets

The government has set itself the target of increasing the percentage of pupils achieving five or more passes by two percentage points each year between 2002 and 2006. The rate increased by only 1.3 percentage points in 2003 and a further on 0.8 in 2004, leaving ground to be made up in future years. But by last year it was realised that that was too ambitious. The target was replaced by the desire to have 60% acheive 5 GCSEs at grades A*–C by 2008. That target requires each of the next four years to have stronger improvement than the last two.

617,000 pupils attempted GCSEs but only 282,000, under half, passed English and Maths

The accuracy of the figures is important as, if the educational standards are not rising in the way the official measure suggests, current government policy might be viewed as being misdirected. The government's initial focus after the 1997 election was on primary schooling and the rising test results were seen as a sign that the policy was successful. But if the improvement in primary school standards is largely illusory, it would be unwise to use it as a model "to justify policies and to promote certain ways of working", not least for secondary schools – the more recent focus of policy emphasis – where there has been no such reported rise in standards.

Prof Tymms said there were two reasons for the inflation of the official data. "Firstly, schools have been trying hard to get better test results as the combined pressures of league tables, Ofsted and targets bite." Accordingly, teachers facing pressure from league tables are training the children in test techniques that can improve test scores without improving what the test measures.

Second, he said, that the standard-setting procedures used between 1995 and 2000 by the Schools Curriculum and Assessment Authority, now the Qualifications and Curriculum Authority, were faulty. "They necessarily use a new test every year and so, every year, they have to decide the cut-off mark...which will correspond to a level 4. This is not easy and a slackness in statistical procedures resulted in a drift in standard-setting." Possible ways that this could have happened included: pre-test benchmark setting occurring earlier in the year (so children are younger) and not under exam conditions, and markers looking more favourably at borderline cases (now the stakes are higher and there is a risk of formal challenge to a mark). All the effects seem to have had a greater impact on KS1 than on any of the other stages.

The important conclusion is that statutory test data should not be used to monitor standards over time – indeed an independent system, that is not part of the "accountability agenda", is required along the lines of the organisations found in a number of other countries. A perfect system for monitoring standards over time would involve the same secret tests being used repeatedly on equivalent samples of pupils of the same age at the same time of year.

Just over half – 53.7% – all 15-year-olds in state maintained schools achieved five or more GCSEs at grades A to C in 2004. There was considerable variation in the performance of local education authorities – the percentage of pupils passing five or more GCSEs ranged from 34% in Hull to 68% in Redbridge – or 93% including the Isles of Scilly. One in twenty four pupils failed to achieve a single pass. (source: DfES, www.dfes.gov.uk, initial figures published in January, final figures in June each year.)

Virtually all of the state schools where over 90% of pupils passed five subjects were selective schools. 162 of the 164 selective state schools fell into this category, while only 32, just under 1%, of comprehensive schools reached that mark. The DfES figures relate to England only. Alternative figures are published by the awarding bodies and a number of newspapers publish summary exam results by school in league table format. A similar trend of improvement is seen in the exam results for A-level passes.

There has also been much debate about grade inflation of public exams for school children. More students achieving higher grades each year could be due to improved learning/teaching or easier examinations/grading. It is likely that both aspects have a part to play with standards falling in part to meet the needs of a larger cohort of children doing the exams in a more inclusive system. In this area, the data are not in doubt – they are perfectly accurate – the problem is the interpretation. As the exam council itself said, "Comparing standards over time is a complex task". (source: "Education, Reform and the State: Twenty-Five Years of Politics, Policy and Practice", R. Phillips and J. Furlong, Routledge Falmer)

Surveys of the amount of homework done by school children show that it has been falling at the very time that enrolments were rising and grades getting better. As the evidence points to homework being important at the secondary level, the rise in grades is surprising. The different grading of various subjects is also a sensitive issue – the harder marking of science, maths and languages (subjects which arguably more directly contribute to the nation's economic competitiveness) has tempted students to take other subjects in their search for higher grades.

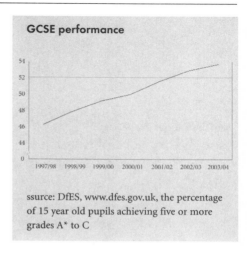

GCSE performance

ssurce: DfES, www.dfes.gov.uk, the percentage of 15 year old pupils achieving five or more grades A* to C

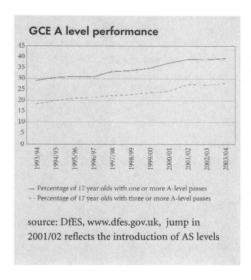

GCE A level performance

— Percentage of 17 year olds with one or more A-level passes
- - Percentage of 17 year olds with three or more A-level passes

source: DfES, www.dfes.gov.uk, jump in 2001/02 reflects the introduction of AS levels

The proportion of 17 year olds gaining at least three grade A 'A' levels has nearly doubled in the last decade to 3.6%

Section 10 • Truancy from school

Around one in five secondary school pupils plays truant at least once a year

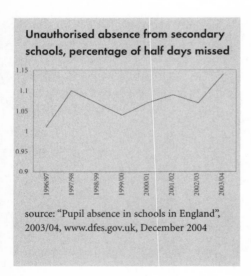

Unauthorised absence from secondary schools, percentage of half days missed

source: "Pupil absence in schools in England", 2003/04, www.dfes.gov.uk, December 2004

27% of primary school children and 17% of secondary school children have truanted without the collusion of their parents

Pupils in state secondary schools miss one in every twelve school sessions, amounting to over 75 million half days in the latest year. Absences from primary schools run at a lower rate, with roughly one in eighteen sessions being missed, yet still amounting to another 60 million lost half days, due to the greater number of primary age children. In total, nearly 150 million school half day sessions were missed in 2003/04 across the state sector, equating to an absentee rate of nearly 7%, about ten full days per pupil.

Most school absences – between 80% and 90% – are authorised by the school, but unauthorised absences – truancy – were at a record high in secondary schools in 2003/04. The rate of 1.1% amounted to over 10 million school sessions missed. (This assumes a little over 150 school days, and a little over 300 possible sessions, per year.) The rate could be higher as there is also some evidence that schools are "over ready" to accept reasons for absence in order to reduce unauthorised absence. (source: "Absence from school", research report 424, www.dfes.gov.uk) Education ministers have said – though official figures do not seem to be available – that 2% of secondary pupils are responsible for almost half of the recorded truancy.

The rate of truancy in the independent sector is much lower – the rate of 0.13% amounting to about 150,000 school sessions missed by the 396,000 pupils who attend independent schools which chose to respond to the government survey. The truancy rate in the independent sector is therefore running at one missed session for every two to three pupils per year, compared to three sessions per pupil in the state secondary sector. Despite the lower rate at private schools, truancy was at a record high in the latest year in that sector too. (source: "Pupil absence in schools in England", 2003/04, www.dfes.gov.uk, December 2004)

In law, parents of children of compulsory school age (5 to 16) are required to ensure that they "receive a suitable education by regular attendance at school". Failure to comply with the statutory duty can lead to prosecution. Local education authorities are responsible in law for making sure that pupils attend school. Schools are required, therefore, to take attendance registers twice a day: once at the beginning of the morning session and once during the afternoon session. Schools must also distinguish between the pupils who are absent with the permission from the teacher and those without. Most truancy reflects bullying, problems with teachers and peer pressure to stay away from school.

There is a considerable divergence between the truancy rates in different authorities – the unauthorised absence from secondary schools is nine times higher in Leicester, the highest rate, compared to Kingston upon Thames, the lowest rate. There is much less divergence between regions – the northeast at 8.5% of half days missed is the highest compared to 7.8% in the southeast, outer London and the East of England.

Estimates suggest that every year in the UK at least 16 children commit suicide because of bullying at school. The true total (including accidental death, misadventure, open verdict etc) could be several times this number. (source: www.bullyonline.org)

Schooling at home?

Around 50,000 families – implying as many as 150,000 (or 1% of the 5–16 population) children in the UK – have chosen educate their children at home. No official figures exist but researchers suggest the number is rising. The reasons for home education vary, but bullying, harassment, religion and a school climate not conducive to learning are often cited.

Truancy black spots

Local education authorities with the highest and lowest rates of unauthorised absence from secondary schools

highest

Leicester	3.04
Bradford	2.83
Greenwich	2.02
Halton	2.71
Salford	2.67

lowest

Dorset	0.46
Tameside	0.46
Shropshire	0.45
Bedfordshire	0.42
Northumberland	0.41
Kingston upon Thames	0.33

source: "Pupil absence in schools in England", 2003/04, www.dfes.gov.uk, December 2004, figures relate to 2003/04

Section 11 • School meals

School meals account for over half of children's chip and pudding intake and over one-third of their soft drink intake

In response to concerns about obesity and the eating habits of children, the Department for Education and Skills (DfES) introduced some limited statutory national standards for nutrition for school meals in England in 2001. School caterers have since had to provide items from the main food groups with a certain frequency.

A survey published in 2004 by the DfES and the Foods Standards Agency (FSA) showed that many schools followed some healthy practices (such as frying in vegetable oil and using semi-skimmed milk), other practices (restricted access to table salt and use of low fat spreads) were followed only by a minority.

One in five 15–16 year olds skip breakfast. School meals provide between a quarter and one-third of the daily intake for children – and more for the 14% of pupils entitled to free school meals (the children from low income households). A 2002 Consumers Association survey found that pizza and chicken nuggets were the most popular main courses, chips the most popular starchy food and baked beans the most popular vegetable. School meals contributed on average less than one portion of the recommended daily intake of five portions of fruit and vegetables.

At school lunch, only one in seventeen pupils chose vegetables other than baked beans and one in sixty five – under 2% – chose fruit

The DfES survey, covering a sample of state schools, found that 83% of schools met the set standards at the beginning of the lunch service but only 47% did by the end as food ran out. Only 82% offered drinking water. The most popular dishes were high fat foods such as chicken nuggets, burgers, pizza and sausages. Chips and soft drinks were also selected by nearly half of children. The less popular low fat main dishes – taken by one in six children – included pasta dishes, stews and curries often served with rice. The lack of availability of chips was a positive influence on reducing pupils' intake of fat.

Of the 688 lunchboxes surveyed, only one salad was recorded. Crisps were found in 69% of lunchboxes and biscuits and chocolate bars in 58%.

More than 5½ billion lunchboxes are packed for children in the UK each year and most children's packed lunches still contain far too much saturated fat, salt and sugar – roughly double the recommended lunchtime intake of saturated fat and sugar, and up to half their daily recommended salt intake. (source: Food Standards Agency, survey of school lunchboxes, September

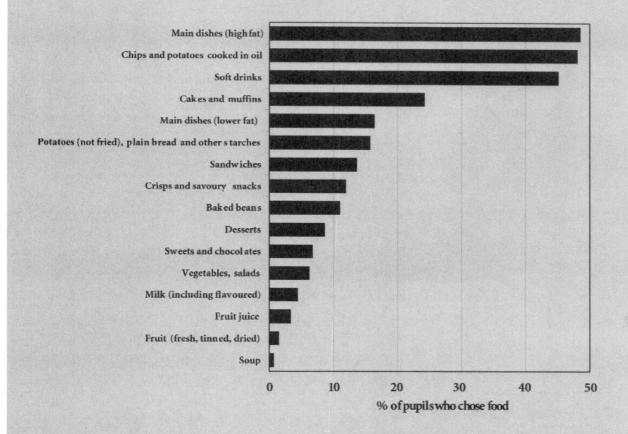

Percentage of pupils choosing specified foods for lunch

% of pupils who chose food

source "School meals in secondary schools in England", FSA and DfES, 2004

2004, www.food.gov.uk) Three out of four lunchboxes (74%) also fail to meet the government nutritional standards set for school meals in 2001.

Sandwiches were present in 82% of lunchboxes and the most popular fillings were ham (27%) and cheese/cheese spread (21%). Brown/granary/wholemeal and softgrain bread was found in only one in eight lunchboxes. Just over half the lunches contained fruit – apples were the favourite (in 18% of boxes) and bananas came second (9%).

Section 12 • University entrance

The number of students in higher education (including overseas students and those at the Open University) has risen from 800,000 in 1980 to 2.3 million

There are 2.4 million higher education students of whom nearly 1 million are part-time

72% of 16 year olds and 58% of 17 year olds are in post-compulsory education

More and more children have been staying on at school after 16 and going into tertiary education. In 1955, only 13% of children had some form of education after the age of 16. By 1975 the proportion had trebled to 38% and then almost doubled again to 72% by 1995. Over one third of 18 to 19-year-olds in Britain enter higher education. The proportion has risen sharply – from less than 5% in 1955, 12% in 1980, to 19% in 1990, to 35% in 2002.

Nearly 410,000 home applications (from British-based addresses) were made in 2003, of which 334,000, some 81%, were accepted. The sharp rise in applications in 1997 reflected students taking advantage of university in advance of tuition fees being introduced in the following year. Otherwise the number of home applicants has been on a rising trend for many years, despite briefly falling at the end of the 1990s. The proportion accepted has also been rising, though did dip in 2003. (source: www.ucas.ac.uk)

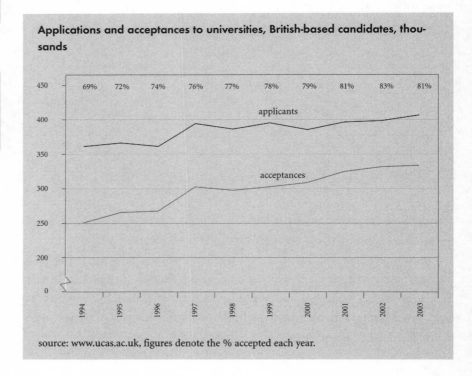

Applications and acceptances to universities, British-based candidates, thousands

source: www.ucas.ac.uk, figures denote the % accepted each year.

Overseas students comprised 11% of all university acceptances but have a different age profile from home applicants. Overseas students form just 8% of those under 21, yet one quarter of those aged 21 to 24. As UCAS processes applications for full-time and sandwich undergraduate courses only, they are likely to exclude a significant number of mature students, as they are disproportionately likely to study part-time. All UK universities (excluding the OU), most colleges of higher education, and some colleges of further education are UCAS members, but as membership changes from year to year, the statistics are not strictly comparable over time. (source: www.ucas.ac.uk)

UCAS data relates to the annual number of applications and acceptances to its member institutions. Each year UCAS reports numbers relating to those applicants who applied or those who were accepted. UCAS does not check if accepting applicants actually enrol on the course to which they were accepted. Details of all student populations are provided by the Higher Education Statistics Agency (www.hesa.ac.uk).

In 2004, there were 333 institutions in the UCAS scheme including universities, colleges of higher education and further education colleges that offer higher education courses. An up-to-date count of universities is available from Universities UK – in 2004, there were 90 universities in the UK and an additional 26 university institutions. They employed 143,000 academic staff, including 13,800 professors. The UK spends 0.8% of GDP as public sector support for the university sector. This is below the average of the OECD countries of 1%, and roughly half of those at the top of the table – such as several Scandinavian countries and Canada.

Various performance indicators – a range of statistical indicators intended to offer an objective measure of how higher education institutions are performing – have been set for all publicly funded HEIs. They currently cover: access to higher education, non-completion rates for students, outcomes for learning and teaching in universities and colleges and research output.

The purpose of performance indicators is to: provide reliable information on the nature and performance of the UK higher education sector, allow comparison between individual institutions where appropriate, enable institutions to benchmark their own performance, inform policy developments and contribute to the public accountability of higher educa-

Sources of university income

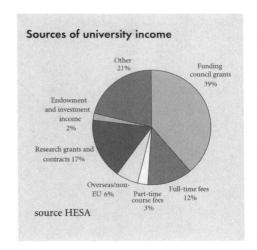

source HESA

State school entrance %

Coutald Art Institute	26
Royal Agricultural College	45
Royal College of Music	45
Oxford	55
Royal Acadamy of Music	57
Cambridge	58
UC London	61
St Andrews	62
Bristol	64
Royal Veterinary College	66
LSE	66
Edinburgh	66
Exeter	67
Durham	68

source: www.hesa.ac.uk, % of first degree entrants, full-time.

First degree entrants, 2002/03

Manchester Metropolitan	6600
Leeds	6400
Sheffield Hallam	5400
Manchester	5100
Birmingham	4900
Nottingham Trent	4900
Central Lancashire	4900

source: www.hesa.ac.uk

Drop out rate, %

Oxford	1.1
Durham	1.4
Cambridge	1.7
Nottingham	1.8
Bath	2.1
Exeter	2.1
:	
:	
London Metropolitan	14
Surrey Roehampton	15
Napier University	16
University of Paisley	19

source: www.hesa.ac.uk, % young entrants not in HE in year following entry, major insitutions only.

tion. HESA says that no meaningful league table could fairly demonstrate the performance of all higher education institutions relative to each other due to the diversity of the sector and believes that the use of a range of indicators and benchmarks is preferable. The indicators concentrate on performance relative to full-time undergraduates. Generally, the changes in these indicators in the last few years have been modest.

Nationally, over 90% of 17 year-olds in full-time education attend schools or colleges in the state sector (source: Department for Education and Skills). 87.2% of young entrants to full-time first degree courses in 2002/03 had attended such schools. Most institutions take more than 90% of their young students from state schools. About one in 9 institutions take less than 70% of their young entrants to full-time first degree courses from state schools (www.hesa.ac.uk). Nearly half of the population of working age are classified in the lower socio-economic groups 4 to 7, where classification is based on current or most recent occupation. Nationally, 28% of young entrants to full-time first degree courses come from this section of the population.

In general, a higher proportion of mature entrants than young entrants do not continue in higher education after their first year. The UK non-continuation rate is 15% for mature entrants compared with 7% for young entrants. The non-continuation rate for young entrants is less than 10% at seven out of ten institutions.

HESA calculates projected outcomes that would be expected from starters at institutions if progression patterns were to remain unchanged over the next few years. The sector averages show that 78% of full-time first degree students starting at an institution are expected to qualify from that institution with a degree, and 14% are expected to get no qualification. A further 6% are expected to transfer to another institution. The projected percentage of students who leave before gaining any award, and who neither return to study nor transfer to another institution, is less than 20% for the majority of institutions.

Statistics on applicants for graduate teacher training courses are available from www.gttr.ac.uk. Information on the country's 102 business schools is available at www.the-abs.org.uk.

Section 13 • **Employment**

The Government set itself the target of having a greater percentage of people in work than ever before by 2010 and has almost met it – though the upward trend seems to have stopped, temporarily at least. The percentage of the working age population in employment has risen steadily since the post-recession trough of 70.3% in 1993 to 74.7% (in Q3 2004), matching the rate seen in 1990. The number of people in work is a record – 27.4 million in 2004 – 1.7 million up on 1997 and 2.9 million up on the trough of 1993. The weaker trend shown by the rate compared to the crude numbers is explained by the growth in working age population – as the population is expanding, the economy needs to generate the extra jobs to stand still.

Throughout the 1980s and 1990s, Britain persistently had a higher percentage of the working age population in employment than the average of all industrialised countries. But the rate in Britain is not exceptional – there are several countries with a higher rate – and neither is the rise in recent years. The Chancellor is understandably keen to proclaim the addition of nearly two million people in work as a great success of his chancellorship. In fact, the increase in jobs in the six years from 1998 to 2003 averages an annual rate of 1%, which is not out of line with the average achieved in all advanced economies. We know nothing about the quality of the new jobs that have been created.

It is also unclear to what extent the robust trends of employment reflect private sector vitality or the rapid expansion of employment in the public sector as there have been no accurate and timely estimates of the number of people employed in the public sector (new data were expected from ONS in March 2005). It seems shocking that the government does not know how many people it employs, but the large number of bodies, many of which are at arms' length from central government, and the complexities of consultants, contractors and part-time working, goes some way to explaining the difficulties. Estimates suggest that the number of public sector workers has increased by 10% since 1998, accounting for over half a million of the new jobs.

> Employment statistics is a messy and tricky area and is in need of some attention from statisticians

> One in six men of working age is now inactive compared to one in nine at the start of the 1990s

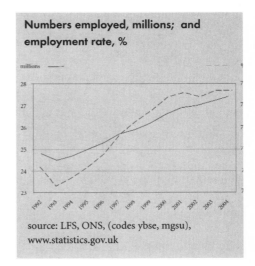

Numbers employed, millions; and employment rate, %

source: LFS, ONS, (codes ybse, mgsu), www.statistics.gov.uk

Employment rates in major countries, 2003

Switzerland	84.1
Iceland	83.2
Norway	76.6
Denmark	75.8
Japan	73.4
Canada	73.3
UK	72.4
Australia	71.6
US	71.0
Germany	69.2
OECD	64.2
France	63.4
Italy	56.3

source: OECD Economic Outlook 75, www.oecd.org

When the employment rates are compared between countries, for example using the figures from the OECD, the UK often appears with a different – lower – rate from that quoted domestically. The OECD gives employment as a proportion of all people aged 15 to 64 years old, while the UK's preferred measure excludes women aged 60 to 64.

The growth in the working age population has also contributed to a rise in the number of people who are defined as economically inactive – those of working age who choose not to work, i.e. are neither employed nor unemployed. The Chancellor rarely mentions that the 7.8 million inactive in 2004 is a record high and is over 1 million up on the low point in the series, seen in 1990. The inactivity rate has been stable between 21% and 22% for a decade, but the stability masks a sharp rise in the male rate and a fall in the female rate. Around 16½% of men of working age were inactive in 2004, up by over 1% since 1997. In contrast, just under 27% of women are inactive, down from over 28% in 1997. There was a much sharper rise in male inactivity from 11½% to 15½ % between 1990 and 1997, and the current government's policies have slowed but not arrested this increase.

Reasons for inactivity

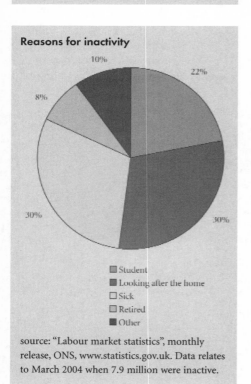

source: "Labour market statistics", monthly release, ONS, www.statistics.gov.uk. Data relates to March 2004 when 7.9 million were inactive.

Economic inactivity of working age people, millions

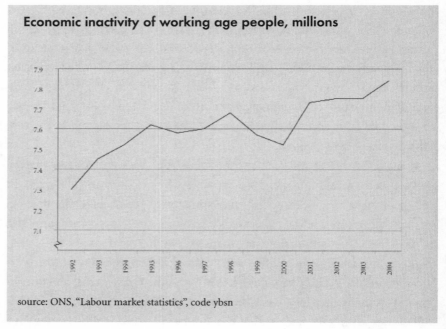

source: ONS, "Labour market statistics", code ybsn

It is easy to confuse the number of people in employment with the number of jobs in the economy. In general, household surveys are used to provide statistics of people in employment, and business surveys are used to provide statistics of jobs. Surveys of individuals have traditionally been very poor at providing an accurate industrial breakdown of employment – people usually do not know what industrial sector their company operates in. The ONS compiles the two series and there is usually a large gap between them – at the end of 2003, 28¼ million people were in employment and there were 30½ million jobs. Much of the apparent discrepancy is accounted for by the 1¼ million people (estimated from a different source) with second jobs and other coverage issues but some differences are unresolved. Indeed, a quality review of the data conducted by the Office for National Statistics, with emerging findings published in March 2004, identified 30 differences between the two surveys which could account for the discrepancies.

People are said to be in work if they do at least one hour of work a week – so that a student doing occasional babysitting would be classified as in work. It has been suggested that it would be better to count as workers only those working, say, at least ten hours a week. Not surprisingly, governments are not keen to make such a change, as it would appear from the headline figures that fewer people are in work.

The number of self-employed was around 3¼ to 3½ million during the 1990s, having risen sharply in the 1980s. The number rose more in 2003 (190,000, 6%) than in any year since 1989, and strongly again in 2004 to surpass the record high of 3.54 million in 1990. Generally the number falls when the economy is strong as more opportunities arise to become an employee, and rises when the demand for jobs slows.

The number of employees in employment has risen every year since the low point in 1993. Since then, employment is up by just over 3 million. The period of strongest growth was between 1995 and 2001. 2002 to 2004 saw much weaker growth – around 100,000 additional jobs each year compared to on average over 400,000 a year in the previous seven years.

The total number of employees is shown for each sector of the economy. Several large sectors dominate the total. The major trend since 1997 has been the decline in manufacturing jobs and the rise in business services and the public sector. The number of employees in manufacturing rose in the mid 1990s (by 200,000 between 1993 and 1998) but fell by over 700,000 since the 1998 peak – equivalent to about 600 job losses each working day.

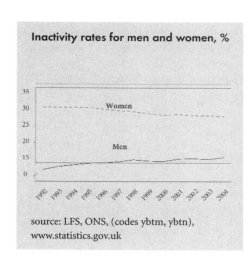

Inactivity rates for men and women, %

source: LFS, ONS, (codes ybtm, ybtn), www.statistics.gov.uk

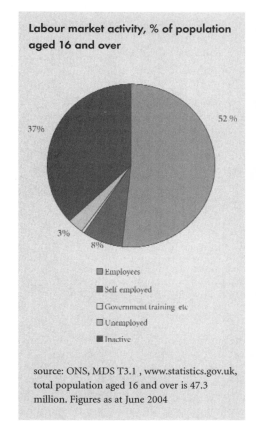

Labour market activity, % of population aged 16 and over

■ Employees
■ Self employed
□ Government training etc
□ Unemployed
■ Inactive

source: ONS, MDS T3.1 , www.statistics.gov.uk, total population aged 16 and over is 47.3 million. Figures as at June 2004

Number of self-employed, millions

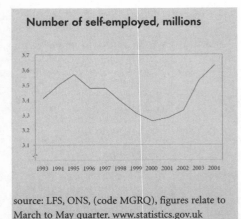

source: LFS, ONS, (code MGRQ), figures relate to March to May quarter. www.statistics.gov.uk

Number of employee jobs, millions

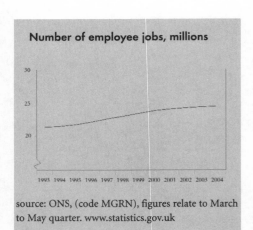

source: ONS, (code MGRN), figures relate to March to May quarter. www.statistics.gov.uk

A hundred years ago the most common jobs were farming and gardening (2.3m), domestic service (2.2m), transport (1.5m) and textile manufacturing (1.5m)

source: 1901 census

The number of employees in agriculture has fallen by over one quarter between 1997 and 2003, to 170,000. (source: MDS table 3.8, ONS, www.statistics.gov.uk)

Employment by sector

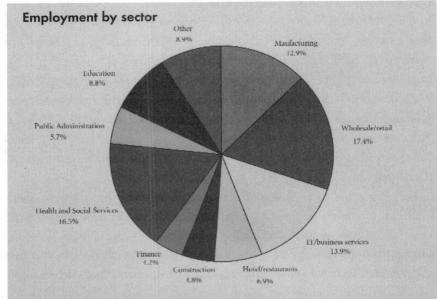

Source: Monthly Digest of Statistics, T3.3, ONS, www.statistics.gov.uk, % figures relate to mid 2004

Quality issues with labour market data

It seems clear that improved statistics are required to measure accurately the increasingly complex dynamics of the labour market where the boundaries between employment, unemployment and inactivity have become increasingly fuzzy. A "quality review" of the labour market data was carried out by the ONS in 2002 (report no 11, www.statistics.gov.uk). It raised a number of fundamental issues about the usefulness and coherence of the current set of outputs and made 28 recommendations. It said, "For a number of years neither producers nor users of labour market statistics have had an agreed conceptual under-standing of the ways in which the separate elements of these statistics fitted together. In the middle of the 20th century, the labour market could predominantly be characterised in terms of (i) men working in manufacturing industries, doing a full time job, and (ii) the unemployed finding work by registering or, later on, by claiming benefits. But nowadays the labour market is far more heterogeneous. Employment is dominated by the service sector; women play a major role in the labour market; flexible, "non-traditional" working arrangements are the norm, and there are multiple routes into employment. The area of labour market policy has become increasingly involved. Labour market statistics underlie a raft of different needs, including macro-economic policy, employment and welfare policies and employment relations policies. And there is a sub-national dimension too, not least in relation to the statistical needs of the devolved administrations."

Workers in Britain clock up just over 900 million hours of work a week. Full-time workers work just over 37 hours a week on average and part-time workers 15½ hours a week

Fortunes of selected industrial sectors

A: Employees in 2003 (000s)
B: Change since 1997 (000s)
C: % change

	A	B	C
Manufacturing	3362	-706	-17
Wholesale and retail	4404	238	6
Business services (incl computing)	3540	564	19
Health and social work	2776	288	12

source: ONS, (codes lmad, lmaz, lmbf, lojv), www.statistics.gov.uk

The largest trade unions, members

Unison	1,289,000
Amicus	1,062,000
TGWU	835,000
GMB	704,000
Royal College of Nursing	360,000

source: www.certoffice.org, annual report 2003/04

The number of working days lost due to industrial action was the lowest in each of 1997, 1998 and 1999 since records began in 1891. Since then, the figure has picked up and the loss of 1.3 million days in 2002 was the highest in any year since 1990. Even so, by historical standards the current figures remain low – every year from the Second World War up to 1990 saw at least one million days lost. (source: MDS table 3.17, ONS, www.statistics.gov.uk)

7.7 million people are members of 197 trade unions compared to nearly 12 million members of 500 unions 30 years ago

Section 14 • Unemployment

Unemployment, millions

Unemployment rate,%

source: LFS, "Labour market trends", December 2004, ONS, all figures relate to the spring quarter, March to May.

The unemployment figures have been one of the most conspicuous statistics in Britain in the post-war period. For many decades unemployment was the focal point for many in politics and economics and it was often cited by voters as the most important policy issue facing the country. The generally lower rates of the last decade means that the attention of the public and policy makers has shifted somewhat, but unemployment remains an important figure.

While unemployment might sound like a simple concept, it is not and there are many different ways of defining it. In Britain, as in many other countries, we have a choice between the long-running figures for those claiming unemployment benefit and a measure derived from the Labour Force Survey. Clearly not everybody without a job is unemployed – many are retired, studying, caring for family members or choosing to take time out from the labour market. The traditional Keynesian concept of involuntary unemployment underpins the Labour Force Survey definition, but deciding who really wants a job, is seeking work and is available for work is hard. Because of these difficulties, much policy now focuses on activity and inactivity rates within the economy, rather than a narrower definition of unemployment.

Unemployment fell from the post-recession peak of 1993 until 2001 and has been broadly stable since. According to the Labour Force Survey the figure was around 1.4 million in mid-2004 (a rate of just under 5% of the economically active population). The claimant count – the number of people receiving jobseekers allowance – is lower at just under 1 million (and 3% of the workforce).

The labour force measure, the generally preferred measure, is derived from a survey of the population on internationally agreed definitions. People are categorised as unemployed if they are ready to start work in two weeks and had looked for work in the past four weeks – or are waiting to start a job they have already been offered.

While many people will fall into both measures of unemployment, some fall into to just one or the other. While the levels of the two series and month-

What is the best unemployment rate?

The unemployment numbers are best expressed as a percentage but this raises the question as to what unemployment should be a percentage of. For many years, the unemployment rate was expressed as the number of unemployed divided by the sum of employees in employment and the unemployed. In the mid-1980s, the self-employed and armed forces were added to the denominator. Unemployment was thus expressed as a percentage of the workforce. That change caused a drop of 1½% in the unemployment rate (though all back data were revised). Sometimes unemployment is expressed as a percentage of the population of working age.

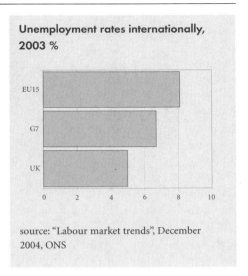

Unemployment rates internationally, 2003 %

source: "Labour market trends", December 2004, ONS

to-month changes might be quite different, the trends in both series, including peaks and troughs, are quite similar.

As there is no single perfect measure of unemployment, there are frequent calls for government to publish a range of numbers. One model would be to replicate the measures published by the Bureau of Labour Statistics in America. These range from a limited measure – U1, people unemployed for more than 15 weeks, to a broader measure – U6, which includes marginally attached workers and part-timers wanting full-time work. At the end of 2004 the official measure (U3) stood at a little over 5%, while U1, the lowest figure, was 2% and U6, the highest, was over 9%.

In Britain, the basic measure would be those unemployed aged over 25 years old. But it would be possible to add those under 25, those available to work but not looking for work, other inactive people who say they want a job, people on government schemes, part-timers who want full-time work, and other working age people on benefits. The attraction of publishing a range of measures is that users can apply the definition that they feel most comfortable given the purpose that they had. It would be preferable to have clearly defined official alternative measures rather than encourage, by default, analysts and commentators to create their own, less well under-stood, measures.

Researchers at the Centre for Regional Economic and Social Research at Sheffield Hallam University have been among the most active in analysing the concept of "hidden unemployment". They calculated that the best estimate

Unemployment fiddles of the 1980s

The so-called "fiddling" of the claimant unemployment numbers, mostly during the 1980s, is the most frequently cited instance of "political interference" in statistics. During the 1980s there were around thirty changes to the eligibility rules relating to unemployment benefit. Each change was defended at the time, with some justification, on the grounds of improved accuracy or practicality, yet because virtually all changes had the effect of reducing the published unemployment totals, the suspicion lingered that one main motive behind the changes was to reduce the damaging political effect of the very high unemployment rates seen in the early 1980s. At the time, the numbers were the responsibility of the then Department of Employment, not the ONS, as is currently the case, fuelling the suspicion. Only five or six of the changes had a material impact on the numbers, but their combined effect was to take about half a million people off the unemployment register, which stood at about 3 million people, a rate of roughly 11%, in the early 1980s. The department did publish estimates of unemployment on each new basis for the earlier periods but as there was no alternative measure from the labour force survey at the time many observers took a dim view of the change. The issue is no longer sensitive due to the availability of timely labour force survey measures and relatively few changes in eligibility to benefits in the recent past.

"Real unemployment" by district, % rate	
Highest	
Merthyr Tydfil	28
Easington	24
Blaenau Gwent	23
Liverpool	23
Glasgow	23
Knowsley	22
Neath Port Talbot	21
Tower Hamlets	21
Lowest	
West Berkshire	2.7
North Wiltshire	2.7
Hart	2.6
Surrey Heath	2.5
West Oxfordshire	2.4

source: "The real level of unemployment 2002", CRESR, Sheffield Hallam University, figures as at July 2002.

for "real unemployment" was 2.8 million, compared to the figure of just under one million on the claimant count, at the beginning of 2002. The largest single group of hidden unemployed, just over one million, are men and women who have been diverted onto sickness related benefits. These account for just over 40% of the total number of people of working age claiming sickness related benefits – and are those people that the researchers felt would have been in work in a fully employed economy. On their calculations, hidden unemployment is disproportionately concentrated in the traditional industrial areas of northern England, Scotland and Wales. In some places – Liverpool, Glasgow, and parts of the Northeast and South Wales – they estimated that hidden unemployment was as high as 20%. (source: "The real level of unemployment 2002", CRESR, Sheffield Hallam University)

One advantage of the claimant count figures is that they are available for small areas. For many years the House of Commons Library has been publishing monthly figures for unemployment by parliamentary constituency. The figures are the number of JSA claimants living in the constituency and the rate expresses this as a proportion of the economically active population in the constituency in 1997. (source: www.parliament.uk, look under "library" in the index) As they do not take into account the ability of people to work outside the constituency, the figures should be viewed more as a measure of relative social deprivation than a mismatch of supply and demand for labour.

These were published by the House of Commons as, until 1999, the ONS did not publish local area unemployment rates as they felt the numbers would be meaningless – most constituencies do not approximate to self-contained labour markets (defined by them as being an area where 70% of the workers in an area work in that area and where 70% of those who work in the area also live there). But in 1999, they decided to publish the number of claimants in an area as a proportion of the number of jobs in the area, regardless of whether the job holders were resident in the area or not. Figures were available for parliamentary constituencies and local authorities. After some criticism and claims that the figures were misleading, the ONS withdrew the numbers from the start of 2003, and replaced them with a rate using the percentage of working age population as the denominator.

The criticism was largely founded on the fact that local area rates calculated on this basis were misleading for some areas, notably because of a large distortion in inner-city areas. Inner-city areas generally have high rates of poverty and high rates of unemployment, yet because the inner cities also "benefit" during the day from concentrations of workers who commuted from the outlying suburbs, the unemployment rate under this measure was lowered as the denominator was inflated by the commuters. It was also felt that this calculation was not a genuine "rate", as the numerator, the number of people unemployed in the area, was not part of the denominator, the number of people working in the area. It was convenient for the government to have figures that produced a lower rate of inner-city unemployment – it would be hard to argue that there was a major problem that required some policy response from the government.

Constituencies with highest and lowest unemployment rates

Highest rates

Birmingham Ladywood	13.0
Birmingham Sparkbrook	10.7
Camberwell & Peckham	10.3
Bethnal Green & Bow	9.9
Poplar & Canning Town	9.8
Hackney South & Shoreditch	9.3
Liverpool Riverside	9.1
Tottenham	9.0
Manchester Central	8.3
West Ham	8.2

Lowest rates

Henley	0.8
Woodspring	0.8
West Dorset	0.8
Northavon	0.8
Wansdyke	0.8
Mole Valley	0.8
Witney	0.7
Mid Dorset & North Poole	0.7
Westmorland & Lonsdale	0.7
Salisbury	0.7

Rank of English constituencies, August 2004, not seasonally adjusted

Why denominators are important – and unemployment is a blunt tool

Something of a fracas broke out in the late 1990s when an analysis of the European labour force survey showed that the unemployment rate for young people in France was roughly double that in Britain – 28% compared to 15%. This shocked French politicians as it suggested that France had a large pool of frustrated jobseekers and discontented youth. Meanwhile the UK was boasting that young people could earn their living easily.

In fact, closer analysis of the figures showed that such an interpretation was highly misleading. In fact both countries had roughly the same number – around 700,000 – of 15 to 24-year-olds who were unemployed. Both countries also has a similar number of people aged 15 to 24 – just over 7 million – implying that the youth unemployment rate as a percentage of the population aged 15 to 24 was just under 10% in both countries. The "misleading" and "shocking" rates pointing to a large gap in fact result from the choice of denominator. It is common when comparing unemployment figures to choose the labour force (the unemployed and unemployed) as opposed to the whole population (employed, unemployed plus the so-called inactive). At the time 4½ million of the French people aged 15 to 24 were in education – and therefore defined as inactive – compared to 2½ million in Britain. Similarly there were just under 2 million of the young French people in work compared to just under 4 million of the British people. Hence, the much larger denominator used in the calculation for Britain meant that a similar number of unemployed was translated into a much percentage.

While the traditional unemployment rate remains useful for some purposes – employers gauging the supply of labour and analysts using the fluctuations overtime as an indicator of economic growth – it is clearly not a meaningful social indicator. Indeed, in this case it could be a perverse indicator. For in the UK, if nearly two thirds of young people are in the labour market, than they are probably not in education. Against the background of the fall in demand for unskilled labourers, the fact that so many of this age group in France remain in education be considered to be an indicator of social policy success. So, while the original percentages seemed to put France at a disadvantage, it is quite likely that the UK's lower rate is, in fact, masking a problem. (source: "Deconstructing the statistics that support European employment policy", Monica Threlfall, Loughborough University, 2002)

The scale of the distortion in the constituency and local authority figures published by the ONS in 2002 and 2004 before and after the change, is quite striking. The rate of unemployment nationally barely changed between the two years and yet the unemployment rate in five inner London local authorities – Tower Hamlets, Camden, Westminster, Kensington and Chelsea, and Southwark – appeared to increase by more than five percentage points. The change in the figures for Islington and Hammersmith and Fulham were just below five percentage points. These are the inner city authorities whose daytime population expands most dramatically due to commuters and, therefore, are the authorities that suffered the greatest distortion in the previous figures. Under the old figures the unemployment rate in Southwark and Tower Hamlets was about 5% in both cases, but under new figures the rates rose respectively to over 10% and over 13%. The change in numbers would give quite a different impression as to the scale of social and economic problems and the nature of possible policy responses required.

Local authority unemployment rates: how change in definition affected the numbers

Unemployment rate %	New definition	Old definition
Tower Hamlets	13.4	5.2
Newham	12.1	8.4
Southwark	10.3	5.1
Lambeth	10.1	7.6
Lewisham	10.1	9.7
Hackney	10.1	7.3
Harringey	8.9	8.8
Islington	8.7	3.8
Hammersmith and Fulham	8.6	3.7
Camdem	8.5	2.0
Wandsworth	7.3	4.3
Westminster	6.9	0.7
Kensington and Chelsea	6.9	1.6

source: "Labour market trends", ONS

Section 15 • New Deal

The government's welfare to work programme – called the New Deal – has been a centrepiece of policy since 1997. It started (nationally in April 1998) as a scheme for out of work young people up to 24 years old (mandatory for those who had been claiming benefits for six months) and offered training and job preparation, but has since expanded into a number of schemes – New Deal for Young People (18 to 24), New Deal 25 plus, New Deal 50 plus, New Deal for Disabled People, New Deal for Lone Parents, New Deal for Partners, New Deal for self-employment, and, even a New Deal for Musicians. (source: www.newdeal.gov.uk)

In Budget 2004, the Chancellor said "The New Deal for young people has helped nearly 480,000 people between 18 and 24 move into employment while the New Deal for those aged 25 and over has helped over 170,000 people get back to work." Overall the government claims that the scheme has helped roughly one million people move from unemployment to employment. The main funding for the various New Deal schemes was the £5.2bn raised in 1997/98 and 1998/99 from the "excess profits" of the privatised utilities. The bulk of the money was spent by the end of 2003/04.

It is perhaps surprising that there are no really useful and relevant statistics that show what has happened to the people who have been on the schemes. Statistics are published regularly showing the number of people on the various schemes and the number of people who have passed through the schemes, but very little information is available about the value of the schemes, in other words how people's lives have been changed by them. How many of a scheme just returned to unemployment afterwards? The New Deal figures released in December 2004 were accompanied by a note explaining data enhancements but the main weaknesses remain. There are a large number of government commissioned reports looking at various aspects but we are still largely left in the dark about what the real impact of the schemes has been.

The various studies conducted on behalf of the DWP cannot be certain about the impact of the scheme and some are more positive than others. One study suggested that after the first two years of the scheme when over half a million people had been through it, youth unemployment was only around 40,000 lower and employment about 30,000 higher – and that each job had come at a cost of £7000. (source: New Deal for Young People: implications for employment and public finances, Employment Service Research Report No. 62, www.dwp.gov.uk) There have been periodic reports of tensions between administrators in DWP (and its predecessor departments) and the statisticians – researchers are fully aware that ministers require the New Deal to be seen to be a success and had the collection of figures be too rigorous and purposeful, there is a chance that they might have pointed to its being an expensive failure.

Statistics for long-term youth unemployment (defined as being out of work for more than six months) have been corrupted by the nature of the scheme, which has contributed a large illusory component to the fall in the numbers. The distortion arises because if after all the New Deal training, education and task force placements a person fails to find a job, they will return to claiming job seeker's allowance (JSA) – but will start as a fresh claimant. After another six months on benefit, they will once again start the New Deal process ensuring that anyone who is unemployed over the long-term, but has regular spells of New Deal activity, fails to become long-term unemployed, according to the statistics.

The New Deal effect will also have reduced the over 25 long-term unemployment rate, and will do so especially from June 2005 when all JSA claimants will have to go on "a mandatory short intensive work-focused course", as foreshadowed in Budget 2004.

This is very unfortunate for economists and statisticians as long-term youth unemployment has in the past been used for analysing the economy. Between 1998 and 2003 the number of youth unemployed for up to six months fell from 232,000 to 209,000. This fall of 23,000 is modest relative to the fall in the number of youths unemployed for more than six months over the same period – a fall of 67,000, from 107,000 to 40,000.

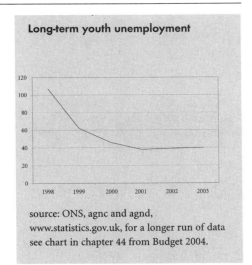

Long-term youth unemployment

source: ONS, agnc and agnd, www.statistics.gov.uk, for a longer run of data see chart in chapter 44 from Budget 2004.

Section 16 • Minimum wage

It is estimated that ¼ million jobs pay less than the national minimum wage (for people aged 18 and over). This constitutes just over 1% of the jobs in the UK. People in part-time work were over three times as likely as people in full-time work to be paid less than the minimum wage, with 2.3% of part-time jobs and 0.7% of full-time jobs falling below the level.

These estimates cannot be used as a measure of non-compliance with the legislation. This is because the survey data do not determine whether an individual is eligible for the minimum wage. For example, it is not possible to identify people such as apprentices and those undergoing training, who are exempt or are entitled to lower rates. (source: www.dti.gov.uk/er/nmw and www.lowpay.gov.uk) The Low Pay Commission estimated in 2003 that just over one million, between 4% and 5% of jobs, were benefiting as a result of the minimum wage. This figure rose to about 1½ million of jobs, around 7% of the total, following the rate rise in October 2004. (source: "Low Pay Commission report", 2004, www.lowpay.gov.uk)

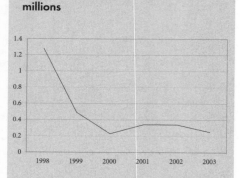

Jobs paid below the minimum wage, millions

source: Labour Market Trends, ONS, December 2004, figures relate to UK, spring of each year, based on the Labour Force Survey and the Annual Survey of Hours and Earnings

People affected most by the introduction of the NMW are likely to be: women, part-timers, seasonal or casual workers, younger employees, people with disabilities, people working for small employers (under 25 employees) and those working in certain parts of the private sector (especially hospitality, retail, social and personnel services, and health-care). (source: www.cipd.co.uk)

What is the minimum wage?

The national minimum wage was introduced in April 1999, with the rate set at £3.60 per hour for those aged 22 or older. It was increased in October 2000 and each October since, rising to £4.85 in October 2004. The minimum wage was set at a level such that about one in 14 workers was directly affected. Compliance with the regulations is thought to be widespread leading to a detectable effect on wage distribution among low earners.

Since April 1999 the Inland Revenue, which is responsible for the enforcement of the minimum wage, has responded to over 320,000 enquiries and handled over 11,000 complaints about non-payment of the minimum wage. Since the introduction of the minimum wage its enforcement officers have identified over £13 million in pay arrears for workers. (source: www.inlandrevenue.gov.uk)

Section 17 • **Equal pay for women**

The publication of the first figures from the Office for National Statistics' new Annual Survey of Hours and Earnings – which replaced the existing and much maligned New Earnings Survey – in October 2004 showed a further narrowing in the gap between male and female earnings. Earnings across the board rose but as the estimate of hourly pay for males rose by less than the estimate of female pay, the gap between the two narrowed. Average hourly full-time male pay was £11.04 compared to £9.46 for women. The pay gap is narrowing but not very fast. (source: www.statistics.gov.uk)

The Annual Survey of Hours and Earnings
The new survey was the first to be designed as part of the ONS statistical modernisation programme and benefits from improved methodologies and statistical tools. There seems little doubt that the numbers from it will be more robust than those from its predecessor survey. Earlier in October, the ONS had published revised figures for previous years resulting from the new methodology.

But the pay gap figures are not all they might seem at first glance. If median earnings are used to construct the gender pay gap, it comes out at 14% in April 2004, compared to 18% using the mean, as the impact of the very high earners (which tend to be men) is removed. The percentages vary according to which of a myriad of job definitions is selected. The part-time pay gap is much larger than the full-time pay gap, with women earning about 60% of men's mean hourly full-time earnings. Women's weekly earnings are just under 80% of male earnings, as men tend to work longer hours and do more overtime. (source: www.womenandequalityunit.gov.uk)

Even when the definition is agreed, there is more to the gap than direct pay discrimination, i.e. where a man and woman are doing the same job but being paid different rates. Because the pay gap is an aggregate concept, not matching person against person, there are lots of reasons other than what most people would see as discrimination that could explain it: the differ-

The Cabinet Office published (November 2003) a summary report of its findings into pay in the civil service which showed a reported average gender pay gap of around 5% in favour of men within pay bands but no evidence of deliberate gender discrimination

(source: www.civilservice.gov.uk)

Over the last three decades, the full-time hourly pay gap has closed considerably from around 30%, to just under 20% now, to the narrowest since the Equal Pay Act came into force, in 1975

ences in the patterns of male and female employment (i.e. differences in the jobs they do), previous employment histories, child care responsibilities and levels of qualifications.

Why is there such a big difference between the mean and the median measure?

The mean is the average, which is calculated by taking the sum of all earnings and then dividing that figure by the number of employees. However, the problem with using the mean is that it is strongly influenced by the very high earnings of a few individuals at the top end of the income curve, which can give a distorted picture of 'average' earnings. For that reason, the ONS now prefers to present the gap primarily in terms of the median. Fifty percent of people in employment earn more than the median, while fifty per cent earn less, so it can be argued that the median gives a truer picture of what is happening to a typical person. Both the mean and median figures are presented here but those organisations interested in drawing attention to the size of the gap tend to focus on the mean rather than the median.

In the absence of any figures from government that highlight "discrimination", a lot of research has been done to unpick the relative importance of the various factors contributing to the causes of the gender pay gap. Even so, it is difficult to come up with a definitive breakdown. One piece of research suggested that discrimination accounted for less than one third of the pay gap. (source: www.womenandequalityunit.gov.uk)

The Equal Opportunities Commission identifies four main causes of the

The incomes of single women in their early 30s are higher than their male couterparts, but at all other ages and household types, male incomes are higher.

Components of the pay gap per hour worked

Component	% of gap
Years of full-time employment experience	26
Interruptions to the labour market due to family care	15
Years of part-time employment experience	12
Education 6 Segregation	13
Discrimination and other factors associated with being female	29

Based on British Household Panel Survey data

pay gap: discrimination, education, labour market rigidities and working patterns. They believe that discrimination (which includes what they call "systematic disadvantage", in other words the work women choosing to do being paid less than the work men choose to do) accounts for just over one-third of the pay gap. The latest analysis concluded that 36% was due to different lifetime working patterns (the tendency to work part-time and looking after children) and 8% was due to women spending less time in education. (source: Equal Pay Taskforce report, "Just Pay", 2001, and "Britain's competitive edge", 2004, www.eoc.org.uk) It is hard to see how micro policy can be pursued efficiently if we do not know how much direct discrimination is occurring.

Some of the differences between the sexes at younger ages appear in official statistics. At A-level, three times as many boys as girls sit the exam in physics while more than twice as many girls than boys sit the exam in English literature. When it comes to apprenticeships, there are 50 boys for every girl in the construction sector and 250 for every girl in the electro technical sector. At university, men outnumber women by five to one in computer science and engineering courses. While women outnumber men by at least two to one in education, languages and "subjects allied to medicine" (excluding medicine and dentistry). It is easy to see how the choice of subject to study can affect the future earnings prospects. (source: "Facts about women and men", www.eoc.org.uk)

The older the age group, the wider the gender pay gap generally becomes. This is partly because as women get older, they are more likely to have spent time out of the labour market caring for children or elderly dependants. The increase in the gender pay gap by age also reflects the gap in qualification levels between men and women. Although the gender gap in education has closed in recent years, the difference is still significant between men and women over 40 years old.

The Prime Minister announced (July 2004) the creation of a Women and Work Commission to examine the gender pay gap and other issues affecting women's employment. Hopefully the so-called Prosser Commission will call for better data when it reports in the autumn of 2005.

Girl apprentices outnumber boys by 7 to 1 in health and social care, by 13 to 1 in hairdressing and by 40 to 1 in early years care – sectors with a tradition of low pay

There are very few occupations which have roughly equal numbers of men and women. Men dominate – by a ratio of at least three to one in professions such as software and ICT, police, marketing and sales, and security guards. Women dominate by at least three to one as office clerks, primary teachers, care assistants, hairdressers, nurses and receptionists. Doctors, solicitors, shelf fillers, chefs and cooks, and secondary teachers are among the few occupations where the gap is less than two to one.

Section 18 • **Sickness, disability and work**

In some local authorities more than one in five men of working age are claiming a sickness benefit

The number of sick and disabled people has risen sharply in the last decade despite the understanding that general health levels are improving, making it a political issue. The number claiming incapacity benefit (IB) for more than six months has risen from 0.6 million in 1981 to 2.2 million in 2004 and according to government surveys, as many as one in five of the population suffer from some form of disability. In mid-2004, about 2.7 million people claimed IB or Severe Disability Allowance compared to 0.8 million claiming jobseeker's allowance (unemployment benefit).

Measuring disability is a classic tricky statistical issue for several reasons, not least because of the differences in the way that "disability" is measured (just how disabled is disabled?) and methodological differences between surveys (dealing with the inevitable sensitivities, sample sizes, question wording, gaining access to disabled people, and measures taken to improve their ability to complete forms etc). In addition, there is a problem of knowing what the reference population is – people of working age, all

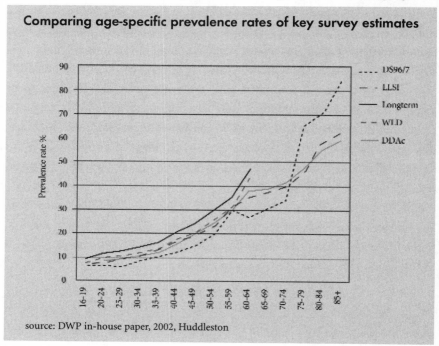

Comparing age-specific prevalence rates of key survey estimates

source: DWP in-house paper, 2002, Huddleston

adults, total population and so forth – as the rate of disability varies considerably by age. Disability rates of under 10% are common for people under the age of 30 rising to over 50% by the age of 80 – and rates are much more volatile between surveys for the older age groups.

Objective surveys asking specifically about disability tend to give lower rates of disability than general surveys. This is a common problem in the measurement of many other phenomena but is amplified in this case not least due to the sensitivity of the topic. But aside from all the measurement problems, the main concern is the number of disabled people of working age and the sharp rise in the numbers during the 1990s.

The government's General Household Survey asks, "Do you have any long-standing illness, disability or infirmity?" and "Does this illness or disability limit your activities in any way?" The chart shows the responses for men aged 25 to 54 (so-called prime age men) and also the trend for those with no qualifications and degree level qualifications. The aggregate measure shows a very slight upward movement over the past two decades, but the rate for those with no qualifications rises sharply during the 1990s.

Figures from the government's Labour Force Survey suggest a rising trend. The question asked changed in 1997 leading to a break in the series but the change did not seem to have a great impact on responses. The question used since 1997 asks whether the respondent had a health problem that was expected to last more than a year and then asked if it limited the kind of work they could do. In this case the aggregate measure for prime age men has risen from below 10% to close to 15% – i.e. close to the figure shown by the GHS.

The 10-yearly population census sheds a bit more light on the issue asking people of working age whether they have a "limiting long-term illness". The figures for men and women together for England and Wales were 8.2% in 1991 and 13.6% in 2001. A similarly defined sample from the LFS would show a rise from 12.3% to 18.4%. The rise shown is similar in both cases even if the levels are different.

There is some evidence from the US to support the idea that health is deteriorating. The National Health Interview Survey reported a 40% rise in disability between 1984 and 1996. The rise among the young was associated with the prevalence of asthma and diabetes. But it is also possible that respondents exaggerate the severity of health problems in order to ratio-

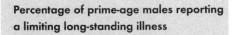

Percentage of prime-age males reporting a limiting long-standing illness

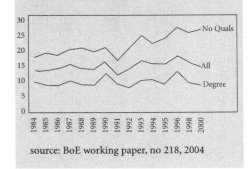

source: BoE working paper, no 218, 2004

Percentage of prime-age males reporting health problem limiting the kind of work they can do

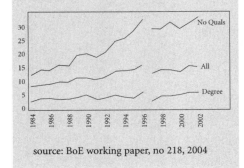

source: BoE working paper, no 218, 2004

The percentage of working age men with a limiting health problem has doubled in the last two decades to 30% for those with no qualifications but stayed at 5% for those with a degree

Doctors get 22 million requests for sicknotes every year and they estimate that 9 million of them are bogus

source: www.healthof the nation.com

There is no single gold standard measure of disability

The major survey sources used by DWP put the prevalence rate of disability at between 15% and 20% in GB. One reason for differences in measurement lies in the survey questions asked. There have been a few specialist surveys of disability in the UK but generally the estimates come from single-item, global questions about disability placed in surveys whose prime concern is not disability. Specialist surveys can more accurately measure functional limitations in daily activities such as mobility and self-care. In comparison, single questions are far more subjective in that they rely on the respondent to self-assess – and they give higher rates of disability.

Three common measures of disability are: self-reported limiting long standing illness, work-limiting disability (questions usually ask respondents about the type of work they could or might do), and whether the respondent is covered by the 1995 Disability Discrimination Act (which defines disability as a "physical or mental impairment which has a substantial and long-term adverse effect on ability to carry out normal day-to-day activities"). National non-specific surveys are thought to underestimate the extent of disability. Part of this reflects a tendency of old people to view their disability as part of the aging process rather than disability as such. The government's target of increasing labour market participation of the "long term disabled" covers those of working age in the second and third categories.

It is vital that users know the definition of figures being used when drawing conclusions. Different measures will more appropriate in certain circumstances. DWP research showed that some users felt the definition used in the surveys was too inclusive and some felt it was insufficiently inclusive. Very little data is available linking disability to demographic factors such as ethnicity and social outcomes such as home ownership or educational achievement. (source: "Review of disability estimates and definitions", DWP, In-house report 128, 2004)

In March 2004, the government announced a crack down on "blue badge fraud" – there are currently 2 million badges issued to people whose mobility is severly limited. The badges allow drivers to park in disabled bays and ignore certain parking restrictions

nalise non-participation in the labour force and/or receipt of disability benefits of one sort or another.

During the 1970s and 1980s the number of prime age men in the UK claiming incapacity benefits was stable and even declining slightly during much of the 1980s. There was, however, a steady upward trend in the number of claimants staying on the benefit for more than six months – rising from 3 in 10 in 1972 to 8 in 10 by 1989. In the 1990s there was what the Bank of England called an "explosion" ("Health, disability insurance and labour force participation", BoE Working Paper no 218, 2004) in the number of prime age males claiming disability. The number rose from under 400,000 in the early 1990s to over 800,000 in 2002.

The sharp rise in incapacity benefits claimants begs the question as to whether it is real or partly accounted for by some so-called disguised unemployment. The unemployment claimant numbers could be lower than they should be as some people who are claiming incapacity benefit are capable of working and should be claiming unemployment benefits. The Bank of England research estimates that as many as ½ million people were shifted from unemployment to sickness benefits during the 1990s. The geographical pattern of sickness claimants – not covered in the Bank paper – seems to support this as the rates are particularly high in areas that suffered from the de-industrialisation of the early 1980s and early 1990s when technological change, shifting trade patterns and privatisation cut the demand for lower skilled employment. The DWP refutes that there are significant numbers on the wrong benefit while some analysts and commentators suspect the figure is greater than the Bank's estimate.

Intriguingly the Bank of England Research Paper shows that the period of large increases in the number on incapacity benefit coincided with the disability system being particularly generous. In the early 1990s, claimants aged between 45 and 59 would receive almost double on the sickness system than the unemployment system. (The figures are based on new claimants and an assumed duration of claim in both cases of more than one year.) The financial attractiveness of disability rose as the so-called earnings-related Additional Pension built up. The relative generosity fell in 1995 when the AP was abolished. It was around that time that the flow onto incapacity benefits eased. None the less, IB is paid at a higher rate than JSA, there is no time-limited contributory element and the benefit is payable with less stringent national insurance payment records.

The Bank's analysis covered the "pull factors" of generous incapacity benefits but largely ignored the "push factors". The late 1980s was also a

> The number of "prime age men" claiming disability benefits doubled in the decade to 2002

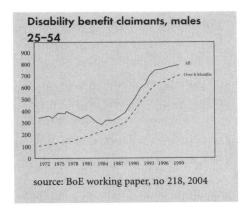

Disability benefit claimants, males 25–54

source: BoE working paper, no 218, 2004

> 500 people a week leave the labour market because of injury at work. Three-quarters of claimants have "subjective" health complaints

The rise in sickness

A group of researchers at the Centre for Regional Economic and Social Research at Sheffield Hallam University have been at the forefront of documenting and explaining the phenomenon. (Source: "A theory of employment, unemployment and sickness", Regional studies, 34.7, 2000, and "Incapacity and unemployment benefit", July 1999) Their notion is that sickness is quite widespread in the economy and that many people hold down jobs despite their illness. But when they become unemployed many are diverted to sickness benefits, creating a form of hidden unemployment. This flow is irrespective of the general level of ill health in the country. In areas of traditionally heavy industry, where occupational ill-health might also be higher, a larger proportion of the unemployed are likely to end up on sickness benefits. The number flowing onto sickness benefits will vary over time as benefit rules change.

time when unemployment benefit became harder to claim and the unemployed were subjected to an increasingly stringent programme of pressure to search for and take increasingly worse jobs. This might push the number of people "incorrectly" on sickness benefit to around ¾ million.

Depending on the age, men are 10–30% more likely than women to be receiving incapacity benefits. During the 1990s the gap between men and women widened at the younger ages (say, under 40s) but narrowed at the older ages. (source: a paper, "Explaining the growth in the number of people claiming incapacity benefits" (2002), written by Trevor Huddleston of DWP, but never publicly released.) The DWP paper also says that, "Faced with long-term detachment from the labour market, these people claimed those benefits that offered the least onerous conditionality and the most generous financial reward." It also concludes that "many of the people who have been receiving incapacity benefits would have been in work in a fully employed economy."

The cost of benefits paid to those claiming they have been disabled by stress, depression and anxiety has risen to more than £2 billion a year, prompting a warning of a burgeoning "can't cope culture". There is uncertainty as to the extent of otherwise healthy men and women are being kept off the unemployment register by being signed off as unfit to work on mental health grounds and the trend towards what some experts claim are benefits for vaguely defined disorders that encourage the work shy.

There is a strong regional disparity in the prevalence of sickness claims. As research by the Institute for Public Policy Research showed, 13% of the working age population in the north east receives some form of sickness and incapacity benefit – compared to just 3% receiving unemployment benefits. ("Working brief", June 2004) Only 5% and 7% respectively claim sickness benefits in the south east and London. Their figures showed that 23% of working age people are on sickness benefits in Easington, a district in county Durham, and over 22% in Merthyr and Blaenau Gwent in Wales. Well-heeled districts in the south east such as Wokingham have sickness benefit rates around 3%.

British insurance companies manage over 300,000 claims – and spend over £1 billion each year – for workplace and road traffic injuries. Research has shown that some people take disproportionately longer to recover than others due to psychological factors and personal circumstances. Between 20% and 30% of injury outcomes are aggravated in some way by psychological factors – with the person taking longer to recover than medical based analysis suggests.

Around one in twenty soft-tissue injuries such as back sprain – and these account for four in five of road traffic claims – become deemed "problematic" and are causing problems a year after the event even if most people have recovered after 6 weeks. In one in twenty cases, the outcomes are seriously adversely affected to an extent that cannot be explained by initial or remaining injury – cases known as ADOs, Apparently Disproportionate Outcome. One in five injury victims exhibit some form of post-traumatic stress disorder and one in seven has associated anxiety one year after the event. (source: "Psychology, personal injury and rehabilitation", ABI/IUAL, 2004.)

The study identified 24 factors that could delay or prevent a return to normal life that were grouped in four categories:

- Environmental – for example, unpleasant work, or low job satisfaction
- Medical – such as the failure of treatment
- Organisational – such as on-going legal proceedings (during which a full recovery would jeopardise the claim) and qualification periods for compensation
- Individual related – such as beliefs about pain and poor coping strategies.

The ABI argued that a "biopsychosocial" approach needs to be used in addition to the traditional approaches used by solicitors, doctors the courts and insurers to make the existing system less "cumbersome, slow and expensive."

If the employment rate of those on disability benefits was raised to that for the whole economy, more than 1½ million extra people would be in work – roughly the scale of the rise in employment since 1997.

Since 1997 the cost of benefits for those suffering from post-traumatic stress has risen from £48 million a year to £103 million. For those certified with depression, annual expenditure has risen from £770 million in 1997 to over £1 billion. Phobic anxiety and all other mental and behavioural disorders absorb £900 million. More than 700,000 people – a quarter of all claims – receive incapacity benefit on the grounds of poor mental health, a 38% increase since 1997. Of those, 230,000 are women, a 60% increase in seven years.

The statistics are contained in a written parliamentary answer from the work and pensions minister, Maria Eagle, to Paul Goodman MP.

Section 19 • Injuries and fatalities at work

Fatal injuries to workers

source: "Statistics of fatal injuries" HSE, 2003/04

Death by type of accident, %

Fall from a height	29
Struck by a moving vehicle	19
Struck by falling or moving object	12
Drowning	9
Electricity	6
Moving machinery	5
Other	20

source: www.hse.gov.uk, data for 2003/04

235 people were fatally injured at work in 2003/04 in Great Britain, a rise of 4% on the previous year. The rate of deaths per 100,000 workers also rose slightly to 0.81. There was a downward trend in the numbers killed in the 1990s to a low point of 220 in 1999/2000 (the figure was last over 300 in 1992/93) and has been flat since at around 250 a year. The extent to which the downward trend is due to health and safety issues or the movement of people out of the more dangerous sectors and the use of newer equipment (that was not usually introduced with health and safety in mind), is unclear.

Nearly half of the deaths to workers occurred in the construction sector (30%) and agriculture, forestry and fishing (19%). The most dangerous industries were scrap and waste recycling, mining and petrol and gas extraction where the death rate is more than ten times the national average. There have been no deaths shown in the deep coal mining figures in the last two years. (source: Statistics of fatal injuries, Health and Safety Executive, 2003/04, www.hse.gov.uk/statistics)

Unusually, the data for the latest year saw one incident cause 21 deaths (9% of the total), when cockle harvesters were trapped by rising tides in Morecambe Bay. This is an extreme example of how the figures can be volatile from year to year and why caution is sometimes needed in interpreting what might appear to be changes in trend. The rate of death is higher among the self-employed as they dominate the most dangerous industries of construction and agriculture.

The rate of death in Britain is low compared to other EU countries. The latest data refer to 2000, cover 14 of the then 15 members (excluding Luxembourg) and are on a different basis to that of the British figures. They show Britain at 1.7 deaths per 100,000 workers compared to the EU average of 2.8. Only Sweden has a lower rate while that in Spain, Austria and Portugal is more than double that in Britain. (source: Eurostat E3/ESAW as replicated in the HSE annual publication.)

The same HSE data set also collates the number of members of public who died in accidents although it is far from clear what the numbers mean. In 2003/04, 371 were counted but most of these – 240 – resulted from acts of trespass or suicide on the railways. In both cases, the figures are the total supplied by companies and others to HSE under the "Reporting of injuries, diseases and dangerous occurrences regulations 1995". Acts of violence at work are counted but other work related deaths are not, such as those arising from: road traffic, civil aviation and merchant shipping accidents. The armed forces and the self-employed when at their own premises are also excluded. For members of the public, therefore, the figures could easily be misleading as they are a (rather limited) measure of deaths on (selected) business premises rather than a full and more useful assessment of suicides or accidental deaths including those occurring in the home or on the streets.

In the last five years, 18 people have been killed at work by an animal

Work related illness

Around 30 million working days were estimated to have been lost in the last 12 months due to work-related ill-health with each person who was off work taking an average of 22 days off – equating to a loss of 1.3 days per worker across the whole economy. The two main medical problems were musculoskeletal disorders (often backache) and stress, depression and anxiety, accounting respectively for about 1.1 million and 0.6 million people. The groups with the greatest prevalence rates were the protective services (fire, police and armed forces) where over 8% of workers reported some form of illness, health and social welfare workers, some categories of construction workers and teachers. An additional 9 million days were lost due to workplace injuries with each person taking an average of 9 days off. Figures for sickness and off-work in the economy at large show much higher rates as the figures shown here include only the HSE's count of work-related illnesses, not counting illnesses which are not put down by respondents as being due to work.

12 million working days were lost last year due to workplace induced back-ache and 13 million due to workplace stress

The HSE also gives data on the number of people who have suffered injuries at work. (source: "Statistics highlights", 2003/04, HSE) The number of injuries to employees rose by 9.4% in 2003/04 to 31,900 while the number of reported over three day injuries rose by 0.9% to 130,200. The survey can not be compared fully with its earlier versions (from pre 1996/97) as they are not on the same basis – the level of information collected and survey design were different.

In 2003/04 39 million working days were lost, 30 million due to work-related ill health and 9 million due to workplace injury

Major injuries to workers, 000s

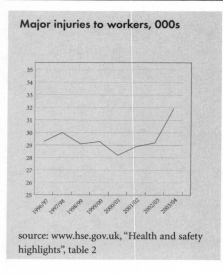

source: www.hse.gov.uk, "Health and safety highlights", table 2

The government has set targets as part of its "Revitalising health and safety" programme to help reduce work-related injuries, ill health and working days lost. The HSE reviews progress against them annually. There is no easy read across from the targets to the data and, as the department says, progress against the targets will be measured using data from a variety of sources, statistical models and new data sources will be required to make "a full assessment of progress". That said some trends seem to be emerging.

The first target is to cut the number of fatal and major injuries by 5% in five years and 10% in ten years from the base year of 1999–00. The rate of major injury rose over the first four years while the employer reported rate of "over 3 day injury" fell. The number of fatal injuries is broadly unchanged over the period. The department says that most of these data are subject to a statistical uncertainty of 5–6% and concludes, "there is no clear evidence of change" in serious injuries, which is in line with the flat trend reported in fatalities.

The target to reduce the incidence, i.e. new cases, of work related ill health by 10% in five years and 20% in ten years looks likely not to be met, according to the HSE. The department concludes from the information that is available that the rise in work-related stress since the basline period is not offset by the small falls in asthma and some other ailments, and the broadly flat trend in musculoskeletal disorders.

The third target is to reduce working days lost per 100,000 workers due to injuries and ill health by 15% in five years and 30% in ten years. The total number of days lost due to workplace injuries and work-related ill health has dipped in 2003/04 from 180,000 per 100,000 in 2000/02 to 170,000, a decline which is not statistically significant.

The HSE estimates that the cost to individuals of ill health and injury is between £10–15 billion a year, with two-thirds due to the former and one third to the latter.

Section 20 • Health Service

Plenty of health service information is available but its value to decision-makers and others is questionable because of its quality, relevance and the shambolic way it is organised. At the most fundamental level, health statistics underpin society's understanding of what is good for us and what is not – and so inform advice about diet and smoking, life insurance premiums, the laws on drug abuse and so on. Health data also indicate which parts of the country are most sick, deprived and in greatest need of services – and so inform the allocation of resources to local authorities, social services and the targeting of national schemes. Thousands of organisations from GP practices to national institutions, university research departments, drug companies, insurance companies, charities and, of course, NHS management, draw regularly on statistical information either in the form of data or as messages taken from analysis of the data. As the Statistics Commission said in its 2004 report on health statistics, "Its importance in shaping the institutions and values of society cannot be overstated."

In the context of health service management – the largest and most politically sensitive public service – the scale of decision-making is vast. Public expenditure on health services in 2004/05 will be a little over £80 billion and is rising rapidly. This equates to around £1,400 annually for every man, woman and child in the UK. The NHS, government, Parliament and citizens all want to know whether this money is being spent as effectively as possible, whether the advice and treatment provided by the NHS is as good as possible, and whether services are as good where they live as they are elsewhere in the UK, and elsewhere in the world.

Many people would expect that relevant figures to make these judgements would meet certain basic standards. The first of the ten "fundamental principles" for official statistics set out by the United Nations in 1994 is that, "official statistics are to be compiled and made available on an impartial basis to honour citizens' entitlement to public information." On this fairly basic level, the Department of Health fails.

Figures on health care in the United Kingdom barely exist. There are two main reasons. First, the Department of Health is focused on the performance

> The English NHS employs over one million people and is said to be the world's third largest employer after the Chinese army and the Indian Railways

Doctors internationally, 2000

Greece	4.5
Italy	4.1
Switzerland	3.5
France	3.3
Germany	3.3
US	2.7
Australia	2.4
Ireland	2.2
UK	2.0
Japan	1.9

source: OECD Health Data, 2003.
Note: definitions used are not always consistent.

Cancer accounts for about
a quarter of all deaths in
the UK and survival rates
are lower than in other
European countries

About 300,000 people
suffer a heart attack each
year

of the NHS and seems not to care about the private sector. Second, the
devolved nature of the NHS makes aggregation from the constituent countries almost impossible. The ONS made one attempt in 2000 by producing
"UK Health Statistics" but that is now out of date and is yet to be repeated.
Even the figures on the English NHS are hard to assimilate, not least because
the Department of Health does not publish an up-to-date compendium of
figures on health care. Some of the aggregations of data which are readily
available on the web site which do contain data – such as the NHS annual
report – are produced on behalf of ministers and do not have the impartiality
expected of standard statistical publications. The latest annual report shows
only figures that indicate an improving trend. But surely some aspects of the
health service are deteriorating? Some data are shown for only a year or two
and others for a decade or more. Why? A casual observer might imagine that

The Wanless report

"Securing our future health: taking a long-term view" - the report
commissioned by the Treasury from Derek Wanless concerning the long-
term resource requirements for the NHS - was published in 2002. It
highlighted a number of problems in the health service, such as the low
levels of health care professionals per head of population compared to
many other countries, the poor use made of ICT, the low standard of
accommodation and food, and capacity problems in the social care
sector. The report frequently referred to the paucity of good quality,
readily available data. It said that, "bringing data together has been a
complicated and time consuming task, as different elements of the data
were held in different places and were not always directly comparable." It
recommended that each of the UK health departments should have a
single source of validated health and social care related information
based on common definitions. The report presented conclusions for the
UK as a whole but said it was forced to base the analysis on an assessment
of only the English situation due to the data comparability difficulties
across the four countries. The review said that it had not been able to
analyse the health needs of different parts of the UK and draw any firm
conclusions about the link between health and socio-economic inequal-
ities due to data difficulties - where figures existed they were often
conflicting. Source: www.hm-treasury.gov.uk

Finished consultant episodes, million

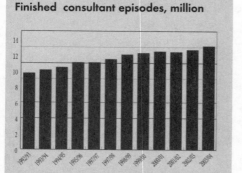

source: www.doh.gov.uk, England, consultant
episodes will be higher than the number of
patients.

The Statistics Commission's review of health statistics

The Commission published its review of health statistics in October 2004. Its six recommendations cover three broad areas: supporting user access to data and analyses, consistency and coherence, and identifying and meeting user needs. It concluded:

1. UK producers of official health statistics should give high priority to developing an easy to use and up-to-date online index to available health statistics, and statistical reports, covering all four countries of the UK. Wherever possible the index should guide the user directly to the figures and supply relevant contextual information and advice on interpretation.

2. UK producers of official health statistics should work together to produce metadata in a consistent format.

3. Producers of official health statistics should consult users afresh about whether there are any specific diseases or medical conditions on which fuller statistical datasets are required and where the cost would be justified.

4. The Department of Health, in consultation with the devolved administrations, should address the inconsistencies in definition and availability of key health statistics and related indicators for the four countries of the UK. In doing so, a fresh assessment should be made of the potential value to decision-makers of UK aggregate data and of the value of consistent data for the four countries within the UK.

5. The producers of official health statistics across the UK should address more systematically the statistical requirements of the large number of organisations that need health data for particular geographical areas.

6. The producers of official health statistics should seek, in consultation with bodies that represent user interests, to identify systematically the use made of health statistics in research and decision-making across the UK.

source: www.statscom.org.uk

More people think that the overall state of the NHS is bad than good, 44% compared to 30%

source: ICM, 2002

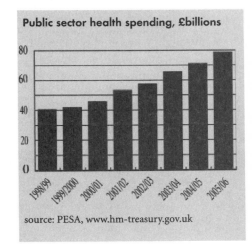

Public sector health spending, £billions

source: PESA, www.hm-treasury.gov.uk

something is being hidden. The Health Care Commission publishes performance indicator information on individual trusts. (www.healthcarecommis-

The NHS currently provides around 300 million meals a year the equivalent of six meals per person in the whole population - spending around £2.50 per person per day, roughly half that spent in the private sector

NHS expenditure, % of GDP

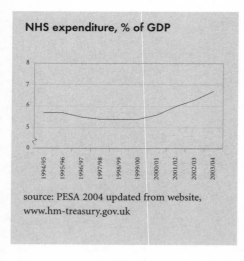

source: PESA 2004 updated from website, www.hm-treasury.gov.uk

Health expenditure per capita, PPP US$, selected countries

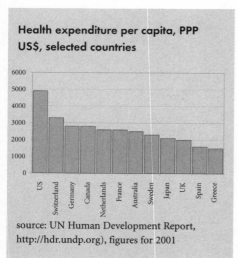

source: UN Human Development Report, http://hdr.undp.org), figures for 2001

sion.org.uk) There are odd snippets of data on www.performance.doh.gov.uk but sadly no readily accessible statistical series.

Hospital Episode Statistics are the backbone of information about admitted patient care delivered by NHS hospitals in England. The data runs from 1989 but is only readily accessible on the internet from 1998/99. The data is hard to compare over years, in part due to the way it is presented on the doh.gov.uk website but also due to definition changes.

Large chunks of data in the web based version of "Health and personal Social Services" publication were not up to date when this book was being written due to "technical and operational problems". It can only be hoped that when the Health and Social Care Information Centre is established in 2005, the provision of data will improve.

Public expenditure on the health service is expected to double from £44 billion 1997/98 to £88 billion in 2005/06. The plans show it rising to £107 billion in 2007/08, two years later. It is also possible to see how total spending on health as a proportion of GDP has developed over the last decade and is forecast to develop in the published plans. Sadly, the Treasury's documents do not allow such comparisons to be made for spending in real terms, i.e. inflation-adjusted, or for any breakdown of the total. A real terms comparison is only possible for the latest outturn year, 2003/04, which shows that expenditure in cash terms between 1996/97 and 2003/04 rose 76%, compared to 48% in real terms. Despite the increase in expenditure, it was only in 2002 that the output of the NHS as a proportion of the total economy surpassed the levels seen in 1996.

According to the OECD, approximately 7½% of UK GDP is accounted for by health expenditure – public and private. On this basis, the UK ranks 11th out of the original EU-15 countries and is relatively low down the rankings among developed countries for expenditure on a per capita basis. Looking purely at public spending on health around the world, there are four countries – Germany, France, Sweden and Denmark – that spend 7% or more of GDP. The UK ranks alongside the US, Australia, Japan, Switzerland, Italy, Belgium and Portugal, all of which spend between 6% and 7% of GDP on the public health service. Several countries, such as the Netherlands, Austria, Spain and Finland, spend between 5% and 6% of GDP on the health service.

Part of the reason for the UK's relatively low ranking in the total

The structure of the NHS

There are a variety of organisations in the NHS - and have been subjected to periodic structural change. "Primary care" is usually the first point of contact for patients and includes GP practices, health visitors, dentists and opticians. "Primary care trusts" plan and commission health services for the local communities - a role previously carried out by health authorities. "Secondary care" is specialised treatment usually provided by hospitals. Hospitals are organised into NHS trusts, which employ the majority of NHS staff, such as doctors, nurses and therapists, along with all the support staff. Performance management, the management of the delivery of local health services and strategies, and ensuring that national health priorities are translated into local plans, are functions carried out by strategic health authorities.

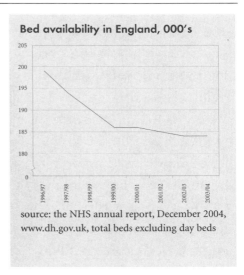

Bed availability in England, 000's

source: the NHS annual report, December 2004, www.dh.gov.uk, total beds excluding day beds

spending on health lies in the modest proportion spent on private sector health – including direct household (out of pocket) spending and private insurance. While Americans spend nearly 8% of GDP, South Africans over 5% and the Swiss just under 5% on private healthcare, the British spend less than 1½% of GDP. The Greeks and the Dutch are among the EU-15 countries spending over 3% of GDP on private healthcare, with only Sweden and Luxembourg among the EU-15 spending less. (source: UN Human Development Report, http://hdr.undp.org)

Throughout the 1980s and 1990s, the number of NHS beds fell – from 362,000 in 1979 to 194,000 in 1997/98. The decline was spread across all categories of medical specialties but was particularly sharp in mental illness and learning disabilities. Since 1997 there has been a further reduction – in all categories except day cases and acute – but at a much less rapid rate and is showing tentative signs of having levelled off. The decline in the number of beds reflects a combination of improved treatments – so that people do not have to stay in hospital for so long as they used to – and the decision that certain categories of patients, such as some who are mentally ill, are best treated in the community. In 2003/04, 68% of elective hospital admissions (3.7 million out of 5.5 million) were day cases, a rise from 62% in 1997/98.

Many of the NHS outputs are on a rising trend. For example, the number of imaging and radiodiagnostic tests carried out have increased from 27.8

In the year to mid-2004, nearly 600,000 people were readmitted in an emergency within 28 days of leaving hospital – nearly 6% of patients

The number of NHS beds in England has halved in the last 25 years

The hospital episodes statistics give very detailed information on hospital treatments. For example, in 2003/04, 263 pedestrians were admitted to hospital following a collision with a pedal cycle. Their average length of stay was four days, half were under 14 years old, and in total they used 1077 bed days

million in 1997/98 to 30.6 million 2003/04. Nearly 680 million prescription items were dispensed in England in the year to September 2004, amounting to nearly 14 items per person during the year. This is a rise of over one third since 1997. But it is unclear to what extent any increased output reflects improved health care, a reduction in waiting lists, rising costs or the deteriorating health of the population.

Figures for the latest year, 2003/04, show that there were record numbers of treatments for cancer (1.098 million), ischaemic heart disease (415,000), stroke (150,000), influenza and pneumonia (673,000), and hip fracture (90,000). The number of people with cancer has been on a steady rising trend, rising by 15% since 1997/98. The number of people treated for asthma, diabetes and heart failure were not at record levels.

The enthusiasm of the Department of Health to proclaim year-on-year increases in activity is somewhat paradoxical, regardless of how accurate

Prevalence and incidence

The term 'prevalence' usually refers to the estimated population of people who are managing a problem at any given time. The term 'incidence' refers to the annual diagnosis rate, or the number of new cases diagnosed each year. Hence, these two statistics types can differ: a short-lived disease like flu can have high annual incidence but low prevalence, but a life-long disease like diabetes has a low annual incidence but high prevalence.

and carefully constructed are the data – it is not always in the population's interest that the NHS is "doing more". Prevention of accidents would be far more desirable for society than increased admissions to hospital casualty departments. Some costs are rising rapidly also. The average cost of each prescription has risen by more than one third since 1997, taking the bill to nearly £8 billion in the year to September 2004. The rising cost could reflect the increasing cost of some or all drugs, or a move to more expensive drugs. (source: NHS annual report, December 2004, www.dh.gov.uk)

The number of NHS treatments – defined as finished consultants episodes – has risen every year over the last decade. In 2003/04, there were 13.2 million hospital consultant episodes, of which just over half involved an operation. Nearly three out of ten (3.8 million) were day cases. As some patients will see more than one consultant during their stay in hospital, they will be recorded twice in these figures. Allowing for this double counting, the figure of admission episodes falls to 11.7 million. There were 270,000 deaths in hospital in 2003/04, roughly one in every 40 admissions.

A survey of GPs revealed that alcoholism, drug addiction, sexually transmitted diseases, stress and obesity are the biggest growth conditions in the GP surgery. Two thirds of doctors reported a progressive and significant increase in the number of cases of childhood obesity. They also believed that for more than a quarter of their consultation patients did not need to see a doctor.

British doctors get 22 million requests for sick-notes every year – and they estimate that nine million of these are suspect and that, at best, nearly a fifth of them are invalid. And nearly three million workers across the country admit they would consider asking their GP for a bogus sick-note – with twice as many men than women saying they would cheat the system. The most frequent causes for sick-note requests are: back pain, depression, work-place stress, other stress related problems and flu. (source: www.healthofthenation.com)

The measures that have been used to describe the productivity of the public health sector as a whole have been widely recognised as seriously misleading as they failed to capture quality increases and the full range of outputs. The Office for National Statistics, along with the Treasury and the Department of Health, are in the midst of a several-year programme of trying to make a sustained improvement in the figures. A review of the future of government output measurement under Sir Tony Atkinson was launched by the ONS and reported at the end of January 2005.

The UK national accounts estimates released in June 2004 were the first to be compiled using more comprehensive information and much greater transactional detail than had been available before on the volume and cost of government health services. The new figures include information on over 1,700 NHS activity types, covering around three quarters by value of all NHS activity, compared to under twenty indicators before. It still does not take account of changes in quality of service. This change brought about a substantial increase in the output of the health service in recent years – roughly doubling the output growth from 10% to 20% since 1998. The improvement in the quality of the government healthcare output estimates was overshadowed at the time of their announcement by concerns that the change, which

At any one time, one in six adults has a mental health problem such as anxiety or depression, although only one in fifty suffers from severe mental illness

Suicide is the most common cause of death among the under 35s

New NHS services, millions
A: calls to NHS direct
B: visits to NHS direct online
C: visits to walk in centres

	A	B	C
1999/00	1.6	0	0
2000/01	3.4	1.5	0.6
2001/02	5.2	2.0	1.1
2002/03	6.3	4.0	1.4
2003/04	6.4	6.5	1.6

source: NHS annual report, December 2004,
www.dh.gov.uk

Hospital star ratings
Some information about the performance of individual trusts is available from the annual performance monitoring activity of the Healthcare Commission. For each type of trust – acute, specialist, ambulance, primary care, and mental health – a variety of data is collected on dozens of topics such as waiting times, financial management, clinical negligence, infection control, cancelled operations and patient complaints. For each indicator, each trust is then graded into one of four categories – pass, borderline, moderate fail and fail. The results are then aggregated and the trust given a star rating of between three and zero. In 2003/04, a total of 590 ratings were awarded to NHS trusts – a quarter were awarded three stars, nearly one half were awarded two stars, almost a fifth were awarded one star and about one in 17 had no stars. The Healthcare Commission only came into existence in 2004, succeeding the Commission for Health Improvement, and it is not yet clear how independent it will be from the Department of Health in setting targets and monitoring performance. The star rating system is discussed further in the chapter on targets. (source: "NHS performance ratings 2003/04", July 2004, www.healthcarecommission.org.uk)

came largely without warning, had been politically motivated following the known concerns of the Chancellor and Prime Minister that there seemed to have been little return in the form of increased output in relation to the large increase in spending in recent years. (source: www.statistics.gov.uk)

The answer to "What do we get for our healthcare spending?" should be measured in terms of "health", but the NHS has very little idea of what results it really produces as it does not routinely measure patients' health-related quality of life (HRQoL). This failure seems to stand in the way of establishing where the real gains in health are to be made, which treatments and modes of delivery are most effective, how hospitals, clinical teams and clinicians are really performing, and where the extra money we plan to spend on the NHS would produce the best results. Productivity is not just about producing more of everything for each pound, it is about doing the right things in the right way as efficiently as possible.

The failure to measure this absolutely fundamental outcome of healthcare has not been due to lack of ways of measuring health related quality of life – measures have existed for many years, have been intensely researched, and have provided well recognised and accepted measures of outcome in clinical trials for decades. Indeed, the NHS has failed to match the simple three-point health-related outcome measure for patients – relieved, unrelieved and dead – devised by Florence Nightingale in the 1860s. There is a statistical disregard, it seems, for measuring the performance of the NHS in terms of patients' health. Such measures, it is argued, are required to explain certain features noticeable in existing crude data, such as the wide variations in the amount of work done by different clinicians in the NHS and the wide and persistent variations in the performance of hospitals. (source: "Measuring success in the NHS", November 2004, www.drfoster.co.uk)

Section 21 • NHS staffing

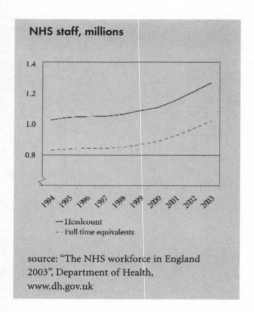

NHS staff, millions

1.4

1.2

1.0

0.8

1994 1995 1996 1997 1998 1999 2000 2001 2002 2003

— Headcount
- - Full time equivalents

source: "The NHS workforce in England 2003", Department of Health, www.dh.gov.uk

Employment figures may be quoted on a headcount or a full-time equivalent basis, with the latter allowing part-time workers to be counted in proportion to the hours of work they do. Most people agree that a full-time equivalent basis is a better measure as it is more likely to reflect the changes in the labour input. Even so, the government continues to prefer a headcount basis – presumably on the grounds that the larger the number, the more impressed everyone will be. Generally the trends in full-time equivalents and headcount move in the same direction and at similar paces, but occasionally the trends will diverge. In 1997, for example, the headcount in the NHS rose by 2,000 while the full-time equivalents fell by 2,000 – presumably as full-time workers were placed by part-timers. As the government promotes flexible working in the NHS, headcount is likely to rise more strongly.

Nearly 1.3 million people (on a headcount basis) were employed in the NHS in England in 2003. This is a rise of about 60,000 over the previous year and an average increase of 37,000 per year since 1997. The figures are not presented in such a way that it is easy to work out how many are providing medical support as opposed to administration. Roughly half of the employees are doctors, qualified nurses and other qualified clinical staff. Almost one third are people offering support to the clinical staff, with the remaining 200,000 (16%) offering infrastructure and administrative support, though this excludes administrators in GP practices. (source: "Annual workforce census", Department of Health, www.dh.gov.uk, figures as at September in each year)

The NHS in England employed 305,000 full-time equivalent qualified nursing staff in 2003 – a rise of 49,000 (19%) compared to 1997. It employed 102,000 doctors – of which 30,000 were GPs and 26,000 consultants – a rise of 17,000 (20%) compared to 1997. The number of NHS "managers" in England has risen by 58% since 1997, but is a much smaller group comprising just 3% of the workforce on the Department of Health narrow definition. Since 1997 the percentage increase in the number of doctors, qualified nurses, ambulance staff and GPs has been less than the increase in the total number of English NHS staff (21%). Management,

Blatant misrepresentation – an example

The Department of Health document "NHS workforce statistics in England 2003" contained a rare example of blatant misrepresentation. The chart on page 9 set out the figures employed in the NHS in each year since 1997. While the 2003 bar was plotted against the correct figure on the left hand scale, it seems, from reading across to the scale, that none of the others were. The 1997 figure appears to be about 60,000 too low. The department defended the chart as being a "representation" and not designed for academics or researchers, who could find the data elsewhere in the document (partly) and on the website. The "fiddle" has the effect of increasing the steepness of the bars in the later years (as the under count is unwound) so that a reader might think that the addition to the health service staffing between 2000 and 2003 was greater than it really was. This misrepresentation was relatively easy to spot given the numbers were plotted against the columns in this chart but that is not so for the others in the document. Are they true representations or not?

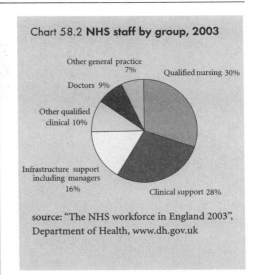

Chart 58.2 **NHS staff by group, 2003**

source: "The NHS workforce in England 2003", Department of Health, www.dh.gov.uk

consultants, clinical support and other qualified clinical groups in aggregate, have seen above average growth over the period. There are no figures for the number of private contract workers employed.

International comparisons of staffing levels are fraught with difficulty largely due to different practices in different countries. Work done by a doctor in one country will be done by a nurse elsewhere, and some specialities such as midwifery barely exist in some countries, where such work is done by doctors and nurses. That said, some figures are published, and Britain does not perform very well. In one count of the number of physicians per 100,000 people, the UK scores 164, below countries such as Romania, the Dominican Republic, Tajikistan, Egypt, Macedonia and Slovenia. The countries that Britain prefers to be compared with all score rather more highly – Ireland, Australia, the US and Sweden at between 200 and 300, and all other developed European countries at above 300. (source: UN Human Development Report, http://hdr.undp.org)

Section 22 • Child immunisation

The number of children being given the combined measles, mumps and rubella (MMR) vaccination fell to an all-time low in 2003/04, with only four out of five having the jab before the age of two. (source: "NHS immunisation statistics, England, 2003/04", www.dh.gov.uk)

Public health officials had hoped confidence was being rebuilt as the long-running controversy over the vaccination – which started in the late 1990s – looked to be going the government's way. The *Lancet* medical journal in 2004 retracted part of the 1998 article in which scientist Andrew Wakefield and colleagues had first raised doubts about its safety, and many doctors now consider the research discredited. But the Department of Health statistics show that only 80% of under-twos had the MMR in 2003/04, a drop from 82% the previous year. The peak year for MMR vaccination was 92% in 1995/96. The figures suggest that many parents are still anxious in spite of reassurances and scientific studies apparently disproving the suggestion in the Wakefield paper that there may be a link between the jab and autism.

The figures, which are collected through the health service, do not include those children whose parents have taken them for individual vaccinations – privately in Britain or overseas – for the three diseases. Such a route is against the government's advice but the lack of statistics means that no one knows what the true vaccination rate is. The data for the reinforcing doses of diphtheria, tetanus and polio given to children in their mid-teens are also thought to be lower than the true position as the data from schools, where many of the jabs are administered, is thought to be incomplete.

The MMR figures vary considerably across the country. Only 8 of the 303 Primary Care Organisations (PCOs) reported a rate of over 90% while 221 (73%) were less than 85%. Those for London are particularly low. Only 70% of under two year-olds received the MMR, and in parts the take-up was lower – 62% in south-east London and 69% in north-west London. Such rates are viewed as "dangerously low" by health experts.

The World Health Organisation recommends 95% take-up of vaccinations to avoid outbreaks of disease – a rate not being achieved for any of the

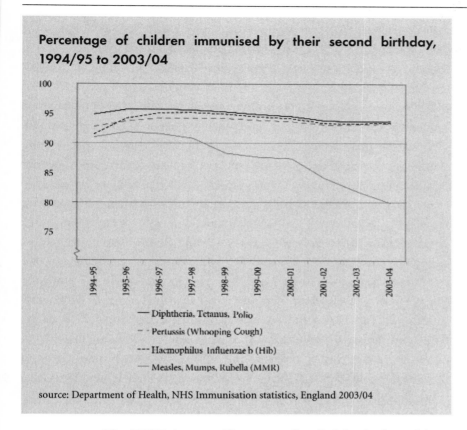

Percentage of children immunised by their second birthday, 1994/95 to 2003/04

— Diphtheria, Tetanus, Polio

- - Pertussis (Whooping Cough)

--- Haemophilus Influenzae b (Hib)

— Measles, Mumps, Rubella (MMR)

source: Department of Health, NHS Immunisation statistics, England 2003/04

Selected immunistaion rates for measles, %

Japan	99
Egypt	98
Spain	97
Mozambique	96
Netherlands	96
Canada	95
Peru	95
Tunisia	94
Albania	93
US	93
Australia	93
Germamy	92
Botswana	90

source: www.who-int, latest data, see website for data definitions

programmes. The WHO has specific targets for diphtheria, hepatitis B, measles, pertussis, polio and tetanus for all countries and other vaccinations for countries at risk. It does not say the MMR must be administered.

The result of the trend in the MMR jab is that the UK now has a lower rate for measles vaccination than many other countries. The WHO website (www.who.int/vaccines-surveillance) shows the latest figures for many countries in the world. Although there are some European countries with rates around the mid-80s (such as France and Italy) most developed countries have rates in the mid to high 90s. Many far less well developed countries have rates in the high 90s too.

Uptake of other vaccinations for children under two was also drifting lower but has not fallen off as it has for MMR. Around 94% of children were immunised against diphtheria, tetanus and polio, compared to 96% in the mid-1990s. The whooping cough, meningitis C and Hib (Haemophilus influenzae b) vaccination uptake was 93%.

Just over half of those waiting for an inpatient appointment are day case admissions

Section 23 • Hospital waiting lists

857,000 people were waiting for inpatient admission to NHS hospitals in England at the end of October 2004 – this is 300,000 fewer than in March 1997. While there seems little doubt that both waiting lists and waiting times have declined since 1997, the statistics for waiting lists have undoubtedly been influenced by some sharp practices which have contributed to the reduction in the numbers (this is discussed at more length in the chapter on targets).

Initially the focus was on inpatient waiting times – the time between seeing the hospital specialist and being admitted, i.e. receiving hospital treatment – as that was the target the government set itself in the run-up to the 1997 election. However, it became clear that the wait from GP referral to hospital specialist could also be long, leading to demand for a new list, named the outpatient waiting list, also to be monitored. Indeed, this list was necessary as one way of reducing the inpatient waiting list would be to increase the outpatient waiting list by increasing the time it takes for people to see the hospital specialist in the first place.

More recently, it has emerged that a third list is required if the patient journey through the NHS is to be fully reflected in the statistics. After seeing the hospital consultant for the first time, the patient might be required to undergo some tests. Any delay for these tests – and no records are kept centrally of what the delays are – would be "hidden" from the two waiting lists currently monitored. That had led to calls for one list to be created that measures the full patient journey from GP to treatment. In the 2004 spending review it was announced that a new target would be introduced – that no one waits more than 18 weeks from GP referral to hospital treatment. New systems are being introduced so that the new target can be operational by 2008. This means that it will have taken ten years from the original 1997 manifesto pleadge to get statistics that reasonably measure the wait as it is experienced by patients.

Fewer than 100 people were waiting last autumn for an inpatient appointment more than nine months, a point beyond which the government wishes to have no one waiting (the NHS implementation plan set a

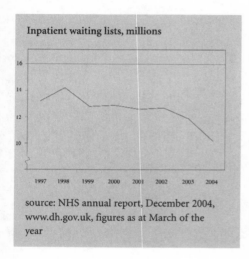

Inpatient waiting lists, millions

source: NHS annual report, December 2004, www.dh.gov.uk, figures as at March of the year

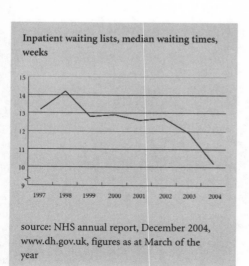

Inpatient waiting lists, median waiting times, weeks

source: NHS annual report, December 2004, www.dh.gov.uk, figures as at March of the year

target to reduce the maximum inpatient waiting time to nine months by the end of March 2004). In October 2003, a year before, there were 39,000 people waiting more than nine months. The very long waits seem to have been largely eradicated, but the median waiting times have fallen less sharply since 1997, from about 13 weeks to about 10 weeks. The government's PSA targets set in 2002 intended that nobody should wait more than six months for inpatient treatment by the end of 2005.

The outpatient waiting – the wait from GP to seeing the first hospital specialist – has also been slower to fall, really showing a decline only from 2003. The number of people who had waited for at least 13 weeks before seeing a consultant has fallen more sharply in the last teo years.

To add to the confusion, there are hospital and commissioner based waiting lists which can differ in length by up to 1% to 3%, with the hospital based figure being the larger. The commissioner based returns exclude all patients living outside England and all privately funded patients waiting for treatment in NHS hospitals. However they do include NHS funded patients, living in England, who are waiting for treatment outside of England and at private hospitals; patients which are not included in the corresponding hospital based returns. (source: "NHS waiting list figures", monthly press release, www.dh.gov.uk)

Figures for waiting time (on a mean and median basis) are also available from the Hospital Episode Statistics series. In the case of the HES, waiting time is defined as the period between the date of the decision to admit to hospital and the date of the actual admission. Days of deferment and suspension are not (yet) taken into account. The "official" waiting list figures provide, in contrast, an indication of the numbers waiting to be admitted on a particular date, and how long they have been waiting up to that date.

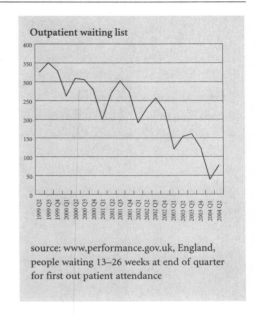

Outpatient waiting list

source: www.performance.gov.uk, England, people waiting 13–26 weeks at end of quarter for first out patient attendance

Median outpatient waiting time has fallen from 7.7 weeks to 7.1 weeks between early 2000 and early 2004

Section 24 • Hospital super-bugs – MRSA

> More people are killed each year by MRSA than by accidents on the road

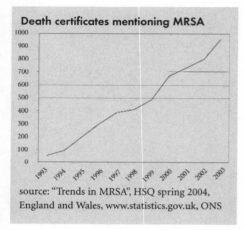

Death certificates mentioning MRSA

source: "Trends in MRSA", HSQ spring 2004, England and Wales, www.statistics.gov.uk, ONS

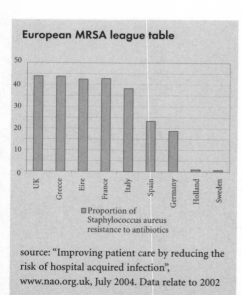

European MRSA league table

□ Proportion of Staphylococcus aureus resistance to antibiotics

source: "Improving patient care by reducing the risk of hospital acquired infection", www.nao.org.uk, July 2004. Data relate to 2002

MRSA, popularly called a "hospital super-bug", is methicillin-resistant Staphylococcus aureus, a common germ resistant to antibiotics. Its prevalence has risen sharply in recent years in response to, it is thought, the less than scrupulously clean environment found in some hospital wards. It is a good example of one aspect of health which has attracted plenty of attention and concern for which little good quality data is available.

It is necessary to rely upon several different sources of information to build up a picture of this dangerous infection. The Department of Health offers little and points those needing data to other sources. An ONS article in 2004 analysed the available data up to the end of 2002 and showed that the number of people who had died where MRSA was mentioned on the death certificate had risen sharply in the last decade from around 50 to 800 a year. It is unclear how much of the rise is due to improved ascertainment and how much is real. It is also impossible to know how many of the people who died, having caught MRSA, would have died in any case as many were already very ill. (source: "Trends in MRSA", HSQ spring 2004, England and Wales, www.statistics.gov.uk) Updated ONS data in February 2005 pointed to nearly 1,000 deaths in 2003.

A new survey from the Health Protection Agency showed that there were 7,300 cases of MRSA in 2002/03, up from 7,200 in the previous year, the first year of the survey. It showed just one detection of MRSA for every 5,800 bed days. (www.hpa.org.uk) A report from the National Audit Office said that at any one time, 9% of patients had an infection that had been acquired during their hospital stay. The effects varied, it said, from extended length of stay and discomfort to prolonged or permanent disability and, in at least 5,000 patients a year, death.

There is little information on the cost of hospital acquired infections. One dated survey suggested that a patient with a hospital acquired infection would normally be two to six times the cost of a patient without such an infection. On average, such patients would stay in hospital for 2½ times as long, equivalent to an extra 11 days. (source: "The socio-economic burden of hospital acquired infection", www.dh.gov.uk) The NAO cost estimate was £1 billion a year.

Section 25 • Private healthcare

Very little information about private sector healthcare is available from the government, but fortunately a certain amount of information is available from non-official sources. The trends in the sector as a whole are often driven by what is happening to the long-term care for the elderly and disabled, which accounts for just over half of total revenues.

It is possible to partition the provision of healthcare services into four possible combinations of private and public, finance and supply – public finance public supply, public finance private supply, private finance public supply, and private finance private supply. Such an analysis helps to understand the private/public mix in healthcare and avoids confusion in the debate on the extent of private involvement. It is striking how different types of activity fall into the four different finance and supply groupings. Elective surgery, for example, is 86% public finance public supply and 12% private finance private supply, leaving only 2% in the other two categories. Dentistry, in contrast, is 51% private finance private supply and 34% public finance public supply, leaving 15% in the private finance public supply category. Some 43% of abortions are public finance public supply and 33% private finance private supply, leaving 24% in the public finance private supply category. Roughly 25% of the long term residential care of mentally ill people is public finance public supply and 75% public finance private supply, leaving negligible amounts in either category of private finance. (source: "Healthcare market review", www.laingbuisson.co.uk)

The proportion of the population covered by private medical insurance has remained between 11% and 12% since 1990. Within the aggregate stability, company paid subscribers have been replacing individual subscribers since 1997. The proportion covered by insurance rose sharply in the second half of the 1980s from about 8½% to 11½%, in part due to the strong economic growth of the time, heavy marketing of the product and the emergence of several new hospitals. There is a strong regional variation in medical insurance penetration – nearly one in five in London and the south east is covered, compared to one in twelve in Scotland, Wales and the north east.

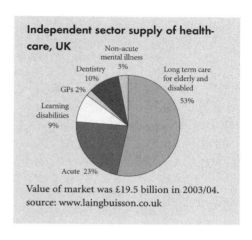

Independent sector supply of healthcare, UK

Value of market was £19.5 billion in 2003/04.
source: www.laingbuisson.co.uk

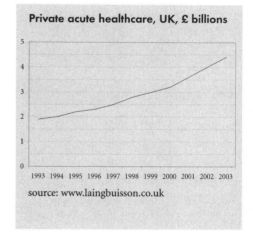

Private acute healthcare, UK, £ billions

source: www.laingbuisson.co.uk

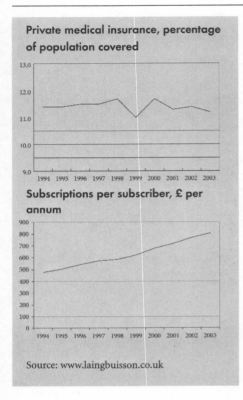

Private medical insurance, percentage of population covered

Subscriptions per subscriber, £ per annum

Source: www.laingbuisson.co.uk

Factors determining the independent sector involvement

The main factors are thought to be:

- The limits that the NHS sets to its responsibilities. The long term care of the elderly, mentally ill and people with learning disabilities are typically shared between the public and private sectors. "Alternative" medicine, infertility treatment and substance abuse are other areas of private sector dominance.
- The lack of any tradition in certain modes of healthcare delivery. The NHS has no tradition in specialised hospice care for the terminally ill. It has also not invested in long-term care facilities, with the result that nearly all long-term geriatric facilities in the NHS still consist of hospital wards.
- The limits of medical insurance cover. Childbirth, for example, is only exceptionally included in medical insurance and as a consequence less than 1% of babies are delivered outside the NHS.
- The marginal cost of care outside the NHS. When the marginal cost of choosing private over public treatment is relatively low and where there is a significant public sector supply constraint, the private sector has flourished. For example, the care of elderly people, abortion and sterilisation, dentistry and the market for spectacles.

Many in the industry believe that private insurance penetration reached a ceiling a decade ago with those who can afford the insurance and want it (most typically middle aged professionals, employers and managers), having already taken it out. Attempts to market insurance to other, less well-heeled individuals have not met with much success. The withdrawal of tax relief for the over sixties in 1997 has also served to dampen demand, as did several years of large premium increases. In the four years from 1999, the premiums for medical insurance rose on average by just over 5% in real terms in each year – higher than in any years except in 1991 and 1992, the years when the strong growth in subscriber numbers ended.

Section 26 • Obesity, smoking and well-being

During the last decade, the average weight for a man has increased by 3½kg (to 82½kg) and by 3 kg (to 69½kg) for a woman. Over much of the period, average height is barely changed at all, although the last two years have shown the early signs of a modest increase in height. In the last decade the proportion of adults with a desirable BMI has fallen to 29% for men and 34% for women. There has been no significant change in the proportion of adults defined as overweight, but there has been a marked increase in the proportion that is obese. Over 22% of both men and women are now obese compared to 13% and 16% respectively and decade ago. The proportion of children defined as obese also rose over the period. (source: Health Survey for England, 2003, Department of Health, www.dh.gov.uk)

What is obesity?

Obesity and being overweight are widely accepted as posing a major risk for chronic diseases, including type 2 diabetes, cardiovascular disease, hypertension and stroke, and certain forms of cancer. The key causes are increased consumption of energy-dense foods high in saturated fats and sugars, and reduced physical activity. Obesity is measured by a "body mass index". The BMI is calculated by taking an individual's weight in kilograms divided by the square of their height in metres. A BMI of between 20 and 25 is defined as "desirable", with 25 to 30 being "overweight", and over 30 "obese". Obesity accounts for 2-6% of total health care costs in several developed countries; some estimates put the figure as high as 7%. The true costs are probably greater as not all obesity-related conditions are included in the calculations. (source: World Health Organisation, www.int.org)

Obesity rates vary considerably between countries. While some eastern European countries, such as the Czech Republic and Hungary, almost match the English rate, the European average for obesity would be close to half of the English figure. There are few countries in the world with much higher rates than in the UK – with the exception of America, it is mostly a disparate

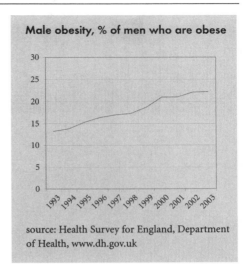

Male obesity, % of men who are obese

source: Health Survey for England, Department of Health, www.dh.gov.uk

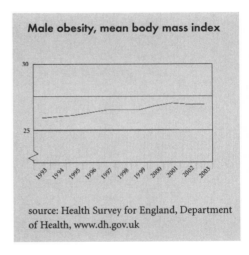

Male obesity, mean body mass index

source: Health Survey for England, Department of Health, www.dh.gov.uk

Britons consume on average fewer vegetables than the global mean. Some countries, including China, Greece, UAE and Turkey, consume at least two and a half times as much

Chocolate consumption per capita, 2003, kg

Switzerland	11.4
UK	9.5
Belgium	8.7
Germany	8.7
Ireland	8.1
Denmark	7.1
US	6.3

source: Euromonitor

bunch of less developed countries, several of which are pacific islands.

The prevalence of smoking is generally in decline, as reflected in the proportion of men who smoke – having peaked at 30% in 1996, the proportion has now fallen to 27%. The percentage of women who smoke has been more stable, but weakened to 24% in 2003. Of the men that do smoke, roughly a third each were classed as light smokers, medium smokers (10–19 per day) and heavy smokers (20 or more a day). Britain is a relatively good performer compared to other countries. In a number of countries, including China, Japan, Turkey, Russia and several other Eastern European countries, over half of the men smoke. Most western European countries, including Germany, France, and Italy, have between 30% and 40% of smoking. Sweden, along with several English speaking countries including America and Australia, have rates a little below that of Britain. (source: UN Human Development Report, http://hdr.undp.org)

A question about the consumption of fruit and vegetables has only been included in the English health survey since 2001. Just over one fifth of men and one quarter of women consume five portions or more a day, and there has been no significant trend in the three year life of the survey.

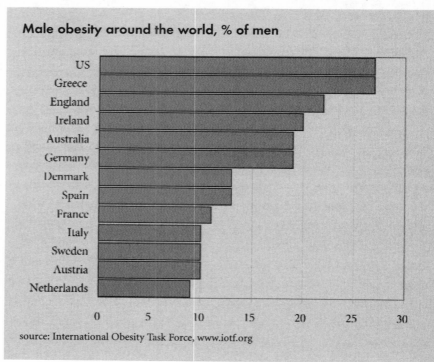

Male obesity around the world, % of men

source: International Obesity Task Force, www.iotf.org

Britons consume nearly 9 litres of ice cream each during a year. Australians, Kiwis, Americans and Swedes consume on average at least 50% more

The prevalence of (self-reported) general bad health and acute sickness have been increasing over the last decade. While self-reported ill-health continues to rise, the percentage of both men and women reporting acute sickness seems to have stopped rising and might be showing the first signs of a decline.

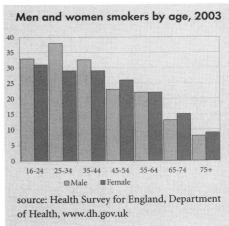

Men and women smokers by age, 2003

source: Health Survey for England, Department of Health, www.dh.gov.uk

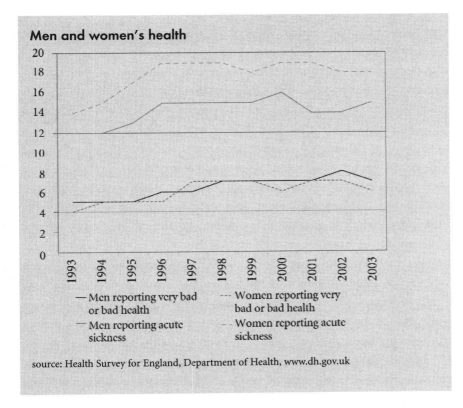

Men and women's health

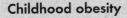

source: Health Survey for England, Department of Health, www.dh.gov.uk

The Britons and the Irish consume at least double the per capita quantity of baked beans than any other nationality

Childhood obesity

There is no consistent measure of childhood obesity over time but the prevalence seems to have risen from about 1% in the 1980s, to 2% in the mid 1990s and as high as 8% and 15% now for 6 and 15 year olds respectively. Contributing risk factors are diet (especially the high intake of certain fatty foods, sugars and sweetened drinks) and physical exercise.

source: www.parliament/post, postnote no 205, 2004

Section 27 • **Teenage pregnancy**

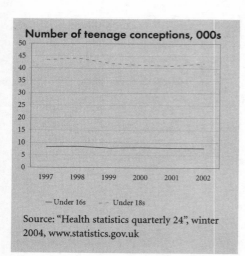

Number of teenage conceptions, 000s

— Under 16s   - - Under 18s

Source: "Health statistics quarterly 24", winter 2004, www.statistics.gov.uk

It is estimated that around 100,000 children in England have a teenage mother. Around 4% of adult men and 13% of adult women report having had a child under 20

Teenage parents tend to have poor ante-natal health, lower birth-weight babies and higher infant mortality rates. Their own health and their children's are worse than average. Teenage parents tend to remain poor and are more likely than their peers to end up without qualifications. They are disproportionately likely to suffer relationship breakdown and their daughters are more likely to become teenage mothers themselves.

In explaining the high rate of teenage pregnancies in England, the Social Exclusion Unit's report identified three factors that stand out: low expectations, a lack of accurate knowledge about contraception, and mixed messages from the adult world. It was also the case that certain features increase the likelihood that a teenage woman would become pregnant. Among the most important were: low social class, having been a child in care, being the child of a teenage mother, having suffered from mental health problems or sexual abuse, being involved with crime, and low educational achievement and not staying in the educational system beyond 16. (source: "Teenage pregnancy", 1999, www.socialexclusionunit.gov.uk)

The report noted that the United Kingdom had teenage birth rates which were twice as high as in Germany, three times as high as in France and six times as high as in the Netherlands – though roughly half that seen in the US. In the 1970s, the UK had similar teenage birth rates to other European countries, but while they have generally achieved dramatic falls in the 1980s and 1990s, the rates in the UK have remained high.

The report also noted that although less than a third of young women are sexually active by the time they are 16, half of those who are used no contraception the first time. Teenagers who do not use contraception have a 90% chance of conceiving in one year and those who do not use condoms are also exposed to a range of sexually transmitted infections. In a single act of unprotected sex with an infected partner, teenage women have a 1% chance of acquiring HIV, a 30% risk of getting genital herpes and a 50% chance of contracting gonorrhoea. Of those who do get pregnant, just over a half of under 16s and just under a half of under 18s opt for abortion. Around 90% of teenage mothers have babies outside marriage and relationships started in the teenage years have a 50% chance of breaking down.

The Teenage Pregnancy Unit – now part of the Children, Young People and Families Directorate in the Department for Education and Skills – was established to lead the delivery of the cross-government strategy. To help make progress, the government highlighted two main goals: to halve the rate of under 18 conceptions by 2010 and get more teenage parents into education, training or employment. Between 1998 (the baseline year for the Teenage Pregnancy Strategy) and 2002 (the latest year for which full figures are available), the conception rate for under-18s in England has fallen by 10%, compared to the interim target to reduce the rate by 15% by 2004.

The rate of progress is flattered by the choice of base year – as under 18 conceptions were particularly high in 1998. The trend could equally be described as being flat as the actual number of under 18 conceptions has remained stable between 41,000 and 44,000 in the last six years, and was at similar levels in the early 1990s. (source: "Health statistics quarterly 24", winter 2004, www.statistics.gov.uk) The percentage of teenage mothers not in learning or work has fallen from 84% in 1997 to 73% in 2003. (source: www.teenagepregnancyunit.gov.uk)

The so-called conception figures are not really conception figures – they count births and legal abortions but exclude miscarriages and illegal abortions.

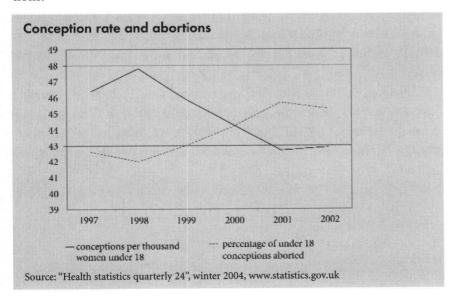

Conception rate and abortions

—conceptions per thousand women under 18

--- percentage of under 18 conceptions aborted

Source: "Health statistics quarterly 24", winter 2004, www.statistics.gov.uk

The rate of under 18 conceptions varies widely across the country – the lowest in Surrey and Sussex with just over three conceptions per 100 under 18s compares to over six conceptions per hundred under 18s in south east London – and as high as one in ten in Lambeth

Births to women under 20	
UK	30.8
Portugal	21.2
Ireland	18.7
Austria	14.0
Germany	13.1
Greece	11.8

All other EU-15 countries had a rate between 6 and 10. Births per thousand women in 1998. Source: UNICEF, a league table of teenage births, July 2001, www.unicef-icdc.org

One in eight conceptions in England and Wales is to a teenage women

Section 28 • Abortion

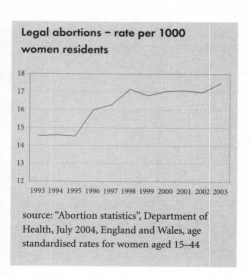

Legal abortions, England and Wales

source: "Abortion statistics", Department of
Health, July 2004

There are three abortions for every ten births in England and Wales

Legal abortions – rate per 1000 women residents

source: "Abortion statistics", Department of
Health, July 2004, England and Wales, age
standardised rates for women aged 15–44

The number of (legal, recorded) abortions in England and Wales was a record high in 2003 at just over 190,000. From the previous peak in 1990, the number declined to a low in 1995 and has risen since. The number of abortions for residents was also a record high at 182,000 – equating to a rate (age standardised) of 17.5 abortions per 1000 women aged 15–44. (source: "Abortion Statistics", Department of Health, www.doh.gov.uk) According to the British Pregnancy Advisory Service, the abortion rate has risen due to continued concern about the safety of contraceptive hormones, especially among young women, and "possibly because abortion is seen by more women as an acceptable way to manage an unwanted pregnancy." (source: www.bpas.org)

The ratio of abortions to births has been rising steadily and is now approaching 25%. This ratio is on a par with other Anglo-Saxon countries such as Canada, US and Australia and above most western European countries, many of which have rates between 10 and 20%. On the basis of 1990s data a woman in England will have nearly 2.2 pregnancies in her lifetime – close to the population replacement rate – but will only give birth to 1.7 children, due to abortions.

In 1992, around 31% of the abortions were on women who had previously had an abortion, up from 25% a decade earlier. One in 47 abortions were to women 15 years old or younger and one in five to women 19 or under.

There were 9,100 abortions for overseas residents in 2003. The number has been broadly stable at between 9,000 and 10,000 since 1995 and is well down on the record high of 57,000 in 1973. Between 80% and 90% of abortions for non-residents are for women from the Irish Republic or Northern Ireland.

Section 29 • **Travel patterns**

British residents travel 750 billion kilometres a year in the country. Roughly 6% of this distance was covered in buses and a similar amount by rail, with the bulk of the rest in car. The love affair with the car has continued unabated in recent years. While the distance travelled by car has increased by 6% over the last 10 years, all other forms of travel – walking, public transport and "other" such as cycling and motorbikes – have seen a fall in the distance travelled. Since 1997 the percentage of households without a car has fallen from 31% to 27%, the number of cars per household has risen from 0.99 to 1.09, and the number of cars per adult has risen from 0.54 to 0.60.

Men make slightly more trips by car than women, and many more as car drivers. Almost half of all trips made by men are as a car driver, compared with only a little more than a third of trips made by women. Just over a quarter of households do not have access to a car, compared with one-third a decade ago. Yet only one-fifth of people live in households without a car as households without cars tend to be smaller than average. (source: National Travel Survey 2003 Provisional Results, Department for Transport, www.dft.gov.uk, July 2004)

People in Great Britain made an average of 1,000 trips each in 2003, 6% fewer than in 1992/1994. But while the number of trip is declining slowly, the distance travelled is increasing – the average Briton travelled 6,800 miles within Great Britain in 2003, an increase of 6% since 1992/1994. This reflected an increase in the average length of trips, up from 6.1 miles to 6.9 miles.

The distance travelled on average by each person each year has risen by more than 40% in the last 25 years even though the number of trips has been broadly stable. (The fall in the number of trips in the last two years could be due to an under-recording of the small trips – See Box.) Over the period, the average time spent travelling has remained at about 360 hours per person per year, or about an hour a day.

The proportion of primary aged children walking to school has declined by about 5 percentage points to 53% since Labour came to power. The propor-

> On average we travel 12 times as far each year by car as by rail

> In the 1970s, each person travelled less than 5,000 miles a year, a figure now approaching 7,000

Average distance travelled by mode of travel in 2003

	miles per person per year	average journey length
Car only - driver	3,275	8.6
Car only - passenger	1,977	9.0
Surface rail	347	31.9
Other local bus	213	4.5
Walk	192	0.7
Van/lorry - driver	191	*
Private hire bus	135	*
Other public including air, ferrieslight rail, etc.	96	41.9
Non-local bus	86	92.6
Van/lorry - passenger	70	*
LT Underground	54	8.4
Bus in London	51	3.8
Taxi/minicab	49	4.1
Motorcycle/moped	36	10.7
Bicycle	34	2.3
Other private vehicles	27	20.0
All modes	6,833	6.9

source: National Travel Survey, 2003, DfT,
* Data not given

Six out of ten cars exceed the 30mph speed limit where it applies. Nearly nine out of ten articulated HGVs exceeds the 50mph speed limit on dual carriageways

tion being driven to school has commensurately increased to 39%. For secondary school pupils there was a similar, though smaller, shift from walking to car use, with a much larger proportion using the bus to get to school.

Adults, on average, make 245 trips on foot each year. Some 70% of these are under 1 mile, and the total distance travelled over a year on average is 169 miles. The number of walking trips fell by over 10% since 1997. Women made 27% of their trips on foot in 2002, compared with 23% for men. The average number of bicycle trips per person per year has fallen from 18 in 1997 to 14 in 2003, and the distance travelled by bike has fallen 10% to 37 miles a year. The number of commuting trips per person and the number of miles have both fallen since the mid to late 1970s, meanwhile the average trip length has risen fractionally to 8½ miles.

The National Travel Survey

The National Travel Survey began in 1988 following a series of ad hoc surveys since the mid-1960s. The sample size was trebled in 2002 so that figures for each year, as opposed to periods, would be available. Figures for earlier years are grouped into three-year periods. There are discontinuities and inconsistencies between the data from the two periods. There is some evidence to suggest that short walking trips have been under-recorded. The figures for London and "deeply" rural areas are particularly volatile. Even though the sample size is over 8,000 households, some of the results are based on small samples and may be misleading. Falling survey response rates mean that the margins of error may be a little larger in the latest years.

One of the more curious data collections by government is for the transport statistics bulletin called "Vehicles speeds in Great Britain". The figure are derived from the Department of Transport's automatic traffic counters. The monitors are "situated away from junctions, hills or sharp bends, at locations where traffic is likely to be free flowing and not near speed cameras," so the figures provide information on the speeds at which drivers choose to travel when their behaviour is not constrained by congestion or other road conditions. The figures do not indicate average traffic speeds across the road network, as an innocent user of the data might imagine. Perhaps unsurprisingly recorded vehicle speeds have been essentially flat for a number of years. The figures do give some indication of the extent of speeding on our roads. For example, more than half of all cars observed at the survey sites on motorways exceeded the speed limit and 20% were travelling at more than 80 mph.

Britons' appetite for overseas travel continues to grow – up by 33% since 1997 to over 61 million in 2003. The number of foreign tourists visiting the UK has been broadly stable since the mid-1990s. The impact of the New York terrorist attacks in September 2001 can be seen in the tourist numbers – especially in the case of visitors to the UK. Spending of foreigners in the UK has remained around the £11–13 billion mark for nearly a decade while Britons' spending overseas has doubeld from £14 billion a year to £29 billion in 2003, creating a large deficit.

Busiest international airports

1. London Heathrow
2. Charles de Gaulle, Paris
3. Frankfurt
4. Schipol, Amsterdam
5. Hong Kong
6. London Gatwick

source: www.rati.com

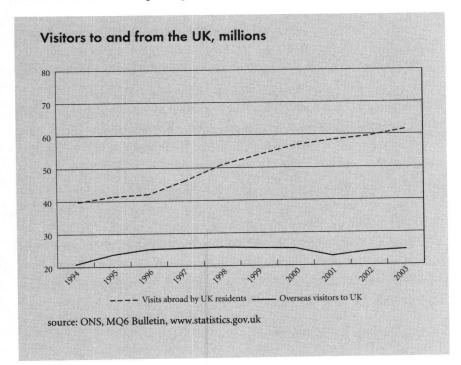

Visitors to and from the UK, millions

- - - - Visits abroad by UK residents ——— Overseas visitors to UK

source: ONS, MQ6 Bulletin, www.statistics.gov.uk

In 2003 UK residents spent 620 million nights overseas

More Americans visit Britain than any other nationality – 3.3 million, ahead of the French at 3.1 million and the Germans at 2.6 million

Section 30 • Vehicles on the road

The number of all types of vehicles on the road continues to grow. 2003 saw another large rise, following the two previous years, to over 31 million registered vehicles. The total number of vehicles on our roads – for which we have no offical estimate – would include the untaxed vehicles and foreign cars on British roads less British cars overseas.

Top ten car registrations in 2004	
Focus	141,000
Corsa	102,000
Fiesta	89,000
206	87,000
Megane	87,000

source: www.smmt.co.uk

Unregistered vehicles

The 31 million total is only registered vehicles – there is no official regularly published series of unregistered vehicles. It is estimated that about 1¾ million vehicles evade vehicle excise duty – and therefore are excluded from the figures – in GB. Around 1.2 million are cars and 0.3 million motorbikes. The rate is around 4% for cars but more than 25% for motorbikes and farm vehicles. A survey conducted by DfT ("Vehicle Excise Duty Evasion 2002"), showed that the trend in evasion is upward with the rate rising by ½% between 1999 (when the survey was last conducted) and 2002. The loss to government in revenue is nearly £200 million. The evasion rate in Northern Ireland is estimated to be at least double that of GB.

Cars dominate the total accounting for just over four out of five vehicles. They also account for 80% of the 4¼ million increase in the number of vehicles since 1997. Several other – smaller – categories of vehicles have increased more rapidly since 1997. The number of motorbikes and scooters has increased by 60% having been stable through much of the 1990s. The

A very misleading number

The DfT publishes ("Vehicle licensing statistics, 2003", table 7) a figure for "unlicensed" vehicles but it is not what it seems. The total of 33.8 million unlicensed cars in 2003 is more than the 26.2 million recorded as licensed! This figure is highly misleading (and probably one of the most misleading bits of official data) as it includes cars that have been scrapped but not reported as such.

Licensed motor vehicles

	Cars	Motor bikes etc	Buses	Goods	Exempt	Other	Total
1993	20102	650	73	428	979	2594	24826
1994	20479	630	75	434	1030	2583	25231
1995	20505	594	74	421	1169	2606	25369
1996	21172	609	77	413	1424	2607	26302
1997	21681	626	79	414	1522	2652	26974
1998	22115	684	80	412	1558	2689	27538
1999	22785	760	84	415	1573	2751	28368
2000	23196	825	86	418	1590	2783	28898
2001	23899	882	89	422	1602	2853	29747
2002	24543	941	92	425	1855	2701	30557
2003	24985	1005	96	426	1887	2808	31207
Change 1997–2003							
000s	3304	379	17	12	365	156	4233
%	15	60	21	3	24	6	16

source: "Transport statistics bulletin, vehicle licensing statistics 2003", Department for Transport

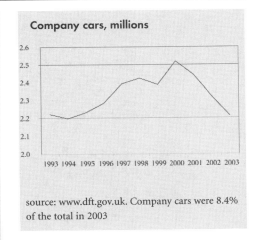

Company cars, millions

source: www.dft.gov.uk. Company cars were 8.4% of the total in 2003

206,000 currently registered cars, under 1% of the total, were first registered before 1985

number of buses and goods vehicles has also risen in recent years. The rise in exempt vehicles reflects the rise in cars for disabled people (from 570,000 in 1993 to 1,010,000 in 2003) and the decision in 1995 to exempt old (pre 1972) cars from vehicle excise duty, allowing over 300,000 cars to register free of charge.

The number of company cars was at a ten year low in 2003 but has been broadly stable over the last decade, falling as a proportion of the total number of registered cars.

The popularity of diesel cars is steadily rising and has nearly trebled between 1993 and 2003 but at around one third of new cars is still under half the proportion of France and Spain.

It seems that the desire of the British people to have ever-larger cars continues. Nearly half of the net increase in registered cars since 1997 has been in the category 1800cc to 2000cc and nearly 80% has been in cars over

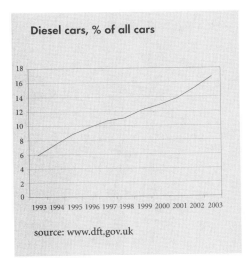

Diesel cars, % of all cars

source: www.dft.gov.uk

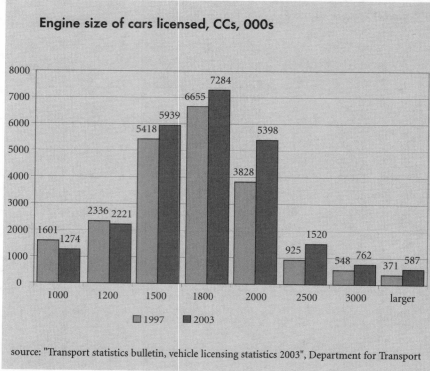

Engine size of cars licensed, CCs, 000s

source: "Transport statistics bulletin, vehicle licensing statistics 2003", Department for Transport

1800cc despite them accounting for just over a quarter of the stock of cars in 1997. The number of cars under 1200cc has fallen in the period.

The figures for the number of registered vehicles are the number registered at the year-end. For those categories that have a strong seasonal pattern, for instance motorbikes (where they are sometimes registered for six months in the summer and then "off the road" in the winter), the true figure is probably higher than that shown.

Nearly 4% of new cars are convertibles compared to under 1% in 1994

The rise of the 4X4

Essential urban fashion accessory or nuisance on the school run? The sales of 4X4 vehicles rose by 20,000, some 13%, in 2004 compared to the pevious year, to 179,000. 7% of new cars are now 4X4s compared to just 4½ % in 2000. The proportion in London is rising – just over 3% of the cars registered in the capital are 4X4s compared to over 6% of those registered in 2004.

source: www.smmt.co.uk

Section 31 • Road deaths

There has been little change in the overall annual road accident casualty numbers over the past decade – every year seeing between 300,000 and 330,000 casualties in Great Britain, dipping to 290,000 in 2003. However, the proportion seriously injured has tended to fall while the proportion with slight injuries has risen. The number of road accident casualties per mile travelled has been showing a downward trend, as the mileage travelled has been trending upwards over the period. The number of fatal road accident casualties trended down until the late 1990s but has been stable at 3,400 in the period since, rising above 3,500 in 2003. This is less than half of the 8,000 deaths recorded in 1966, the post-war peak year.

The number of road accident casualties involving illegal alcohol levels fell back in 2003 from a decade high figure of 20,100 in 2002. Much of the rise in the last three years is accounted for by casualties defined as "slight", although the number of fatalities rose to 560 in 2003, a figure that was surpassed only once in the last decade (in 1996).

The percentage of drivers and riders who are killed while over the alcohol limit has risen from a low of 15% in 1998 to 19% in 2003. This has coincided with the fall in the number of breath tests conducted.

There is a major question mark over the completeness of the data as research has shown that many non-fatal injury accidents are not reported to the police. In addition, some casualties reported to the police are not recorded and the severity of injuries tends to be underestimated. The combined effect of under-reporting, under-recording and misclassification suggests that there may be 2¾ times as many seriously injured casualties than recorded in the figures and 1¾ times as many slightly casualties. There are particular problems with the drink-drive figures for two reasons: not all drivers can be breath tested at the time of an accident – only about a half are currently tested – and for drivers killed in the accident, a post-mortem blood sample is not always available, for example, if the person dies some time after the accident.

Any tendency to mis-record – and any changes in the trend of mis-recording – could have important consequences for the ability of the

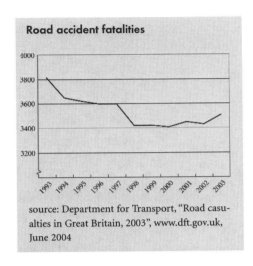

Road accident fatalities

source: Department for Transport, "Road casualties in Great Britain, 2003", www.dft.gov.uk, June 2004

Teenagers are 30 times more likely to be involved in a drink drive accident than the over sixties

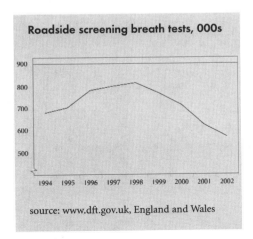

Roadside screening breath tests, 000s

source: www.dft.gov.uk, England and Wales

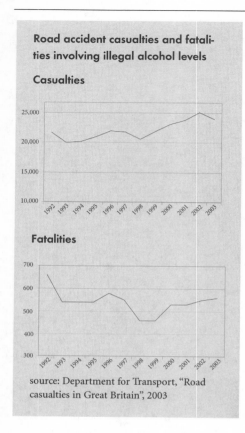

Road accident casualties and fatalities involving illegal alcohol levels

Casualties

Fatalities

source: Department for Transport, "Road casualties in Great Britain", 2003

Drink drive accidents

Age	Rate*
17 to 19	31
20 to 24	18
25 to 29	10
30 to 34	5
35 to 39	4
40 to 49	3
50 to 59	2
60 or over	1

* per hundred million miles driven
source: www.dft.gov.uk - GB 2002

government to be sure that it has achieved its road safety targets. In 2000, the government set new targets for a reduction in the number of casualties: to achieve a 40% reduction in the number of people killed or seriously injured in road accidents by 2010, compared with the average for 1994/98; a 50% reduction in the number of children killed or seriously injured; and a 10% reduction in the slight casualty rate, expressed as the number of people slightly injured per 100 million vehicles kilometres.

Figures for reported casualties in 2003 indicate: the number of people killed or seriously injured was 22% below the baseline, the number of children killed or seriously injured was 40% below, and slight casualty rate was 16% below the baseline. But the decline of 22% in the number of people killed or seriously injured is made up of a fall of 24% in the number of people seriously injured (33,700 in 2003 compared to 44,100 in the baseline period) and only a 2% fall in the number of people killed (3,500 in 2003 compared to 3,600). Given the concerns about under and mis-reporting, it might well be that the fall in the number of seriously injured purely reflects changes in reporting habits. If so, little progress would seem to be being made to making the nation's roads any safer. On the other hand, as the number of miles travelled is rising, the rate or deaths and accidents would be recorded as being weaker. Alas, for some series, such as children on bikes, no such data exist. (source: www.dft.gov.uk)

The improvement in road safety has only occurred for some categories of road users. The number of pedestrians and pedal cyclists killed in 2003 was in both cases well below the baseline average. In contrast, the number of motorcyclists killed has increased by nearly 50% and the number of car users and drivers of goods vehicles has remained broadly unchanged.

The selection of a five-year average as the baseline against which to measure future performance is a most interesting one. Had the figures for 1998 alone been chosen, or perhaps an average of 1997 and 1998, the percentage changes seen to the latest year's figures would be quite different. Because the trend for the sum of all categories of casualties among pedestrians and cyclists was falling during the averaging period, the selection of the five-year baseline average has the effect of flattering the extent of the decline since the targets were set in 2000. The percentage fall for all casualties among pedestrians by 2003 is 22% using the five-year average baseline but only 19% compared to 1998. Similarly, the decline in casualties among cyclists is reported as 30% but would only be 26% compared with the 1998 figure.

The relative safety of modes of transport is frequently debated. It is noteworthy that the statistics look very different for fatalities per journey compared to fatalities per kilometre travelled. Each journey by air is more likely to lead to death than each journey by car, yet each kilometre travelled by car is far more likely to lead to death than each kilometre travelled by plane. Similar care has to be taken when comparing deaths on different types of roads. In terms of kilometres travelled, motorways are the safest roads in the UK with 18 accidents per 100 million kilometres, while those in built up areas are the most dangerous with 73 accidents per 100 million kilometres travelled. (source: RAC report 2003)

In the EU in 1998 42,687 road users were killed in crashes, compared with 186 rail passengers and 25 airline passengers. (source: FIA Foundation and AA 2003) The UK's performance is as good as any other country in the EU. The UK has only one third as many road deaths in relation to its population size as Portugal and Greece, and under half as many deaths as Luxembourg, Belgium, France and Spain.

When it comes to car accidents, speeds make a big difference. Hit by a car at 35mph a person is twice as likely to be killed as someone hit at 30mph. (source: DETR 2000) Hit by a car at 40mph a pedestrian has an 85% chance of being killed, at 30mph he has a 45% chance of being killed, while at 20mph the risk falls to 5%. (source: www.pacts.org.uk)

Men commit nine times as many motoring offences as women in England and Wales. In 2002, men committed 97% of dangerous driving offences, 94% of offences causing death or bodily harm, 89% of drink or drug driving offences, 85% of careless driving offences, 83% of speeding offences, 84% of offences involving neglect of traffic signs and directions or of pedestrian rights and 77% of obstruction, waiting and parking offences. (source: Home Office/DfT)

There is patchy information on the contributory factors to road accidents. A review of road accident statistics in 1997 suggested that such figures be collected. The proposal was not adopted but fifteen police forces chose to participate in a trial – they have been collecting information on causes since 1999, covering about a quarter of road accidents. A further review carried out in 2002/03, expressed some concerns about the trial

Fatal casualties by road user type

	1994–98 average	2003	change %
Pedestrians	1008	774	-23
Pedal cyclists	196	114	-39
Motorcyclists	467	693	48
Car users	1762	1769	0
Goods vehicle	118	116	-2
All road users	3578	3508	-2

source: Department of Transport

For every mile travelled, death is 140 times as likely in a car compared to an aircraft and 45 times as likely on a bike than in a car

Fatalities per billion passenger kilometres

Air	0.02
Bus/coach	0.3
Rail	0.4
Water	0.8
Van	1.0
Car	2.8
Pedal cycle	30
Foot	48
Motorcycle/moped	130

source: www.transport2000.org.uk, data for 2000

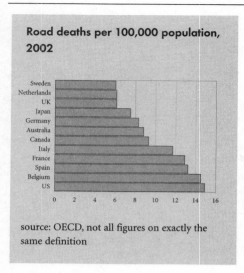

Road deaths per 100,000 population, 2002

source: OECD, not all figures on exactly the same definition

system but concluded that the information was of value. Accordingly, a substantially revised specification will be introduced for accidents from the start of 2005 and will be adopted by all police forces. The new data will not be directly comparable with the data collected in the trial.

Five of the fifteen precipitating factors listed in the trial data accounted for over 80% of accidents. These were: failed to avoid a vehicle or object in the carriageway, loss of control of vehicle, failed to give way, pedestrian entered carriageway without due care, and poor turn or manoeuvre. The most commonly coded contributory factors in fatal accidents were excessive speeds, careless, thoughtless or reckless behaviour, inattention, lack of judgement of own path, and failed to judge other person's path or speed. (source: www.dft.gov.uk)

Section 32 • Driving licences

The proportion of young people – aged 17 to 20 – with a full driving licence has fallen in the last decade from nearly half (48%) to just over a quarter (28%). In the early 1990s at its peak, nearly 54% of young men and 42% of young women had driving licences but the rates have now fallen to 31% and 24% respectively. (source: National Travel Survey, 2003, DfT, www.dft.gov.uk) The total number of 17–20 year olds with licences has fallen from 1.4 million to just over 800,000 – though part of that decline reflects the demographic trends that have seen a fall in the number of young people.

The explanation for the fall has been put down to rising running costs for motoring (especially for fuel, insurance and tax that have not been offset by lower new car prices for a group that generally runs second hand cars), improved public transport, police targeting of young drivers, the growth in higher education (a near doubling of the proportion of youngsters in education to four out of ten means fewer have the finances to run a car), and the introduction in 1996 of a theory component of the test. (source: General Insurance Monthly, September 2004, Association of British Insurers, www.abi.org.uk) The proportion of people in their 20s holding a licence has remained constant over the last decade suggesting that a delay in driving is being seen rather than anything more fundamental.

Car insurance costs have risen much more rapidly than other insurance – car insurance has roughly doubled since 1996 while building and contents insurance has risen by less than 20% (according to the AA British Insurance Premium Index, www.theaa.com). The AA says that a 17 year old man might pay nearly £3,000 for a year's insurance on a small car, falling to £1,700 at 18, £1,100 at 19 and £500 at 21, assuming a clean licence and full "no claims bonus". Sex seems to make a big difference in driving insurance risk with men much more at risk – due more, it seems, to behaviour and psychological functioning than driving skill. (source: "Sex differences in driving and insurance risk", www.sirc.org)

The proportion of women holding full driving licences has increased every year since records began, most recently rising from 54 to 61% in the

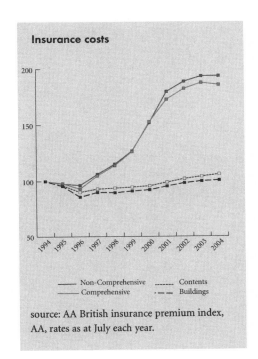

Insurance costs

Non-Comprehensive .... Contents
Comprehensive ─ ▪ ─ ▪ Buildings

source: AA British insurance premium index, AA, rates as at July each year.

decade since 1992/1994, while the proportion of men holding licences has remained remarkably stable at 81%. Licence holding among all those aged 60–69 rose from 57 to 73% over this period. Men in their 40s have the highest holding rate at 91% while the lowest rate is among women under 20 (24%) and women over 70 (27%).

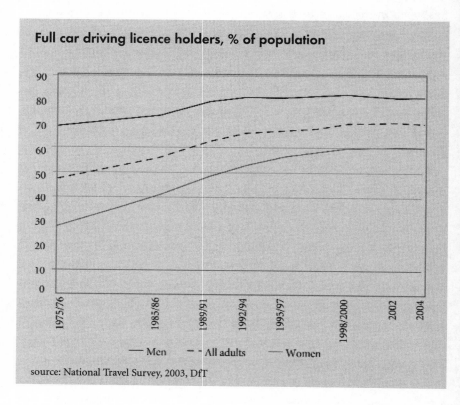

Full car driving licence holders, % of population

source: National Travel Survey, 2003, DfT

Section 33 • **Petrol**

A litre of standard unleaded petrol cost 85 pence during November 2004, 28 pence higher than the typical price of 57 pence average seen in 1996. The price also reached 85p per litre in June 2000 – a 50% increase in four years – leading to widespread blockades and protests. The price fluctuates according to the global market for oil, but around three quarters (the proportion fluctuates even when taxes are stable due the volatility of the crude oil price) of the price of unleaded petrol in Britain is accounted for by taxes and duties – this is the highest rate in the EU – and amounts to a whopping 300% tax on petrol. (source: www.theaa.com)

Justifying the sharp tax increases, the government says there are sound environmental reasons for levying fuel taxes, believing that the people who use the most fuel and pollute the atmosphere the most should pay for the damage they are causing. There are several EU countries with tax rates on unleaded fuel close to the UK figures, but non have diesel rates as high. In defence for raising petrol prices, the government says that on average over the last ten years the overall cost of motoring has not risen in real terms. (sources: www.farmersforaction.org, www.fuelprotest.com)

The Association of British Drivers has a calculator on its web site which estimates the tax paid each year on the fuel used to drive a car a given mileage at the appropriate fuel economy rate. (source: www.abd.org.uk)

There has been a dramatic decline in the number of filling stations in Britain from about 18,000 in 1992 to just over 11,400 in 2004. Petrol retailing is a high volume low margin business and increased competition, particularly from supermarkets, has squeezed margins. Coupled with the investment needed to attain the standards now common on the forecourt and stricter environmental legislation, a lot of sites have closed. (source: www.ukpia.com)

If anyone wanted to know how many vehicles run on Liquefied Petroleum Gas (LPG), Natural Gas and hydrogen, there would be no point looking in DVLA statistics that do not distinguish between these vehicles. Statistics from the DVLA (PQ of October 2003) show that there are 41,400 vehicles running on all road fuel gases. But this understates the number of

> For every £50 spent on a tank of petrol, £37 is tax. Excluding tax and duties, a litre of unleaded petrol or diesel would cost around 20p

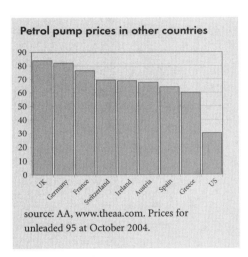

Petrol pump prices in other countries

source: AA, www.theaa.com. Prices for unleaded 95 at October 2004.

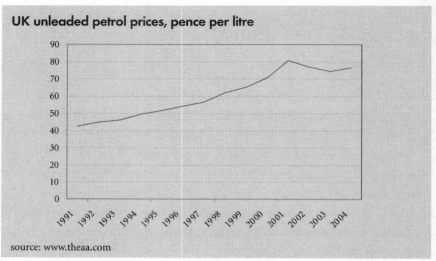

source: www.theaa.com

33 billion litres of motor fuel are sold each year in the UK (source: www.rmif.co.uk)

vehicles because not all conversions to alternative fuelling are notified to DVLA. Industry sources suggest there are around 100,000 vehicles currently running on LPG, around 850 on natural gas (CNG and LNG, compressed and liquid natural gas, respectively) and only a few prototype/demonstration vehicles in UK running on hydrogen. At the same time, the Energy Saving Trust said that there were around 1,300 LPG, 19 CNG and 7 LNG refuelling sites in the UK and no sites giving public access to hydrogen.

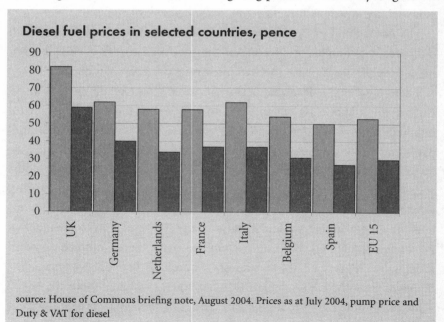

source: House of Commons briefing note, August 2004. Prices as at July 2004, pump price and Duty & VAT for diesel

Section 34 • Uninsured drivers

The estimated 1 million drivers – one in 20 – on British roads without insurance are both a cost to law-biding users and an added danger on the roads. No robust estimates exist but a figure of around that level is agreed by the DVLA, Motor Insurance Bureau, Association of British Insurers and motoring organisations – but is thought to be conservative and on a rising trend. Some targeted police campaigns have found as many as one in five driving uninsured.

Accidents involving uninsured drivers cost around £½ billion a year- and certainly more than the £250 million raised by the MIB in 2003. This is sharply up from previous years - £34 million in 1991 and £100 million in 1995. The average cost of each settlement has risen (largely due to the rise in personal injury costs) but so too has the number of claims – 53,000 in 2003 from 44,000 in 1997. In addition, some costs are met directly by insurers. The Greenaway Report said, "remarkably, there is hardly any information on which to draw to provide an accurate estimate of the total costs", adding that they could be of the same order of magnitude as the MIB levy. Greenaway said that, "the public policy interests would be served by more complete and more accurate information" from insurers about the costs of uninsured drivers. (source: Greenaway Report into uninsured driving, August 2004, www.dft.gov.uk) This adds around £30 to the insurance premium of each law-abiding motorist.

Research has shown a link between the misuse of vehicles and crime. Offenders view the chances of being caught as slim – a survey conducted by the ABI showed that 89% of drivers think there is more chance of being caught for speeding than driving uninsured – and the penalties minor – the average fine is £150–200.

Third party insurance is a standard requirement in developed countries. In the UK, it is provided in an extensive and diversified market with gross premiums of £9 billion in 2001. In some countries third party cover is provided by the state via a direct levy on road duty or fuel. Non-compliance is high in the UK in absolute and relative terms compared to other EU countries – estimated at 5% in the UK compared to 1% in many others. (source: Association of British Insurers, www.abi.org.uk)

Many uninsured drivers are young, unqualified and often driving non-roadworthy vehicles. The breakdown of those found to be guilty of being uninsured (in England and Wales) showed that 90% were male, 60% were under 25, and most lived in urban areas

The cost of comprehensive car insurance has risen by 86% in the last decade according to the AA

The ABI points to a strong link between serious motoring offences, estimating that uninsured drivers are:

- 10 times more likely to have been convicted of drink-driving
- 6 times more likely to have been convicted of driving a non-roadworthy vehicle
- 3 times more likely to have been convicted of driving without due care and attention

Section 35 • Motoring offences

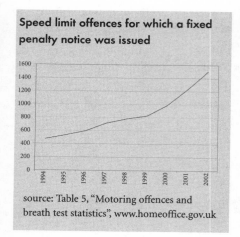

Speed limit offences for which a fixed penalty notice was issued

source: Table 5, "Motoring offences and breath test statistics", www.homeoffice.gov.uk

Some 11.8 million motoring offences were dealt with by the police or penalty charge notices in 2002 (2003 data is published in spring 2005). This is the highest number ever and 11% up on 2001. It represents 425 offences for every thousand vehicles, again a record high. (All the data in this section relate to just England and Wales due to the different legal systems in the other parts of the UK.)

The number of offences has risen steadily over the last decade reflecting the arrival of the penalty charge notice issued by local authorities for parking offences. Since the launch of PCNs in 1994 the number issued has risen sharply – up 21% in the year to 6.4 million in 2002. There has been a partly commensurate drop in the number of police-issued fixed penalty notices. In 2001 PCNs accounted for over half of all motoring offences for the first time. In 1995, a PCN was issued for every seven cars while in 2002 one was issued for every four cars.

There has been some degree of stability over recent decades in the number of police actions taken with regard to causing death, dangerous driving,

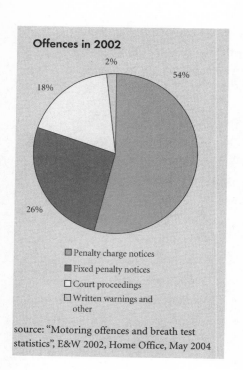

Offences in 2002

- Penalty charge notices
- Fixed penalty notices
- Court proceedings
- Written warnings and other

source: "Motoring offences and breath test statistics", E&W 2002, Home Office, May 2004

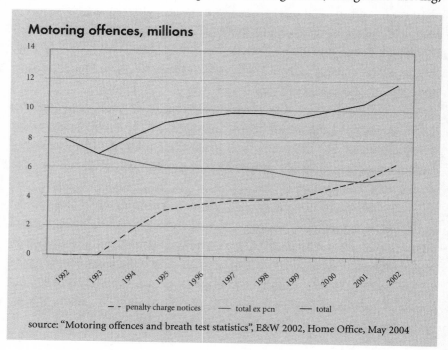

Motoring offences, millions

penalty charge notices — total ex pcn — total

source: "Motoring offences and breath test statistics", E&W 2002, Home Office, May 2004

careless driving and unauthorised theft of a car. But the numbers relating to drink driving, licence and insurance issues, vehicle condition and speeding have all shown strong upward trends. The number of speed limit offences has risen very sharply in the last decade – more than doubling to 1½ million between 1997 and 2002 – largely reflecting the advent of speed cameras. Cameras provided the evidence for 85% of speeding offences.

Despite the sharp rise in offences, the number of proceedings at magistrates' courts for offences relating to motoring has been steady at just over 2 million in recent years. Nearly half of the sentences of immediate custody given for motoring offences at all courts were for offences of driving while disqualified. Causing death or bodily harm was most likely to be dealt with by a custodial sentence – four out of five findings of guilt in recent years. Just under half the convictions for driving while disqualified and dangerous driving attracted sentences of immediate custody.

The number of breath tests for alcohol conducted on motorists was at a ten-year low in 2002 having fallen by nearly 250,000, 30%, since the peak in 1998. Yet the number who tested positive was the highest – at over 100,000 – pointing to a higher "success" rate – now standing at 18%.

The variation in the use of breath tests between police forces is striking. At one extreme, Derbyshire conducts one test a year for every 25 residents and North Wales one for every 35. This compares to Hertfordshire and the West Midlands conducting barely one-tenth as many, just one for every 250 residents. The national average is one a year for every 90 residents.

Penalty charge notices for parking and the associated vehicle wheel clamping and towing away are still predominantly features of life in London, but they are spreading to other local authorities. In 1999, over 9 out of 10 notices were given in London, a proportion that dropped to three-quarters in 2002. The number given in the rest of England almost quadrupled in the last four years.

The figures come from administrative sources and are particularly prone to associated problems such as changes in practice, different practices in different police forces (such as completeness of reporting failed breath tests) and processing problems in police authorities (if computer systems malfunction). Changes in legislation give rise to new offences and can cause similar cases to shift between categories over time.

Motoring offences dealt with at magistrates' courts, 000s

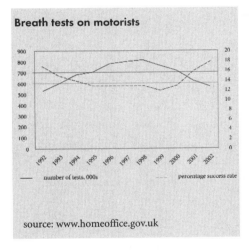

source: www.homeoffice.gov.uk

Breath tests on motorists

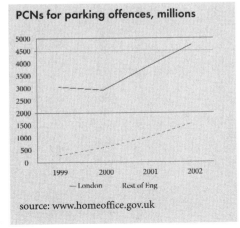

source: www.homeoffice.gov.uk

PCNs for parking offences, millions

source: www.homeoffice.gov.uk

Section 36 • Abandoned cars

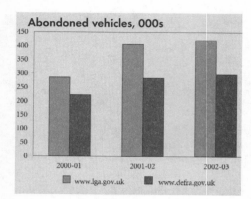

Abondoned vehicles, 000s

Legend: www.lga.gov.uk | www.defra.gov.uk

Why are cars being dumped?

Owners of old cars used to sell them to scrap merchants for a few pounds. But new European legislation (the "End of life vehicles directive" of 2000 which promotes the recyclability of vehicles) coupled with rising dismantling costs, tougher MOT tests, increased crime and the decline in demand for spare parts have changed the situation. Owners now have to pay to have the cars taken away. Unless they live in a local authority offering a free service. In some countries, the responsibility for disposing of cars rests with the manufacturers (and that should largely be the case in the UK after 2007).

(source: www.lga.gov.uk, www.ieep.org.uk, www.renewal.net, www.apse.org.uk and www.dti.gov.uk/sustainability

---

The number of abandoned vehicles removed from the streets of England rose to 300,000 in 2002/03, according to Defra. This is a rise of 8% in the year after a rise of 39% in the previous year and accounts for about one in six of the two million cars scrapped every year. The Liberal Democrats said there were enough abandoned cars to fill the M25 and the figures suggest that at least one in fifty households dumps a car each year.

The Local Government Association published the results of a one-off survey in 2004 which suggested the scale of the problem was larger. It said that 829,000 vehicles were reported as being abandoned by local authorities and that some 420,000 of these were destroyed. It is not clear why the estimates differ to the extent that they do – the inclusion of Wales in the LGA figures should not account for the figure being 35% higher and the definition of what constutites an abandoned car is similar in both cases. The survey gave additional information not covered by the government survey. It said that only 7% of authorities had prosecuted for the offence of abandonment as they felt the costs of doing so would not be justified by the impact on the abandonment rate. (source: "Abandoned vehicles", 2004, www.lga.gov.uk)

Statistics for abandoned vehicles removed and destroyed were first compiled by Defra for 2000/01 following the launch of a new survey on the topic – started in response to the perception that the practice was becoming more widespread. (source: "Municipal waste management survey", 2002/03, August 2004, www.defra.gov.uk)

In the latest year, London topped the league with 94,500 vehicles, 29 vehicles per 1,000 households, and accounted for one-third of the abandoned cars. The abandonment rather in other regions is now rising fast – the rate in the north east and Yorkshire nearly doubled in the last two years while that in London has been flat. As most old cars are owned by the poorer members of society, greater proportions of dumped – and often torched – cars are in the poorer neighbourhoods where generally local authorities are less well placed to pay for the disposal of the cars.

Section 37 • Rail performance

The distance passengers travelled on the rail network had been reasonably constant at between 28 and 33 billion kilometres in the thirty years up to the mid-1990s. In the late 1990s, however, there was a decisive break, with passenger kilometres rising sharply to top 40 billion in 2003/04. The bulk of this rise has occurred in the London and south east region, boosted by commuters, which accounts for about half of passenger kilometres in the country. As a result of fare increases and the rise in journeys, passenger revenues have risen sharply to nearly £4 billion in 2003/04, a rise of over 50% since 1996/97. (source: "National rail trends", Yearbook 2003/04, Strategic Rail Authority, www.sra.gov.uk)

There is something of a problem with this data leading to a break in the series in 1999/00. The rail industry's central ticketing system does not correctly record sales of certain products. A robust estimate of the use of these products has been included in the figures since 1999. While the adjustment can be large for some operating companies, the impact is relatively minor at the national level.

The "public performance measure" (PPM) was introduced in 2000 to give a better indication of the performance of the country's railways. It measures the performance of individual trains against the planned timetable. The planned timetable is usually the same as the published timetable with amendments reflecting pre-published engineering announcements. There was a very clear drop in performance in 2001 following the Hatfield accident in October 2000, especially in the long distance sector where the moving annual average performance fell from over 80% in the summer before the accident to almost 60%, by the end of 2001. In the year to March 2004, the best performing operator had just over 90% of trains arriving on time, compared to the worst which had just 70%.

The number of complaints about the rail service is at a record low of just 78 per 100,000 passenger journeys, down from 120 in 1998/99 and a peak of 131 in 2000/01. A change in the number of complaints does not necessarily indicate a change in the performance by the industry as a number of other factors can affect the volume of complaints. Advertising, improved

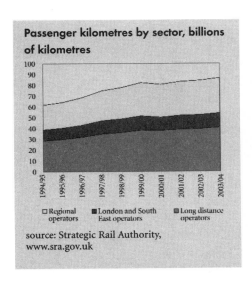

Passenger kilometres by sector, billions of kilometres

Regional operators | London and South East operators | Long distance operators

source: Strategic Rail Authority, www.sra.gov.uk

81% of trains ran "on time" in 2003/04 – a train is deemed as being on time if it arrives within five minutes of the planned arrival time (or within ten minutes for long distance operators)

The number of passenger journeys rose above one billion for the first time in 2003/04 – over two-thirds of these journeys were in London and the south east

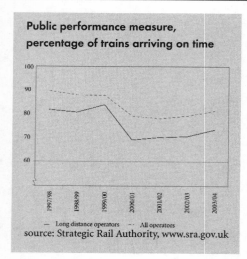

Public performance measure, percentage of trains arriving on time

— Long distance operators   - - All operators
source: Strategic Rail Authority, www.sra.gov.uk

In the latest year, passenger kilometres rose by 3% and passenger journeys increased by 4% yet train kilometres increased by only 1% – despite revenues increasing by 3%

availability of pre-printed complaint forms, and the opening of complaints telephone lines are likely to prompt a larger volume of complaints than would otherwise be the case. A shift in the type of journeys being made on the rail system can affect the number of complaints as the propensity to complain varies across customer types – commuters and regular same route travellers are less likely to complain about an individual journey than business or leisure travellers who make more infrequent rail journeys. The number of phone calls made to the national rail enquiry scheme in 2003/04 was the lowest since records began in 1998. Some 6% of calls made received no reply.

The amount of freight carried on the railways declined steadily from a peak in 1988/89 to a low point in 1994/95. It then rose sharply during the second half of the 1990s to a peak in 2001/02, but has fallen back since. The trend, including the recent weakness, is largely driven by the transportation of coal. Coal accounts for one quarter of the net tonne kilometres of freight moved, but nearly half of the freight lifted (freight lifted is the mass of goods carried on the network and takes no account of the distance travelled).

According to the national passenger survey, nearly three-quarters of passengers are satisfied or very satisfied with their overall journey, a figure which has been broadly stable of the last two or three years. Customer opinions of train services are collected twice a year from a representative sample of passenger journeys. Satisfaction with 27 aspects of service can be compared over time.

Section 38 • Train safety

The latest year – 2003/04 seemed a good one for rail safety as many risk variables were reduced. There was a year on year fall in the number of collisions and derailments – and no train accident fatalities. (source: HSE annual report on railway safety, 2003/04, www.hse.gov.uk/railways)

This positive news would seem to be endorsed by the trend in train incidents per million train miles travelled. From a level of one "significant incident" per million miles in 1975, the rate in the latest year dropped below 0.2 per million for the first time. While some years see a rise due to the erratic nature of the incidents, the trend has been continuous over the period and the last three years re-established the decline after three years of plateau. This measure is attractive as it allows for the rise in the number of train miles. The total number of "significant train incidents" fell to 63 last year compared to a five-year average of 93.

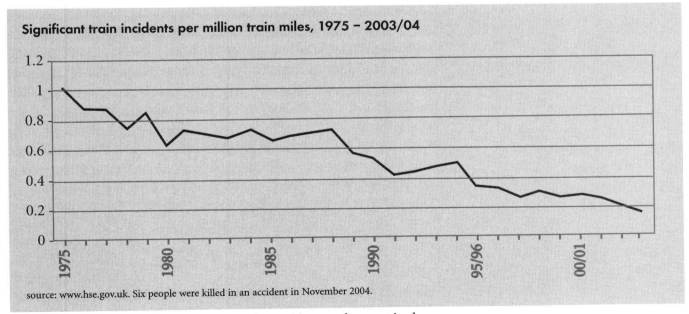

Significant train incidents per million train miles, 1975 – 2003/04

source: www.hse.gov.uk. Six people were killed in an accident in November 2004.

But a gap seems to have emerged between the positive trend set out in those figures and the perception of declining train safety. One reason why perceptions of safety have dipped could be the occurrence of major incidents. The

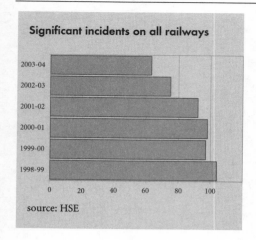

Significant incidents on all railways

source: HSE

seven train accident fatalities in 2002/03 (one incident at Potters Bar) hit confidence, given that the five years 1997/98 to 2001/02, saw three major incidents at Southall, Ladbroke Grove and Great Heck, killing 7, 31 and 10 people respectively. So the 55 deaths in the seven years since 1997/98 compare to the previous seven-year period which saw only one major incident, the Cowden accident killing five people. But it is unclear whether this is a trend or just "bad luck" – major catastrophes do not come evenly over the years.

Figures can look very different according to the precise definition – deaths, major or minor injuries, to passengers, workers or all on the train network, or the number of incidents – and whether looked at in crude terms or as rates. A careful selection of the statistics can show a convincing case for improvement or deterioration in the trend.

Signs of concern can also be seen in other accident figures. There were in fact ten deaths due to train accidents in 2003/04 but as they occurred in eight different incidents (typically a train hitting a bike or car on a level crossing) and did not involve passenger deaths, the year was perceived as a "good" one.

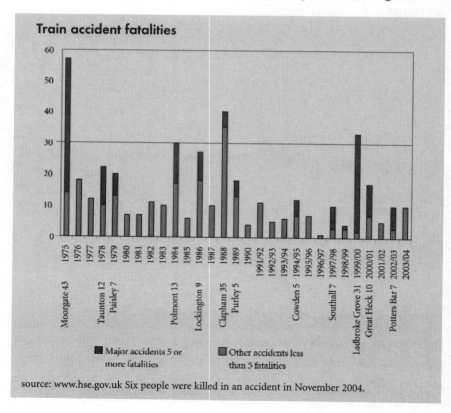

Train accident fatalities

■ Major accidents 5 or more fatalities   ■ Other accidents less than 5 fatalities

source: www.hse.gov.uk Six people were killed in an accident in November 2004.

It is common to look at the death toll excluding the major incidents of five of more deaths – and on that count, the figure of ten in 2003/04 is high, indeed, the highest in one year since 1991/92. It compares to three in the previous year and an average of just over four per year in the past decade.

The casualty figures for "all incidents" are also showing little sign of improving. The figure of 39 deaths in 2003/04 was down on the 49 in the previous year but the same or higher than three of the last five years. The figure of 39 was below the previous five-year average of 46 but up from the five years before of 37. The 39 deaths in 2003/04 were comprised 12 passengers, 9 railway employees and 18 other members of the public, but excluded those deemed to be suicides or trespassers. Ten were killed in train incidents (none of which were passengers), 19 in other "movements" (such as falling out of a carriage, off a platform or being struck by a train while working) and 10 in non-movement incidents (such as electrocution, falls and incidents on stairs). A total of 4,876 people received hospital treatment in 2003/04 as a result of such incidents.

The government aims to reduce by 10% each year the "incidence of train accident precursors that could lead to a catastrophic event", namely signals passed at danger, track quality issues, level crossings and so forth.

But other figures have been improving in recent years. The fall in "significant collisions" – to 12 last year compared to a five-year average of 24 – follows improvements in a range of aspects of safety. Derailments fell to 6 compared to a five-year average of 9. The number of signals passed at danger (SPADs) fell to 378 from 401. The train protection warning system was completed at the end of 2003 (having become a requirement in 1999), and that seems to be helping to reduce the consequences of serious SPADs. The death figures would seem to point to investment in future going to protect those who come into to contact with the train system but are not on trains - or indeed those travelling by other means, such as car or bike, where the number of deaths per year is much higher.

The number of broken rails fell for the fifth year in succession even though the number of "track buckles" rose sharply (to 137 from 21) as a result of the hot summer in 2003. There are 8,000 level crossings on the GB network (down by 250 in the latest year) and misuse by the public remains a major factor in the number of incidents – leading to 17 fatalities in the last year.

> Of the 63 "significant" train incidents in 2003/04, 30 were caused by technical defects, 26 by staff error, one by management failure and six by other factors

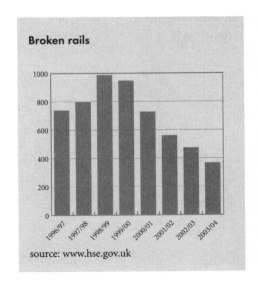

Broken rails

source: www.hse.gov.uk

Children killed on the railways

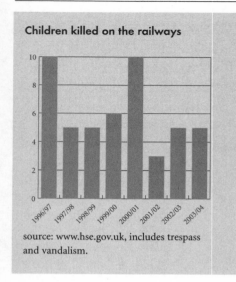

source: www.hse.gov.uk, includes trespass and vandalism.

The minor/heritage railway sector is thriving – operating 384 track miles, catering for 12 million passengers and employing 1,100 staff augmented by 11,000 volunteers

International comparisons?

It is difficult to compare statistics on railway safety between different European countries because the statistics are collected and defined in different ways. However, the European Rail Transport Statistics Regulations established common rules for producing rail statistics. The first set of data will be compiled at the end of 2004 allowing the comparison of European rail networks.

Last year 335 people were killed or seriously injured trespassing on railways. People often do not hear a train coming until it is too late – modern trains move with the minimum of noise. A train cannot slow down or stop as quickly as a car – a train travelling at 60 mph needs more than half a mile to come to a stop. Many railways work using electricity at voltages of 750 volts for a ground level conductor rail to 1,500 volts or 25,000 volts for an overhead line system. The electric current on any of these systems is only ever switched off for maintenance work. This means that in most cases even if a train is not present the electricity will be on and will be more than enough to kill if touched. Climbing on top of trains or holding metal objects in the air near an overhead cable can cause instant death as the current from overhead cables can spark across a gap of several feet.

Section 39 • **Value of a life**

The Government needs estimates of the value of saving a life or serious injury in road accidents for use in the appraisal of road schemes. Official estimates ("Highways Economics note no.1" DfT, www.dft.gov.uk, 2002) values a fatal accident at £1.25 million. A serious injury is valued at £140,000 and a minor injury at £11,000.

In 2002, the 222,000 injury accidents on Britain's roads (of which 3,100 were deaths) are therefore deemed to have a cost benefit value of £12.8 billion (in 2002 prices). An additional 3.3 million damage only incidents were valued at nearly £5 billion, taking the total value of the prevention of all road accidents to about £17.8 billion.

These values include: the loss of output due to injury (the expected loss of earnings), ambulance and medical costs, and human costs (to represent pain, grief and suffering to the casualty and others, and, for deaths, the intrinsic loss of the enjoyment of life). These are not actual costs but cost benefit values representing the benefits that would be obtained by the prevention of road injuries. The value of preventing an accident is greater than these numbers relating to individuals for two reasons – most incidents involve more than one casualty and some costs not specific to causalities, such as damage to vehicles and other property and police time, are not included.

Section 40 • Economic growth

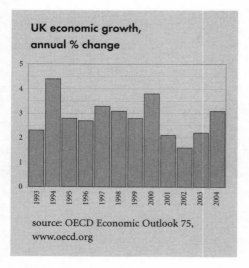

UK economic growth, annual % change

source: OECD Economic Outlook 75, www.oecd.org

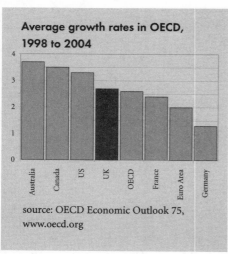

Average growth rates in OECD, 1998 to 2004

source: OECD Economic Outlook 75, www.oecd.org

The Chancellor has claimed that "boom and bust" and "the old British disease of stop-go" are a thing of the past. In his Budget statement in March 2004, he said, "I can now report that Britain is enjoying its longest period of sustained economic growth for more than 200 years". In his 2005 Budget it was the most sustained period of growth since 1701. The Chancellor is not renowned for his modesty and many of his claims merit close inspection. Even if aggregate economic growth has been reasonably stable under Labour, some of the components have been extremely volatile and some have been on a very weak trend. (See section on Economic Stability.)

The claim about the longest period of sustained growth for 200 years might be thought hard to verify due to lack of quality data over much of that period but, in fact, sources point to a 15 year period of uninterrupted growth from 1959 to 1973 inclusive which is longer than the current expansion of 12 years. (source: "International historical statistics, Europe 1750 to 1988", Mitchell, Stockton Press) That period does not count for the Chancellor as there were occasional quarters when output fell even though the annual figures were always positive.

The Chancellor, perhaps not surprisingly, also fails to mention that the last fall in output was in the second quarter of 1992, meaning that the first half of this period of stable growth occurred under a Conservative government which, arguably, put in place many of the foundations for the current stability. Even if the Chancellor is somewhat economical with the truth, it is the case that the UK is the only G7 country not to have had at least one quarter of falling output since the turn of the millennium. (Budget 2004, page 16) But this begs the question as to whether it has any statistical – the figures are naturally volatile – or economic significance – falling output over such a short period as a single quarter is unlikely to be damaging to the economy.

By constantly repeating the theme of "stop-go", the Chancellor creates a politically advantageous myth. Recessions did not occur that frequently before Gordon Brown became the Chancellor. According to data from the International Monetary Fund, Britain has had only three spells of falling

GDP since its records began in 1959. In the other 40 or so years, the economy grew. While a major and persistent recession lasting a year or more would seem to be in no one's interest, a quarter or two of fractional declines in GDP, defined as "bust" by the Chancellor, would barely be noticed and not be an unmitigated disaster for the country.

Since 1997, growth has averaged 2¾%, while the strongest annualised growth in any quarter was just over 4.1% (at the end of 2003) and the weakest was 0.8% (early in 2003). While this average growth rate is not unhealthy it is by no means exceptional in the context of Britain's recent history. In the 1950s, 1970s and 1980s, the annual growth rates averaged around 2½%. In the 1960s the growth rate was higher – just over 3%. Indeed, in three of the six years from 1998 to 2003 inclusive, growth was slower than in any of the five years 1993 to 1997.

International comparisons suggest that the UK performance has been average since 1997. In the seven years from 1998 to 2004, UK growth averaged 2.7% compared to 2.6% for the whole OECD area, in effect the industrialised world. The UK was ahead of the Euro area (2.0%) but well behind other anglo-saxon countries such as the US, Canada and Australia.

In the world's premier economic league, composed of the 20 largest economies measured by their gross national income, Britain was ranked sixth in size in 2001 but only tenth in the average rate of growth over the five years to 2003. The UK has experienced higher economic growth than the US in only two of the seven years of the Labour government between 1998 and 2004. Similarly, UK growth was faster than in Australia in only one of the seven years and in three compared to Canada. The majority of countries below the UK are those pegged to the Euro. The average annual GDP growth in the UK since 1997 has been only a ¼% greater than that of the G-7 countries. (source: "Gordon Brown's boasts", Centre for Policy Studies, www.cps.org.uk, 2004)

The GDP figures, along with many other government statistics, are frequently revised. Due to the sensitivity and importance of the GDP numbers, the ONS publishes frequent guides to the scale of revisions. Following considerable investment and improvements in the figures in the last decade, the revisions are now much smaller.

There are also definitional issues to consider. For example, GDP is measured at market prices in the national accounts. Gross value added (GVA) is

What is recession?

International convention normally defines a "recession" as being two successive quarters of falling GDP. This definition acknowledges the fact that minor cyclical fluctuations in output (say, over just one quarter) are commonly experienced throughout the world - and could even be due to changed timing of holidays, extreme weather conditions or statistical volatility. In America, the authorities found this a little too simplistic and mechanistic with the consequence that they now have a more subtle definition. A recession is defined by the National Bureau of Economic Research as, "a significant decline in economic activity spread across the economy, lasting more than a few months, normally visible in real GDP, real income, employment, industrial production, and wholesale-retail sales. A recession begins just after the economy reaches a peak of activity and ends as the economy reaches its trough. Between trough and peak, the economy is in an expansion. Expansion is the normal state of the economy; most recessions are brief and they have been rare in recent decades." (Source: www.nber.org)

The total value of the UK at the end of 2003 was £5,344,000,000,000 (£5.3 trillion) —just over half of which is housing

It is a shame that Britain does not have an independent body to ensure that the economic data are robust and to interpret the data (and to determine the length of economic cycles)

measured at basic prices which exclude taxes less subsidies on products. The difference between these two measures shows the contribution to growth of taxes less subsidies (this essentially means the contribution of VAT and excise duties). On average in the four years 2001 to 2004, tax increases added one quarter of one percentage point to economic growth. (For a fuller description of the impact of choosing different measures of GDP, see the section on public spending.)

Economic growth and quality of life

What about the gap between economic output and the quality of life? Output has doubled in the last 30 years but surveys suggest life satisfaction has remained flat. The GDP figures give no indication of whether the costs of economic growth have exceeded the benefits - a particular concern of anti-globalisation protesters. GDP is the sum of an economy's money transactions and takes no account of issues which are important to quality of life, such as safety, health, the environment and the family. These cannot be easily measured in money terms. The failure of GDP to include activities such as leisure, caring for children or the elderly, and housework can also lead to baffling consequences. For example, if you employ a cleaner to clean your home rather than clean it yourself, the payment of the wage will increase national income and economic growth even though your house is no cleaner under the new arrangements. Some countries, including the UK, are starting to produce so-called satellite accounts to quantify activities such as housework or the environmental impact of economic activity. These are not part of the official growth figures but they do allow the scale of the activities or the trends to be compared. The development of national balance sheets or indicator scorecards in the future might allow the non-monetary services to play a large part in policy.

(sources: www.worldvaluessurvey.org, Eurobarometer at http://europa.eu.int, www.andrewoswald.com, www.neweconomics.org)

Section 41 • Economic stability

The Treasury has set itself ten objectives which it reviews in its annual report. The first three relate to "maintaining stability at home and overseas", with the first being the maintenance of "a stable macroeconomic framework". In the 2004 annual report, the Treasury says that it is on track to meet this PSA target set in 2002. In justifying this conclusion it refers to the stability of inflation, the meeting of the fiscal rules and the effective handling of the financial consequences of the action in Iraq.

Even if the Chancellor's vision of stability applies to the aggregate GDP figures it certainly does not apply to many of the important components. The manufacturing sector, for example, has seen no growth at all during the period of Labour government. Indeed, manufacturing output in 2003 was fractionally lower than that recorded in 1997 while service sector output was 23% higher. Some components of manufacturing have performed disastrously – the textile, leather and clothing industry, for example, has contracted by one quarter since 1999. Meanwhile some components of the service sector have performed very (too?) strongly – real estate, renting and business services grew by 17% and the retailing sector by 16% in the three years to 2003.

This points to a much less balanced economy than in, for example, the decade before the Labour government. Between 1987 and 1997 manufacturing output increased by 17% and service sector output by 29%. Total industrial output – manufacturing plus the output from primary industries including the oil sector – grew only fractionally in the UK between 1997 and 2003 compared to much stronger growth in the EU and the US.

The personal sector has been booming. Family spending – defined as real household final consumption – has grown very strongly in recent years, rising by an average 3¾% a year since the second quarter of 1997, compared to 2¾% for total growth. In every year from 1996 to 2004 inclusive, real private consumption expenditure grew faster in the UK than in the industrialised world as a whole. (source: OECD Economic Outlook 75, www.oecd.org) Retail sales, for which monthly figures are available, has grown even faster with growth averaging about 5% in each of the last three

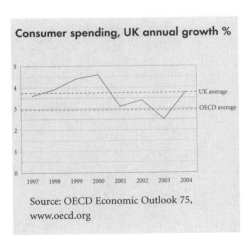

Consumer spending, UK annual growth %

Source: OECD Economic Outlook 75, www.oecd.org

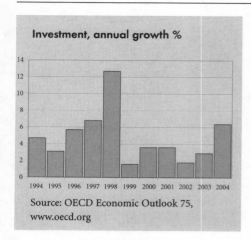

Source: OECD Economic Outlook 75, www.oecd.org

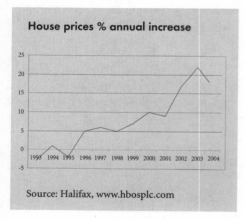

Source: Halifax, www.hbosplc.com

years. Nominal growth has not been much higher suggesting that there have been strong pressures on the retail sector to keep prices unchanged. The housing market, the strength of mortgage equity withdrawal and the boom in credit have been the antithesis of stability during the last decade. As indicated by the Treasury's own data, 2003 and 2004 saw the emergence of a range of weaker consumer indicators such as deteriorating consumer confidence and a fall back in the number of housing transactions.

The growth in private sector earnings has been greater than the growth in public sector earnings up to and including 2000, but growth in public sector earnings has been greater in the last three years. The last time public sector earnings grew faster than those in the private sector was in 1991 and 1992 during the last recession. Private sector earnings growth of 3% in 2003 is the lowest since the Treasury's records began in 1991. (source: "Data pocketbook", www.hm-treasury.gov.uk, November 2004)

The recent story for investment has been mixed and not very balanced. There was a surge in investment in 1997 and 1998 driven by the private sector, but in the five years since it has grown slowly – more slowly than the economy as a whole. Business investment fell in 2002 and 2003. Government spending on investment his risen sharply since 2001, rising by over 60% in the three years to 2003. Manufacturing investment fell in 1999 and has fallen every year since. In the period since 1997, manufacturing investment has fallen by about the same amount as government investment has risen – by a little over £6 billion a year.

In contrast the housing sector has been very strong with significant real terms price increases occurring every year since 1999.

Section 42 • Black economy

It is difficult to define a shadow (underground, black, illegal, clandestine, cash, parallel, criminal, non observed) economy and even harder to measure its size. Normally the shadow economy is defined to include all not officially recorded productive activities that should be part of GDP – normally they are hidden from the authorities to avoid paying tax – but the lack of an agreed definition adds to the difficulty of making an accurate estimate in any country to be comparable with one from elsewhere. The direct approaches to measurement are based on surveys and the examination of tax returns, while the indirect approaches analyse the discrepancies between what would be expected and what is actually observed with respect to spending, employment, and the use of money.

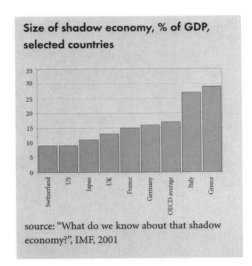

Size of shadow economy, % of GDP, selected countries

source: "What do we know about that shadow economy?", IMF, 2001

Academics have estimated that the sub-economy could be worth anything between £50 billion and £130 billion a year and could involve from 1.4 million to 3.6 million workers. However, it cannot be accurately measured because of its 'hidden' nature — examples are illegal migrants working secretly in Britain or an unemployed man undertaking undeclared work. The International Monetary Fund (IMF) has estimated that shadow economies have now reached an average of 17% of national wealth for OECD countries, including a figure for the UK approaching this average.

These estimates of the black economy are in addition to any allowances already included in the GDP figures. Most countries implicitly include some allowance for illegal activities in GDP because the incomes generated from them will in good part be spent on legal goods and services – and the sum of expenditure must equal the sum of incomes.

The shadow economy could also help to explain the large gap in the census figures after around a million fewer people were recorded as living in England and Wales in 2001 than previous figures suggested. In general, the non-observed economy is heavily concentrated in a small number of sectors. In heavy industry, rail and air transport, government services and banking, for example, there is little scope for shadow activities, which are much more common in sectors such as home repairs, retail, taxis and catering. (source: "Measuring the non-observed economy", OECD statistics brief, November 2002)

While underground activities mean that government revenues are forgone (from taxation and social security contributions), they are value creating and introduce a dynamic element into the "official" economy – the vast bulk of these activities are thought to be legal but just not registered. The ramifications for policy making are greater than just people failing to pay tax while still using public services – many of the unregistered people could return to "the official world" in time to claim their retirement state pensions, and the underground economy provides a cover for illegal activities and terrorists.

Not all illegal activities are productive – only those involving an exchange of goods and services between willing buyers and sellers would be included. For example, fraud, protection rackets, and theft would not be included, but "fencing", the trade in stolen goods, would be included. In the case of Britain, the Office for National Statistics estimated that the inclusion of illegal activities, namely drugs, prostitution, gambling and fencing, would add between 1 and 1½% of GDP. International organisations such as Eurostat and the OECD have been keen to include aspects of the shadow economy in the official GDP figures – but most countries are unwilling to put the effort into making such estimates, thinking it better to turn a blind eye.

Although non-observed activities are a significant component of industrialised economies, they are a much larger problem in developing economies and Eastern Europe. The incremental changes from year to year in the extent of unofficial activity in an industrialised economy is quite modest – so that while the level of activity might be poorly measured, the growth rates over time should remain fairly accurate. In Eastern bloc countries, however, the replacement of central planning by unrestricted and often chaotic free markets has largely undermined the traditional statistical reporting system. In these countries particularly, the inability to accurately measure these activities casts a shadow over the accuracy of the GDP figures.

Section 43 • Interest rates

Interest rates have been historically low in Britain since 1993. From the peak of 15% in 1989, the base rate fell to 6% in January 1993 and reached a low point of 5¼% in February 1994. It then drifted up (and was renamed the repo rate when Labour took office in 1997) to reach a peak of 7½% in June 1998. The rate then followed a general downward trend to reach a low point of 3½% in July 2003 before edging higher again. Short-term rates averaged just over 6% in the five years from 1993 to 1997, and just over 5% in the seven following years. Chancellor Brown's policies, notably letting the Bank of England set interest rates, would appear to have helped keep inflation and thus interest rates low but the impact of his policies on rates has not been as dramatic as he often suggests. The period of very high and very volatile interest rates had apparently ended before Labour came to power in 1997.

What are short and long term interest rates?

The base or repo rate is a key policy tool of governments. The rate will be raised if there is a need to slow the economy or reduce the rate of inflation. Short term – 3 month – market rates are heavily influenced by base rate movements. Long term interest rates – say 10 year rates – are determined by the market for bonds and depend largely on the propects for inflation (lower inflation implies lower rates) and the scale of government borrowing (more borrowing implies more bonds being issued).

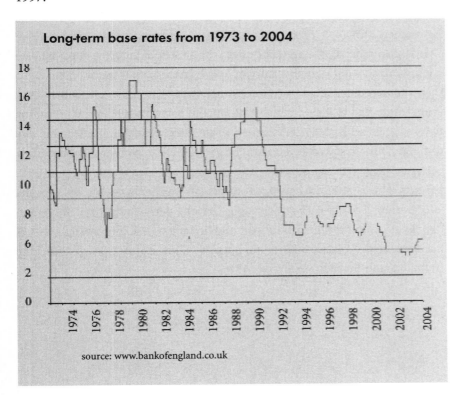

Long-term base rates from 1973 to 2004

source: www.bankofengland.co.uk

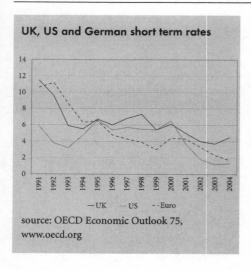

UK, US and German short term rates

source: OECD Economic Outlook 75,
www.oecd.org

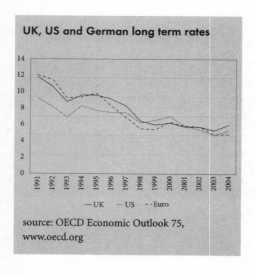

UK, US and German long term rates

source: OECD Economic Outlook 75,
www.oecd.org

Indeed, the phenomenon of low interest rates is something that has been affecting all industrialised countries, not just the UK. In the five years 1993 to 1997 prior to the Labour government, short term interest rates in the UK averaged between 1% and 1½% above German and US rates – narrower than the current differential and suggesting that the low rates of recent years are not the result of policies pursued in the UK. Interest rates in the Euro area, on average broadly the same as UK rates in the five years up to and including 1997, have been about 2% lower in the seven years since. Low interest rates are of course a double edged sword – businesses, individuals and politicians prefer interest rates to be lower rather than higher, other things being equal, but persistently low interest rates are usually a sign of economic malaise in the country (as is currently the case in Japan and the Euro area).

2003 saw the start of the rise in the interest rate cycle in the UK, increasing the differential above the corresponding US rates for 2004 to 3%, the highest since 1992. UK rates were more than 2% above Euro rates in 2003, the highest since 1998. (source: Source: OECD Economic Outlook 75, www.oecd.org and "Data pocketbook", www.hm-treasury.gov.uk, November 2004)

It is also true that long term rates – the rates of interest applicable to borrowing on a ten year government bond – have been lower under Labour than the previous Conservative administration – roughly 5% in the seven years from 1998 to 2004 inclusive, compared to nearly 8% in the preceding five years. As with short-term interest rates, however, not all of this is due to the policies followed by Chancellor Brown. For example, the differential between long term rates in the UK and the Euro area is the same in both periods. The differential compared to the US was just over 1% lower in the later period. There are also early signs that the period of narrowing differentials has come to an end – as the public sector deficit increases, 2004 is likely to see the widest differential between UK long-term rates and those in the US and the Euro area since 1997.

Section 44 • Inflation

Inflation has been very stable for the last decade. The economic boom of the late 1980s gave rise to a period of high inflation but the rate fell in the ensuing recession and was heading downwards well before the mid-1990s. As with economic growth, the Chancellor has been economical with the truth as to the origins of the current low inflation. He is naturally keen to emphasise the impact of his decision in 1997 to establish a monetary policy committee and give the Bank of England "operational responsibility for setting interest rates" – a limited form of central bank independence. But policy measures taken earlier in the 1990s, such as the ultimately disastrous decision to join the exchange rate mechanism in 1990, and the more successful setting of an inflation target of 1% to 4% in 1992, clearly had some impact on reducing the rate of inflation. Inflation in the seven years from 1997 has averaged 2½%, exactly the same rate as recorded in the previous four years. (source: "Data pocketbook", www.hm-treasury.gov.uk, November 2004)

It is true to say that policymakers in developed countries have found inflation relatively easy to control in the last decade. Most countries have adopted some form of inflation target pursued by central banks with some degree of independence from the political process. There have also been very few external shocks and both non-fuel commodity prices and manufactured dollar-priced imports have fallen in recent years, reducing inflationary pressure. The upturn in oil and other commodity prices in the last year or two coupled with persistently high house price inflation should make the environment for policymakers in the UK more challenging looking forward.

There is a difficulty making international comparisons of inflation rates as most countries have their own unique precise definition. Since the late 1990s some comparison has been possible between the countries of the EU due to the introduction of a harmonised measure in the run-up to monetary union. On the basis of a harmonised measure the rate of inflation has been lower in Britain than the EU average since 1993.

The RPI has been a constant – and trusted – statistic for measuring consumer inflation since the 1950s. Most "inflation linking" – in fields such as pensions, tax rates, savings and so on – still uses the main RPI. But it was

Components of the RPI, weights for 2004	
Food and soft drinks	10.6
Alcohol and tobacco	4.6
Clothing and footwear	6.2
Housing and utilities	10.3
Furniture and household eq'ment	7.5
Health	2.2
Transport	15.1
Communication	2.6
Recreation and culture	15.0
Education	1.6
Restaurants and hotels	13.7
Other	10.6

source: ONS, MDS T18.2, www.statistics.gov.uk

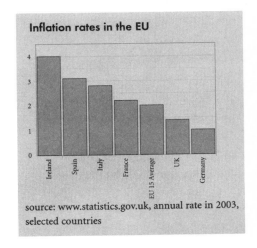

Inflation rates in the EU

source: www.statistics.gov.uk, annual rate in 2003, selected countries

What is inflation?

The language of inflation can be confusing due to the loose or ambiguous use of words. Generally, however, there is said to be inflation when there is a broad-based and sustained rise in prices in the economy. The rate of increase may be gradual (creeping inflation) or large and accelerating (hyperinflation). If the rate of inflation is falling, there is said to be disinflation. Occasionally prices fall, which is called negative inflation or deflation. Price indices are frequently referred to as deflators and are used to convert, i.e. deflate, figures in current prices into constant prices. This statistical process is called deflation. There are many price indicators measuring different prices or groups of prices. While the RPI is the most commonly used measure, other indicators include: the gold price, oil price, commodities, producer input and output prices, house prices, consumers' expenditure deflator and the GDP deflator. While a low and stable rate of inflation is deemed desirable, very low inflations is associated with below tred economic growth.

deemed unsuitable for monetary policy as it includes mortgage interest payments that move largely in line with interest rates. This has a perverse effect – as interest rates are increased (generally to slow the economy and bring inflation down) the inflation rate rises. This led to the introduction of the RPIX, the RPI excluding mortgage interest rates, so that the Treasury and Bank of England had a better measure for policy making. At the end of 2003, the Chancellor changed the target to be the CPI (consumer price index), which was previously known as the EU's harmonised index of consumer prices (HICP). The target was set at 2% on the new measure replacing a target of 2½% on the old. Due to differences in the way the two indices are calculated, the targets are broadly similar.

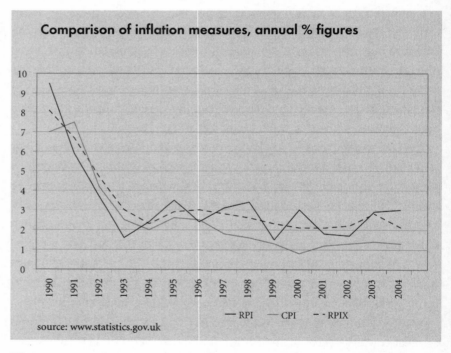

Comparison of inflation measures, annual % figures

source: www.statistics.gov.uk

There was another unexpected change to the calculation of the inflation numbers in February 2004 with the introduction of so-called hedonics – a way to measure quality change in the products that people buy. While many products have little or no quality change during the course of a year or two, some products, such as cars, computers and cameras, can change very rapidly. Measuring the inflation rate to apply to a computer, for example, which from year to year has both falling prices and improving quality, is very hard.

Hedonics, which essentially breaks down the product into its various components, pricing each one, is the new and preferred – albeit labour-intensive – way of measuring quality and price change for these difficult products.

The introduction of hedonics has tended to reduce the recorded rate of inflation. Accordingly, there was some concern when this methodology was partially introduced that the resulting reduction in the rate of inflation could be damaging to those whose savings, benefits or pensions depend on the inflation rate. Estimates made at the time suggested that the Chancellor could benefit from both increased tax revenues (due to lower indexation of tax allowances) and reduced public expenditure by up to £100 million a year. There was some concern that the failure of the Chancellor to convene the RPI advisory committee to sanction the change given that he retains ultimate control over the inflation numbers, coupled with the lack of fore-warning from the ONS about the change, hinted at political manipulation of the figures. The Statistics Commission subsequently reported that the technical change was merited but felt that the institutional arrangements for the RPI – with the Chancellor (uniquely for data covered by the National Statistics branding) having the final say over the figures – were inappropriate and that ONS communication on this occasion had been inadequate. (source: www.statscom.org.uk, report of September 2004)

The monthly RPI press release from the ONS is full of data on the various components and the Bank of England's quarterly bulletin is a very thorough analysis of the current inflationary pressures. It is regrettable that the ONS still does not publish breakdowns of the RPI showing how inflation affects different groups such as pensioners, students, single people, council house tenants etc. The failure to publish inflation rates for different types of households might explain why people sometimes feel that the inflation numbers are not accurately reflecting the price pressures they experience. A good part of the explanation might be that the different components of the RPI move very differently over time. Between 1997 and 2003, the prices of clothing and leisure goods actually fell while those for tobacco, housing and leisure services rose by more than a third. No regional figures are published for the UK, but they are available for some other countries. (source: www.statistics.gov.uk/rpi and www.bankofengland.co.uk)

Inflation rates by sector, change in prices (%) between 1997 and 2004

Tobacco	53
Housing	49
Leisure services	39
Fares	28
Catering	27
Housing services	25
Whole RPI	19
Personal goods and services	18
Alcohol	17
Motoring	11
Fuel and light	8
Food	7
Household goods	4
Clothing	-19
Leisure goods	-20

source: ONS, MDS T18.4, www.statistics.gov.uk

At any one time, only about one third of households face an inflation rate within 1 percentage point of the average rate

source: IFS

Section 45 • Trade and competitiveness

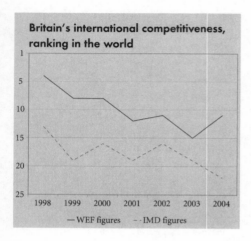

Britain's international competitiveness, ranking in the world

— WEF figures   - - IMD figures

Trade balance in goods and services, $bn

	2004	Change since 1997
Canada	37	-25
France	21	-20
Germany	124	+96
Italy	6	-42
Japan	107	+59
Spain	-21	-27
Switzerland	28	+13
UK	-74	-76
US	-526	-425

source: OECD, Economic Outlook 75

One consequence of the weakness of manufacturing has been the appearance of a large trade deficit – since going into deficit in 1998 its cumulative size has risen to £135 billion over six years. No other country has seen a comparable fall with the exception of the US. The US trade deficit is roughly the same as the UK's after allowing for the size of the economy. The deficit seems to be more structural than that which arose during the period of strong economic growth in the late 1980s. And, for all of the Chancellor's talk about Britain being a "truly enterprising economy", his stewardship as Chancellor has seen Britain's share of world exports fall from 5½% in 1997 to 4.9% in 2003. While many other industrialised countries – France, the US and Japan, for example – have also experienced a fall in export share over the period, some have not. Germany's share has risen by nearly one percentage point and in others such as France, where the share has fallen, the decline seems to have been arrested and is now being reversed.

Britain's falling competitiveness is confirmed by a number of international surveys which showed the country's ranking on the slide. On the basis of the global competitiveness report published by the World Economic Forum (www.weforum.org), which is designed to enhance "the understanding of the key factors which determine economic growth, and explain why some countries are so much more successful than others in raising income levels and opportunities for their respective populations", the UK has fallen from fourth place in 1998 to eleventh in 2003. Similarly, the Institute for Management Development (www.imd.ch) shows the UK's ranking on the basis of a "competitiveness scoreboard" has fallen from 13th in 1997 to 22nd in 2004. The UK scores 72, compared to the US with a top score of 100, and comes below the other Anglo-Saxon countries in the report such as Ireland, New Zealand, Canada and Australia.

Section 46 • Productivity

Productivity – a measure of the ability to create goods and services from a given amount of inputs such as labour, materials and capital – is one of the most basic foundations of economic analysis. Chancellor Brown has described productivity as "a fundamental yardstick of economic performance" and has set a target of raising the UK's rate of productivity growth and narrowing the productivity gap with our competitors.

A high national productivity level typically indicates efficient production of goods and services and a competitive economy – and it is increased productivity that opens the door to the achievement of higher rates of economic growth. This is not always the case, however, as productivity growth can also occur during periods of recession as businesses cut jobs in an attempt to become more efficient.

The main source of productivity increases is the use of more and better "capital stock", namely investment in machinery and equipment, along with skills, innovation, competition and enterprise. Despite its importance, productivity is painfully difficult to measure with any certainty and accuracy. The Chancellor claims to have boosted UK productivity performance but most experts feel a longer run of data is required before drawing such conclusions. (source: "Productivity in the UK: benchmarking UK productivity performance", March 2004, www.hm-treasury.gov.uk)

Productivity is usually measured in terms of output per hour worked, a measure which makes comparisons between firms, industries and countries somewhat easier, though there are different ways of measuring it, such as output per worker, output per job, adjusting for different skill levels and total factor productivity. The measure of output per worker can easily be affected by a change in the composition of the workforce – a shift towards part-time workers, for example, could lead to a larger number of employees and yet unchanged hours work and unchanged output, hence an apparent fall in productivity. Some people have advocated measuring the output per person of working age, which while not a measure of productivity, indicates how efficiently an economy includes all of the potential workers in productive employment.

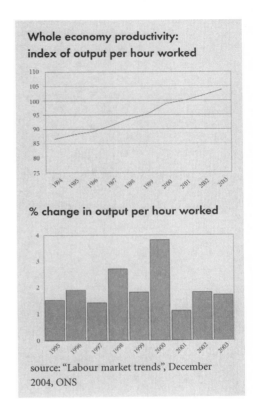

Whole economy productivity: index of output per hour worked

% change in output per hour worked

source: "Labour market trends", December 2004, ONS

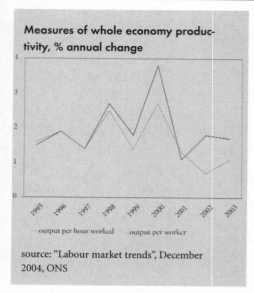

Measures of whole economy productivity, % annual change

output per hour worked　　output per worker

source: "Labour market trends", December 2004, ONS

The main whole economy productivity measure published by the ONS is based on output per worker, and is measured as the ratio of an index of gross value added at basic prices over an index of employment, but the ONS also publishes an output per hour measure. As there are many different measures of "national output" and labour market activity, there are many different measures of productivity. Indeed, both the Bank of England and the Treasury publish their own subtly different measures. The various measures from the various suppliers are different in any given year, but over a number of years show broadly similar trends. In recent years the growth in output per hour has generally been stronger than the growth in output per worker as the rise in hours worked has been less strong than the growth in employment levels.

Apart from all the definitional difficulties, the figures can also be very erratic from quarter to quarter. The ONS press release announcing the third-quarter figures for 2004 (published in December 2004) showed that in the previous eight quarters, the quarter on quarter growth in output per worker had fluctuated between a fall of 0.3% and a rise of 1.1%. The annual growth rate had fluctuated between a rise of 0.6% and a rise of 2.9%. The different industrial sectors can also reveal markedly different trends in output per job. In the year to the third quarter of 2004, the food, textiles/clothing and rubber/plastic sectors saw productivity fall while the electrical/optical and transport equipment sectors saw double digit growth.

Until now, ONS has not published productivity estimates for the individual service industries because of known quality issues with the data. However, a range of improvements are now being made to the output measures and these provide an opportunity for the statisticians to re-assess the potential for extending productivity estimates to the services industries. Some limited data – either annual figures or groupings of various industries together – are expected to be published shortly.

UK productivity growth over the long-term – the average over the last three decades – is around 2% per annum and this is below a number of international competitors, such as France and the US. In the UK a lower proportion of people have higher skills than in the US, and fewer have intermediate skills than in Germany or France. UK firms under UK ownership have significantly lower productivity than UK firms under foreign ownership.

The slower growth has led to a "productivity gap" opening up between the UK and a number of other countries. On an output per worker basis, the G-7 average in 2002 was around 13% higher than the UK figure, and on an output per hour basis the gap was around 12%. The gap is spread across a wide range of industries – of thirty industries studied, UK productivity was below that in the US in 26 industries, below France in 25, and below Germany in 21, in 2003. On a per worker, but not the per hour, basis the UK's productivity is similar to Germany's. (source: "Labour productivity", Labour market trends, November 2004, ONS)

In October 2004, the ONS published for the first time some "experimental" international comparisons of GDP per hour worked. On this basis the UK was only ahead of Japan (85.0 with the UK set at 100) in 2003, but behind Germany, France and the USA, with France being the leader (at 129.4). The figures are experimental in the sense that they do not meet the quality criteria of National Statistics – the per hour figures are of good quality when following the trends in one country over time, but the different methodologies used in each country to derive their numbers mean they are less reliable for cross-country analysis.

Total factor productivity captures the contribution to output of other more intangible factors: innovation, managerial skill, organisation, competition and chance. It is an appealing measure of the economy's efficiency as it attempts to measure output per unit of all inputs, and hence captures how effectively inputs are used together. However, in practice it is difficult to calculate and is often measured as the residual – as productivity nets off the contribution of physical and human capital.

The measurement of government output is even more complex than the measurement of private-sector output. Sir Tony Atkinson was asked in December 2003 by the National Statistician to undertake a review of the future development of measures of government output and was reported in January 2005.

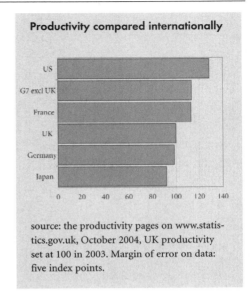

Productivity compared internationally

source: the productivity pages on www.statistics.gov.uk, October 2004, UK productivity set at 100 in 2003. Margin of error on data: five index points.

Section 47 • Insolvencies

There were over 100
personal bankruptcies
each day in the last year

The number of bankrupts or personal insolvencies (in England and Wales) was a record high in 2003 as people found the debt levels harder to live with. The 16% rise in 2003 took the figure over 35,000. The number of corporate insolvencies was a record high of 16,300 in 2002 but fell back in 2003 to 14,200, below the mid-point of the range seen since the mid-1990s.

Numbers of personal insolvencies, 000s

	Bankruptcy orders	Individual voluntary arrangements	Total	Change %
1996	21.8	4.5	26.3	-0.2
1997	19.9	4.5	24.4	-7.0
1998	19.6	4.9	24.5	0.4
1999	21.6	7.2	28.8	17.3
2000	21.5	8.0	29.5	2.5
2001	23.5	6.3	29.8	0.8
2002	24.3	6.3	30.6	2.7
2003	28.0	7.5	35.6	16.4

source: Department of Trade and Industry quarterly press release, www.dti.gov.uk

The term 'bankrupt' is used to describe insolvency. Insolvencies are dealt with under the 1986 Insolvency Act. A bankruptcy order can be made when a court is satisfied that there is no prospect of the debt being paid. Individual voluntary arrangements allow debtors to come to an agreement with their creditors. Personal insolvencies (dealt with under different legislation) were also at a record high in Scotland in 2003.

Section 48 • Government borrowing

The government borrowed £630 over and above tax receipts for every UK resident to fund public expenditure in 2003/04. Public borrowing is high – the outturn for 2003/04 in the March 2004 Budget was £37 billion, 3.4% of GDP. The UK would in 2003/04 have failed to comply with the 'Excessive deficits procedure' of the EU, had the UK joined the Euro, which says that the deficit should be below 3% of national income.

The deficit has risen sharply. Just two years before, the public sector was in balance. It has risen more sharply than the Chancellor expected. The eventual outturn of 2003/04 was nearly three times higher than the £13 billion forecast in the 2002 Budget.

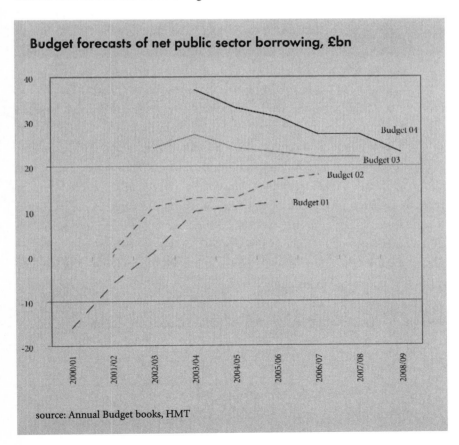

Budget forecasts of net public sector borrowing, £bn

source: Annual Budget books, HMT

The 3.4% deficit in relation to GDP is higher than the average seen in the 1990s (3.3%) and the 1980s (2.2%). This is despite the economy performing well – often the deficit has risen in times of recession – and taxes rising. While Budget 2004 showed the public finances to be on track to meet the rules the Chancellor has set himself as part of the "Code for fiscal stability" in 1998, media reports since suggest most forecasters do not expect them to be met. Set out in detail in the Budget each year, the 'Golden rule' says that there will only be borrowing for investment and that current expenditure should match current receipts over the economic cycle. The 'sustainable investment rule' says that net government debt will be set at a "stable and prudent" level (defined as below 40% of GDP).

Rules should not be interpreted by the rule maker. The rules, which the Chancellor says play a key role, have met with a lukewarm response. The Institute for Fiscal Studies says, "There is nothing sacrosanct about these two rules, nor are they necessarily optimal." (source: www.ifs.org.uk) The golden rule is highly dependent on the period defined by the Chancellor as the economic cycle – in some other countries, such as the US, the economic cycle is independently determined. The rule also ignores the fact that some types of public spending might be more desirable than others. The rule is less onerous than the one used for Euroland countries – they must balance all expenditure (including investment) over the cycle.

The Chancellor has also tweaked the rule. Initially the surpluses and deficits in each year were aggregated pounds, but now each year's deficit is converted into a percentage of GDP and then aggregated. He has also more recently referred to the size of the cyclically adjusted deficit – i.e. adjusted for the state of the economic cycle, allowing for the fact that there would be more borrowing when the economy is less buoyant – this has the effect of giving him a little more wriggle room. Conveniently for the Chancellor, given that he is close to breaking his rule, this has the effect of increasing the benefits of the early years of surplus and decreasing the disadvantage of the later years of deficit. Every little helps. The Chancellor refers some of his assumptions and decisions for scrutiny by the National Audit Office but the process would be much more credible if he referred all of his assumptions.

During the 1980s, the data show that the golden rule (had it existed) would have been missed in cash terms, but met in terms of cyclically adjusted figures since the economy under-performed over much of the decade. In the first half of the 1990s the current budget was in deficit – it averaged over 4% of GDP. The situation was much healthier in the second half of the decade.

There are many names given to measures of the annual public sector deficit. The preferred measure used by the government changed in the late 1990s from the public sector borrowing requirement (PSBR) to public sector net borrowing (PSNB). One major difference between the two is that the PSBR is based on cash payments not accruals (i.e. amounts due in or relating to a given period). This has a major impact when there are, for example, large sales of government assets or privatisations. In 2000/01, the government raised £22½ billion from the sale of the third generation mobile phone spectrum licenses. This cut the PSBR (recently renamed the public sector net cash requirement, PSNCR) by the full amount yet was spread over 20 years in the PSNB. This allowed the Chancellor to claim both that the receipts had been used to pay down debt in that year (and cut debt payments accordingly) and also score £2 billion of receipts a year going forward to make the accounts look more favourable. Indeed, more than once the Chancellor has claimed that he is "paying off more debt in one year than all the debt paid off in the whole of the last 50 years taken together". (source: speech to the British Chambers of Commerce, April 2004)

The UK's fiscal position has deteriorated much more under Labour than has the balance of any other industrialised country over the same period, with the exception of the US. The general government financial balance went from a very small surplus in 1998, the first full year under Labour, to a deficit of 3¼% in 2003. This deterioration of over three percentage points is far greater than that seen for the euro area countries as a whole (just under half a percentage point). But the deterioration is even more concerning given there was a surplus of nearly 4% in 2000 – in the three years since the fiscal position has deteriorated by 7% of GDP. This is a sharper deterioration than seen in the US and almost double that seen in the industrialised countries over the same period.

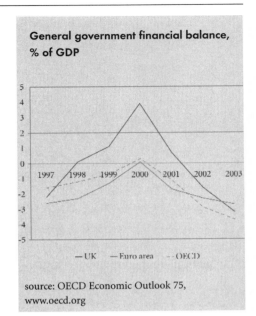

General government financial balance, % of GDP

source: OECD Economic Outlook 75, www.oecd.org

Section 49 • Government debt

Debt levels, £billions

Debt as % of GDP

source: Government deficit and debt, ONS first release, August 2004, www.statistics.gov.uk

Government debt is at its highest ever in nominal terms – £437 billion at the end of 2003. As a proportion of GDP – around 40% – it is the lowest since the early 1990s. Government debt in relation to GDP falls during periods of strong economic growth such as in the 1980s (leading to the low figure in the early 1990s) and again in the second half of the 1990s (leading to the current low figure) – as the strong growth boosts GDP, increases tax revenues and restrains the growth of public expenditure. The current position is healthy but not unprecedentedly so.

There are many definitions of debt. The Chancellor's preferred definition happens to deliver a lower figure than that preferred by the statisticians in the ONS and that commonly used in the EU. The rationale for the Chancellor's target debt level of 40% has never been set out – the EU chose a figure of 60% for the Maastricht Treaty but using a different definition of debt. The common EU definition of debt shows Britain's position in a less favourable light – the debt to GDP figure is about 6 percentage points higher – for example the ratio for 2004/05 is 41% according to the EU compared to 34½% as defined by the Treasury. The British debt is well below that in most other major countries – the corresponding internationally defined average for the G7 is 82%, with France, Germany and US all between 60–70%.

The UK has for some years had lower debt than many other countries, this is more due to the higher rates of inflation in the UK in the 1970s and 1980s eroding away the debt rather than spending restraint in the recent past on the part of the current or previous governments.

In 2004/05, public sector net debt is forecast to be 34% of GDP – a little lower than the average in the 1980s (41%) and the 1990s (37%). As the figure was just below 40% of GDP in the last year of the Conservative government (1996), it is clear that the bulk of the difference between Britain and its competitors does not reflect policy of the current government. Indeed, given the healthy state of public finances in the late 1990s and early 2000s, it is perhaps surprising that debt was not paid off more quickly. The position can also quickly reverse – the borrowing in 2003 (£35 billion when defined as general government's net borrowing) was greater than the sum of repayments in the four years from 1998 to 2001 (of £32 billion). Britain's debt burden has been below the average in all OECD members and the euro area in every year since 1986.

The Chancellor has also been keen to make much of the reduction in the country's debt interest payments. In the decade up to the 1997 election the net interest payments ranged between 2% and 3½% of GDP, so the fall to 1½% in 2003 is good if not record-breaking. The OECD average for 2003 is 2% and about 10 countries have a burden which is lower than Britain's.

National debt

The Bank of England quietly announced in the November 2003 edition of "Monetary and Financial Statistics" that it was ending the publication of a figure for the national debt. It said that there were now other more comprehensive and meaningful measures. It is true that the national debt – defined as the total gross national liabilities of the National Loans Fund – had become something of an anachronism, but as it had survuved for 315 years, it seemed a shame to stop one of the most enduring series. At the end of March 2003 the national debt stood at £448,006,333,944. (source: www.crnd.gov.uk and www.bankofengland.co.uk)

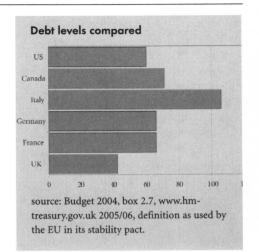

Debt levels compared

source: Budget 2004, box 2.7, www.hm-treasury.gov.uk 2005/06, definition as used by the EU in its stability pact.

Section 50 • Public spending

General government outlays as percentage of GDP

	1997	2005	Change
Canada	44.3	39.9	-4.4
France	54.9	53.4	-1.5
Germany	49.3	47.1	-2.2
Ireland	37.2	35.8	-1.4
Japan	35.1	36.6	1.5
UK	41.0	43.3	2.3
US	34.9	35.2	0.3

source: Economic Outlook 75, table 25, www.oecd.org

It is surprisingly difficult to measure the scale of government activity and how it has changed in Britain despite the central political importance of this issue

Given Parliament's control of the purse strings has always been one of the foundation stones of British democracy it is perhaps surprising that consistent figures – both across branches of government at any one time and in any one area over time – of public sector activity are not more readily available.

Both the Treasury and the Office of National Statistics can be criticised for letting this situation arise. The problems involved in quantifying and tracking the size of the public sector may well mean that there is no unambiguously correct way to approach the problem. Even so, it does seem that the ONS has, on the one hand, been too keen to accept the demands of the international bodies for internationally comparable data leading to definitions and concepts which are far from intuitive to other users of the data and, on the other, failed to stand up to the Treasury to publish enough useful information in an accessible way for those watching policy in the UK.

That said, it is clear the Labour government has increased the size of the public sector significantly. The 2004 budget showed that public sector spending was planned to rise to about £580 billion (over 42% of GDP) by 2007/08, compared with spending of £320 billion (39% GDP) in 1997/98. This increase has been paid for by higher taxes and higher public sector borrowing. The shift under the Labour government is clearly one to high public spending and high taxation. The definition of government outlays used by the OECD is different from the measure used by the Chancellor, but on the harmonised measure, the UK is the only major country to have experienced a rise of such magnitude in government spending between 1997 and 2005. The exceptional position of the UK is even more striking if the period from 2000 to 2005 is isolated. The Chancellor's spending spree started in 2000 when the ratio of public spending to GDP was 37%. By 2005, the ratio is expected to have increased by over six percentage points – a rise which is nowhere near matched by any other large country.

The Chancellor sets out his public spending plans for the coming three years, every other year. (The plans are available on the Treasury web site, www.hm-treasury.gov.uk) Public expenditure was under reasonably tight control in the late 1990s because Gordon Brown decided, by and large, to stick to the existing Conservative plans, but since 2000 spending has risen sharply.

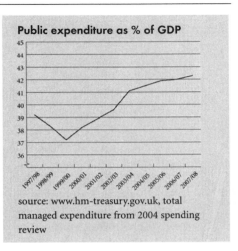

Public expenditure as % of GDP

source: www.hm-treasury.gov.uk, total managed expenditure from 2004 spending review

Why public expenditure data is a minefield

Definitions of public expenditure are many and include departmental expenditure limits, annually managed expenditure, total managed expenditure, current and capital expenditure, numerous "accounting adjustments". The figures can be in cash terms or real, inflation-adjusted, terms or as a percentage of GDP. The figures might relate just to central government, or general government (central government plus local authorities) or the whole of the public sector (general government plus public corporations and other trading bodies). Some figures are given by sector and others by department. There is expenditure which is voted by Parliament and non-voted spending. The involvement of the private sector in so many diverse ways – public private partnerships, privatisation, and subcontracting, for example – across the public sector has also made the figures more complicated and harder to understand. The Chancellor has also created a number of "kitties" – such as the "invest to save" and the "capital modernisation" funds – which complicate the tracking of public expenditure. There is an end year flexibility scheme which allows departments to carry-over some unspent money to the following year. And a whole new system called resource accounting budgeting has recently been introduced replacing the previous accounts which could be in either cash or accruals terms. The Chancellor often creates his own definitions of spending aggregates rather than using those which are part of the national accounts or internationally agreed – this means that data published regularly by the Office for National Statistics is not easy to relate to plans set by the Treasury.

Given the complexities of public sector data, it is left to the Treasury and ONS to present data which clearly show trends in a helpful manner. Despite the explosion in the size of the budget red book since Gordon Brown became Chancellor, it has lost much of the simple factual information that characterised earlier financial statements. Partly by design, it seems, the Treasury not only fails to help the reader, but at times seems to obfuscate

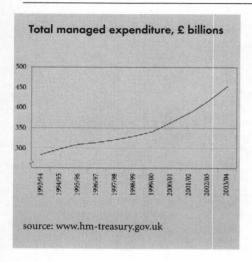

Total managed expenditure, £ billions

source: www.hm-treasury.gov.uk

Public expenditure: the big spenders

A. total spending in 2003/04 £bn
B. spending as a percent of GDP
C. change in real terms since 1997/98

	A	B	C
Social protection	152.1	13.6	16
Health	75.0	6.7	45
Education	59.4	5.3	37
Defence	27.4	2.5	13
Public order and safety	27.3	2.4	39
Debt interest	22.7	2.0	-34
Transport	15.6	1.4	46
Total	453.4	40.6	22

source: www.hm-treasury.gov.uk

even more. A perfect example of Treasury-induced complication is the creation of tax credits, which count as negative taxation rather than additional spending on social benefits. The Treasury document "Public expenditure statistical analyses" runs to nearly 200 pages and contains many breakdowns of expenditure for any one inclined to invest the time to understand. The long runs of data contained in the document often stop at the current year making it impossible to put plans in an historical context. Only one table in this document has data covering a 30 year period. Many tables only cover a five or ten year span – a far too short period.

There are a number of reasons why there are so few truly consistent measures over time of public expenditure as a proportion of national output. The points to be made here are intrinsically boring – being mostly about public sector accounting concepts – but the data definitions can have a crucial impact on the political debate. The first is that definitions of the public sector itself vary widely, particularly when allowances are made for the existence of quasi-government bodies and public corporations. An attempt was made to limit these problems by using the concept of "general government" which is central government plus local authorities, therefore excluding public corporations. Certainly this allowed for a reasonably consistent analysis during the Thatcher years which saw many industries such as gas, electricity and water supply, removed from the public corporations sector into the private sector. But the distinction has become ever more blurred in recent years. (source: "Is high public spending good or bad for you?", March 2002, David Smith, Williams be Broe)

The second reason for the inconsistent measure of public spending burdens over time concerns the definition of national output used to scale the various spending magnitudes. For most of the early postwar period it was accepted that the correct measure of GDP to use was the "factor cost" measure, which excluded indirect taxes and subsidies. This was because the factor cost measure provides a more accurate indication of the national output available to support public consumption. The alternative "market price" measure of GDP, which is gross of indirect taxes, would rise if there were a switch from direct to indirect taxation, even if nothing else has changed.

This might seem like a trivial accounting detail until the scale of the difference is appreciated. In recent years the market price measure of national output has been around £150 billion higher than the factor cost measure, a difference of around 15%. The consequence is that the share of total general government expenditure of money GDP would vary from say about 38% using the market price measure up to about 44% with the factor cost measure. (There would be a similar gap of around six percentage points looking at the share of taxes in GDP.)

While the figures presented in any Treasury or ONS press release spanning perhaps five years are likely to be on a consistent definition, the sheer variety of definitions means it is most unlikely that figures taken from a different source for any point further in the past are going to be comparable. This did mean, for example, that when tax and spend figures were being discussed in the run up to the 2001 general election, the outturn figures for the previous three or four years under the Labour administration were being compared with figures set out in the 1997 election manifesto of the Conservatives. It was never noticed that these two sets of numbers were based on different definitions and were therefore not comparable.

It seems that the market price measure of GDP was adopted in place of the superior factor cost measure, about 30 years ago by the then Labour government, with the aim of cosmetically massaging down the public spending, tax and borrowing burdens in the face of concern that these were becoming unsupportable. That "new" practice was maintained by the Conservative government. The present government's policy of raising extra revenue through higher specific duties has also had the politically convenient effect of pushing up the market price measure of GDP, and correspondingly suppressing the reported tax spending burdens. However, this is relatively small beer when compared to some of the other accounting practices deployed by the Chancellor, such as treating tax credits – which are extra public expenditure – as negative income tax, thereby not increasing social spending.

The accurate measurement of the government spending and tax burden became more difficult following the changes to the national accounts associated with the introduction of the so-called ESA95 in 1998. This new internationally agreed structure of national accounts erased a number of established features of the UK economic landscape. Among the more important of the changes is that the European Union now appears as a separate fourth

Largest defence budgets, $billion	
US	376.2
Japan	41.4
UK	41.3
France	34.9
Germany	27.4
China	22.4

source: "The top 10 of everything", 2004, www.dk.com

Seven countries have per capita defence spending at least 50% greater than the UK – Qatar, Israel, Kuwait, US, Singapore, Saudi Arabia and UAE

The state and its beneficiaries are spending around £70 for every £100 spent in the private sector

Public sector productivity

The introduction of the ESA95 also led to changes in the measurement of government productivity. This change affected the volume and implied cost of government spending but not the value. Changes to the data were only implemented from 1994 onwards, which makes it hard to know how comparable the earlier data are with today's figures. A further significant change to the measurement of public sector productivity was made in 2004. The ONS has set out a clear explanation of how the choice of the deflator for government expenditure affects the value/volume splits in the public accounts. There is little that a lay reader can do other than accept the best figures available from the ONS. But it is clear that the evaluation of how far increased government spending is generating greater outputs or improved outcomes rather than disappearing in higher costs is a debate which is going to continue for many years. There was some controversy when the figures were published in 2004 as there was little warning and hence suspicions that the change was politically motivated. The Statistics Commission said at the time that too little information had been published for them to form a view as to the appropriateness of the changes. The Atkinson review, commissioned by the ONS, reported in January 2005. (source: "Measuring government services output", ONS, October 2004, www.statistics.gov.uk and www.statscom.org.uk)

Wasteful spending?

Does the government waste £50 billion a year? Examples include: fraud and mistakes in the benefit system (£4.1bn), Network Rail inefficiency (£2.5bn), aspects of the CAP (£1.8bn), local education authority waste (£1.1bn), quangos (£0.5bn) and the Treasury's refurbishment (£0.3bn)

source: www.taxpayersalliance.com

arm of government, in addition to central government, local authorities and public corporations. As a result, measures of the general government tax burden, for example, now exclude VAT and other government revenues raised on behalf of the EU, an amount equal to nearly 1% of national output.

Another major change following the introduction of ESA95 is that many publicly funded activities which were once included in general government, such as NHS trusts and universities and some colleges of higher education, now appear in different national accounts categories, such as public corporations or non profit making institutions serving households. The reported size of general government also fell through the exclusion of municipal services such as regional airports and housing associations. All such changes make it more difficult to use the traditional measure of general government spending expressed as a ratio to national output.

The regular chopping and changing of definitions is something that has irritated econometric modelers who need long runs of consistent seasonally adjusted quarterly data – just what they do not get.

The rise in public expenditure has been paid for in part by increased taxation. The OECD figures show that taxes as a percentage of GDP are expected to rise from 38.8% in 1997 to 40.4% in 2005. This is at a time when the rates for the whole of the euro area and for the whole of the OECD area have fallen by two percentage points. The percentage of GDP taken in taxes is expected to have fallen between 1997 and 2005 in France, Germany, Ireland, Italy, and the US. (source: OECD Economic outlook table 26, www.oecd.org)

The ratio of tax and public spending to GDP can be looked at in a more controversial way. The public expenditure or tax ratio to GDP of 41%, could be seen as £41 being spent by the government or raised in taxes by the government for every £59 being spent by the private sector or being retained from income by the private sector.

Research from the European Central Bank suggests that many governments fall short of the three countries – Japan, US and Luxembourg – that are most efficient in the provision of their public services. It suggests that if the UK were as efficient as the best, public spending would only need to be 84% of current spending in order to maintain services. Such a level of spending would allow the spending to GDP ratio to fall to around 35%. The government is implementing the Gershon on review to make public sector savings primarily by relocating civil servants away from London. (source: "Public sector efficiency: an international comparison", July 2003, www.ecb.int) The Conservatives have promised even greater savings.

The longer-term rise in public expenditure

The long-term rise in the share of national resources absorbed by the state is one of the most striking economic features of the 20th century in the UK (and abroad). The proportion rose from about 10% of national income at the start of the century to between 25% and 30% in the interwar period. A further sharp rise came in the 1960s and 1970s as the welfare state became more widely established with public expenditure rising above 40% of national income by 1980. The ratio then fell during much of the time of the Conservative government before rising again in the late 1990s.

Section 51 • **Taxation**

Prior to the 1997 election, Labour gave a commitment that the income tax rates would not rise – and they have not. But that does not mean that many people are not feeling the pressure from higher taxes. A common – and very simple – way of looking at the tax burden is to set total taxes as a proportion of national output. From a ratio of just below 35% in 1996/97, it rose to 37½% in 2001/02 following the large tax increases in the early years of the Labour government, before settling back as the economy grew and taxes rose by less.

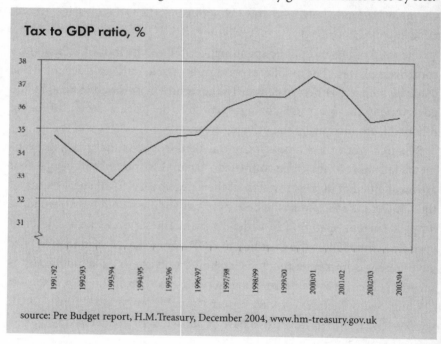

Tax to GDP ratio, %

source: Pre Budget report, H.M.Treasury, December 2004, www.hm-treasury.gov.uk

The Conservatives say that there have been 66 tax increases under Labour (though there have been over 100). They estimate that the value of the tax increases in the third year after the announcement in each budget (not all tax increases are achieving full revenue in the first year due to phasing etc), up to and including the 2004 budget, is around £34 billion (excluding council tax). Summing the take from each during the first three years following its announcement amounts to £76 billion.

The 66 Tax Rises

2 July 1997
- Mortgage tax relief cut
- Pensions Tax
- Health insurance taxed
- Health insurance taxed again
- Fuel tax escalator up
- Vehicle Excise Duty up
- Tobacco duty escalator up
- Stamp duty up for properties over £250,000
- Corporation Tax changes
- New Windfall Tax on utilities

17 March 1998
- Married couple's allowance cut
- Tax on travel insurance up
- Tax on casinos and gaming machines up
- Fuel tax escalator brought forward
- Tax on company cars up
- Tax relief for foreign earnings abolished
- Tax concession for certain professions abolished
- Capital Gains Tax imposed on certain non-residents
- Reinvestment relief restricted
- Corporation Tax payments brought forward
- Higher stamp duty rates up
- Some hydrocarbon duties up
- Additional diesel duties
- Landfill Tax up

9 March 1999
- NIC earnings limit raised
- NICs for self-employed up
- Married Couple's Allowance abolished
- Mortgage tax relief abolished
- IR35: Taxation of personal services companies
- Company car business mileage allowances restricted
- Tobacco duty escalator brought forward
- Insurance Premium Tax up
- Vocational Training Relief abolished
- Employer NICs extended to all benefits in kind

source: www.conservatives.com

- VAT on some banking services up
- Premiums paid to tenants by landlords taxed
- Duty on minor oils up
- Vehicle Excise Duties for lorries up
- Landfill tax escalator introduced
- Higher rates of stamp duty up again

21 March 2000
- Tobacco duties up
- Higher rates of stamp duty up again
- Extra taxation of life assurance companies
- Rules on Controlled Foreign Companies extended

17 April 2002
- Personal allowances frozen
- National Insurance threshold frozen
- NICs for employers up
- NICs for employees up
- NICs for self-employed up
- North Sea taxation up
- Tax on some alcoholic drinks up
- New stamp duty regime
- New rules on loan relationships

9 April 2003
- VAT on electronically supplied services
- IR35 applied to domestic workers
- Betting duty change
- Tax on red diesel and fuel oil up
- Controlled Foreign Companies measures on Ireland
- Vehicle excise duty up

17 March 2004
- New 19 per cent tax rate for owner-managed businesses
- New tax on private use of company vans
- UK transfer pricing introduced
- Increase in rate of tax on trusts
- Increase in tax on red diesel fuel
- Increase in tax on other road fuels (including LPG)

Every April
- Council Tax up

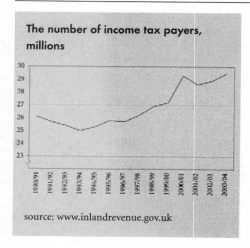

The number of income tax payers, millions

source: www.inlandrevenue.gov.uk

Major tax receipts in 2003/04, £ billions

Income tax	118.3
National insurance	72.5
Corporation tax	28.6
Stamp duties	7.5
Other Inland Revenue	1.1
VAT	69.1
Fuel duties	22.8
Tobacco duties	8.1
Alcohol duties	7.6
Other Customs & Excise	8.0
Vehicle excise duties	4.8
Business rates	18.4
Council tax	18.8
Other taxes and royalties	11.2
Total taxes	396.7

source: Pre Budget report, H.M.Treasury, December 2004

There are several ways of indicating how the tax burden is increasing. It is possible, for example, to split the year into two parts – during the first period all your income goes to the taxman and during the second it goes to you. In 2004, the so-called "Tax Freedom Day" fell on 30 May, implying that all your earnings up until that point were paid in tax. The consequence of Budget 2004 was to increase the tax burden – Tax Freedom Day was pushed later by three days compared to 2003. Adding in the public sector borrowing expected in the year, pushes Tax Freedom Day out to 11 June. (source: www.adamsmith.org) It is also possible to use the same methodology but apply it to the week rather than the year. On this basis, all the income for someone working a standard Monday to Friday week is paid to the tax man up until 9.30 on a Wednesday morning. (source: www.taxpayersalliance.com)

The number of taxpayers was broadly stable in the early and mid-1990s, but has risen since 1997. The number of payers of both income tax – up by 3½ million since 1997 – and corporation tax is at a record high. The number of death estates paying inheritance tax has also risen sharply – from 18,000 in 1997/98 to 30,000 in 2003/04. (source: www.inlandrevenue.gov.uk)

The amount of tax paid has also risen sharply. Gross Inland Revenue taxes, primarily income tax, corporation tax and stamp duty, have risen by 50% since 1996/97 to £228 billion in 2003/04 – and are forecast to rise by another 20% to £274 billion in 2005/06. Stamp duty has risen particularly sharply, trebling during the last seven years.

Tax credits, worth just over £4 billion in 2003/04, are netted off the tax figures given by the Treasury, as they count them as negative tax rather than public expenditure (in contrast to how the ONS treats them in the national accounts). The Treasury says that it was necessary to treat them as a negative tax for policy reasons, but the action also has the happy coincidence – so far as the Treasury is concerned – of reducing the tax take figures and ratios. Income tax and national insurance account for just under half the tax take.

It would be helpful if the Treasury (or ONS) would publish figures indicating how a "typical family" or a number of common household types have seen their tax burden move over the years. Some companies do publish such estimates but it is hard to vouch for their accuracy. One estimate suggested that an owner-occupier man earning £40,000 with two children (and an average consumption of fuel, beer, etc) would have seen his tax bill (in real terms) rise from £15,700 in 1997 to £18,200 in 2004, equivalent to a rise to 35.1% of income compared to 32.0% in 1997. (source: http://www.smith.williamson.co.uk)

Wasted tax and lost benefits

Nine out of ten UK adults, more than 40 million people, "wasted" an estimated £5.7 billion in 2003/04 in unnecessary tax. That works out at an average of £132 per taxpayer. Or, putting it another way, all taxpayers waste enough money to create a new millionaire every day for the next 15 years, buy enough petrol to drive a Mini to the sun and back 7000 times or rent a video for every person in the UK every month for 2 years. At the same time, around £2 billion of tax credits are going unclaimed either because families do not realise they are entitled to them or they find the forms too difficult or time-consuming to complete. (source: IFA Promotion, www.taketaxaction.co.uk)

Section 52 • Council tax

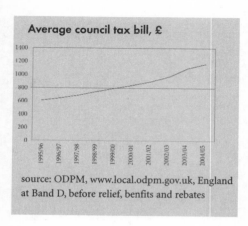

Average council tax bill, £

source: ODPM, www.local.odpm.gov.uk, England at Band D, before relief, benfits and rebates

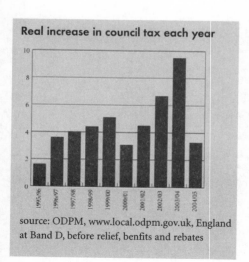

Real increase in council tax each year

source: ODPM, www.local.odpm.gov.uk, England at Band D, before relief, benfits and rebates

Council tax bills have risen sharply in recent years – by 70% since 1997/98 in England. Between 1997 and 2004, five counties have suffered cumulative increases above 90%: Devon, Norfolk, Cambridge, North Yorkshire and Worcestershire. The fear of anticipated rises in 2005 leading to some counties seeing their tax bills double since 1997 prompted the Chancellor to make a £1billion subsidy available as part of his pre-Budget report in Decmber 2004.

Normally, changes over time or differences between councils are analysed using the Band D council tax for a two adult dwelling. This ensures a like for like comparison is being made as the mix of dwellings by value – and it is value that determines the council tax bands – will differ from one authority to another.

All categories of local authorities – the London boroughs, metropolitan districts, unitary authorities and shire districts – in aggregate, and most regions, have broadly similar levels of council tax, between £1,100 and £1,200. The highest council tax in Britain is £1,294 in Sedgefield local authority, the Prime Minister's constituency. The average for inner London is lower than elsewhere as Westminster and Wandsworth – the two authorities with the lowest levels of council tax at just over £600 – bring down the average. The average council tax per dwelling in England was £967 in 2004/05, somewhat below the average for the Band D dwelling. (source: www.local.odpm.gov.uk)

Council tax has risen in recent years as the proportion of total local authority expenditure met by government grants has fallen. The 61% of the spending of local authorities in England and Wales met by government grants in 1998/99, had fallen to 58% by 2002/03, with non-domestic rates and especially council tax taking the strain. In the eight years since 1997/98, the real increase (i.e. the rise above the rate of inflation) in Band D council tax in England has been between 3% and 10%. When council tax was introduced in 1993/94 it financed 21% of local government "revenue" expenditure (or about 15% of total expenditure – note comparisons of ratios are tricky as expenditure can be measured in different ways: revenue, total or

Why has council tax increased so sharply in recent years?

The increases were caused by two principal factors. First, spending by councils went up by more than had been allowed for in the grant settlement. Second, the effect of the grant regime – whereby 75% of funding comes from central government – means that each 1% that councils add to spending above amounts allowed for in the grant settlement, increases council tax by 4%. The causes of increased spending by councils included: cost pressures such as pay and price increases, increases in national insurance contributions and pension costs; additional demand pressures, including, for example, the need to provide social services to increasing numbers of elderly people; national policy priorities, such as the requirement to increase funding for schools by an amount determined by government or to meet national waste recycling targets; and, local policy priorities, such as additional spending on highways. (Source: www.audit-commission.gov.uk)

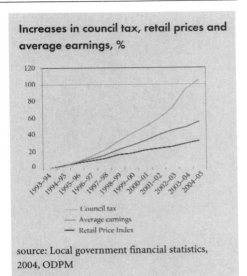

Increases in council tax, retail prices and average earnings, %

source: Local government financial statistics, 2004, ODPM

current and in gross or net terms). The proportion stands at 26% in 2003/04. About 1/7 of the tax bill is funded by means-tested council tax benefit.

Local authorities gross expenditure and income was £98 billion in 2001/02 in England. After deducting sales, fees, charges, receipts and other non-grant income, the overall cost to the central and local taxpayer of local authority

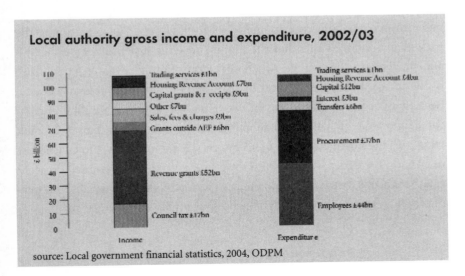

Local authority gross income and expenditure, 2002/03

source: Local government financial statistics, 2004, ODPM

Local authorities account for one quarter of the nation's public expenditure and 9% of national income

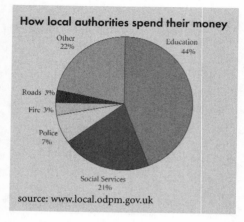

How local authorities spend their money

Other 22%
Education 44%
Roads 3%
Fire 3%
Police 7%
Social Services 21%

source: www.local.odpm.gov.uk

Problems with council tax

There have been many protests in the last couple of years from people finding higher rates of council tax increasingly hard to meet. Increases have been 6%, 8%, 13% and 6% in the last four years, considerably faster than earnings and inflation. People on low and fixed incomes, particularly pensioners, have been particularly stretched. Campaigners want the tax restructured taking into account, at least in part, ability to pay. (source: www.axethetax.org.uk) The Government has announced an inquiry into local government funding that will examine how to make the council tax system "fairer and more sustainable". The Government has already indicated that council tax should be retained but reformed and that there were strong arguments for shifting the balance of funding towards more local funding, but only if the methods for doing this were both feasible and desirable. The inquiry will take into account the revaluation, in 2007, of domestic property and report to the Deputy Prime Minister and the Chancellor by the end of 2005.

services was about £75 billion, equivalent to £1,500 per head. (source: "Local government financial statistics, 2003", www.local.odpm.gov.uk) The comparison of expenditure on particular services over time is fraught with difficulty due to changes in local government responsibilities.

There is broadly a gradient in spending per head by local authorities from the north to the south, with both revenue and capital expenditure higher in the northern regions and lower in the south. The exception to the pattern is London, which has the highest revenue expenditure per head – one-third above the average. Much of the variation in revenue expenditure is due to the difference in levels of spending on social services and police. Because of regional differences in house prices, there is a big difference in the proportion of properties in the different council tax bands in each region. In the north east, 86% of all properties are in Bands A to C, whereas in London the figure is only 44%. However the variation in council tax yield is less than this disparity would suggest, as regions with low value properties tend to have a higher average Band D council tax.

Tax collection rates

Local councils have improved their in-year council tax collection rates. In 1997/98, 95½% of "net collectable debits" were collected in England – this had risen to 96½% in 2003/04. The lowest collection rate was in inner London – at 88% – but it had risen to 92% in the latest figures.

Section 53 • Housing stock

The million pound home is almost becoming commonplace. In 2003, some 3,149 were sold in Great Britain. Although this was fractionally down on the 2002 figure, it was more than a ten-fold increase on seven years ago and looked set to be surpassed in 2004, judging by the figures for the first six months of the year. (source: Halifax, www.halifax.co.uk) Despite the rise in numbers, they account for under one half of one percent of all sales. Nine out of ten million pound sales were in the south east and two out of three in London. One-third of all £1 million plus properties were in the London boroughs of Westminster and Kensington and Chelsea.

Seven out of ten homes are owner-occupied and the proportion has edged up just fractionally over the last decade, from 66% in 1990, 68% in 1997 to 71% in 2003. Around 60% of these are being bought with the aid of a mortgage suggesting that just over 40% of the nation's households are affected by fluctuations in the mortgage rate. In the last decade the proportion of households in social rented accommodation has drifted down from 22% to 18% while that in private rented has remained stable at 10–11%. 2002 and 2003 saw the largest rises in the private rented market in the decade reflecting the rise in the buy-to-let market. (source: "Housing in England 2002/03", ODPM, and "Housing finance", number 64, Council of Mortgage Lenders, 2004)

If sales are representative of the whole housing stock, there would be around 43,000 properties worth over £1 million at mid 2004 in Great Britain

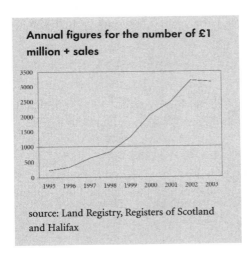

Annual figures for the number of £1 million + sales

source: Land Registry, Registers of Scotland and Halifax

Trends in tenure, %

	owner-occupier	social rented	private rented	Total, millions
1993	68	22	10	19.6
1994	69	22	10	19.8
1995	68	21	10	20.0
1996	69	21	10	19.2
1997	68	21	11	20.1
1998	69	20	11	20.3
1999	70	20	10	20.4
2000	71	19	10	20.6
2001	70	19	10	20.7
2002	71	19	10	20.9
2003	71	18	11	20.9

source: Survey of English Housing, www.odpm.gov.uk

The proportion of home-owners has risen from under one-quarter in 1920, to a half in 1970 and now to seven out of ten – there are nearly 15 million owner occupier households compared to 4 million fifty years ago

The number of homes has risen steadily since 1997 to 20.9 million. The 4% rise over the period reflects a rise of 8% in owner-occupied homes and a 10% fall in social rented homes. The number of homes rented from councils has fallen even faster as the number of housing association homes has risen. The housing shortage has not been helped by the reduction in the net growth of new homes each year. There have been an average of nearly 20,000 fewer homes added to the stock in each of the last three years than in the three years before due to reduced new completions and an increase in demolitions.

Dwelling stock: estimated annual gains and losses, Thousands of dwellings

	1993/94	1994/95	1995/96	1996/97	1997/98	1998/99	1999/00	2000/01	2001/02	2002/03
Gains to dwelling stock:										
Housebuilding completions	147.7	158.0	154.6	146.2	149.6	138.6	141.8	133.7	130.1	137.9
Conversions (net gain)1	7.5	9.9	8.9	8.6	2.8	4.2	3.5	2.8	5.1	3.8
Change of Use	..	..	..	..	11.6	15.9	13.9	9.2	14.8	16.2
Non-permanent dwellings additions	..	..	..	..	0.2	0.2	0.3	0.3	0.3	0.7
Losses from dwelling stock:										
Slum Clearance (non LA owned dwelling demolished)	3.9	3.0	2.7	2.9	1.3	1.3	1.4	1.7	1.6	1.2
Other Demolitions	5.2	5.8	4.8	4.1	12.8	13.2	15.8	18.3	24.7	22.0
Change of Use	..	..	..	..	0.7	1.4	0.8	0.7	0.8	1.2
Non-permanent dwellings losses	..	..	..	..	0.1	0.2	0.1	0.3	0.3	0.2
Net gain in year	146.2	159.0	156.0	147.8	149.3	143.0	141.3	125.0	122.8	134.0

source: ww.odpm.gov.uk

Different types of families tend to live in different types of accommodation. Nearly three-quarters of couples with dependent children are in homes they are buying with a mortgage, compared to just one-quarter of single people. Single people are over-represented in the renting groups – renting more than average from both social and private landlords. In contrast, couples without children are over-represented among owner-occupiers. "Other multi-person households", mainly students and young professionals, is the group most likely to be renting privately, especially furnished properties.

Household type by tenure, England 2002/03

	Couple, no dependent children	Couple, dependent children	Lone parent, dependent children	Other multi-person household	All one person households	Total %
Owned outright	42	8	6	27	35	29
Buying with a mortgage	41	73	31	27	24	42
All owners	83	81	37	54	60	71
Rented from:						
Council	6	8	32	13	18	12
RSL	3	5	16	5	9	6
All social rented sector tenants	9	12	47	19	27	18
Rented privately:						
Unfurnished	6	6	14	12	9	8
Furnished	1	1	2	15	3	3
All rented privately	8	7	16	27	13	11

source: ww.odpm.gov.uk

People who own their homes outright tend to have lived in them for a long time – three-quarters have lived there for over 10 years. In contrast, four out of five private sector furnished renters have moved within the last three years.

Most people are satisfied – 48% very satisfied and 37% fairly satisfied – with the area in which they live. Only 3% are very dissatisfied. The most commonly reported problem is crime closely followed by traffic, in turn followed by vandalism and litter and rubbish.

Since 1997, buying a home with a mortgage has become less affordable. For all mortgage holders, the mortgage payments amount to just 13% of gross income in 2001/02. But for the lowest fifth of earners the payments are 28% of gross income, up from a low of 22% in 1996/97. Nearly one third, 29%, of households currently buying on a mortgage have increased the amount borrowed since the property was purchased.

The supposed desire of the English to have a garden is borne out by the data that shows 85% of households have access to one. Only 9% have no access to any outside space – a balcony, yard or garden. Access to outside space is much higher for owner-occupiers. 64% of households have double glazing in all windows and a further 14% have double glazing in some windows. One third of all households have no private parking facilities

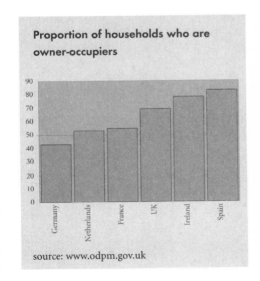

Proportion of households who are owner-occupiers

source: www.odpm.gov.uk

Length of residence by tenure

A: less than 3 years
B: more than 10 years

	A	B
Owned outright	8	76
Buying with a mortgage	27	37
All owners	20	54
Rented from:		
council	25	45
RSL	32	29
All social rented	27	40
Rented privately:		
unfurnished	62	18
furnished	80	6
All rented privately	66	15
All tenures	25	46

source: Labour Force Survey 2003 and the
Survey of English Housing 2002/03.

The most common names for houses in the UK are The Cottage, Rose Cottage and The Bungalow

available to them – yet just over one third of households who do not currently need private parking have it nonetheless. Nearly nine out of ten households are able to park in the street near their accommodation. 83% of households had no parking restrictions in their street.

Access to outside space by tenure, % 2001/02

	owner-occupier	social rented	private rented	Total
Garden	92	69	62	85
Patio or yard	4	4	13	5
Roof terrace or large balcony	1	3	2	1
Has none of the above	3	24	24	9

source: Survey of English Housing, ODPM,

Second Homes
The Survey of English Housing estimates that there are 175,000 second homes in the country (excluding those held purely for investment reasons). It says that half of these are owned as a holiday home but one in five is a pied-a-terre for the purposes of work. The survey has reported a figure between 150,000 and 200,000 each year for the last decade – at a time when all the anecdotal information pointed to more people buying. The population census recorded a fall in the number of second homes between 1991 (240,000 homes) and 2001 (135,000) but the figures are widely thought to be unreliable. The decline could reflect more people cashing in on high property values and, in some cases, buying overseas.

There are about 860,000 empty homes in the UK, equivalent to 3.4% of the dwelling stock. Over 7½% of dwellings were empty in Burnley and Liverpool and less than ½% in the Isles of Scilly, Berwick-upon-Tweed and Cambridge. (source: www.halifax.co.uk)

Section 54 • Housing market

Are Britain's homeowners sitting on a nicely appreciating asset or is the value of what is often a family's biggest asset stagnating or falling? In the last year, as the market has turned, the various house price indices have been giving quite different messages leading to confusion that affects economic policy makers as much as individuals. The confusion is compounded by the unfortunate desire of the media to look at the latest month on month change rather than a smoothed annual rate of change. Luckily, despite the differences in the house price measures available, over a period of a few years, looking at annual rates (rather than actual price levels), the various series give a broadly consistent message.

While an Englishman's home might be his psychological castle, its economic status is ambiguous and unique. An owner-occupied home is both a "durable good" – providing a flow of rents to the owner or "services" to the occupier – and a tradable asset. Often of course, it will also be a family's largest purchase – and debt.

And when it gets down to measurement, several special characteristics of house prices make it a very difficult task. The first problem is created by the variety of the housing stock – the simple but crucial fact is that no two homes are exactly the same. While two houses in a street will usually exchange hands for a broadly similar amount, the difference in the price achieved can sometimes differ by more than the whole market inflation rate in that year.

Second, the price is rarely known other than to the parties involved in the sale, with the advertised or asking price sometimes being as poor a pointer to the sale price as surveyor valuations. How can the figures allow for some sales including fixtures and fittings and others not?

Third, houses are sold infrequently. According to the Bank of England, 7% of the housing stock was sold on average each year in the 1990s. This is equivalent to each home being sold once every 14 years.

And what is the best way to compile an index series from raw data? A simple average of transactions in a particular period is not perfect for every use. It is useful to measure the value of turnover but that is not the

The perfect price index
The perfect index is one that includes only completed transactions at the right price, is timely and is adjusted both for seasonal variations and changes in the mix of housing bought and sold.

Lending for home purchase, £bn

source: "Housing Finance", ww.cml.org.uk

2003 was the first year since the late 1980s in which fewer than one in a thousand homes were repossessed for mortgage arrears

same as the total value of the housing stock or the price of a representative house. Finally, mix adjusted or constant quality measures, which try to standardise information to make it easier to compare prices over time, are not easy to calculate and are rarely transparent. The different methodologies – hedonic regression, mix adjusting and repeat sales – can give very different results.

Close scrutiny of the various measures available rapidly shows that they are all measuring subtly different things over slightly different time periods. In a competitive field, the indices that have come closest to giving a definitive picture in recent years are those from the Office of the Deputy Prime Minister (ODPM), the Land Registry (with monthly interpolation and forecasts made by the Financial Times) and monthly series from the mortgage lenders Halifax and Nationwide. Hometrack and Rightmove, estate agent websites, are among those who have more recently added their own measures, while both the Royal Institution of Chartered Surveyors and the House Builders Federation already produce qualitative surveys of sentiment in the market.

Civil servants have been calculating a house price index for 35 years – theirs is the longest running index in the country – but being quarterly, rather than monthly, and published some time after the period to which it related, it was not widely followed. The Treasury and Bank of England asked some years ago for a reliable official index, so that the policymakers would not be subjected to confusion when the figures from Halifax and Nationwide – certainly the two series most closely watched in the 1990s – gave conflicting messages. The ODPM, which is responsible for the government's housing policy, obliged with revamped figures after much haggling among various government departments.

None of the existing indices is perfect – each has its faults or omissions. Looking forward, the "ultimate target" of creating a house price index for England and Wales that also reflects cash purchases might be only five years away. The Land Registry's long-term plans for E-conveyancing will improve the timeliness of the data and the proposed development of a National Property Databank will allow it to be mix adjusted. Such an index could be extended to cover the whole of the UK pending the commitment of the regional administrations in Scotland and Northern Ireland. At that stage the nation will be as close to having a perfect index as possible. Until that

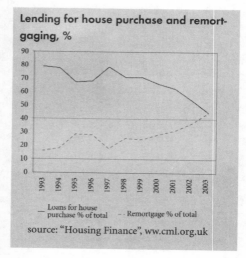

Lending for house purchase and remortgaging, %

— Loans for house purchase % of total   - - Remortgage % of total

source: "Housing Finance", ww.cml.org.uk

time – and it could be another boom and bust away – the Land Registry/FT and ODPM indices will meet most needs.

But even a perfect index is likely to show that house prices are volatile from month to month, with any sharp movements in one month usually quickly reversed. A Bank of England study concluded that "monthly changes in house price inflation do not individually contain much information about whether the medium-term inflation rate is rising or falling". Persuading the media to interpret the "perfect" index correctly might take even longer than creating the numbers in the first place. (source: www.ft.com/houseprices, www.acadametrics.co.uk, www.odpm.gov.uk, and the Bank of England Quarterly Bulletin, spring 2003, www.bankofengland.co.uk)

Two major reports were published in 2004 on the "British obsession". The Barker report on housing (source: 'Delivering stability: securing our future housing needs', March 2004) set out the background and prospects for housing and the Miles review of the mortgage market (source: "The UK mortgage market: taking a longer-term view, March 2004) made recommendations to remove obstacles to the development of a larger market for fixed interest rate mortgages. Both reports were sponsored by the Treasury and can be found on their website. (source: www.hm-treasury.gov.uk)

The Barker report said that "the UK has experienced a long-term upward trend in real house prices, 2.4% per annum over the last 30 years, creating problems of affordability. In addition, the volatility of the housing market has exacerbated problems of macroeconomic instability and has had an adverse effect on economic growth. To improve macroeconomic stability and deliver greater affordability for individuals a lower trend in house prices is desirable:"

It said that in order to deliver a trend in real house prices of 1.8% an additional 70,000 houses each year in England might be required. To bring the real price trend in line with the EU average of 1.1% an extra 120,000 houses each year might be required.

The report set out a range of policy recommendations for improving the functioning of the housing market which inlcuded: government setting a goal for improved market affordability, additional investment building-up to around £1½ billion per annum to deliver social housing to meet

Average real house price inflation, 1971–2001, %	
UK	3.3
Spain	3.3
Ireland	3.1
Netherlands	2.8
Belgium	2.1
Average	1.8
Italy	1.5
Denmark	1.3
France	1.2
Finland	0.7
Germany	0.1
Sweden	0.0

source: "Review of Housing Supply", Kate Barker (HM Treasury), 2004

House price inflation has been higher in the UK than in most other countries. Only Ireland, Spain and Netherlands came within ½% of the UK's real rate of 3.3% between 1971 and 2001

Number of mortgages, millions

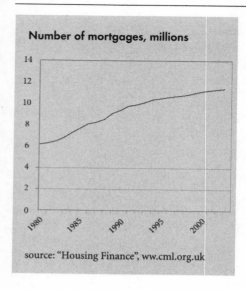

source: "Housing Finance", ww.cml.org.uk

Buy to let mortgage advances

A: Gross new advances in period (thousands)
B: Gross new advances in period (£ billons)
C: Mortgages outstanding at end of period

	A	B	C
1998	na	na	28.7
1999	44.4	3.1	73.2
2000	48.4	3.9	120.3
2001	72.2	6.9	185.0
2002	130.0	12.2	275.5
2003	187.8	19.3	408.3

source: www.cml.org.uk

projected future needs, and a range of local schemes to provide financial incentives to house building.

The number of mortgages is at a record high – 11½ million by mid 2004. The number has increased every year but at an increasingly modest rate. The growth since 1997 has been the lowest for a generation. As the population growth has been hardly any greater than the growth in the number of mortgages, the ratio of people to mortgages has been stable in the last four years and little changed since the late 1980s at around 5¼ people per mortgage. Lending for house purchase has soared in recent years. The amount lent doubled between 1997 and 2003 to £122 billion. The rate of growth is comparable with that of the mid to late 1980s.

While mortgage lending for house purchase has risen sharply, lending for buy-to-let and remortgaging have both risen more sharply. The gross new advances each year for buy-to-let properties have risen from almost nothing in the late 1990s to 190,000 advances worth nearly £20 billion in 2003. Remortgaging became as large as loans for house purchase in 2003, with both accounting for just over £120 billion in 2003 alone.

A recent Bank of England article shed light on the link between gross equity withdrawal and consumer spending, concluding that the bulk of gross withdrawals is not consumed in the near term. Those who sell a property without purchasing another one and those who trade down are more likely to pay off debt or save withdrawn equity than spend the proceeds. Remortgagors and those who obtain further secured advances are likely to spend the equity, but the Bank estimated that their equity constitutes only about a quarter of total gross withdrawals. Of those who spend equity, financing home improvements rather than purchasing consumer goods appears to be the most important use of funds – consistent with the relatively weak relationship between consumption and mortgage equity withdrawal recently observed in aggregate data. (source: "Housing equity and consumption", Bank of England QB, www.bankofengland.co.uk)

The number of new home loans fell in 2003 (from a record high in 2002) having been broadly stable between 1.1 million and 1.4 million since 1997. Yet the proportion that is first time buyers has fallen from above a half to under one-third. Affordability for all buyers has deteriorated sharply since 2001.

The number of mortgages in arrears and the number of possessions has fallen sharply during the last decade. The number of mortgage possession actions entered (and not all orders result in the issue and execution of warrants of possession) was at a high in 1998 but then fell steadily, rising in 2003. (source: Department of Constitutional Affairs, www.dca.gov.uk)

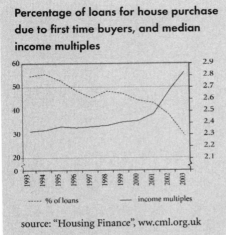

Percentage of loans for house purchase due to first time buyers, and median income multiples

source: "Housing Finance", ww.cml.org.uk

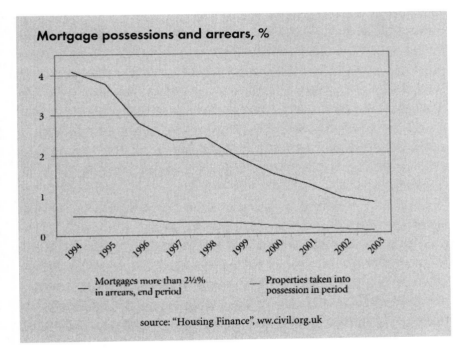

Mortgage possessions and arrears, %

— Mortgages more than 2½% in arrears, end period

— Properties taken into possession in period

source: "Housing Finance", ww.civil.org.uk

Section 55 • Saving, debt and borrowing

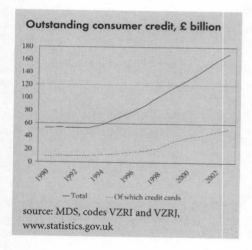

Loans secured on dwellings, £ billion

source: "Economic trends", code AMWT, www.statistics.gov.uk

Outstanding consumer credit, £ billion

— Total   --- Of which credit cards

source: MDS, codes VZRI and VZRJ, www.statistics.gov.uk

Over 1,600 different credit cards are available in Britain

It has been widely reported that Britain is in the grip of a "credit binge" – total UK personal debt broke through the £1 trillion (£1,000,000,000,000) barrier in July 2004 and is still rising. The amount of personal debt is increasing by £1 million every four minutes, having risen by 13% in the last year. (source: www.creditaction.org.uk)

The bulk of this borrowing is made up of mortgages – total secured lending on homes was £867 billion by the final quarter of 2004 – and consumer credit to individuals – some £183 billion in November 2004. This points to an average household debt in the UK of approximately £7,500 (excluding mortgages) and £43,000 (including mortgages), nearly £18,000 per person. A little over half of the mortgage debt and about one sixth of the credit card debt is held by British banks (source: www.bba.org.uk), with building societies, foreign banks and other lenders accounting for the remainder.

The rapid rise in debt, which now equates to about 140% of annual incomes, compared to just over 100% a decade ago, is a concern to government policy-makers and the Bank of England for two reasons – any adverse economic shocks such as increasing unemployment or higher interest rates would make it harder for people to meet their debt repayments, affecting the economy and the outlook for monetary policy, and should an increasing proportion of borrowers fail to repay that debt there could be an impact on financial stability. (source: www.bankofengland.co.uk) The rate of growth of consumer credit seems to have slowed in 2003, but the amount of credit continues to grow.

There are around 60 million credit cards in the UK and two thirds of adults have at least one card. The UK has more credit cards in circulation than any other country in Western Europe, having overtaken Germany to become the most card intensive country in Europe. The UK accounts for 40% of the £500 billion credit market in the EU. The number of plastic cards in issue has reached 160 million meaning the average adult now has nearly four plastic cards. (source: "The consumer credit market in the 21st century", December 2003, www.dti.gov.uk and Datamonitor)

While most people who have taken out credit have an agreeable experience, roughly one in five has some difficulty and one in twenty experiences serious over indebtedness. Over indebtedness is a phrase used for households which spend more than 25% of their annual income repaying consumer credit (a situation that 5% find themselves in) or spend 50% of their annual income repaying consumer credit and mortgage debt (6%). Those people that have some difficulty with debt repayments are spread fairly evenly across society, but serious over indebtedness is predominantly a problem for the less well-heeled in the lower social categories. (source: "Taskforce on tackling over indebtedness", second report, 2003, www.dti.gov.uk)

Between 1 and 4% of credit card customers are thought to be in severe financial difficulties suggesting that around 500,000 people have balances which they are struggling to pay off. The level of interest rates charged on different credit cards varies dramatically, with APRs on credit cards found to be available in one study in the range of 7% to 30%. There were other cards marketed to low-income groups that had APRs approaching 40–50%. One in five people are borrowing money just to pay household bills, and one in four are struggling to meet bills and credit repayments. Six million families are already struggling to keep up with credit commitments at a time when borrowing is rising. (source: "Transparency of credit card charges", Treasury committee, House of Commons, December 2003, www.parlaiment.uk and National Consumer Council, www.ncc.org.uk)

A survey of clients of the Citizens Advice Bureau, the national problem-solving charity, revealed that the three main reasons for suffering debt problems, were: a sudden change in personal circumstances – resulting typically from job loss, relationship breakdown or illness; low income – the consequences of living for a long time on a low level of income; and over-commitment. The CAB bureaux dealt with nearly 1.1 million debt-related issues in 2003/04, a figure that includes housing and utilities-related debts. But the CAB said that consumer debt is by far the biggest type of debt problem for which people come for help, and it is increasing more than other debt problems. (source: October 2004, www.citizensadvice.org.uk)

The amount of debt being chased by Britain's bailiffs has soared by 70% over the past two years to a record £5 billion. The typical household falling into difficulty owes £25,000, spread across an average of 15 different

The average family accumulates 18% of their annual borrowing in December by spending twice as much than in any other month of the year (British Retail Consortium)

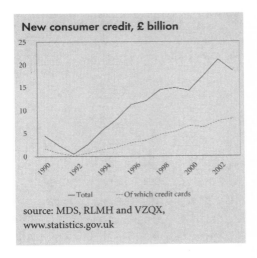

New consumer credit, £ billion

— Total   ---- Of which credit cards

source: MDS, RLMH and VZQX, www.statistics.gov.uk

246 plastic transactions took place every second in the UK in 2003

Participation rates in unsecured debt, %

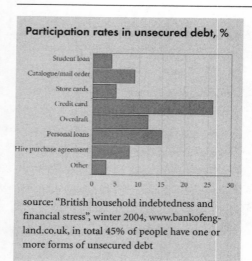

source: "British household indebtedness and financial stress", winter 2004, www.bankofengland.co.uk, in total 45% of people have one or more forms of unsecured debt

The average loan given out by a pawnbroker is £100 and 85% are redeemed within the statutory six-month period (www.dti.gov.uk)

3 million households do not have a current account. "Despite the introduction of the Basic Bank Account in 1999 the number of households operating outside the financial mainstream has not fallen significantly" – Budget 2004

Financial ignorance

A large minority of the population has little knowledge of basic financial concepts. Nearly four out of five people do not know that APR refers to the interest and other costs of a loan, four in ten admit they do not understand mortgages or ISAs, and a third lack confidence in their financial affairs. One in five did not understand the concept of inflation. Nearly a third did not know that insurance products are designed to protect their owners from unforeseen events. Only 30% could calculate 4% on £2,000 over two years. (source: by Mori for the Institute of Financial Services, www.ifslearning.com)

lenders. 20 million cases have been passed to debt collectors over the past year. (source: www.creditaction.org.uk) Graduates in 2004 owed £12,200 on average, an increase of £4,000 on 2003, a rise from £3,700 over five years. (source: "Money matters survey", 2004, www.natwest.com)

A large proportion of the population has no savings. The government's Family Resources Survey shows that over half of the households in Britain have less than £1,500 in savings and over half of those have no savings at all. There is always a question mark over the quality of these estimates as many people prefer not to reveal such details, but the overall message remains clear. Households with children have much lower levels of savings than the average. This is perfectly understandable as the costs of bringing up children eat into disposable incomes and many families find that there is little if any money left over to save. At the more prosperous end of society, the figures suggest that only 18% of couples with children have savings of over £10,000, compared to 29% of couples without children and 43% of pensioner couples. The position is even worse for single people with children, as only about 3% are estimated to have savings of more than £10,000. (source: www.dwp.gov.uk/asd/frs)

In recent years the government has offered tax incentives to encourage saving. Personal equity plans (PEPs), started in 1987, ran until 1999. They allowed people to invest in equities tax-free, subject to a subscription limit of £2,400 in the first year, rising to £6,000 in 1990. During the scheme's lifetime, £69 billion had been invested in 20 million accounts. Tax exempt special savings accounts (TESSAs) were established in 1991 and operated until 1999 at which point £30 billion was invested in 5.4 million accounts. They allowed up to £9,000 to be saved over five years and all interest earned was tax-free provided the savings were left in the accounts for five years.

The Labour government replaced both of these schemes with individual savings accounts (ISAs). These schemes, building on the experience of TESSAs and PEPs, included three components: cash, stocks and shares, and life insurance. The annual subscription limit is £7,000, of which no more than £3,000 can go into cash. By September 2004, after 5½ years of operation, £126 billion had been saved in ISAs. (source: www.inlandrevenue.gov.uk)

Popularity of savings vehicles %

A: UK
B; highest region
C: lowest region

	A	B	C
Current account	88	93	78
Other account	32	39	19
Tessa	8	11	6
ISA	32	39	19
Stocks and shares	24	32	15
PEP	9	11	5
Unit trust	5	7	3
Premium bonds	23	32	5

source: www.dwp.gov.uk/asd/frs, in most cases the region of highest ownership is the south east and the lowest is Northern Ireland

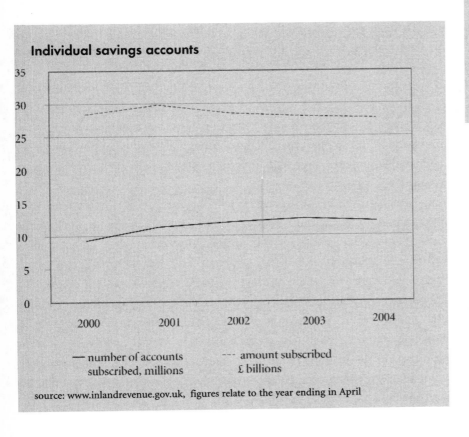

Individual savings accounts

— number of accounts subscribed, millions   --- amount subscribed £ billions

source: www.inlandrevenue.gov.uk, figures relate to the year ending in April

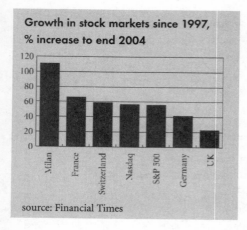

Growth in stock markets since 1997, % increase to end 2004

source: Financial Times

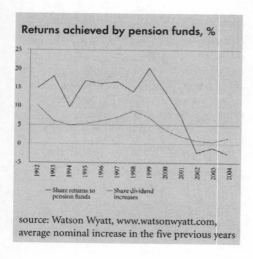

Returns achieved by pension funds, %

— Share returns to pension funds   — Share dividend increases

source: Watson Wyatt, www.watsonwyatt.com, average nominal increase in the five previous years

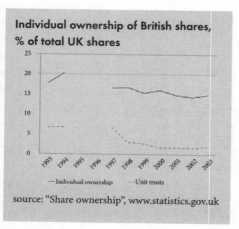

Individual ownership of British shares, % of total UK shares

—Individual ownership   Unit trusts

source: "Share ownership", www.statistics.gov.uk

Section 56 • Investments

The equity market has performed less well in the UK since 1997 than in most other countries – both the FTSE 100 and FTSE all share indices have been outperformed by the German, French, Swiss, Spanish and Italian markets in Europe as well as the Nasdaq and S&P 500 in America. In the last eight years the American market (S&P 500) has risen by 56% and the European market (FTSE Eurofirst 300) by 44%, compared to just 23% rise in the FTSE 100. The rise in the UK market is barely above the cumulative inflation rate, pointing to negligible rural growth over the period.

The explanation for the relative poor performance of the UK probably reflects a combination of: the removal of tax credits for pension funds, the weakness of the dollar and the damage to profits and earnings on the back of new regulation and extra taxation (including the £5 billion windfall tax on privatised utilities to pay for the New Deal). The estimated cost of new regulations is several times greater than the benefits to companies from the cut in the corporation tax rates. Some members of the government have also shown hostility to business, particularly criticising profits when they are deemed to be too high and launching campaigns against what has been said to be a "rip off Britain".

It is very hard to measure accurately the impact of new regulation on business but three organisations – the British Chamber of Commerce, the Institute of Directors and the Confederation of British Industries – have all made some effort. The British Chamber of Commerce lists over 30 different measures introduced since 1997 with an annual recurring cost of around £7 billion. The most expensive single item has been the Working Time Directive, accounting for around one third of the total cost, but other regulations concern parental leave, trade union recognition, works councils, tribunals, and the administration costs of the working families tax credits, student loans, data protection, disability discrimination regulations and stakeholder pensions. Tax increases and the national minimum wage also added to business costs. (source: "The stock market under Labour", CPS, www.cps.org.uk, 2004)

The returns made on the investments linked to interest rates have also been lower in recent years. Although low short-term interest rates are

Who owns British shares?

Individuals directly own less than 15% of UK shares - valued at £204 billion at the end of 2003. This proportion has declined steadily over many years – in the 1960s, individuals owned over half of the market. Individuals also directly own most of the shares held by unit trusts – accounting for a further 2% of ownership. Nearly one third of the market is owned by overseas investors. Insurance companies and pension funds each own between 15% and 20%.

widely perceived to be a good thing – businesses and individuals can borrow more freely – they are, of course, damaging for those people who have savings in bank and building society accounts. The nominal return on short term fixed interest products fell to just 4½% in 2003, the lowest in modern times. The nominal returns to savers were well over double that in the early 1990s. Real returns – that is after adjusting for inflation – are also sharply down on a decade before. The returns on long-term fixed interest investments, based on the FTSE over 15 year gilt index, have been even more disappointing. Following two very good years in 1997 and 1998, returns have been persistently low. Even though there were bad years from time to time in the past, it is rare to see several years of such low returns – as reflected in the five-year moving average.

The cumulative impact of these low figures means that pension funds achieved an average return in the three years from 2001 to 2003 of barely 2½%, compared to the three year average of over 10% at any point in the previous two decades.

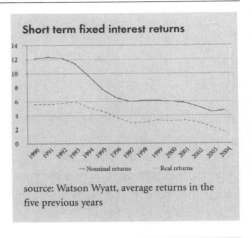

Short term fixed interest returns

source: Watson Wyatt, average returns in the five previous years

Long term fixed interest returns

source: Watson Wyatt, based on the FTSE over 15 year gilt index

Britain's biggest companies at the end of 2004

	Market value £billion
BP	108.7
HSBC	100.5
Vodafone	93.7
Glaxosmithkline	72.7
Royal Bank of Scotland	55.6
Shell	42.6
Barclays	38.1
HBOS	33.6
Astrazenaca	31.4
Lloyds TSB	26.7

source: FT

Section 57 • **Rich and poor**

> Of the households with a monthly income of over £1000, two-fifths live in London and the south east and just one in 50 households in each of the north east, Wales and Northern Ireland
>
> source: Family Resources Survey, 2002/03

Income by percentile, £ per annum

percentile	pre-tax	post-tax
1st	4,800	4,800
5th	5,800	5,700
10th	6,900	6,700
50th (median)	15,500	13,600
90th	36,200	30,000
95th	49,200	38,000
top	107,100	74,300

source: Inland Revenue Statistics and House of Commons research paper, 04/70, September 2004.

The terms income and wealth are often used interchangeably yet are very distinct concepts. Income represents the flow of resources over a period, received either in cash or kind. Wealth on the other hand describes the ownership of assets valued at a particular point in time. There are significant practical difficulties in measuring wealth and this is reflected in the paucity of statistics. The Office for National Statistics has launched a new survey on the topic but results will not be available for several years.

Similarly, the terms earnings and income are often used interchangeably, but earnings refer to one aspect of an income stream, that received from paid work. There are other sources of income, such as that from savings and investments, benefits and pensions. Earnings account for the majority of most people's income, with 93% of total income received by those paying income tax being earned income. However, income from investments is disproportionately received by those higher up the income distribution, so its inclusion is important when looking at distributions and inequality.

There are many ways of defining income – it can be gross or net, that is after taxes, benefits and credits have been taken into account. Income data can be presented at different stages of redistribution, from original income, through the addition of cash benefits and deduction of direct and indirect taxes, to final income. Sometimes household income data include the income of non-profit institutions serving households – the ONS has agreed to separate out such income, starting in 2005. Each measure has strengths and weaknesses and no single measure is necessarily correct or incorrect. But the different measures will often tell different stories.

Most of the income data are derived from two large social surveys run by the Office for National Statistics – the expenditure and food survey and the family resources survey. There are some key differences between the surveys so the results from the two are not comparable. A quality review of income statistics, conducted by the ONS, assessed the nine official income-related surveys and recommended greater harmonisation between them.

Most measures of income inequality show a broadly flat trend over the last decade though on some measures income inequality in Britain is now higher (fractionally) than at any time in the previous 18 years of Conservative rule. The latest figures relate to 2002/03 and in some cases show a reduction in inequality compared to 2001/02. Data for later years will be needed to ascertain whether this is the start of a new trend. The persistently high inequality reflects income changes at both extremes – at the very top end incomes have risen rapidly, and at the bottom, incomes have grown very slowly, possibly due to non-take-up of means tested benefits or an increase in the number of people whose incomes are temporarily low. (source: "The effect of taxes and benefits on household income", ONS, May 2004, and "Poverty and inequality in Britain: 2004", IFS, commentary 96)

> For a decade, four out of five adults have seen the gap between rich and poor as too large. Yet only two out of five feel that the government should redistribute from richer to poorer people
>
> source: British social attitudes survey, NCSR, 2004

Measuring inequality

The Gini coefficient is the most widely used indicator of income inequality, although there are a number of other measures. It summarises the overall deviation from equality in a given income distribution into a single figure. Gini coefficients are commonly expressed as a percentage between 0 and 100, rising with increasing inequality: 0% representing complete equality and 100% representing complete inequality. Gini coefficients have the advantage of simplicity - expressing inequality in a single number - but they are often supplemented by alternative or additional measures of inequality, such as income ratios. Income ratios compare two different points in a given income distribution. For example, one might compare incomes at the bottom of the upper decile (top 10%) of the income distribution with those at the top of the lowest decile (bottom 10%), or the ratio of the 90th percentile compared with the 10th percentile. These measures have the advantage of being unaffected by extreme values at either end of the income distribution, which in any case are thought to be measured less accurately in the surveys.

Separate figures are available from the Inland Revenue showing the distribution of income tax payers. Between 1996/97 and 2004/05 (projections), the share of total income tax liabilities of the top 10% rose by three percentage points, while the lower 90% of the distribution saw their share of total liabilities fall.

There are very limited figures available measuring wealth and those that do exist are of questionable value. The Inland Revenue publishes figures

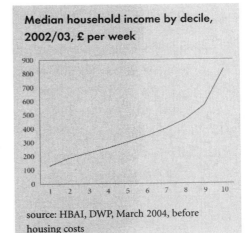

Median household income by decile, 2002/03, £ per week

source: HBAI, DWP, March 2004, before housing costs

The wealthiest 1% of adults own nearly one quarter of the wealth, the richest quarter own three-quarters of the wealth and the richest half own 95% of the wealth

Percentage shares of equivalised total original and disposable incomes by quintile groups for all households

	93-94	97-98	02-03
Original income			
Bottom	2	2	3
2nd	6	7	7
3rd	14	15	15
4th	25	25	25
Top	52	51	50
Disposable income			
Bottom	8	8	8
2nd	12	12	12
3rd	16	16	17
4th	23	23	23
Top	42	42	41

source: Economic Trends, June 2004

The poorest fifth of the population earns just one 40th of the income

based on the value of estates at the time of death which suggest that the richest quarter owns three quarters of the wealth. If dwellings are excluded, then the value of marketable wealth is even more concentrated amongst the wealthy – the top 1% owned about one third of the wealth and the top 10% own nearly three quarters. The strength of the housing market in recent years has caused a greater gap to open up between those with some wealth and those without. Wealth is far more unevenly distributed than income – the Gini coefficient of 70% for wealth is as much as double that for income (depending on which measure is chosen).

The last decade has seen more stability – "no consistent trend" in the words of the ONS – than the previous decade in terms of income distribution. The figures show that the top one-fifth of earners have maintained their share – just over a half – of original pre-tax incomes (excluding benefits) for well over a decade. The proportion has been between 50% and 52% every year since 1990, having risen sharply during the 1980s from 44% in 1980. There was a drop in the proportion in 2002/03 to 50%, the latest year for which data are available, which might point to a decline in the future. The bottom one-fifth has had 2 or 3% of original income every year since 1980. (source: "The effects of taxes and benefits on household income", ONS 'Economic Trends', June 2004, www.statistics.gov.uk)

A similar pattern – though at less dramatic levels – is shown for gross income (earnings plus benefits), disposable income and post-tax (excluding indirect taxes) income. For disposable incomes, the top one-fifth have 43% in 2002/03 compared to 8% for the bottom fifth.

Generally households in the top half of the income distribution pay more in taxes than they receive in benefits, and the reverse is true for those in the lower half of the distribution so that the net effect of taxes and benefits is to reduce the differences between households. In 2002/03, the top fifth of households had an original income of around £60,300, roughly 15 times as much as the £4,000 average of those in the bottom fifth. In the two previous years the ratio was larger – more unequal – 18 to 1. After taking account of taxes and benefits, the ratio falls to 4 to 1.

Cash benefits play the largest part in the redistribution. Direct taxes except council tax also redistribute. Although the households on higher incomes spend absolutely more on council tax, it represents a lower proportion of income. Indirect taxes on the other hand are regressive, taking a

The effects of taxes and benefits by quintile groups on all households (with ratio of top/bottom households), 2002/03

	Bottom	2nd	3rd	4th	Top	All	Ratio
Income, taxes and benefits per household (£ per year)							
Original income	4 030	9 610	19 320	33 080	60 310	25 270	15
plus cash benefits	5 640	6 010	4 250	2 500	1 390	3 960	0
Gross income	9 670	15 630	23 560	35 580	61 700	29 230	6
less direct taxes and employees' NIC	910	1 900	4 000	7 270	14 650	5 750	16
Disposable income	8 760	13 730	19 570	28 310	47 050	23 480	5
less indirect taxes	2 750	3 140	4 180	5 340	6 990	4 480	3
Post-tax income	6 010	10 590	15 390	22 970	40 060	19 000	7
plus benefits in kind	5 700	4 960	4 370	3 970	3 070	4 410	1
Final income	11 710	15 550	19 750	26 940	43 130	23 410	4

source: Economic Trends, June 2004

higher proportion of income from those on lower incomes as the higher earners channel more of the their income into savings and mortgage payments which do not attract tax. The proportion of income of the lower earners consumed by indirect taxes is exaggerated by the fact that the group's recorded spending is invariably above its recorded incomes – pointing to, among other factors, income from black market or 'informal economy' activities, borrowing to finance expenditure, the consumption of savings, and the use of severance payments or inheritance tax receipts which are not recorded in the survey. The higher income groups do pay more in indirect taxes in cash terms – £7,000 per annum compared to £2,750 for the lowest fifth. The receipt of benefits in kind – such as state provided education and health – also fall as income rises, adding to the redistribution.

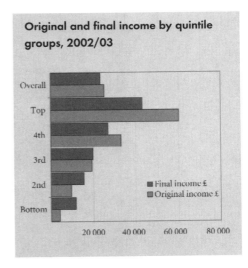

Original and final income by quintile groups, 2002/03

Income tax is the most progressive tax – the lowest paid fifth pay under 4% of incomes in tax compared to 18% for the top earning fifth. Yet the position looks different in cash terms – of the total income tax paid, the lowest two quintiles pay about 7% while the top two pay 81%. The proportion of national insurance paid rises to the fourth quintile when the earnings cap comes into play. While lower income groups typically pay half as much council tax as the top earners, they pay three times as much proportionately.

What is equivalisation?

Many figures relating to incomes are on the basis of equivalised income – adjusted to take into account the size and composition of households. This means that a larger household will be lower down the income distribution than a smaller one with the same absolute income. It means that a particular level of equivalised income equates to different actual income levels depending on household composition. Hence in 2002, 60% of median household income before housing costs was equivalent to £187 per week for a couple with no children, £140 per week for a single adults, and £273 per week for a couple with two school-age children. The ONS figures are thought to be quite reliable though there is always a question mark over the accuracy of some numbers, such as those for the recorded incomes of the self-employed, and definitions, for example, of what constitutes a household. When looking at figures, check to see if they include all households, some might exclude pensioners for example.

Taxes as a percentage of gross income for all households by quintile groups, 2002/03

	Bottom	2nd	3rd	4th	Top	All
Direct taxes						
Income tax	3.5	6.3	10.3	13.4	18.3	13.5
Employees' NIC	1.3	2.5	3.8	4.7	3.9	3.8
Council tax & Northern Ireland rates	4.6	3.4	2.9	2.3	1.6	2.4
All direct taxes	9.5	12.2	17.0	20.4	23.7	19.7
Indirect taxes						
VAT	10.7	7.8	7.2	6.3	5.0	6.4
Duty on alcohol	1.6	1.0	1.1	0.9	0.7	0.9
Duty on tobacco	3.2	2.2	1.4	0.8	0.4	1.0
Duty on hydrocarbon oils & Vehicle excise duty	3.2	2.3	2.3	2.1	1.4	1.9
Other indirect taxes	9.8	6.8	5.8	4.8	3.8	5.1
All indirect taxes	28.5	20.1	17.7	15.0	11.3	15.3
All taxes	37.9	32.2	34.7	35.5	35.1	35.0

Average incomes, taxes and benefits by quintile groups of all households, 2002/03

	Bottom	2nd	3rd	4th	Top	All
Average per household (£ per year)						
Quintile points (equivalised £)		11 196	15 516	20 860	29 575	
Original income						
Wages and salaries	2 451	7 054	14 915	26 647	45 273	19 268
Imputed income from benefits in kind	13	34	105	365	1 107	325
Self-employment income	584	659	1 326	2 385	7 150	2 421
Occupational pensions, annuities	584	1 362	2 200	2 531	3 696	2 075
Investment income	235	357	550	909	2 836	978
Other income	165	146	218	247	250	205
Total	4 032	9 613	19 315	33 084	60 312	25 271
Direct benefits in cash						
Contributory						
Retirement pension	2 090	2 666	1 859	1 271	734	1 724
Job seeker's allowance	57	14	22	6	6	21
Incapacity benefit	334	371	277	88	49	224
Widows' benefits	33	22	44	29	69	39
Statutory Maternity Pay/Allowance	2	5	13	28	69	23
Non-contributory						
Income support	1 035	653	391	144	5	446
Child benefit	480	395	373	353	245	369
Housing benefit	745	757	338	99	1	388
Job seeker's allowance (Income based)	164	26	23	2	2	43
Invalid care allowance	40	72	41	8	3	33
Attendance allowance	36	136	142	31	7	71
Disability living allowance	158	366	365	157	53	220
Disabled Persons Tax Credit	1	8	3	-	7	4
War pensions/War widows' pensions	5	17	45	48	20	27
Severe disablement allowance	21	14	42	38	6	24
Industrial injury disablement benefit	24	24	13	35	14	22
Student support	38	72	33	43	56	48
Government training schemes	16	12	4	6	1	8
Working Families Tax Credit	256	275	147	64	18	152
Other non-contributory benefits	106	105	71	49	24	71
Total cash benefits	5 640	6 013	4 247	2 498	1 390	3 958
Gross income	9 673	15 625	23 563	35 581	61 702	29 229
Direct taxes and Employees' NIC						
Income tax	343	980	2 432	4 765	11 286	3 961
less: Tax relief at source[1]	3	3	4	4	8	4
Employees' NI contributions	130	395	894	1 677	2 408	1 101
Council tax and Northern Ireland rates[2]	681	701	752	852	967	791
less: Council tax benefit/Rates rebates	238	174	77	20	4	103
Total	914	1 899	3 997	7 270	14 650	5 746
Disposable income	8 759	13 726	19 566	28 311	47 052	23 483
Equivalised disposable income	8 314	13 233	18 111	24 816	45 024	21 899
Indirect taxes						
Taxes on final goods and services						
VAT	1 032	1 215	1 688	2 245	3 102	1 856
Duty on tobacco	312	338	324	296	249	304
Duty on beer and cider	67	78	117	156	163	116
Duty on wines & spirits	86	83	142	181	263	151
Duty on hydrocarbon oils	241	280	409	591	693	443
Vehicle excise duty	69	85	125	165	189	127
Television licences	83	82	93	101	105	93
Stamp duty on house purchase	42	43	74	121	273	111
Customs duties	17	19	25	31	42	27
Betting taxes	41	46	61	55	49	50
Insurance premium tax	23	28	42	57	79	46
Air passenger duty	7	13	21	29	43	23
Camelot National Lottery Fund	43	54	62	68	48	55
Other	12	8	17	13	39	18
Intermediate taxes						
Commercial and industrial rates	164	186	238	300	402	258
Employers' NI contributions	240	271	347	437	585	376
Duty on hydrocarbon oils	109	124	158	199	266	171
Vehicle excise duty	22	25	32	40	54	34
Other	142	161	206	259	347	223
Total indirect taxes	2 752	3 139	4 180	5 345	6 990	4 481
Post-tax income	6 006	10 587	15 386	22 967	40 063	19 002
Benefits in kind						
Education	2 496	1 766	1 623	1 521	848	1 651
National health service	2 978	3 029	2 635	2 363	2 117	2 625
Housing subsidy	80	74	43	20	2	44
Rail travel subsidy	12	12	14	30	63	26
Bus travel subsidy	54	53	42	38	35	44
School meals and welfare milk	79	27	9	2	0	23
Total	5 699	4 961	4 367	3 975	3 065	4 413
Final income	11 705	15 548	19 752	26 941	43 128	23 415

1 On life assurance premiums.
2 Council tax and Northern Ireland rates after deducting discounts.

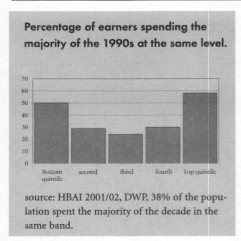

Percentage of earners spending the majority of the 1990s at the same level.

source: HBAI 2001/02, DWP, 38% of the population spent the majority of the decade in the same band.

Nearly half of all adults spent one year in poverty during the last decade

Over the medium term the income distribution displays a certain rigidity. Those with high incomes tend to keep them in the years that follow and those with the lowest tend to have difficulty rising up the scale. Half the people in the lowest 20% in 1991 we were still there a decade later. Over the ten year period from 1991 to 2000, just under a half of individuals spent at least one year and 15% spent at least five years in households with below 60% of median incomes. (source: HBAI, DWP)

A serious loss is the annual article in the ONS publication Economic Trends, showing how the tax and social security burdens in Britain compared with those in other leading countries. This has not appeared since March 1999 when the latest information still referred to the Conservatives' period in office. There is no proof, of course, that the government has suppressed this article or any of the figures that used to be published. However, the loss is a blow to the democratic accountability of policymakers.

Section 58 • **Pensions**

The Pensions Commission report, launched in October 2004 (source: "Pensions: challenges and choices", www.pensionscommission.org.uk), contained a damning summary of the quality of information available on this important topic. The report's overall conclusion was that "present data sources are significantly deficient as a basis for some aspects of evidence based policy. This is in part because they have not been designed to answer the questions we now need to consider and in part because of significant errors in past data gathering and analytical approaches. Some improvements will come on stream over the next year, but these will not transform data availability in the key areas where information is currently deficient."

Appendix A of the report covered the data adequacy issue and ran to 22 pages of detailed comments and recommendations. It said that the problems with data from the employers, schemes and administrative sources on trends in pension provision, membership and contribution rates, are "moderate". Regarding data on individual wealth and savings behaviour and on individual pension scheme participation, it said the problems were "severe".

Worst of all, the commission said that the problems associated with data for the total level of pension contributions and benefits have been "exceptionally severe", but are now being addressed by the ONS. It said that its assessment of the level of total private pension saving in the UK is "hampered by significant errors and uncertainties in National Statistics." Raw data provided by insurance companies on pension contributions includes a large element of double counting, and ONS procedures have in the past only succeeded in removing a portion of this. In addition, it said, "there are several significant methodological errors and inconsistencies in the way that ONS have been manipulating the data, introducing errors to estimates of benefits as well as contributions."

The commission said that revised figures published by the ONS in July 2004 took account of most of their concerns, but the figures in the 2004 blue book, the annual flagship publication on the economy from the ONS, still contain the errors. The commission said the results of the errors was to "hugely" overstate the figures. It said the correct figure for the annual

The Pensions Commission
The Commission was appointed by the government in December 2002 with the remit "to keep under review the regime for UK private pensions and long-term savings, and to make recommendations to the Secretary of State for Work and Pensions on whether there is a case for moving beyond the current voluntarist approach."

Data difficulties

There are particular difficulties collecting data about pensions and wealth. For a start, pensions are very complex and most people are not regularly aware of what their own pension entitlements are likely to be worth and therefore find it hard to answer the survey questions even if they wanted to. When it comes to wealth most people are unwilling to respond – at least accurately – to surveys. It seems likely that richer people in particular may not wish to participate – explaining why surveys of individual saving do not aggregate up to national institution-based totals. At the more modest level, tests have shown that when people are counting their savings they often omit some balances, such as those in non-interest-bearing accounts. It is also difficult to define debt, for example, as many people will under estimate it as they do not think, for example, of goods being paid for in instalments as debt.

contribution level to personal pensions was about £14 billion rather than the £20 billion figure in the blue book. Contributions to insurance company managed occupational schemes are around £7 billion per year, according to the commission, compared to the blue book figure of £21 billion. In aggregate this means that the ONS was over-estimating the contributions made to these two type of scheme by £600 for every working age person each year.

Some progress is being made. The Pensions Commission welcomed the work of the pension statistics task force that has been set up to improve the aggregate data, the new questions added to a survey of earnings, and the prospect of improved information from increased data sharing between government departments.

But the commission also says that the new wealth and assets survey planned by the Office of National Statistics should be a "major" priority. It needs this to support longitudinal analysis, analysis of pension rights accumulation among all age groups, analysis of the impact of inheritance on asset accumulation, linkage to administrative records and analysis of expectations and attitudes that influence savings behaviour. The ONS has started working on the trailing of the survey but no date for its launch has yet been given.

The commission also asked for:
- the employers' pension provision survey to be undertaken every two years
- additional information to be gathered on group personal pension schemes and trustee based occupational schemes
- improved coordination among government departments for research into the ageing and health debate
- improved cross departmental coordination and high-level credibility checks of information
- improved data on consumption patterns in old age and also people's attitudes and expectations

One table in the report presented the personal sector balance sheet for the end of 2003. The fact that the figures were rounded to the nearest £50 billion and given for only broad categories of assets and liabilities, indicated the data difficulties that the commission was experiencing. It shows that pension rights account for less than half of personal sector wealth, with the

Personal sector balance sheet, £ billion

	Asset	Liabilities
Cash and deposits	650	150 (debt)
Equities and bonds	350	
Insurance company policies	300	
Unquoted equity	100	
Residential housing	3,000	750 (mortgages)
Pension funds	1,300	
Unfunded public sector pension rights	500	
Accrued state pension rights	1,100	
Total	7,300	900

Source: "Pensions: challenges and choices", www.pensionscommission.org.uk

rest being made up of housing wealth and non-pension financial wealth such as equities, bonds and insurance policies.

The report also identified the numbers of people from the working age

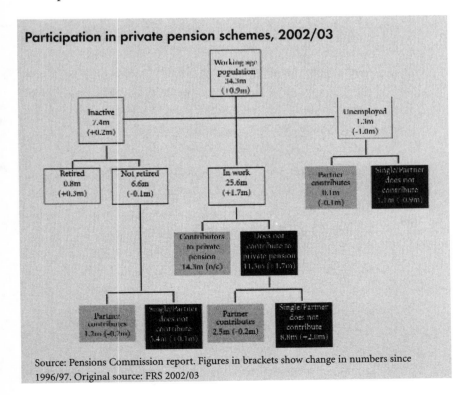

Participation in private pension schemes, 2002/03

Source: Pensions Commission report. Figures in brackets show change in numbers since 1996/97. Original source: FRS 2002/03

population who fell into the main "at risk" categories. From the working age population of a little over 34 million the main at risk categories were: the 5 million who are inactive, not retired and either single or with a partner who does not have a pension; the 9 million who are in work who do not contribute to a private pension and are either single or have a partner does not contribute; and finally the one million who are unemployed who again are either single or not have a partner who contributes. These numbers are large enough but the report showed how, since 1996/97, over a million extra people have slipped into these at risk categories.

A contributory factor to the pensions problem is the growing number of men who no longer work in the later years of their working life. In the last thirty years, the proportion of 50–64 year old men working had fallen from nine out of ten to barely six out of ten. Clearly it is harder to save if income is lower. The largest proportion of those working age men who are inactive, but not "retired", fall into the lowest wealth groups categories.

Section 59 • Pensioners

Of the 59¼ million people living in the UK in 2002, about 6½ million were men aged 65 to 74 and women aged 60 to 74, and nearly 4½ million were aged over 75. In total 10.9 million, 18½% of the population, were over retirement age. Of the total, nearly 4 million were men and 7 million were women. (source: "Population trends", number 117, autumn 2004, www.statistics.gov.uk)

The number of pensioners has grown from 9.7 in 1976 to 10.9 million in 2002, roughly double the growth rate of the population as a whole. Pensioners formed 17.2% of population then compared to 18.4% now. The biggest change over that time has been the increase in the number of elderly pensioners with the number of people aged over 85 doubling.

The Department of Social Security bases its figures on the financial well-being of pensioners on the Households Below Average Income dataset (see the section on poverty), which in turn is based on the Family Resources Survey. This covers Great Britain and measures the number of "pensioner units" as that is the number of benefits it hands out. In 2002/03, the latest year for which figures are available, it is estimated that there were 6.8 million pensioner units, of which approximately 2¾ million are pensioner couples. As the data are based on the family resources survey, it does not reflect the situation of the roughly 280,000 pensioners in care homes. The exclusion of Northern Ireland makes little difference to the aggregate figures as pensioner incomes there are broadly similar to those in Great Britain. Northern Ireland was included in the survey for the first time in 2002/03, so the figures are expected to be converted to a UK bases in due course. Due to changes in the survey, consistent figures are not available for periods prior to 1995.

Measuring the financial well-being of pensioners is fraught with difficulty and it is relatively easy by careful selection of statistics used to present their position as reasonably healthy or quite dire. It is also true that the distribution of pensioners across the income scale is very similar to that of the distribution of the whole population, so that some look quite poor while others look quite wealthy.

There are 10.9 million pensioners in the UK – and the same number of children aged under 15

The Elderly population of the UK

A: 1976 number in millions
B: 2002 number in millions
C: percentage change

	A	B	C
all ages	56.216	59.232	5.4
under 16	13.797	11.759	-14.8
16 to 64/59	32.757	36.567	11.6
65/60	9.663	10.905	12.9
65/74	5.112	4.965	-2.9
75/84	2.348	3.341	42.3
85/89	0.390	0.737	89.0
90 and over	0.147	0.387	163.3

source: "Population trends", number 117, autumn 2004, www.statistics.gov.uk

There would seem to be some good news. Pensioner incomes in aggregate have grown faster than average earnings across the economy as a whole over the last eight years. Net income for pensioners has grown in real terms by 25% since 1994/95, compared to real average earnings growth of about 13% over the same period. Net income after housing costs has grown more quickly – up by 34% in real terms since 1994/95 – partly because pensioners are now more likely to own their own home outright than they were in 1994/95.

Of course these changes in average income reflect not only the changes experienced by individual pensioners, but also the composition of the pension group, for example as new retirees with higher incomes join the group and as increasing life expectancy leads to a growing proportion of pensioner couples. A couple would also be defined as a pensioner couple if the man has reached retirement age but has a younger wife who is still working, so that the "pensioner" couple benefits from the woman's earnings. For what are described as "historical reasons", a couple where the woman has retired but a younger man is still working, is not a pensioner couple and is excluded from the main analysis.

The state pension was first introduced in 1909 and the foundation for a universal contribution related pension was layed in the 1940s. The state provides a basic level of pension provision to which everyone has access, providing a minimum level of retirement income. The basic state pension is payable from the state pension age which is currenly 65 for men and 60 for women. The basic state pension is a redistributive, flat rate pension available to everyone who has made appropriate contributions. Between 1974 and 1979 the state pension was increased annually by the greater of the increase in national average earnings or the increse in the retail prices index. Since 1979, annual increase have generally been linked to the RPI.

The government suffered from something of a "pensioners' revolt" from late 1999, when they announced that the basic pension increase in April 2000 would be 75 pence, to £67.50 a week. Although this figure was the "right one", i.e. that it was the appropriate increase given the (very low) rate of inflation in the previous year, it was the lowest increase for many years. The increase in both of the previous years has been a little over £2. In the following year the government raised the basic pension by £5, over double the rate implied by the increase of inflation, and the largest nominal

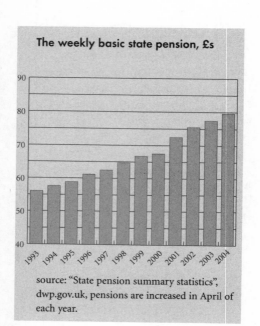

> The government spends about 5% of GDP on pension benefits, less than most other countries

The weekly basic state pension, £s

source: "State pension summary statistics", dwp.gov.uk, pensions are increased in April of each year.

increase for over a decade. To avoid any recurrence of such low increases, the government has said that in future the pension will be uprated each year by the greater of 2½ % or the rate of inflation. (source: www.pensionspolicyinstitute.org.uk)

Accordingly, there has been a steady decline since the beginning of the 1990s in the ratio of the state pension as a proportion of average earnings. This ratio will continue to decline so long as pensions are linked to the rate of inflation, since earnings traditionally grow faster than inflation, and for some pensioners the basic pension remains the lion's share of their income. For the poorest fifth of pensioners, which are heavily dependent on the basic state pension, it typically accounts for between 80% and 90% of their income. A pensioner couple in the richest fifth of pensioners, finds that the state pension contributes only about one fifth of their income, with the rest being made up primarily from occupational pensions but also often from investment income or earnings.

Older pensioners tend to be poorer than younger pensioners. This is partly because they are less likely to work (and therefore have no earnings), partly due to cohort effects (older pensioners are much less likely to have an occupational pension), and partly due to the length of time since retirement (as benefits tend to be uprated in line with inflation, not earnings). A single recently retired pensioner has an average income of £246 compared to just £190 for pensioners over 75.

For pensioners as a whole, state benefits account for half of income and occupational pensions just over one quarter. Earnings and investment income each account for just under 10%. Although nearly three-quarters of pensioners had some investment income, for over half of those, the income received was less than £8 a week. (source: "The pensioners incomes series, 2002/03", www.dss.gov.uk) The contribution of occupational pensions, personal pensions and earnings, to pensioner incomes have all grown in recent years, while the contribution of the state pension has fallen and the contribution from investment in recent years has been more volatile but on a broadly flat trend. Those components that have increased reflect both an increased number of people receiving and increased amounts for those that do receive.

> Following the pensioners' revolt in 2000, the state pension has had a larger percentage increase in the last four years than in the previous six, despite low inflation

State pension equalisation

The state pension age for women is due to increae from 60 to 65 between 2010 and 2020, giving women equality with men. A survery, conducted in early 2004, showed that six out of ten working age people were aware of the increase. Older respondents, perhaps unsurprisingly given their proximity to retirement, were much moe likely to be aware of the change. Only 43% of women who will be affected by the increase corerctly identified the age at which they will become entitled to a pension. Men and women were both equally aware while those in work were much more likely to have heard of the increase than those who are economically inactive.

source: "Public awareness of state pension age equalitsation", November 2004, www.dwp.gov.uk

Section 60 • Child poverty

Is poverty a big problem?

The proportion of children living in poverty grew from 1 in 10 in 1979 to 1 in 3 in 1998 and is now just under 30%. The UK has one of the worst rates of child poverty in the industrialised world. Nearly one half of poor children live in a household headed by a lone parent and even where an adult has a job, the doubling of the number of low paid jobs since 1977 to over 6 million, a fifth of the workforce, means that work is no guarantee of escape from poverty. As a consequence, one in three poor children do not have three meals a day and lack adequate clothing, particularly shoes and winter coats. Poverty affects life chances – being born into poverty can damage educational achievements and shorten life expectancy by about seven years. (source: www.ecpc.org.uk)

In September 1999 the government published its first annual "Opportunity for all" report setting out a strategy for tackling poverty and social exclusion. Earlier that year the Prime Minister had stated that the government would commit to eradicating child poverty within 20 years. In November 1999 the Chancellor announced an intermediate goal of halving child poverty by 2010. In 2000 a further target was announced to reduce the number of children in poverty by at least a quarter by 2004/05.

As the fashions for different definitions of poverty change over time there is a problem in monitoring medium to long-term commitments. The traditional approach to measuring poverty involves looking at how many people live in households below particular low income thresholds. The government is measuring its 2004/05 child poverty target by looking at the number of children in households which have incomes below 60% of median equivalised household income in that year.

The government has been helped in reducing the number of children in poverty by the overall demographic situation. The number of under 16s in the UK fell by around a quarter of a million to 11¾ million in the four years to 2002. This means that even if the proportion of children in poverty was constant, the actual number would be falling.

The government has stated that progress is being measured on both a before housing costs and an after housing costs basis. As 3.1 million children were living in relative low income poverty in 1998/99, the target for 2004/05 is 2.3 million or fewer on a before housing costs basis. On an after housing costs basis, 4.2 million children were in poverty in 1998/99, so the target for this measure would be 3.1 million or fewer. Sampling and other errors in datasets such as the "Households below average income" survey from DWP, mean that care needs to be taken when making inferences based on estimated differences of less than 150,000. This means that it could be argued that an outturn of 3.0 million is not statistically different from just over 3.1 million, and therefore consistent with failure to hit the target.

The figures for this measure in 2004/05 will not be available until spring 2006, however, the broad consensus is that the measures taken to date,

What is poverty?

There are inherent problems and dilemmas in trying to define poverty and how it relates to other concepts such as social exclusion – and no single measure has universal acceptance. Definitions of poverty generally make a distinction between absolute and relative poverty, in other words a distinction between needs which remain broadly fixed and those which change as societies develop and grow more prosperous. Poverty thresholds based on social assistance benefit rates have some authority in that they show how many people have incomes below that that the state considers the minimum adequate level. This assumes, however, that benefit levels themselves are sufficient to avoid poverty and that some rationale exists for their current levels – neither is obviously the case. There have also been attempts to establish thresholds based on estimates of minimum need. This involves drawing up a priced list of goods and services relevant to each family type that are deemed necessary to meet a minimum standard. The main problem with this approach is that it inevitably involves judgments about minimum need. Similarly a subjective poverty line can be derived by asking members of the public about the adequacy of different income levels. Deprivation indicators, showing a list of items that people have deemed as necessities, can also be used.

The terms poverty and social exclusion are sometimes used interchangeably, yet they are not necessarily synonymous. Social exclusion in Britain generally includes poverty and low income, but is broader and addresses some of the wider causes and consequences of poverty, often being used as a shorthand term for what happens when people or areas suffer from a combination of linked problems such as unemployment, poor skills, low incomes, poor housing, high crime, bad health and family breakdown. If a median income target is the focus of policy, it is likely to skew policy excessively towards tax credits and means tested benefit changes, and away from improving public services for children which might have a greater impact on their well being over the longer term.

Monitoring poverty

The New Policy Insitute has established an annual analysis of 50 indicators of poverty. Its latest assessment (in December 2004) showed that over 5–6 years, 18 were improving and 8 were getting worse. In the latest year, 10 were improving and 7 getting worse. over both time periods most were "steady". www.poverty.org.uk and www.npi.org.uk

Has "social exclusion" become a popular concept because it is even harder to quantify than poverty?

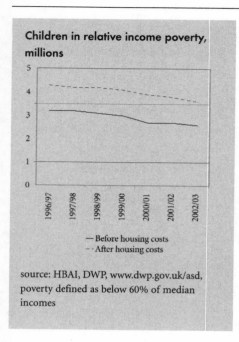

Children in relative income poverty, millions

— Before housing costs
-- After housing costs

source: HBAI, DWP, www.dwp.gov.uk/asd, poverty defined as below 60% of median incomes

Children in poverty on different measures, millions.

Income threshold	Below median	Below mean
40%	na	1.3
50%	1.3	2.9
60%	2.7	4.7
70%	4.3	na

source: Households below average income, DWP, 2001/02, there were 12.8 million children in GB.

notably on tax credits and real terms increases in child benefit, are likely to mean that the near-term target is met, at least when income is measured before housing costs. Meeting the target when income is measured after housing costs will be more challenging. At one level the Chancellor is able to buy his way to success with this target. The Institute for Fiscal Studies has estimated that a £5 per week increase in child tax credits will cost £1.75 billion and lift nearly 400,000 children out of poverty. (source: IFS, briefing note 42, www.ifs.org.uk).

The main problem with using a poverty threshold based on a proportion of median income is that any such threshold is essentially arbitrary. There is no inherent reason why any particular proportion should be considered the threshold below which people can be said to be in poverty. The "Households below average income" series gives figures based on various thresholds and stresses that no single measure should be given particular weight. The choice of threshold makes a big difference – a 60% of median earnings threshold leads to 2.7 million children in poverty (on the basis of the figures for 2001/02), while cutting it to 50% reduces the number of children in poverty to 1.3 million and increasing it to 70% puts 4.3 million children in poverty.

Some commentators like to focus on the number of people living in households where income is less than 50% of the mean income. The choice between median and mean also makes a big difference. The 2.7 million children living in families below 60% of median earnings becomes 4.7 million children living below 60% of mean earnings. Poverty lines derived from means are less desirable as the fluctuation of earnings for the highest earners can introduce perverse consequences. For example, the immigration of a number of high earning families into the UK (as is thought to have occurred in recent years) would bring more families into poverty on the mean basis than with the measure based on the median, which would be more or less unaffected by such change. The UK used to present figures in terms of the mean but it was agreed Europe-wide in 1998 that the median was the preferred way forward.

It has also been widely noted that a relative poverty target, one which moves each year with changing median income, makes the government's task more difficult than if it had instead opted for an "absolute" or fixed threshold set at 60% of median income as it stood in 1996/97 uprated by the rate of inflation. The relative basis for the target means that benefits need to rise at least as fast as median incomes, as opposed to inflation, just to stand still. This has been likened to trying to pull the poorest up over a moving line while the richest get richer – like running up a down escalator. On the basis of a real terms median income target, around 1¾ million of the original 3.2 million children would have left poverty (by 2002/03 the figure was 1.5 million) compared to around half a million under the relative measure.

Despite reducing the number of children in poverty, less progress has been made in terms of the population as a whole. In 2002/03, there were 12.4 million people living in households with incomes below 60% of the median. While this figure is down by 1.4 million under Labour, the number of working age adults living in such households – at 4.9 million – is barely changed since 1996/97. The number of pensioners living in poverty – 2.1 million – is also barely changed over the period.

After allowing for direct social transfers, the UK had 17% of its population living on incomes below 60% of the national median income in 2001. This is just above the average for EU-15. Before making allowance for social transfers, the UK had 29% of its population living on incomes below 60% of the national median, just behind Ireland, the highest in the EU. The table also shows that the impact of transfers to low income households in Britain is second only to that in Sweden. The figures do not allow for housing costs, the inclusion of which would probably make the UK position worse. Both before and after social transfers, the risk of having relative low income was greater in the UK than in the average of the countries that joined the EU in 2004 (though the data in some countries was less timely and less robust).

The EU has not updated figures published in 1996 which showed the proportions in poverty in each country compared with a single EU-wide income threshold. On that basis the risk of low income poverty in the UK was a little below the EU average (14% compared with 17%), due to incomes in Britain on average being higher than those other EU countries. The UK appears in a similar position in the EU league table of child low income poverty. Figures are also published in the UN's "Human development report" and by UNICEF – both of which gave a similar message. (source: www.un.org/esa and www.unicef.org)

As explained, the meaningful comparison of incomes of different families requires adjustment to take account of variations in size and

Percentage of children in families below 60% of national median equivalised income

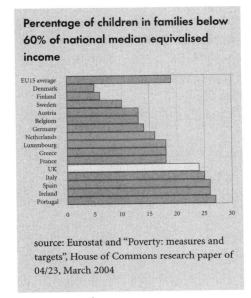

source: Eurostat and "Poverty: measures and targets", House of Commons research paper of 04/23, March 2004

The complex language of poverty
The IFS report on poverty in Britain in 2004 concluded that since the mid 1990s, there has been an unusual combination of "slightly rising income inequality and yet falling poverty". This has arisen as the gap between the very rich, especially the richest ½ million and the rest has got wider. But at the same time, many lower income families have seen their income rise faster than average. (www.ifs.org.uk)

What is persistent low income poverty?

Persistent low income poverty looks at how the composition of those living in low income poverty changes over time, and how many years they spend there. The figures are of interest because if low incomes are more transitory, and the composition of the group changes rapidly, then being on a low income in any given year can be considered less of a problem. For example, pensioners may find themselves on low incomes for a number of years, while many people who are unemployed or are on a career break will be on low incomes for only a short period. Figures about persistent low income poverty are derived from the British Household Panel Survey and are published in "Low income dynamics" from the DWP. There is also a concern that the incomes of people at the lower end of the scale - and especially those who are self-employed - are often inaccurately recorded.

composition of households. This is achieved using so-called equivalence scales. As countries move to greater consistency with the methodology used, there could be some impact on the relative performance of the countries.

During 2002 and 2003 the government held a consultation exercise to determine what child poverty measure should be used to judge whether the government has hit its targets of halving child poverty by 2010 and eliminating it by 2020. The conclusions were announced in a DWP paper, "Measuring child poverty" published in December 2003. It said that success in meeting the targets is to be gauged using a "tiered approach", with three separate measures:

- an income poverty measure based on the low income thresholds fixed in real terms, to see the if the very poorest families are seeing their incomes rise in real terms.

- a measure based on relative low income thresholds to measure whether the poorest families are keeping pace with the growth of incomes in the economy as a whole, and

- a measure combining both low income and material deprivation, to provide a wider measure of people's living standards.

The report said that poverty is regarded as falling when all three indicators are moving in the same direction. But beyond that it is not clear at this stage exactly how progress overall is to be quantified – indeed, the range and nature of the indicators suggests that it will be impossible to say categorically that poverty has been eliminated by 2020. Some commentators have suggested that the more recent comments from government to be "among the best in Europe" on relative child poverty amounts to a softening of the targets. It is also proposed that the new child poverty measures will only use income before housing costs – which is the easier target to achieve and leads to lower estimates of child poverty. The impact of ignoring housing costs is most dramatic in inner London where nearly a half of children are at risk of poverty including housing costs but less than one third excluding housing costs. The campaigning group "End Child Poverty", says the commitment should be met by "truly removing children from poverty not just removing them from the statistics". (source: www.ecpc.org.uk and "Poverty: measures and targets", House of Commons research paper of 04/23, March 2004)

The deprivation indicators to be used for the third tier poverty measure were arrived at following an analysis of existing data sources. The set of indicators relating to children – for example, a holiday away from home for at least one week a year, swimming at least once a month, access to leisure equipment such as a bicycle, and going on a school trip at least once a term – were chosen in order to discriminate between poor and not poor families. These questions will be included in the Family Resources Survey from 2004 and the results will be first available in 2006.

The 2.7 million children in poverty are generally in families that have certain characteristics compared to the rest of the population – lone parent families, families with no or few working members, heavily dependent on state benefits and without savings. Adults at risk of poverty were also tended to be elderly pensioners, those of Pakistani or Bangladeshi descent, the disabled, those with no educational qualifications and those living in inner London.

Characteristics of children in poverty, % of children

A: Children in poverty
B: All children
C: Chance of child being in poverty in this family type

	A	B	C
Lone parent	38	25	32
Lone parent not working	30	14	45
Two parents in f/t work	0	13	1
Workless household	45	18	52
Four or more children	22	11	40
White ethnicity	78	88	18
Not a benefit recipient	32	61	11
Live in South/SE/SW	21	30	14
Live in inner London	14	14	30
Live in Scot/NW/Wales	31	26	25
Live in LA/Hass property	50	25	42
Mortgage holder	30	59	11
Less than £3000 savings	90	73	26

Note: Poverty defined as children in households with incomes below 60% of median. Before housing costs.
source: HBAI, DWP, 2001/02

Risk of relative low income poverty in the EU

A: percentage of the population below 60% of total national median income
B: percentage after direct social transfers

	A	B
Ireland	30	21
Greece	23	20
Portugal	24	20
Spain	23	19
Italy	22	19
UK	29	17
France	24	15
Belgium	23	13
Luxembourg	23	12
Austria	22	12
Denmark	21	11
Germany	21	11
Netherlands	21	11
Finland	19	11
Sweden	27	10
EU total	24	15

source: Eurostat structural indicators and "Poverty: measures and targets", House of Commons research paper of 04/23, March 2004.

Section 61 • Homelessness and begging

Rough sleepers

Year	Rough sleepers
1998	~1800
1999	~1600
2000	~1150
2001	~650
2002	~550
2003	~480

source: ODPM and House of Commons library, www.parliament.uk

The very nature of homelessness makes it hard to come by accurate figures – the populations are transient, as is the state for many people and homelessness itself is hard to define. Many homeless people are secretive and on the margins of society. Plenty of anecdotal information exists and many bodies (social services, health authorities, local authorities, probation services, charities etc) collect some information but there is no systematic collection of data over time. As one paper from Crisis, the national charity of homeless people, said, "We live in a world of targeted social problems and unless a problem is officially defined as a problem and unless it can be framed and explained statistically, then we are not able to tackle it." (source: "Not just another form", www.crisis.org.uk)

The rough sleepers unit of the ODPM, created in 1999 to tackle the problem, collects figures from each local authority and presents them on the website periodically. In 2003, it was estimated that there were about 500 rough sleepers compared to 1,850 in 1998. About half are in London. Figures are presented in a detail which is almost too detailed to be true. Eight authorities including the Isle of Wight and Wolverhampton, are, for example, down as having one rough sleeper. The list excludes all the authorities that (sensibly) were not so precise and indicated they had between 0 and 10 rough sleepers. So the total could be rather higher – indeed would be three times higher at around 1,600 if each of those 228 authorities that declared 0–10 rough sleepers, in fact had five. (source: www.odpm.gov.uk) Any figures based on a street count are likely to be an underestimate. Flow or period estimates are more meaningful than one night counts. Crisis estimates, on the basis of a count conducted in 2000, that there were 11,500 people sleeping rough during the year in Great Britain. (source: Homelessness factfile, Crisis, 2003)

Crisis estimates that 95% of homelessness is hidden, with rough sleepers accounting for just one in 500 of the homeless. It estimates that as many as 400,000 people could be homeless in England – the same as the population of Bristol, Dorset or two average London boroughs. Crisis says that this estimate is derived from the numbers placing themselves in bed and breakfast

Four out of five homeless people take drugs and a half take crack and heroin

accommodation each year, those in shelters, hostels or squats, "absconded" asylum seekers, rough sleepers and those in overcrowded accommodation, for example on relatives' floors. A growing number of the homeless are single people who are even harder to pin down and count. It says that many of these people live in "appalling conditions without security and privacy".

To qualify for local authority housing, an applicant must be pregnant, have dependent children, be "vulnerable" due to age or disability, have lost a home in a natural disaster or be fleeing domestic violence. With social housing in short supply many people with depression, anxiety, substance abuse or suffering from other traumatic experiences such as unemployment, illness or bereavement either do not qualify or are in ignorance of their rights, Crisis says.

Around 137,000 households were accepted as homeless under the provisions of the legislation by local authorities in 2003/04 and the number has risen every year since 1997. The highest rates of homelessness – nearly 1% of households – is in London and the lowest, at less than half the rate, is in the south east of England. The number in temporary accommodation at the end of 2003 was 95,000, up 13% up on the previous year and more than double the figure in 1997. About seven out of ten were white with the remainder from ethnic minorities. One out of five was homeless as they could no longer stay with relatives and one out of five due to relationship breakdown.

Of the *Big Issue* sellers in London, one quarter have been homeless for less than six months and one quarter for more than five years

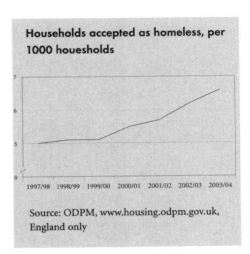

Households accepted as homeless, per 1000 houesholds

Source: ODPM, www.housing.odpm.gov.uk, England only

Households in temporary accommodation arranged by LAs

	Bed and Breakfast	Hostels/ womens' refuge	Leased dwellings	Others	Total
1997	4.5	8.7	14.0	17.6	44.8
1998	7.2	9.8	17.4	19.4	53.8
1999	8.0	9.7	19.8	24.7	62.2
2000	9.9	10.8	25.2	27.2	73.1
2001	11.9	9.8	25.7	30.6	78.0
2002	12.5	9.6	34.1	27.6	83.8
2003	8.4	10.2	47.3	29.2	95.1

Source: ODPM and House of Commons Library

Nearly one in 150 households is homeless

Begging

Begging is an aspect of the homelessness problem. One survey showed that two-thirds of those begging do so every day and over half had slept rough the previous night. Similarly over a half had a mental or physical health problem. Virtually all beggars are under 40 years old in contrast to those drinking on the street who were more evenly spread over the age range. One-third of beggars made between £20 and £30 per day, with over three-quarters making between £10 and £40. Money made was spent in almost equal proportions on food, tobacco, alcohol and drugs. Four out five came into contact with the police every week. (source: Crisis, "Walk on by", www.crisis.org.uk)

The Government set a target in 2002 that by March 2004 no homeless family with children would be accommodated in B&B hotels except in an emergency and even then for no longer than 6 weeks. When the target was set, there were around 4,000 homeless families in England who had been living in B&B for more than 6 weeks and who were placed there by a local housing authority as a discharge of a homelessness duty. The ODPM announced that by mid-2004, only 26 families with children had been in B&B for over 6 weeks. The achievement of this target will be sustained, according to the ODPM, by new legislation which means local authorities can no longer discharge their homelessness duties by placing families in B&B for longer than 6 weeks.

Homeless people often have certain traits: mental illness (four times as common as in the population at large), disputes with parents or step parents (33% of homeless gave this as a contributory reason), have been in care (one-third), served in the armed forces (one in four), marital breakdown (one in eight), ex-prisoner (half), victim of violence or abuse (40%), evicted from their homes due to failure to pay rent, suffering from health problems (the rate of TB is 25 times higher among the homeless), and be unemployed and in debt. (source: Crisis, "Hidden homelessness brief", www.crisis.org.uk)

A link has been made between homelessness and substance abuse. Crisis has shown over four out of five homeless people had used a substance other than alcohol in the last month and a similar proportion had started using at least one new drug since becoming homeless. Substance abuse can often deepen the homelessness problem as those who are drug dependent as almost twice as likely to be excluded from homelessness services. (source: "Home and Dry?", Crisis research paper)

Section 62 • Civil servants

The number of civil servants (including defence staff but not the armed forces) reached a peak of just over 750,000 in 1976 and fell over the following two decades to a low point in 1998. Since then, the number has risen by 62,000 (17% to 421,000 in April 2003). Half yearly figures, published in October 2004, showed a provisional rise of a further 9,000 in the period to April 2004. The numbers are affected by privatisation and contracting out (and shifting boundaries in the public sector), work volumes (such as falling numbers on unemployment benefit, increased immigration work loads and rising prison populations), and the coming and going of policies such as the New Deal. About three quarters of civil servants work in executive agencies rather than for the government departments directly, leading to considerable delegation on staffing issues including pay.

Figures are normally expressed in a full-time equivalent basis. The head-count corresponding to the 517,000 is 547,000. It is difficult to track the exact numbers by department due to creation of new departments, mergers of existing departments and changes of responsibility. All the major group-ings of departments have experienced double digit percentage rises over that period. In 2002, one quarter of civil servants earned £13,720 a year or less and one quarter earned over £23,070. (source: Civil service statistics, annual publication, www.cabinet-office.gov.uk/statistics)

Sickness absence continues to be a significant operational and financial

> The rise in civil servants in the last year equates to over 300 every week.

The number of civil servants, full time equivalents, 000s.

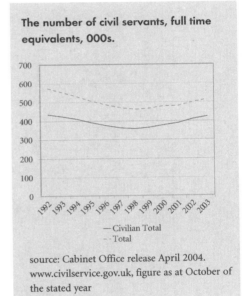

— Civilian Total
- - Total

source: Cabinet Office release April 2004. www.civilservice.gov.uk, figure as at October of the stated year

The largest civil service departments

Total staff in civil departments – 421,000

Other 20%

Work and Pensions 30%

Transport 5%

Customs & Excise 5%

Legal Departmnets 7%

Home Office 16%

Inland Revenue 18%

source: www.cabinet-office.gov.uk, April 2003

> Total public sector employ-ment will be 5.29 million in 2005, up from 4.71 million in 1997

source: www.iod.com

The civil service is now the size of Sheffield (estimated at 513,000 in 2001)

Change in staff numbers in major departments, 000s

A: Education, work and skills
B: Chancellor's departments
C: Home and Legal
D: Total ex defence
E: Defence
F: Total with defence

	A	B	C	D	E	F
October 1998	120	86	77	359	103	462
April 2003	133	104	94	421	91	512
Change, 000s	13	18	17	62	-12	50
%	11	21	22	17	-11	11

source: www.cabinet-office.gov.uk, MDS table 3.4 – components may not add to totals.

burden on the civil service, with an estimated cost of nearly £400 million in 2003, representing 4,886,000 working days lost. The average number of working days of sickness absence per staff year rose from 9.8 in 2002 to 10.0 in 2003, equivalent to 4.4% of working days. Some 36% of staff went the whole year without a recorded spell of absence and 70% lost five working days or less. Female employees on average took nearly three more working days sickness absence per year than their male counterparts – thought in part to reflect the growing number of females trying to balance work and family responsibilities. Research suggests a link between female absence and dependants, as females whose children are no longer dependant or females in higher paid roles do not have significantly higher absences than males in equivalent roles. The number of days of sickness decreases with seniority. (source: "Analysis of sickness absence in the civil service", October 2004, www.civilservice.gov.uk)

The large departments (more than 5000 staff) with the highest sick rates (12 or more days a year) were the Child Support Agency, Prison Service and Job Centre Plus. The most common reasons for absences of more than 10 days were either "mental illness" for "symptoms ill defined". The most common reasons for absences of one or two days were problems related to

The number of special advisers in government has doubled since 1997 and the cost has nearly tripled to £5.3 million in 2003/04

the respiratory or digestive systems. At the time of publication, the statisticians said "the quality of the data supplied over the last few years and especially this year has given the Cabinet Office cause for concern", noting missing, incorrect and duplicate data.

The cost of sickness absence was £786 per civil servant in 2003

The Gershon efficiency savings

Chancellor Gordon Brown announced hefty reductions in civil service numbers as part of the 2004 Spending Review in July 2004. He said that "efficiency programmes will deliver gains of over £20 billion a year by 2007/08 increasing resources available for front-line priorities". He said that the programmes set out plans for a reduction of over 80,000 civil service posts, and for the relocation of 20,000 posts out of London and the South East (following on from the Lyons review of public sector relocation in March 2004). It was announced that by 2008 there will be increased workforce numbers in health, education and criminal justice and that streamlined administration of support functions will lead to a reduction of 84,000 positions. The departments expected to have the largest reductions in staffing were: the Department for Work and Pensions (40,000), Defence (15,000) and the Chancellor's departments (mainly Inland Revenue and Customs and Excise, 17,000). The scale and speed of the planned relocation to the regions is high compared to earlier exercises – it is estimated that in the 40 years since 1963 close to 80,000 civil service jobs were relocated out of London. (source: www.hm-treasury.gov.uk and "The Lyons and Gershon reviews and variations in civil service conditions", House of Commons library, www.parliament.uk)

There are 190,000 trained people employed in the British armed forces, a number that has been broadly stable during the decade. Over half are employed in the army. (source: MDS table 3.6, ONS, www.statistics.gov.uk) Around 2.4 million people are employed in English local authorities with almost another half a million employed in Wales and Scotland. The number employed in England has risen by over a quarter of a million (12%) since the low point in 1998. In the previous decade the number of employees had fallen by nearly 400,000. It is unclear how contracting out has affected the reliability of these numbers as an indicator of services provided the authorities. (source: MDS table 3.7, ONS, www.statistics.gov.uk)

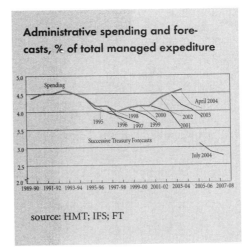

Administrative spending and forecasts, % of total managed expediture

source: HMT; IFS; FT

Section 63 • **Police strength**

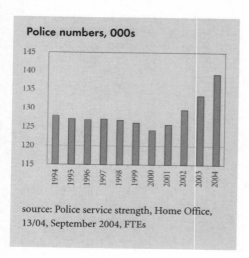

Police numbers, 000s

source: Police service strength, Home Office,
13/04, September 2004, FTEs

Police officers internationally

Italy	472
France	381
EU average	337
Ireland	306
Germany	289
England and Wales	281
US	230
Japan	179

source: "International comparisons of annual
justice statistics, 2001",
www.homeoffice.gov.uk, officers per 100,000
population in the period 1999 to 2001.

There were 140,000 police officers in England and Wales in March 2004 (on a full-time equivalent basis), a 5% rise on the previous year. As most are full-time, the headcount figure was just a little higher at 142,100. (source: "Police service strength", Home Office, www.homeoffice.gov.uk, September 2004)

The rise in police numbers in the last four years follows a number of years of decline to the low point in 2000. The published total for 2002 was the first to surpass the total inherited by the Labour government in 1997. (This comparison is based on the old definition of police numbers that was replaced in 2003. Figures are still produced on the old basis to allow comparison over time.) Of course, police numbers alone, despite being politically sensitive, are not a perfect measure of policing activity – reduction in bureaucracy, civilianisation of the workforce, the use of IT and outsourcing can all improve a police officer's productivity.

Police officers comprised 66% of the 214,400 people (full-time equivalent) working in the police service. Small fractions of the remainder were accounted for by traffic wardens and community service officers but most were support staff. The number of police staff rose by 9% in the latest year. Just over 13,000 officers joined the service in the latest year and 7,000 left. Wastage rates (the number leaving as a proportion of total strength) is close to 5%, with individual forces ranging between 3% and 9% (Bedfordshire and Sussex).

All 43 police forces saw an increase in their numbers in the latest year. The largest percentage increases were in Manchester, Avon and Somerset and Cumbria, each of which was up by at least 8%. The Metropolitan Police Service is by far the largest in the country, accounting for 21% of all officers in England and Wales.

Over 7,000 people in the police service (3.3%) were not available for duty due to career breaks, maternity leave and so forth. Community Service Officers – civilians employed by the police in a highly visible, patrolling role and introduced in 2002 and expected to increase in number to 4,000 by 2006 – are sometimes included in numbers being quoted.

Data quality problems

There had been some concerns about the quality of the Home Office's police figures (notably in correctly counting the numbers of ethnic minorities employed and measuring the results of the efforts to increase staff numbers) so the Home Office set up a Police Numbers Task Force in 2001 to make recommendations about how improvements could be made. The Home Office was also aware that the figures as they stood would probably not meet the requirements of being of sufficient quality to remain classified as National Statistics, when the time came for them to be quality assessed. Changes made included: adding in British Transport Police (which is funded by and formally falls under the rail industry), isolating the number of staff actually available for duty, reconciling the numbers of joiners and leavers with the totals, and presenting headcount and full time equivalent figures (so that any shifts in the number of staff that are part-time would not distort the figures). The new basis for the figures was first used for the figures relating to March 2003. See www.homeoffice.gov.uk

Police corruption and misconduct, % of cases

Disclosure of information	33
Inappropriate association with criminals	11
Drug dealing	11
Inappropriate use of police intelligence	10
Sexual favours or other payments	9
Other	26

Reports of unethical activity from just one police force. "Police corruption in England and Wales", Home Office report 11/03

The number of traffic wardens employed by the police has fallen from 5,000 in 1994 to 1,700 in 2004. As any urban dweller would realise, this decline does not reflect an easing of parking restrictions, but instead the ability of local authorities to employ the wardens directly through contractors. No central estimate of the number of wardens employed locally is available. This raises a question as to whether the people employed in other contracted out services, such as catering in a police station, would be included in the police figures. The Home Office expects that many contracted out staff are included but cannot be sure.

The Police Service of Northern Ireland has about 7,500 staff and nearly 4,000 reserves (www.psni.police.uk) and the Scottish police numbers about 15,700 (www.spf.org.uk). The Scottish Executive does not publish regular figures.

Section 64 • Crime

The number of violent crimes recorded by the police rose above one million for the first time in 2003/04, trebling since 1997

Adults as victims of violent crime, % of people

	Men	Women
Domestic	0.4	0.7
Mugging	1.0	0.7
Stranger	2.7	0.8
Acquaintance	1.9	0.9
All violence	5.4	2.9

source: BCS, "Crime in England and Wales", Home Office 10/04

So is crime at a record high and rising, or at a fifteen year low and falling? It depends on which figures you look at. There are two main sources of data – crime recorded by the police and the British Crime Survey – and they do often point in different directions. Nearly 6 million crimes were reported to the police in 2003/04, up from the low point of 4½ million in 1997. But these figures are susceptible to changes in the public's willingness to report crime – around 95% of vehicle thefts are reported compared to only 30% of acts of vandalism. People often do not report incidents as they perceive them to be too trivial, they sustained no loss or they believed that the police would or could not do much about them.

There is also a problem with variations in recording practices among police forces – an inconsistent approach meant that different forces might not record the same crime, or record crimes to differing degrees. Changes made in 1998 and 2002 – adding new and alleged offences to the list of crime types and introducing common standards for recording crime across police forces – have led to an increase in recorded crime, making it look like more crimes were committed, when that might not be the case. For example, the Home Office estimates that the total figure for all crime in 2002/03 was 10 per cent higher than it would have been under the old system, but not all crime types are equally affected – burglary in a dwelling was inflated by an estimated 3 per cent.

The British Crime Survey in contrast, which despite its name covers just England and Wales, is run by the Home Office and measures crime by asking people about their experiences. Sporadically carried out since 1982, it is now done annually and is generally considered the most authoritative assessment of crime levels – though most analysts feel that the best picture of crime is obtained by looking at both series together.

While it does not claim to count all crimes that occur, it does provide a more consistent measure of trends over time. But the survey does not cover crimes against businesses, crimes where there is no direct victim (such as drug dealing), crimes against victims younger than 16, and crimes that have involved deaths, like homicide (in good part because the victims cannot be interviewed). Also the nature of the survey means that there is no local area data. It does promote a more victim-oriented approach, identifying those most at risk of different types of crime, helping in the planning of crime prevention programmes and looking at people's attitudes, such as how much they fear crime. Overall it is estimated that 58% of crimes are not reported to the police, 31% are reported and recorded in the crime survey, with the remaining 11% being reported to the police but not recorded in the survey. (source: "Crime in England and Wales 2003/04", July 2004, Home Office, www.homeoffice.gov.uk)

Virtually all categories of BCS crime fell in the year to 2003/04. In contrast, about half of the crime types recorded by the police rose in the latest year. Violence against the person rose by 14%, criminal damage by 9% and sexual offences by 7%. Domestic burglary and theft of and from vehicles both fell. There were just over 10,000 firearm offences in 2003/04, roughly double the number recorded in 1998/99, when separate figures were first collected. Some 442 of these offences resulted in a serious injury and 1860 resulted in a slight injury – rises in the year of 5% and 11% respectively.

Rates of crime vary considerably across the country. The amount of personal crime in London is roughly double that in the East Midlands, West Midlands, southwest, northeast and Wales. Household crime in Yorkshire is roughly two thirds higher than in Wales. Crime is also consistently lower in rural areas compared to urban areas, and higher in inner city than urban areas.

The total number of crimes recorded by the police seemed to be on a gentle downward trend during much of the 1990s, but notwithstanding various definitional and procedural changes, seem to have edged up in the last few years. The Home Office says that "the increases seen in recorded crime continue to result largely from changes in recording practices", but no one really knows. As the reporting rate for some crimes is still quite low, it is possible that the number of recorded crimes will rise in the years ahead even if the actual crime level remained stable. Paradoxically, an increase in the number of police officers and an increase in police activity could lead to an increase in reported crime.

In 2003/04, there were 21 violent offences recorded by the police for every thousand people in the population, a rise from just 7 per thousand in 1997. Yet the number of violent crimes in the BCS fell fractionally over the

Young men are twice as likely as young women to be victims of violent crime

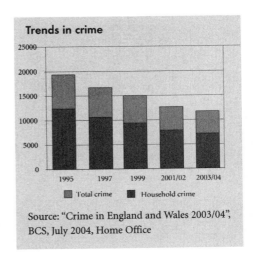

Trends in crime

Source: "Crime in England and Wales 2003/04", BCS, July 2004, Home Office

There is roughly a one in four chance of being a victim in any year of one of the crimes recorded in the crime survey. Roughly 3% of people are subjected to a domestic burglary each year and just under 10% of car owners subjected to vehicle thefts.

Nearly 700 crimes are recorded every hour of which nearly 100 are burglaries

Trends in recorded crime

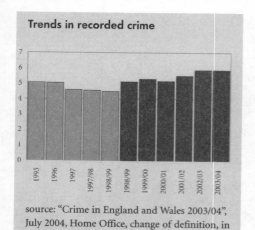

source: "Crime in England and Wales 2003/04", July 2004, Home Office, change of definition, in 1998/99

period. There were 130 recorded crimes for every thousand people in the latest year compared to 88 in 1997. While 74% of people who are the victim of a crime in 2003/04, were only a victim once in the year, 13% were a victim twice and another 13% were a victim three or more times. The high rate of repeat victimisation largely reflects domestic violence and crimes by acquaintances. For mugging, 90% of victims were a victim only once and a further 9% were a victim twice in one year.

Changes in recorded crime since 1997

	2003/04	Change 1997-2003/04
Murder	850	15%
Violence against the person	955,700	281%
Child abduction	920	136%
Sexual offences	52,100	57%
Female rape	12,400	97%
Robbery	101,200	60%
Burglary	818,600	-19%
Theft and handling stolen goods	2,268,100	5%
Fraud and forgery	370,900	137%
Criminal damage	1,205,600	37%
Drug offences	141,100	509%

Footnote: figures make no allowance for definitional and procedural changes
source: "Crime in England and Wales 2003/04", July 2004, Home Office

In the latest year, two thirds of the public thought crime in the country as a whole had increased in the previous two years, with about one third believing that crime has risen "a lot". While high, these proportions are both down by about 5 percentage points compared with the previous year. People continued to show a more positive perception of crime in their own area than nationally – under a half of the public thought that local crime had increased with one in five believing that local crime had increased "a lot".

The risk of becoming a victim of burglary varies considerably across households with different characteristics and between households situated in different localities. Overall, 3.2% of households in England and Wales interviewed for the crime survey had experienced at least one domestic burglary in the previous 12 months. But the rate of burglary was much

British Transport Police crime

The BTP is the national police force for railways throughout England, Scotland and Wales. They also police the London Underground and a number of local transport systems. Their crimes are collected separately from the mainstream police. Over half of the recorded crimes on the transport systems involved theft, 16% were criminal damage and 14% were offences involving violence against the person. Robbery represented 3% of recorded crime and sexual offences under 1%. Most crime types, including violence against the person, sexual, robbery, burglary, criminal damage and drugs, rose in the latest year by between 8% and 14%.

Fear of crime, percentage of people very worried about burglary and violent crime

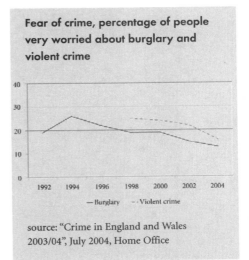

source: "Crime in England and Wales 2003/04", July 2004, Home Office

higher for certain categories of households: for example, a lack of home security measures led to a rate of 18%, head of household under 25 years old 9%, single-parent 9%, living at the address for less than one year 6%, affluent urban area 6%, private renters 6%, and inner-city area 5%.

The figures for the detection of crime are fraught with difficulties. The Home Office assessment is that while the detection rate has fallen for two decades, and from 29% in 1998, it has probably been stable in the last two or three years at around 23½%. For a crime to be counted as detected, the following must have happened: an offence committed and recorded, a suspect identified, the availability of sufficient evidence to charge the suspect, and the victim informed that the offence has been "cleared up". Some crimes are not counted as detected even though the offender is apprehended for another offence, and some crimes are counted as detected when the victim might view the case as far from solved. Changes in counting rules in 1998, changes in the definition of the detection in 1999,

A household headed by someone under 25 is four times more likely to be burgled than one headed by someone over 65

Offences and offenders

Detections are counted on the basis of crimes, rather than offences. So, for example, if six offenders are involved in a robbery and all are arrested and charged, it counts as one detection. Alternatively, if only one of the six is identified and charged, while the other five remain unidentified and go free, this also counts as one detection. Accordingly, care should be taken when comparing detection data with conviction data, as the latter count individual offenders, whether former count crimes.

Audit Commission investigation into police reporting of crime

The report said, "Reducing crime and making places safer is only possible if the police have access to reliable and timely information. Consistent and effective crime recording, backed up by robust management systems, is vital in setting national crime reduction targets, tackling local priorities, instilling public confidence in crime statistics and helping to bring offenders to justice."

In 2002 the Association of Chief Police Officers introduced the National Crime Recording Standard (NCRS) with the support of the Home Office. The standard seeks to promote greater reliability and consistency in collecting and recording crime data. The Audit Commission reviewed crime recording in all 43 police authorities and forces in England and Wales in 2003 and again in 2004. The reviews tested compliance with the new rules against a selection of crime categories and examined the management arrangements in place to ensure compliance. Each authority and force has been given a traffic light rating of green, amber or red."

The review shows, "that more rapid progress is needed. Most forces are improving and making progress in achieving the overall standard of good practice. Last year 12 forces were rated green, this year 17 meet the exacting overall standard. However, the majority are not yet fully compliant and a few still have some way to go. Last year 10 forces had serious problems to resolve, warranting a red rating. This year 4 forces have received this rating, including the largest force in the country, the Metropolitan Police. Almost 18 per cent of all recorded crime is within the Metropolitan Police area. The fact remains that 60 per cent of forces have still to achieve the overall Home Office standard. In some cases crime recording performance has deteriorated and there remain variations in the quality of crime data between forces." (source: www.audit-commission.gov.uk, December 2004)

Captial punishment in the UK, key dates	
Last beheading in England	1747
Last burned at the stake	1789
Last public hanging	1868
Last woman hanged	1955
Last man hanged	1964

and the new reporting standards in 2002 will all have affected the quality of these numbers. Detection rates are highly variable according to the crime – property crime is low at 15% while violence against the person is higher at 50%.

Section 65 • **Murder**

858 cases of murder, manslaughter (unlawful killing without any malice being expressed or implied) and infanticide – taken together termed homicide – were recorded by the police in 2003/04. This represented a large drop from 1045 in the previous year, but due to a quirk of the homicide data – that they are counted in the year in which they are recorded by the police – 172 of the murders in 2002/03 were by Harold Shipman but occurred in earlier years. Excluding the Shipman murders, there was a modest decline from 873 to 858. That runs against the trend as the number of homicides has been rising steadily since the early 1960s when there were typically less than 300 a year.

Each year a modest number of the homicides recorded by the police are reclassified as other offences following police and court action. Similarly, as with Shipman, murders from earlier years can be added to later years data when the crime is discovered. (source: "Crime in England and Wales 2003/04", Home Office)

Since the 1960s, the rate of homicide in Scotland has been higher than in England and Wales. An international comparison made by the Home Office shows a homicide rate of 1.1 per 100,000 population in England and Wales, compared to 2.2 in Scotland in 2.6 in Northern Ireland. (source: "International comparisons of criminal Justice Statistics 2001", Home Office, October 2003) The number of murders in Scotland is more volatile than in England with the rate generally trending up, as below the border. However, due to two years – 1995 and 1996 (with the latter boosted by the Dunblane massacre) – with a very high number of murders, the latest figure is not a record high. (source: "Homicide in Scotland, 2003", November 2004, www.scotland.gov.uk)

In Scotland, unlike England and Wales, the first figure seen in their tables is the number of "cases". A case is counted for each act of homicide regardless of the number of victims. The Dunblane tragedy was recorded as one case, whereas in England it would have resulted in the recording of 17 offences, and Lockerbie in 1988 was also counted as one, rather than 270. The number of victims and accused are also published along side the case figure.

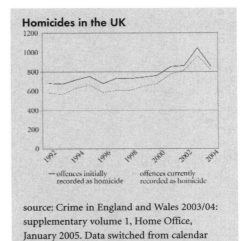

Homicides in the UK

source: Crime in England and Wales 2003/04: supplementary volume 1, Home Office, January 2005. Data switched from calendar year to financial year in 1997.

The Shipman murders

Dr Harold Shipman was convicted in January 2000 of murdering 15 of his patients while he was a GP in Manchester. The public inquiry reporting in July 2002 identified a further 172 victims. These extra homicides were recorded at that time by Greater Manchester Police and appear in the 2002/03 homicide figures. It is thought he might have killed up to 260 people during his career and is the UK's most prolific convicted serial killer. He was found dead in his prison cell in January 2004.

Roughly two-thirds of Scotland's murders occur in Glasgow

Homicides in Scotland

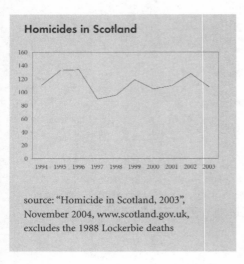

source: "Homicide in Scotland, 2003", November 2004, www.scotland.gov.uk, excludes the 1988 Lockerbie deaths

The overall risk of being a victim of homicide is 19 per million population

Just over one third of murdered women were killed by their partner, ex partner, lover or other family member.

It is more difficult to compare the rate in Northern Ireland because of the particular security situation prevailing, but the number of homicides fell to 33 in 2003/04 from 45 in the previous year. 11 deaths – all civilian – were put down to the security situation in 2003, two less than in 2002. (source: "Recorded crime in Northern Ireland", www.psni.police.uk and www.nisra.gov.uk)

For many crimes it is difficult to know the real prevalence as either or neither of the two principal sources – the police recorded crime figures and the British Crime Survey – might have the right figure. For homicide, however, it is thought the police recorded figures are reasonably accurate. The main uncertainty seems to be issue of undiscovered murders. There are roughly 200,000 people (of which one third are children) who go missing every year and, while virtually all are traced, it is estimated that several hundred are not found. In 2003/04, the National Missing Persons Bureau register recorded nearly 2,500 people missing in the UK for more than 14 days – it is not known how many are eventually found. It might well be that some of these people have been murdered – and the crime not discovered. (source: www.missingpersons.org)

A third of homicide victims are female and two thirds of them knew their killer (excluding the Shipman cases). In contrast, only 40% of male victims knew their killer. Men were most likely to be killed by a sharp instrument (about one third of homicides) with shootings accounting for another 10%. In 2003/04, the detection rate was 92% for murder and 71% for manslaughter.

The homicide rate in England and Wales is one of the highest in Western Europe. A small number of countries have a homicide rate which is much, much higher – South Africa (with over 21,000 homicides in the latest year) has by far the highest rate followed by Russia (with over 33,000 homicides) and the ex Soviet Baltic states, and the US with a rate 3½ times that of the EU average. In the period 1997 to 2001, the homicide rate in England and Wales rose by 19%. Of the countries in the Home Office study, 14 saw their rate rise over the period and 22 saw it fall, and only four countries had a larger increase than England and Wales. (source: "International comparisons of criminal Justice Statistics 2001", Home Office, October 2003)

Figures are also available for homicide rates in capital cities. The countries that have a high rate generally have capital cities with a high rate and

Recorded serious violence, 2003/04

Murder	716
Manslaughter	136
Infanticide	1
Attempted murder	884
Threat or conspiracy to murder	22,232
Child destruction	8
Causing death by dangerous driving	445
Causing death by aggravated vehicle taking	63
Wounding or other act endangering life	19,358
Endangering railway passenger	7
Total	43,850

source: "Crime in England and Wales 2003/4", Home Office

Homicide around the world

South Africa	48.8
Russia	22.2
Lithuania	10.4
US	5.6
Northern Ireland	2.9
Turkey	2.7
Scotland	2.2
Australia	1.8
France	1.8
England and Wales	1.8
Netherlands	1.4
Germany	1.1
Spain	1.1
Japan	1.1

Footnote: homicides per hundred thousand population for selected countries. Table uses latest available data, normally relating to the period 2000 to 2002
source: "Crime in England and Wales, 2003/04", supp. vol 1, Home Office, January 2005

vice versa, but there are some differences. London's homicide rate of 2.6 is a little higher than the average for the EU capital cities of 2.3, and is above the rate for Madrid, Rome, Paris and Berlin, but lower than that in Amsterdam, Stockholm and Vienna. Belfast's figure of 5.9 is well above that of Edinburgh of 1.4, and the highest in Europe excluding the ex Soviet states.

"Yardie killings"

2001/02 saw 97 firearms-related homicide killings, a record high and more than double the annual average seen in the second half of the 1990s. The killings are concentrated in small areas of large cities and are often linked to drug-related feuds. Young black males are heavily over represented as victims and offenders – about one in three men involved in male on male firearm killings is black. (source: "Reducing homicide", Home Office report, 01/03)

Section 66 • **Prison population**

There were 135,000 new prisoners ("first receptions") in 2003, broadly the same as in 2002

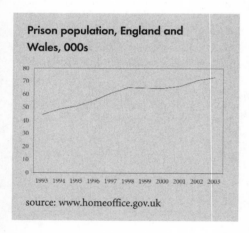

Prison population, England and Wales, 000s

source: www.homeoffice.gov.uk

In the last decade, the number of lifers and those serving less than six months have risen most rapidly

The average population in custody in England and Wales during 2003 was 73,000, an increase of 3% compared to 2002 and came after a rise of 7% in the previous year – and is the highest annual figure ever recorded. The total had risen to 75,200 by October 2004 (based on the Home Office monthly figures, "Population in custody – monthly figures", www.homeoffice.gov.uk). The 2003 total represents a rise of 20% from 1997 and over 60% in the last decade. The number of female prisoners increased to 4,400, an increase of 65% since 1997.

Ethnic minority groups made up 22% of the male and 29% of the female prison population, roughly three times the proportion in the population at large. The imprisonment rate for black people at 1.1 per hundred of the population is roughly seven times higher than the rate for whites or south Asians. Around 10% of the male prison population and 20% of the female prison population were known to be foreign nationals. (source: "Offender management caseload statistics, 2003", December 2004, and previously published as "The prison population in 2002", www.homeoffice.gov.uk)

The increase in the prison population reflects the increased use of custodial sentences at court and an increase in the average length of sentence (from 21 months to 28 months during the last decade) and comes despite a small fall in the number of adults being sentenced in a Crown Court. Just over half, 53%, of the 6,010 prisoners considered for parole in 2002/03 were released. Six out of 10 prisoners discharged from prison in the first half of 2001 were reconvicted of a "standard list offence" within two years of release, and younger prisoners were more likely to reconvict.

Prison is expensive – during 2002/03, it cost an average of £745 per week to keep someone in prison and to build a new prison costs about £130,000 per prisoner place. There are currently 137 prisons holding men, women and children in England and Wales and two new prisons are planned in the expectation of a continued rise in the prison population. There are currently ten privately managed prisons – eight were built and are run by the private sector and two were built by the public sector but are run by the private sector under contract. Two prisons which began life managed by the private sector have been brought into public management. The private sector prisons accommodate just under 10% of prisoners. The prison estate includes one prison ship, HMP The Weare, moored off Portland, Dorset. (source: www.howardleague.org and www.prisonreformtrust.org.uk)

What is the right ratio?

During 2002, concern about prison overcrowding led Britain's senior judge, Lord Woolf, to discourage judges and magistrates from sending criminals to jail. The facts at the time suggested that the prison population was rising when crime was falling - and Britain already had more people in jail per head of population than the rest of Europe. The implication is that judges and magistrates are deploying a rather barbaric instrument when everyone else in Europe prefers a more gentle approach.

But a closer look at the figures can suggest a different interpretation. The best comparison might not be the traditional one, i.e. between the number of prison inmates and the total population, but between the number of prisoners and the volume of crime. A country with a high level of crime would expect, other things being equal, to have to put more people in jail. As England and Wales has one of the highest crime rates among industrialised countries, the high rate of incarceration might be justified.

In the EU the average number of prisoners per 100,000 population in 2000 was 87, compared with 124 in England and Wales. But if the number of prisoners is compared to the number of recorded crimes, a different story emerges - the EU average was 17.7 for every 1,000 crimes and the figure for England and Wales was 12.7. In other words, England and Wales has fewer prisoners in relation to the crime level than the EU average. In fact, 9 out of the EU-15 countries had rates of imprisonment that were the same or higher. France was higher, Spain much higher and Germany the same.

Comparison with countries outside Europe reveals a similar pattern. In 1999, Canada had 123 prisoners per 100,000 population compared with England and Wales, but 15.9 prisoners per 1,000 recorded crimes. Japan had only 43 prisoners per 100,000 population but 25.3 per 1,000 recorded crimes. Looked at this way, it could be argued that prison in England and Wales is under-used. (source: "Does prison work?", www.civitas.org.uk) (The latest figures for the prison population rate per 100,000 of population are available in the "World's prison population list", www.homeoffice.gov.uk)

One quarter of new prisoners were under 21 and one quarter were over 34 years old

Top crimes for prisoners under sentence, October 2004

Total in prison	61,300
of which:	
violence against the person	14,400
drugs offences	10,400
burglary	8,500
robbery	8,400
sexual offences	5,900

source "Population in custody - monthly figures", www.homeoffice.gov.uk

More African Caribbeans went to prison in 2002 (11,500) than went to a British university (8,000)

Length of prison sentence

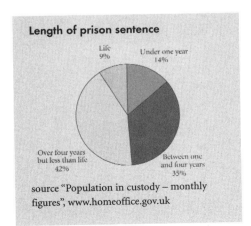

source "Population in custody – monthly figures", www.homeoffice.gov.uk

Foreign nationals in custody

Total number	9,137
of which:	
Jamaica	2,450
Irish Republic	700
Nigeria	450
Pakistan	350
Turkey	250

Footnote: England and Wales only
source: "Population in custody, quarterly brief,
Q1 2004", www.homeoffice.gov.uk

There were just over 5,400 prisoners serving life sentences in mid-2003, of which roughly two-thirds were convicted murderers

Over 9 million people are held in penal institutions throughout the world – of which roughly half are held in the US, Russia and China

The International Crime Victim Survey

The ICVS is the most far reaching programme of standardised sample surveys to look at householders' experience with crime, policing, crime prevention and feelings of safety in a large number of countries. The project was established due to the inadequacy of offences recorded by the police for comparing crime in different countries and the absence of any alternative standardised measure.

Police figures are problematic for comparative purposes because the vast majority of incidents the police know about are notified by victims, and any differences in propensity to report in different countries will undermine the comparability of the amount of crime counted by the police. Moreover, official police figures vary because of differences in legal definitions, recording practices, and precise rules for classifying and counting incidents.

A number of countries have independently mounted crime or 'victimisation' surveys (such as the BCS in England and Wales) to assess national crime problems – and the ICVS mirrors that approach. Such surveys ask representative samples of the population about selected offences they have experienced over a given time. They are interested in incidents whether or not they are reported to the police, and indeed, the reasons why people do and do not choose to notify the police. They thus provide both a more realistic count of how many people are affected by crime and - if the surveys are repeated - a measure of trends in crime, unaffected by changes in victims' reporting behaviour or administrative changes in recording crime. Three surveys have taken place since 1989. (source: "International crime victim survey", http://ruljis.leidenuniv.nl/group/jfcr/www/icvs)

Section 67 • **Prisoner deaths**

Prisoners often suffer victimisation at the hands of other prisoners. Evidence from some other countries such as the US, Canada and Australia suggest that the most extreme case of violence – homicide – is on the increase. In 2004, the Home Office published a report to assess the state in the UK. (source: Home Office report 46/04, "Prisoner on prisoner homicide", www.homeoffice.gov.uk/rds)

Between 1990 and 2001 there were 1,352 deaths of offenders in prisons in England and Wales. Over half (56%) were self-inflicted and another large share (42%) were due to natural causes – just 26 (2%) were homicides, equating to just over 2 per year. The number in any year ranged from 5 to zero. The number of deaths occurring in high security prisons and youth offender institutions were proportionately higher than the number in local and lower category prisons.

Various theories have been put forward to explain the phenomenon: overcrowding, sex (either to rape or to avoid being raped), mental illness, ethnicity, prison type and drugs. The number of homicides in Britain (out of prison) was declining until the 1970s but has since been edging up (more than doubling since 1970 to 833 in England and Wales in 2003/04, www.homeoffice.gov.uk/rds), pointing to a more violent society in general. Often, the researchers noted, the death seemed largely due to the personality and psychopathology of the assailant.

Contrary to the emerging data from some other countries, the number of homicides in prisons in England and Wales is at worst stable, and declining as a proportion of prisoners. The decline has occurred in the number of deaths in high security prisons and could be explained by the change to a more secure and ordered regime following high profile escapes in 1994 and 1995 and the recommendations in subsequent reports. The profile of the prison homicide victim and assailant was similar to the general prison population.

Three are two sources of data on violence in prisons – prisoners self-reporting and official prison records – and both can be subject to measurement error due respectively to either under/over reporting or discretionary

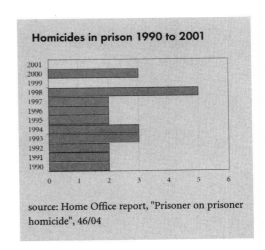

Homicides in prison 1990 to 2001

source: Home Office report, "Prisoner on prisoner homicide", 46/04

Deaths during or following police contact

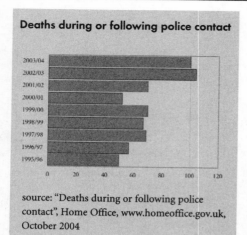

source: "Deaths during or following police contact", Home Office, www.homeoffice.gov.uk, October 2004

There has been a fourfold rise in the number of deaths following police car chases since 1997, so that they now account for 1% of road fatalities

decision-making. Under reporting by prisoners will occur if they fear retaliation from those they report or they accept that higher levels of violence is part and parcel of prison life. The report said that the true extent of prisoner homicide was probably higher than the recorded figures show with the researchers noting a number of cases where homicide seemed likely but other outcomes – accidental death or suicide – had been recorded. The unavailability of data on less serious outcomes than death is a failing.

Deaths from police contact

People can also die during or following police contact. Of the 100 people who died in this way in 2003/04, 38 were as a result of road traffic incidents involving the police, 38 occurred in or following police custody (of which 7 took place at police stations), one was the result of a shooting incident, and 23 took place during or following other types of contact with the police.

The number of breaches of prison discipline is rising year on year but not as rapidly as the number of prisoners, so the rate is falling. There were 145 offences for every 100 prisoners in 2003, down 3% from 2002 and down 36% over the decade. The most common offences were disobedience/disrespect, unauthorised transactions and violence. (source: "Offender management caseload statistics, 2003", December 2004, www.homeoffice.gov.uk)

Section 68 • Northern Ireland conflict

The conflict in Northern Ireland has been an important issue for British governments for nearly four decades. From the time of the first civilian shooting in the summer of 1969, the "troubles", as they have been referred to, have rarely been out of the news for long. Around 3,600 people have been killed and over 30,000 injured as a direct result of the conflict. Civilians accounted for more than half of the fatalities, and over half were people under 30 years of age. More than nine out of ten deaths were of men.

Despite the Northern Ireland conflict being one of the most researched and widely reported conflicts in the world, there is far from total agreement about some of the basic statistics relating to it, for example, the number who have died as a result. There are several lists of those who have died, compiled by different organisations, groups of people and individuals. Most of the lists coincide on the majority of deaths where, for example, someone has been killed in a shooting or bombing incident and one of the paramilitary groups has claimed responsibility.

Over 1,000 people a year are injured in Northern Ireland as a result of the "troubles" despite the peace process

Conflict deaths in Northern Ireland 1969- 2003

source: Police Service of Northern Ireland, www.psni.police.uk

Casualties as a result of paramilitary style attacks have been higher in the last three years than at any time since records began in 1988

Conflict injuries in Northern Ireland

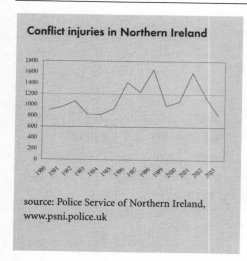

source: Police Service of Northern Ireland, www.psni.police.uk

"The troubles"

The troubles is a euphemism commonly used to refer to the most recent period of civil and political unrest, from 1968 to the present. The conflict is usually explained in terms of the different constitutional aspirations of the two main sections of the community in the region. Many Catholics consider themselves to be Irish and nationalist in political outlook, that is they would like to see the whole island of Ireland reunited and independent of Britain. Most Protestants consider themselves to be British and unionist in political output, that is they want Northern Ireland to remain part of the UK.

However, there are a significant minority of cases where a death is included in one list but not in another. Should a shooting be counted where no organisation has claimed responsibility, or where an elderly person dies of a heart attack after witnessing a violent incident? Do you count someone who is killed when struck by a military vehicle, or someone who commits suicide in direct response to some aspects of the conflict? The main sources of data are: the "official" count of the number of people killed collected by the police, the Irish information partnership database, the Sutton index of deaths, the "Cost of the troubles project", and a number of individuals' databases. (source: http://cain.ulst.ac.uk)

Many people believe that the current period of violent conflict is almost at an end. However, Northern Ireland continues to experience violence not only from those paramilitary organisations which are "active", which did not declare a ceasefire, but also from some organisations who are supposed to be on ceasefire. Accordingly, the period of "peace" since the first ceasefire is has been an imperfect one. While the average number of deaths each year in the last decade has been significantly lower than in the previous 25 years, the number of people injured as result of the security situation has been higher than at any time since the early 1970s.

The population balance in Northern Ireland is changing. The 1991 population census estimated that 58% were Protestants and 42% Catholic. But as the Catholic population is growing more rapidly, the gap between the two narrowed in the 2001 census. The question in 2001 about community background said that 53% had been brought up as a protestant

Organisational responsibility for deaths

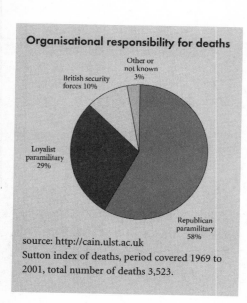

source: http://cain.ulst.ac.uk
Sutton index of deaths, period covered 1969 to 2001, total number of deaths 3,523.

compared to 44% as Catholic. The school population figures suggest that just over 50% of under 16-year-olds are Catholics. The change in the population balance is one reason why most people believe that "power sharing" is preferable to "majority rule". (source: www.nisra.gov.uk)

97% of people in Northern Ireland say there is a problem with organised crime, and three quarters of those surveyed thought that the paramilitary organisations were mainly responsible. Almost three quarters of those surveyed said that they associated drug dealing with organised crime, while 36% associated protection and extortion, 34% armed robbery and 26% fuel smuggling. (source: "Views on organised crime in Northern Ireland", bulletin 4/2004, www.nio.gov.uk)

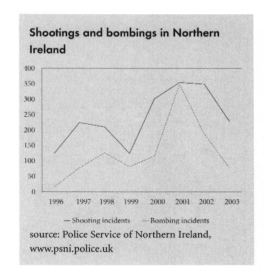

Shootings and bombings in Northern Ireland

— Shooting incidents --- Bombing incidents

source: Police Service of Northern Ireland, www.psni.police.uk

Significant dates

- March 1969 - first explosion
- August 1969 - first civilian death from shooting
- February 1971 - first British soldier killed by IRA
- 1971 to 1975 - internment
- March 1972 - the introduction of direct rule
- January 1972 - "Bloody Sunday", most killed (14) in a single shooting incident
- November 1974 - most killed in one explosion in England (21 in the Birmingham pub bombing)
- 1981 - hunger strike
- November 1985 - the Anglo-Irish agreement
- 1993 to date - the peace process
- April 1998 - the Good Friday agreement
- July 1998 - the first meeting of the Northern Ireland Assembly
- August 1998 - most deaths from a single explosion, 29 killed in Omagh bomb

Section 69 • Alcohol

The number of drinking days

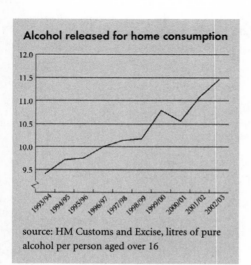

source: ONS GHS 2002, % of all adults aged 16 and over in a typical week

Alcohol released for home consumption

source: HM Customs and Excise, litres of pure alcohol per person aged over 16

Reliable data on drinking (along with other vices) is notoriously difficult to get – not least because people who stray from what is considered to be average behaviour will often feel they have something to hide.

"Binge drinking", curently perceived as a problem, relates to drinking large amounts of alcohol in a relatively short space of time. It has been defined statistically as drinking above double the recommended daily benchmark on at least one day in the previous week. Using this measure, one-fifth of men drank more than eight units and one in ten women had drunk more than six units on at least one day during the previous week. (A unit of alcohol is 10ml of pure alcohol, roughly equivalent to a half pint of beer, a single shot of spirits or a small glass of wine.)

The average weekly alcohol consumption (in England in 2002) was 17 units for men and 7½ units for women. One quarter of men and one fifth of women aged 16 and over drank on average more than 21 and 14 units a week respectively. The Department of Health used to advise, until the mid-1990s, that drinking below these levels was unlikely to damage health. Drinking at these levels among men has remained stable during the last decade while the number of women drinking this amount has increased by nearly half over the same period.

The government advice about healthy drinking was amended in the mid-1990s to state that regular consumption of between three and four units a day for men (and between two and three for women) does not accrue significant health risk. Data on this new basis is available from only 1998 so longer term trends have to be viewed in terms of weekly average consumption. (source: "Statistics on alcohol, England, 2004", Department of Health, September 2004)

A quarter of men and four out of ten women did not have a drink during the survey week. A quarter of men had drunk on five or more days during the week. Around two-fifths of men had drunk more than four units on at least one day during the week. The proportion who had drunk more than four units varied sharply with age ranging from nearly a half of men aged 16 to 24, to just one in seven men aged 65 and over. Young people are more likely to drink above the government-defined sensible limits than older people, who drank more frequently on average but in smaller amounts.

So far as international comparisons are concerned, the UK appears in the middle of the league table – drinking more per capita than the Australians, Finns and Americans but less than the French, Irish and Germans. Over the longer run, alcohol consumption has been rising steadily since the end of the Second World War. The modest rises of the last decade or so have largely been driven by an increased consumption of wine.

Both men and women in minority ethnic groups other than the Irish were less likely that the general population to drink. Some 7% of men and 3% of women fall into the category of chronic drinkers – people who consume more than 51 and 36 units a week respectively – and are at an increased risk of cirrhosis, cancer, suicide and premature death.

Roughly the same percentage of adults are assessed as being dependent on alcohol. In most cases the level of dependence is mild, but in five cases

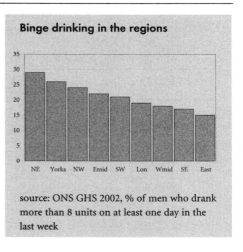

Binge drinking in the regions

source: ONS GHS 2002, % of men who drank more than 8 units on at least one day in the last week

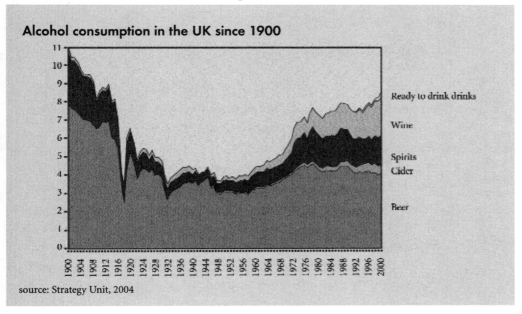

Alcohol consumption in the UK since 1900

Ready to drink drinks

Wine

Spirits
Cider

Beer

source: Strategy Unit, 2004

per thousand the dependence is moderate or severe. The incidence of mild alcohol dependence is strongly related to age. For men, one in nine of those aged over 16 is said to have a mild dependence, but this ranges from one in four men in their early twenties to less than one in ten for all ages over 40.

The Irish drink the most and the Bangladeshi the least

The world's beer drinkers, pints per person annually	
Czech Republic	278
Ireland	265
Germany	217
Austria	188
Luxembourg	177
Denmark	174
Belgium	173
UK	171

source: "The top ten of everything", www.dk.com, data for 2001

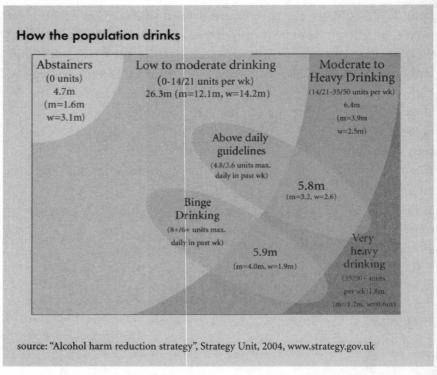

How the population drinks

source: "Alcohol harm reduction strategy", Strategy Unit, 2004, www.strategy.gov.uk

About a quarter of pupils aged 11 to 15 drink alcohol each week – a proportion that has remained broadly flat since the mid-1990s. One in twenty 11-year-olds has a drink each week compared to roughly half of 15-year-olds. The amount consumed by those youngsters that are drinking has increased during the late-1990s but has been stable since 2000. The UK is near the top of the international league tables showing the proportion of young people who have been drunk before the age of 13 and the proportion of young people who frequently became drunk during the course of the last year. (source: www.ias.org.uk)

One third of women who drink give up alcohol during pregnancy, and of the two thirds who continued to drink while they were pregnant, 97% drank one unit a day or less on average.

Many of these numbers do not look extreme but it has been estimated that alcohol misuse costs England around £20 billion a year. (source: "The alcohol harm reduction strategy", Cabinet Office, www.strategy.gov.uk, March 2004) The Cabinet Office report identified four groups of harm:

● Health. The cost to the NHS of alcohol misuse has been estimated at £1.7

billion each year – accounting for one in 26 bed days. It is estimated that up to 22,000 premature deaths in England are associated in some way with alcohol misuse. Around 21,000 people were admitted to hospital due to "injuries" acquired while under the influence of alcohol in 2002/03. This is an increase from 16,700 in 1995/96. The number of accidents involving poisoning by exposure to alcohol has almost doubled over the same period to 1,100. There were over 40,000 hospital admissions in 2002/03 with a primary diagnosis that was related to alcohol. The principal problems were liver disease (11,400), dependence syndrome (9,900), acute intoxication (7,600), and withdrawal state (6,800).

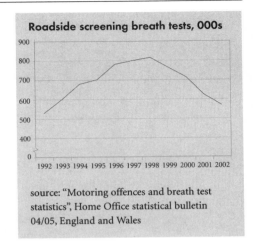

Roadside screening breath tests, 000s

source: "Motoring offences and breath test statistics", Home Office statistical bulletin 04/05, England and Wales

- Crime and antisocial behaviour. Each year around half (1.2 million) of all violent crimes and around one third of all domestic violence incidents are linked to alcohol misuse, with an annual cost to the nation estimated at £7.3 billion.

- Workplace. Roughly 17 million working days are lost each year as a result of alcohol misuse – costing about £6.4 billion. The cost reflects absenteeism, recovery from binge drinking and the loss of productivity and profitability. Up to a quarter of workplace accidents are thought to be linked to alcohol misuse. (source: www.alcoholconcern.org.uk)

- Family and society. The human and emotional impact of alcohol-related incidents is very hard to measure, but marriages which involve alcohol misuse are twice as likely to end in divorce than those that do not. Around one million children are thought to be affected by parental alcohol abuse.

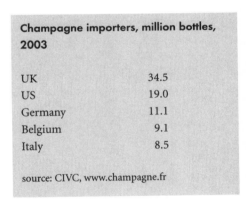

Champagne importers, million bottles, 2003

UK	34.5
US	19.0
Germany	11.1
Belgium	9.1
Italy	8.5

source: CIVC, www.champagne.fr

The 6% of road traffic accidents involving illegal alcohol levels resulted in over 20,100 casualties in 2002 – a 7% increase in the year and the first time over 20,000 since 1990. The number of people killed or seriously injured in drink drive accidents in Great Britain fell below 3,000 in 1998 and 1999. Since then, however, it has been rising by just under 5% a year. There were 530 drink and drive related deaths in 2001 and 560 in 2002 – with the exception of 1996, the latest year is the highest death toll since 1992. In addition to those fatalities around 2,700 people were seriously injured in drink drive accidents in 2001 and 2,800 in 2002.

There were 102,000 proceedings in magistrates' courts for offences relating to driving after consuming alcohol or taking drugs in 2002 in England and Wales. This was higher than the 96,000 in 2001 but fewer than

15% of road deaths occurred when someone was driving while over the legal limit for alcohol

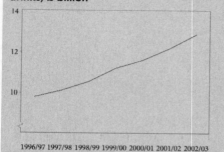

Government tax revenues from alcoholic drinks, £ billion

1996/97 1997/98 1998/99 1999/00 2000/01 2001/02 2002/03

source: "Statistics on alcohol, England, 2004", Department of Health, September 2004

recorded in any year between 1990 and 1998. The number of roadside breath tests increased in most years during the 1990s to a peak of 816,000 in 1998. In five years since, the number of tests conducted has declined each year, to 570,000 in 2002, the lowest since 1992.

In 2001, around £200 million was spent on advertising alcoholic drinks,

Government tax revenues from the import and sale of alcoholic drinks are high and rising. In 2003/04, the receipts from duty on alcoholic drink were over £7½ billion. The total of duty receipts rose every year during the 1990s and has risen by 32% since 1997/98. Total government receipts from alcoholic drink are typically about 75% higher once VAT and excise duty have been included, pointing to total tax revenues in 2003/04 of over £13 billion.

more than double the amount spent on advertising soft drinks. It is estimated that £600–800 million is spent on promotion and marketing of alcoholic drinks. (source: www.alcoholconcern.org.uk and www.ias.org.uk)

Section 70 • **Sex**

The last decade might have seen a greater sexual revolution than occurred during the 1960s – certainly the proliferation of television and cinema with gay and lesbian individuals seems to have inspired particularly more young adults to reflect on their sexuality, with increased and more varied sexual behaviour. The problem is that robust statistical evidence is hard to find. This is partly because funding for sex research has not been available – either because it was not seen as a life or death issue, or because when it was, those affected were in minority sexual groups often disapproved of by the wider society. (source: "Sexuality and statistics", Radical Statistics, no 83, 2003) Information on the occurrence of diseases can be found in the Health Protection Agencey's annual report (www.hps.org.uk), but that only covers some NHS clinics. The National Survey of Sexual Attitties and Lifestyles is a valuable source but it has been conducted only twice (in 1990 and 2000) and the data are not readily available to the public.

Yet information about sexual practices would be helpful – partly because public information and education has merit, but also it would be easier to deal with public policy issues when they arise. That was true in the 1980s when the Aids epidemic first surfaced and could be the case now, as the prevalence of various sexually transmitted diseases is on the rise. The number of people diagnosed with HIV has more than doubled in the four years to 2003, so that more than 10% of the ever-diagnosed cases were diagnosed last year. Better information would also shed light on the extent of sexual ignorance and sexual violence. The last few years have seen pharmaceutical companies getting involved in research on sexual functioning, as various drugs made to improve sexual performance have come onto the market.

All the traditional statistical problems linked to sampling are magnified when it comes to sex. Survey refusal rates are typically very high, there are large differences in response rates according to age, social class, sexual orientation and ethnic background, and no one can ever be sure how truthful responses are. People often only volunteer for surveys on sensitive subjects if they have a particular point of view to put over. Surveys

All the major sexually transmitted diseases – syphilis, gonorrhoea, chlamydia, genital warts and HIV – were at record high rates of occurrence in 2003

Treatment for HIV costs between £½ million and £1 million over the course of a lifetime

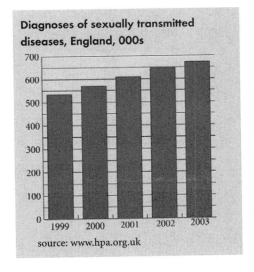

Diagnoses of sexually transmitted diseases, England, 000s

source: www.hpa.org.uk

One in eight 16 year old girls has used the morning after pill

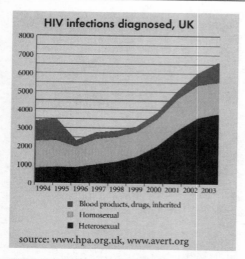

HIV infections diagnosed, UK

- Blood products, drugs, inherited
- Homosexual
- Heterosexual

source: www.hpa.org.uk, www.avert.org

80% of HIV infections that were probably acquired through heterosexual intercourse are thought to have been acquired outside the UK, while 84% of HIV acquired through homosexual intercourse was acquired in the UK

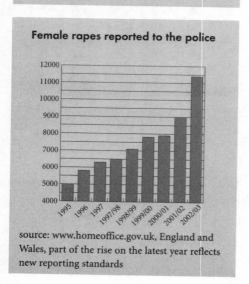

Female rapes reported to the police

source: www.homeoffice.gov.uk, England and Wales, part of the rise on the latest year reflects new reporting standards

conducted using only university student volunteers will not be representative of the whole society.

Nowhere are the difficulties greater than with the issue of rape. Estimates of the number of rapes committed in England and Wales each year range from a high point of about a quarter of a million down to some fraction of the 11,400 which were reported to the police in 2003/04 – of which roughly one in ten lead to conviction or caution. The proportion of women over 16 who, according to surveys, have had forced sexual intercourse ranges from less than 5% to more than 50%. And what about men? Some surveys have suggested that they suffer unwanted heterosexual intercourse at a similar rate to women – though only one male rape is reported to the police for every 13 female rapes.

As rape is sex without consent, the definition of consent is pivotal. The problem is that consent is very rarely present as a single act – the difficulties found in a court of law are present in the field of statistics too. The complexities and subtlety of consent – which could amount to not saying "no", the nodding of a head, accepting an invitation to go to bed, or not resisting increasingly adventurous advances from a man, more often than not at a time when alcohol or drugs can be affecting judgement – mean that there is a natural human frailty in attempting to answer questions on such topics some time after the event.

The statistical variation in prevalence rates generally arises according to how inclusive and wide-ranging are the definitions of rape. The simple question, "Have you been raped?", generally conjures up the image of a stranger leaping out of the bushes with a knife, and normally leads to a conclusion that the prevalence is low. At the other end of the spectrum would be found a woman who did not initially want to have sex perhaps but became persuaded to accept the situation in the heat of the moment, perhaps also feeling a little trapped in the situation, or perhaps under the influence of alcohol or drugs, or perhaps out of a sense of obligation. Either at that time or afterwards, the woman perhaps realised that she had had sex when she did not want to. The inclusion of cases like this will lead to a much higher rate of prevalence for non-consenting sex.

Section 71 • Transsexuals

There are no accurate figures for the number of transsexuals. The government has said that there might be around 5,000 transsexual people in the UK who will apply for legal recognition when the Gender Recognition Panels – set up to allow transsexuals to have legal recognition in their acquired sex – begin in 2005 accepting applications and roughly 300 new applicants each year. (source: Department for Constitutional Affairs, www.dca.gov.uk) The combination of the social stigma attached to being transsexual and a widespread lack of awareness of the true nature of the condition – and something that is often kept hidden – means it is only possible to collect statistics on the numbers of declared transsexuals and such figures undoubtedly represent only a proportion of those affected.

What are transsexuals?

Transsexuals are people with the deep conviction that their gender identity (believing oneself to be a man or a woman) does not match their appearance and/or anatomy. This condition is called gender dysphoria or gender identity disorder. The incongruity between identity and body is sometimes so strong that individuals are driven to present themselves in the acquired (opposite) gender. The government has stated that gender dysphoria is a medical condition that may need treatment and that that treatment may be carried out by the NHS (as well as privately).

Not very long ago estimates of the rate of occurrence of male-to-female transsexuality might have been around 1 in 100,000 of the male population. Today, with the greater awareness and openness that exists, some estimates now put the figure at greater than 1 in 10,000 – about 5–6,000 in Britain. It is known that other chromosomal or intersexed conditions can have rates of occurrence of, or approaching, 1 in 1,000 of the population and it may well be that this is the true order of magnitude of transsexuality. Rates of occurrence of known female-to-male transsexuals are significantly lower, typically being around a third to a quarter of the rate for male-to-female transsexuals. This rate has varied somewhat with time and between different parts of the world suggesting that varying cultural factors might play a role in the decision to be open about the condition.

However, when a number of the lobby groups ended the collection of data in October 2004 on the number of trans individuals who are likely to take advantage of the provisions of the Gender Recognition Act, it recorded just under 1000 people. (source: www.gendertrust.org.uk) Those replying were spread evenly over the age range, most had completed their transition in the last decade, and the number moving from male to female outnumbered the movers from female to male by over three to one.

There is no single common approach in other countries to transsexualism, however, all EU states except Ireland give legal recognition to gender change, as do a number of other countries in Europe and the Commonwealth and many American States. (For additional information see www.pfc.org.uk.)

Transsexuals and the census

For most people, the ten-yearly census is just another form to fill in but for transsexuals, it raises the question of how to legally and truthfully answer the question about sex. Because UK law has not fully recognised trans people in their true gender, the possibility arose that it would be impossible to provide a "truthful" answer that also matched legal requirements. As there is a legal obligation to complete the census form accurately, transsexuals faced an unpleasant dilemma. The Office for National Statistics did announce in advance of the 2001 census that transsexuals can give an answer which is both "truthful" and legal. It said trans women should record their sex as female if they believe that to be correct, even though their birth certificates will still say 'male' and that trans men should record their sex as male if they believe that to be correct, even though their birth certificates will still say 'female'. As there was no checking of census form responses against birth certificates, however, the census did not yield a figure for the number of transsexuals and the country.

Section 72 • Class – and other classifications

Statistics are usually compiled from a large set of individual observations. In order to make conclusions, these observations need to be grouped or 'classified'. A classification assigns items to categories according to shared characteristics and it provides a framework for the description and comparison of statistics. Classifications facilitate the accurate and systematic arrangement of data according to common properties so that the resulting statistics can be easily reproduced and compared over time as well as between different sources.

Classification might seem to be a dull issue, but is in fact an essential and deceptively important part of statistics. One of the key principles of the National Statistics Code of Practice is the promotion and use of common statistical frames, definitions and classifications. In the UK, three widely-used standard classifications are the: Standard Industrial Classification (SIC), Standard Occupational Classification (SOC), and the National Statistics Socio-economic Classification (NS-SEC). Other classifications are used throughout the government statistics machine, some having been developed by government departments while others have been taken directly from European or international use, and a range of other classification systems are available in the private sector, primarily from the marketing industry.

From 2001 the National Statistics Socio-economic Classification has been used for all official statistics and surveys. It replaced Social Class based on Occupation (formerly the Registrar General's Social Class) and Socio-economic Groups. This change was agreed following a major review of government social classifications commissioned in 1994 by the Office of Population Censuses and Surveys (now part of the ONS). The NS-SEC is an occupationally based classification but has rules to provide coverage of the whole adult population. The version of the classification which will be used for most analyses has eight classes, the first of which can be subdivided. For complete coverage of the population, the three categories "students", "occupations not stated or inadequately described", and "not classifiable for other reasons" are bundled together as "Not classified". In the census, the not clas-

The history of social classification

At the beginning of the 20th century, society was conceived as divided into three basic social classes (the upper, middle and working classes), but as researchers studied the problem they added intermediate categories. In the 1920s, a proper class scheme was made possible by the introduction of the first classification of occupations. This led to the introduction of a five class scheme which was used for the analysis of infant and occupational mortality and fertility. This structure not only gave a stronger emphasis to 'skill' than its predecessors, but there is a suggestion that it was constructed in the light of knowledge of mortality rates thereby producing the mortality gradients so cherished by researchers. (source: www.soc.surrey.ac.uk/sru)

The highest proportion of routine and semi-routine jobs occurs in the north east, 29% of the total, and the lowest in London, 15%

sified group made up one quarter of the population. The new official classification replaced the long-standing social class scale which classified people into five groups (represented by roman numerals), one subdivided.

The revision of government social classifications had to take account of a number of issues that had arisen with its predecessor systems. Principal among these are the unit of analysis problem (should a household continue to be categorised on the basis of the occupation of its head or the principle earner?), the relationship between gender and class, the appropriate reference occupation for the retired, the unemployed and other significant economically inactive groups (not all economically inactive people are in the same social category), and the even thornier problem of the relevance of "class" analysis to contemporary society and social scientific explanation.

It is probably inevitable that, for both pragmatic (they are based on routinely and widely-collected data) and theoretical reasons (it remains the case that a person's employment situation is a key determinant of life chances), an occupationally-based classification will remain at the heart of scientific and policy analyses for the foreseeable future. The operational categories of the NS-SEC can be aggregated to produce approximated classifications on both of the old bases using a mapping scheme set out on the ONS web site, www.statistics.gov.uk.

The old government socio-economic classification

I - Professional etc occupations

II - Managerial and technical occupations

III - Skilled occupations, subdivided into:

(N) non-manual and (M) manual

IV - Partly-skilled occupations

V - Unskilled occupations

The new government socio-economic classification

	% of UK, 2003
Higher managerial and professional occupations	10.8
subdivided into :	
1.1 Large employers and higher managerial	
1.2 Higher professional occupations	
Lower managerial and professional occupations	22.2
Intermediate occupations	10.3
Small employers and own account workers	7.7
Lower supervisory and technical occupations	9.4
Semi-routine occupations	13.3
Routine occupations	9.8
Never worked and long-term unemployed	16.5

source: Regional Trends, 38, ONS

While this single social classification has tidied up data coming from government sources, the private sector has been busy creating its own classifications. Terms like 'ABC1', based on the National Readership Survey categories, as a definition of consumer types, are often used to describe a profile of users or target customers. There are now a number of commonly used demographic, lifestyle and geodemographical classifications, such as Acorn produced by CACI and Mosaic produced by Experian, which are mainly used by marketing professionals, researchers and social and lifestyle commentators. Geodemographics combine the analysis of demographic lifestyle with geography that in turn has considerable value for companies involved with marketing or deciding where to establish new retail or entertainment locations.

The proven principle is that people living in similar neighbourhoods generally exhibit similar lifestyle and spending tendencies, and that as people change, they tend to move areas. The movement of people between different areas – as they move from being a student, to a flat share with other young professionals, to setting up the family home, and then settling elsewhere for retirement – is far greater than evolution of particular locations in the country. (source: for links and further information – www.mrs.org.uk and www.businessballs.com)

Such geodemographic classifications are used by marketing professionals to measure and target consumers. There are about 1.7 million postcodes in the UK with each accounting for around fifteen addresses on average. The Acorn and Mosaic classifications allocate every postcode area in the country to, in the case of Acorn, one of 54 neighbourhood types in 17 categories, and in the case of Mosaic, one of 61 types in 11 groups.

While few people will actively use these classifications, they are becoming a more common sight in commercial research papers. The classifications provide a thought-provoking profile of the range of different people in the country. (source: www.caci.co.uk and www.uk.experian.com. The Acorn profile, along with a brief description, for any postcode can be found on www.upmystreet.com)

National Readership Survey social grade definitions

A – upper middle-class, higher managerial, administrative or professional
B – middle class, intermediate managerial, administrative or professional
C1 – lower middle class, supervisory or clerical, junior managerial, administrative or professional
C2 – skilled working class, skilled manual workers
D – working class, semi and unskilled manual workers
E – those at the lowest level of subsistence, state pensioners or widows, casual or lowest grade workers

source: www.nrs.co.uk

Insight social value groups

	% of UK population
Self-actualisers	18%
Innovators	8%
Esteem seekers	23%
Strivers	10%
Contented conformers	24%
Traditionalists	11%
Disconnected	7%

Footnote: Sample descriptions: "strivers" – attaching importance to image and status as a means of enabling acceptance by their peer group, "disconnected" – detached and resentful, embittered and apathetic – www.insightmc.com

Section 73 • **Countryside**

Life expectancy is longer in the countryside and the number of deaths for under ones (a key measure of well-being) is lower – 4.1 per thousand births against 5.6 in urban areas

Things in the local area which most need improving

	Rural	Urban
Low level of crime	16	34
Clean streets	11	28
Low level of pollution	6	13
Education servcies	6	13
Open spaces and parks	3	11
Traffic congestion	14	24
Community activities	4	12
Public transport	34	25
Shopping facilities	18	12
Sport/leisure facilities	17	13

source: Countryside Agency report 2004, Mori. Note: 22 questions were asked and this table shows those where the gap between rural and urban was greatest

Until the late 1990s there was little information about the state of the countryside but as each year passes more becomes available. A major source of information (for England at least) is the Countryside Agency, the statutory champion and watchdog working to make "the quality of life better for people in the countryside" and "the quality of the countryside better for everyone". It is funded by the Department for Environment, Food and Rural Affairs (Defra).

2004 saw the first formal validation and adoption of new rural-urban indicators following cross-government co-operation. The latest figures show that about 14.1 million people (28% of the total) are defined as living in rural areas. But the population is not stable due to migration. According to the Countryside Agency's annual report, the migration from urban to rural is running at four times the rate of migration from the north of the country to the south. The only age group which does not have net migration to the rural areas is the 16–24 year olds – the young it seems are still tempted by the charms of the city. (source: www.countryside.gov.uk)

Life does not seem to be as bad in the countryside as is often portrayed. A survey conducted in 2004 by Mori asked town and country dwellers what is most in need of improving in their area. In all bar five of the 22 questions, the rural dwellers felt there was less need for improvement. The only three subject areas where those living in the country pointed to a clearly stronger need for improvement than their urban counterparts were: public transport, shopping and leisure/sport facilities.

Reducing recorded crime and the fear of crime is one of the government's stated rural "objectives" despite recorded crime being much higher in urban than rural areas. The incidence per thousand of population for burglary, violence against the person, theft of or from a car and sexual offences are roughly double in urban areas. Robbery is seven times as common in urban areas. Crime is lower in rural areas but rising in some categories while urban areas are generally experiencing a decline (from a higher level). The British Crime Survey – supposedly a better measure of crime (for those crimes that are covered by the survey), as many people do not report crimes to the police

– showed a rise in the number of rural dwellers experiencing violent crime in the year to 2002/03 and no change in burglary and vehicle related theft. There has been a slight decline in the fear of crime in both rural and urban areas.

Access of country dwellers to key services is one of the government's "headline rural indicators" but has generally fallen between 2000 and 2003. The sharpest fall has been in access to post offices while there has been an increase in the access to cash points and petrol stations. The increased occurrence of superstores and mini superstores at petrol stations are among the challenges faced by traditional village shops. Government policy is to maintain access to schools in part because they can be a vital focus for community life. 67 primary and 42 secondary schools closed in 2003 ("State of the country", 2004).

Another of the government's headline rural indicators relates to access to housing for the disadvantaged. Social housing accounts for only 13% of the

Percentage of rural households within set distances of key local services

	Distance	2000	2001	2002	2003
Bank and building society	4km	78	76	76	76
Cash point	4km	79	89	91	90
Post Office	2km	97	94	91	91
Petrol station	4km	87	86	94	93
Primary school	2km	92	92	92	91

source: SE regional research laboratory, "State of the countryside", 2004, www.countryside.gov.uk

housing stock in rural areas compared to 22% in urban areas. The stock has declined faster in the countryside than in built up areas adding to the pressure on housing affordability. Homelessness in the countryside has been rising faster since 1999 (when the figures started) but it still barely half the level (per 1000 inhabitants) of that seen in urban areas. The number of priority homeless in need of temporary accommodation is nearly seven times higher in urban areas (82,000 against 12,000 in 2002/03). The higher rates for urban areas could reflect the tendency of the homeless to head for towns. The number has risen in both years since 1999/2000 (by 62% and 44% respectively).

Stock of dwellings in public sector, %		
	Rural	Urban
1997	17.6	24.6
2000	14.1	23.6
2003	13.4	24.6

source: ODPM

In 2002, 80% of rural based adults had a driving licence compared to 68% of those in urban areas, reflecting in part the dependence on car travel

Percentage of households close to a bus stop			
	Population		
	over 250,000	3,000 –10,000	under 3,000
1996-98	97	70	35
1999-2000	98	73	48
2002	98	75	48

source: Dept of Transport in "State of the Countryside", 2004, GB, households within a 13 minute walk of a bus stop with a service of at least once an hour

In 2001 there were 135,000 second homes in England, 64% of which were in rural areas. Second homes account for 0.7% of the stock in so-called accessible rural areas and 2.5% in remote areas. Second homes are, however, concentrated in certain areas – Lake District, Northumberland and the coastal areas of Devon, Cornwall and Norfolk. Seven "output areas" have at least 9% of their housing stock classified as second homes: Isles of Scilly (25%), Berwick-upon-Tweed (14%), South Hams (13%), South Lakeland, Penwith, North Cornwall and Scarborough. Affordability of housing in rural areas has got worse in recent years – as it has everywhere.

The government set a target of increasing the percentage of rural residents who live within a 10-minute walk of an hourly bus service from 37% to 50% by 2010. The figures show that it rose from 35% to 48% by 2000 and was unchanged in 2002. This suggests that the target is on track to be met but also that most of the progress was made in bus access in the early years of the rural bus subsidy grant.

Government's headline rural indicators from the Rural White Paper
- Geographic availability of key services in rural areas
- % of people in rural wards in low income bands
- Educational qualifications of young people in rural areas
- Proportion of population disadvantaged in access to housing
- Proportion of households within a ten minute walk of an at least hourly bus service
- Recorded crime and fear of crime
- Employment activity and unemployment rates
- Proportion of market towns that are thriving, stable or declining
- New business start ups and business turnover
- Farming and non-farming income and agricultural employment
- Countryside quality – biodiversity, tranquillity, heritage and landscape character
- Farmland bird population
- River and air quality
- People using the countryside and type of visit
- Community vibrancy: number of meeting places, voluntary and cultural activities and parish elections.

source: www.defra.gov.uk

The government has set a number of targets but often the data did not exist. Either it still does not exist, or has been created but there is no history to judge against or was a proxy for what was trying to be measured.

The Countryside Agency has attempted to measure the scale of "food localisation", the extent to which food is being produced and consumed locally. The index, produced experimentally in 2004, uses indicators such as the number of organic farmers, local producers advertising in local directories, and the number of farmers' shops and markets. It showed that southern England performed well while the north east and Merseyside performed less well. It also noted that in many areas (except Kent and Devon, for example) the areas that scored well as producers were often not very good consumers, with production tending to dominate in the western part of the country and consumption in the east.

Urban hell?

There are 426 agglomerations in the world with over 1 million people. London is 19th with nearly 12 million people, Western Europe's largest. 51 of the agglomerations are in the US

source: www.citypopulation.de

Hunting

The prospect of a hunting ban had been one of the most highly charged political subjects of the last few years. There are no offical data related to the activity but the Burns enquiry, established in 1999, conducted plenty of research and offer probably the most widely accepted figures. It included a review of previous research which found some wild and varied estimates of all aspects of hunting. Burns estimated:

- There were 302 registered hunts in England and Wales
- Fewer than 1,000 people are employed directly by hunts, but around 6,000 to 8,000 full-time equivalent jobs depend on hunting of which about half are grooms.
- The average annual income of a hunt is just over £50,000, of which half comes from subscriptions and donations and a quarter from social events.
- 45,000 horses are used wholly or primarily for hunting and a substantial proportion would become redundant in the event of a hunting ban.
- Around 20,000 working dogs are employed in hunting and the majority would be destroyed as re-homing is not viable.
- 250,000 people are involved in organised hunting with dogs.

source: Burns Enquiry, 2000, www.huntinginquiry.gov.uk. Examples of additional figures which are conflicting are available on www.supportfoxhunting.co.uk, www.countryside-alliance.org, www.league.uk.com and http://hsa.enviroweb.org

Section 74 • Organic food

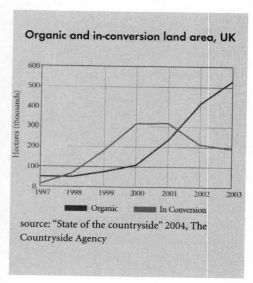

Organic and in-conversion land area, UK

source: "State of the countryside" 2004, The Countryside Agency

Sales of organic food exceeded £1 billion in 2003 for the first time and are growing at around 10% a year ("State of the countryside", annual report 2004, Countryside Agency, www.countryside.gov.uk). While the amount of land producing organic crops has risen every year, the area under conversion was lower in 2002 and 2003 than the previous two years as concerns have arisen about public support for the products. In 2002, 263 new farmers brought 20,000 hectares into the conversion scheme against a target of 650 and 45,000 respectively.

Imports accounted for over half (56%) of organic food and drink sold in the UK during 2002/03 – though this is a falling proportion from 65% in 2001/02 and 70% in the previous year. Soil Association figures show that the size of the organic grocery market is continuing to grow but at a slower rate than in the 1990s. People who choose organic food may do so for many reasons: they think it tastes better, believe that it is safer, more nutritious, better for the environment or better for animal welfare, or perhaps simply because it is more 'natural'. The FSA view is that, "the current scientific evidence does not show that organic food is any safer or more nutritious than conventionally produced food." (source: www.food.gov.uk)

There is little official data on organic farming – the government coming to the topic rather late in the day. The Department for Food and Rural Affairs (www.defra.gov.uk) does have some limited data (for England) but one of the main sources, the Soil Association's "Organic food and farming report" 2003, (www.soilassociation.org), is not available free of charge.

The Food Standards Agency conducted a survey on consumer attitudes to food standards in 2003 which showed that 6% of households claimed to contain at least one vegetarian member. The rates were slightly higher but still under one in ten for younger people and social categories AB. The rates were also a bit higher for those living in England and from black and minority ethnic groups. Some 4% ate fish but not meat. (source: www.vegsoc.org)

Section 75 • Mad cows

BSE (bovine spongiform encephalopathy) has a long history originating with the first recording of scrapie in sheep in 1732 leading through to the formal identification in a cow in 1985 and its spread to several herds in 1987. Changed regulations regarding animal feed were, at the time, regarded as measures to protect animal health, though the risk that BSE posed to human health had not been ignored. Officials at the now-defunct agriculture ministry (MAFF) had been concerned from the outset that BSE might pose a risk to human health as diseased cattle were going into the human food chain. While scrapie was not transmissible to humans, there was no certainty that the same would be true of BSE. In March 1996, the government did announce the possible link between BSE and cases of vCJD (variant Creutzfeldt Jakob Disease) in humans.

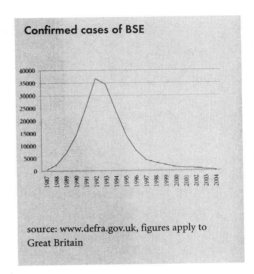

Confirmed cases of BSE

source: www.defra.gov.uk, figures apply to Great Britain

In 1996, when the link first became apparent, the then Government decided to ban the feeding of mammalian meat and bone meal to all farmed livestock, to strengthen controls on the removal of Specified Risk Material (SRM), and to introduce the Over Thirty Month (OTM) rule prohibiting the sale for human consumption in the UK of meat from cattle aged over 30 months at slaughter. Studies had suggested that cattle presented a much higher risk to consumers in the year before the onset of clinical disease which occurs at an average age of 5 years. The rule thus excluded higher risk cattle. One of the main public health control measures is the removal of SRM, which is estimated to remove over 99% of infectivity in cattle.

By 1996, however, the incidence of BSE had declined sharply from the peak year – 1992 – and the disease is now largely under control. Indeed, in April 2004 the European Food Safety Authority (EFSA) agreed that the UK's BSE risk status should be reduced from "high" to "moderate" (the same as most other EU countries). A crucial determining factor for the UK achieving the reduced risk status, was the ability to demonstrate that the incidence rate had fallen below the recently amended internationally agreed limit of 200 cases per million within the cattle population aged over 24 months, calculated over a 12 month period.

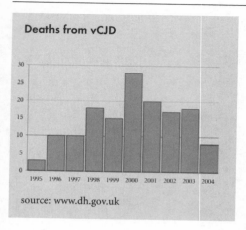

Deaths from vCJD

source: www.dh.gov.uk

Key findings from the BSE enquiry

The enquiry concluded:

● BSE caused a harrowing fatal disease for humans. Families all over the UK have been left wondering whether the same fate awaits them.

● A vital industry was dealt a body blow, inflicting misery on tens of thousands for whom livestock farming is their way of life. They have seen over 170,000 of their animals dying or having to be destroyed, and the precautionary slaughter and destruction of very many more.

● BSE developed into an epidemic as a consequence of an intensive farming practice - the recycling of animal protein in ruminant feed. This practice, unchallenged over decades, proved a recipe for disaster.

● In the years up to March 1996 most of those responsible for responding to the challenge posed by BSE emerged with credit. However, there were a number of shortcomings in the way things were done.

● At the heart of the BSE story lie questions of how to handle hazard - a known hazard to cattle and an unknown hazard to humans. The Government took measures to address both hazards. They were sensible measures, but they were not always timely nor adequately implemented and enforced.

● The Government did not lie to the public about BSE. It believed that the risks posed by BSE to humans were remote. The Government was preoccupied with preventing an alarmist over-reaction to BSE because it believed that the risk was remote. It is clear that this campaign of reassurance was a mistake. When on 20 March 1996 the Government announced that BSE had probably been transmitted to humans, the public felt that they had been betrayed. Confidence in government pronouncements about risk was a further casualty of BSE.

The slaughter of animals was the most visible part of the government response to the problem. By March 1996 approximately 160,000 cattle affected by BSE had been slaughtered – a total now at 180,000. In addition, about 35,000 cattle suspected of BSE, but not confirmed to have the disease, have been slaughtered. These figures can be compared with over 3.3 million cattle slaughtered and destroyed under the Over Thirty Month Scheme in the period from March 1996 to the end of 1999.

Foot and Mouth

Another mass cull of animals – around 4 million and mainly sheep – occurred in 2001 during the foot and mouth epidemic. Britain was declared foot and mouth free in January 2002.

The Department of Health publishes a press release each month detailing the latest information about the number of known cases of Creutzfeldt Jakob Disease. This includes cases of variant CJD – the form of the disease thought to be linked to BSE. At the end of 2004, there were 106 confirmed deaths from vCJD. In addition there are have been 39 probable deaths but without neuropathological confirmation, and an additional two deaths where the confirmation is pending, making a total of 147 deaths. In addition, there are five probable cases of vCJD where the individuals are still alive. Normally it is only possible to confirm the diagnosis with a post mortem.

An inquiry into BSE was announced in Parliament in December 1997, to establish and review the history of the emergence and identification of BSE and new variant CJD in the UK, and of the action taken in response to it; and to report to ministers. (source: www.bseinquiry.gov.uk) The outbreak of BSE is predominantly a problem for the UK, but other countries have also suffered.

Confirmed cases of BSE, up to and including 2004

Ireland	1439
France	940
Portugal	910
Spain	474
Switzerland	452
Germany	353
Belgium	126
Italy	160

Source: www.defra.gov.uk

Section 76 • Animal testing

Scientific procedures involving animals, millions

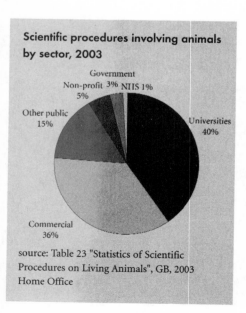

— Commercial — Public and non-profit - - Total

source: Table 23 "Statistics of Scientific Procedures on Living Animals", GB, 2003 Home Office

Scientific procedures involving animals by sector, 2003

Government 3%
Non-profit 5%
NHS 1%
Other public 15%
Universities 40%
Commercial 36%

source: Table 23 "Statistics of Scientific Procedures on Living Animals", GB, 2003 Home Office

The official figures do not answer the questions that are most likely to be asked – how many animals are killed, how many are subjected to testing that makes them suffer and to what extent do animals suffer during the testing?

They do show the number of animals that were used for the first time in any given year regardless of how often and for how long they were used. Each procedure is counted in the year it began and all are equal regardless of its nature or duration. It is unknown how quantitatively different these measures are from those that would be ideal. Procedures are counted in the data if they are covered by the Animals (Scientific Procedures) Act of 1986 and deemed to cause "suffering, distress and lasting harm." The re-use of an animal following the initial experiment is only permitted under certain circumstances. The data are collected from the establishments that are licensed under the Act.

The annual figures (only annual data are available) published by the Home Office (for GB) showed that the number of procedures rose 2.2% in 2003 to 2.79 million, the highest number since 1994. The number had declined steadily until the late 1990s and after several stable years it now seems to be on an upward trend. (source: www.official-documents.co.uk/document/cm62/6291/6291.pdf and Home Office, www.homeoffice.gov.uk, September 2004.)

Little information is given about the nature of the procedures but the bald figure – that there are nearly 3 million procedures – can conjure up a picture of immense suffering even if many of the procedures are breeding or taking a blood sample.

Most – 85% – of the procedures were on rodents with most of the rest on fish (6%) and birds (4%). Dogs (0.25%), cats (0.04%), horses (0.3%) and non-human primates (0.23%) collectively amounted to less than 1% of procedures. The number of procedures on non-human primates rose 21% to 4,800 in 2003 to a nine-year high. The number of procedures on mice was the highest since 1988 and the number on ungulates (animals with hooves) was also the highest since records began. The number on rats and rabbits was a record low.

How good are the figures?

The figures are not classified as National Statistics suggesting that they are of lower quality than many other figures or are subject to political pressure of one form or another. The Home Office points out the publication of statistics is not a statutory requirement and that the current publication "more than adequately meets" the requirement to publish only "such information as is considered appropriate". A broad indication of what the 2003 figures were going to show was on the BBC radio on the morning of 7 September despite the data not being released until later in the day - another indication that the numbers are not fully under the control of the statisticians. The Statistics Commission sensed a suspicion of "leaking", an attempt to "set the agenda", and investigated the event.

The Home Office announced in June 2003 that it had asked the Animal Procedures Committee to carry out a review of the statistics. (The report was due to be published by the end of 2004 but was running late, www.apc.gov.uk) A variety of issues are likely to be addressed, including:

- The development of a measure of suffering and the life experience of animals used in testing through use of a scoring system.
- The opinion of the House of Lords Committee that the data are hard to read and interpret.
- Whether genetically bred "normal" animals should continue to be classified as a "procedure". It has been argued that they should be separately categorised if the intention is to produce a normal animal.
- Anti vivisection groups have claimed that the current figures understate the degree of cruelty as many animals are killed without being involved in experiments as a result, for example, of over breeding.
- An expansion of the data on the particularly emotive topic of non-human primates.

It seems that no changes to the data will be made for 2 or 3 years. The procedures for collecting the data last changed in 1995 ruling out in many cases the possibility of longer runs of data.

Roughly half as many procedures take place now compared to 50 years ago and the government says that the number is minimised by the licensing

European league table for animal experiments, millions

1	France	2.3
2	UK	1.9
3	Germany	1.6
4	Italy	1.0
5	Belgium	0.8
6	Netherlands	0.6
7	Sweden	0.3
8	Denmark	0.3

source: www.ebra.org, EBRA, 1999 data

system in place. Yet many bodies – such as the British Union for the Abolition of Vivisection (www.buav.org), RSPCA, www.navs.org.uk, www.animalaid.org.uk and www.uncaged.co.uk – campaign for further cuts. They often say that the official figures understate animal suffering as they exclude "incidental" deaths for example those killed as a result of being surplus to requirements due to over breeding or dying before experiments. Caged animals used for breeding, which are killed at the end of their breeding life, are also excluded. One group – vivisection-absurd.org.uk – has estimated the number of animals involved in animal testing could be three times as many shown in the government figures – around 7½ million. They estimate this equates to an animal dying in a British laboratory every 4 seconds. There is no way of reconciling all the estimates and arriving at the "truth".

The government published a strategy in 2004 to tackle animal rights extremists and protect the scientific community and claims that the UK's licensing system is "the tightest in the world" and permits only essential research with clear medical benefits.

Upward pressures on the numbers comes from new molecular biology techniques (leading to new areas of research and an increase in the number of genetically modified animals) and EU pressures to increase the use of animals for human health and safety purposes. Breeding procedures accounted for the rise in 2003 and has been on an upward trend for the last decade.

About 40% of procedures used some form of anaesthetic to alleviate the severity of the procedures. The number of procedures in universities and medical schools has now overtaken (since 2000) the number in commercial premises. (These are the two types of institution responsible for the largest number of procedures.) The number in the public (and non-profit making) sector was a record high in 2003 having increased steadily since the mid-1990s and by 25% since 1997. The number in the commercial sector has fallen to a record low and makes up just over one-third of the total.

France conducts most animal experiments in Europe followed by the UK and Germany according to the latest data from EBRA, relating to 1999. The UK conducts most experiments on birds, agricultural animals and primates. France tops the league for rodents and Germany for rabbits and dogs.

Section 77 • Household waste

The UK produces over 400 million tonnes of solid waste per year – supposedly enough to fill London's Albert Hall every hour. But most of this comes from industry and commerce – notably mining, agriculture and construction.

There were 29.3 million tonnes of municipal waste collected in England in 2002/03, over half a tonne per person. The annual rise of 1.8% was lower than that seen on average since the survey began in 1996/97. The proportion going to landfill has declined from 77% to 75% in the latest year and for the first time the actual amount sent to landfill fell. (source: "Municipal waste management survey", 2002/03, The Department for Environment, Food and Rural Affairs, August 2004, www.defra.gov.uk)

The 7.3 million tonnes not sent to landfill (up from 6.4 million in the previous year) had some sort of value – for recycling, composting, energy recovery or the manufacture of "refuse derived fuel". Of this, the proportion incinerated has remained stable while that being recycled rose by two percentage points to 15½%. Nearly one-third of the recycled household waste was compostable, a similar proportion to the amount of paper and card that was recycled. Glass and scrap metal/white goods each made up just over 10%.

There is a competing set of data available from the Chartered Institute of Public Finance (Cipfa) in its "Waste Collection and Disposal Statistics

What is household waste?
Household waste includes household bin waste and also waste from civic amenity sites, other household collections, recycling sites, litter collections and street sweeping. Household waste represents about 90% of municipal waste, which is collected and managed by local authorities. It makes up just 8% of total waste arisings. Households pay less than £1 per week on average for these services. The total cost of all waste services in 2003/04 was £2.4 billion according to Cipfa, a 7% rise in the year, with households accounting for about one-third. Source: www.environment-agency.gov.uk

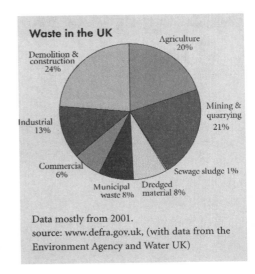

Waste in the UK

Data mostly from 2001.
source: www.defra.gov.uk, (with data from the Environment Agency and Water UK)

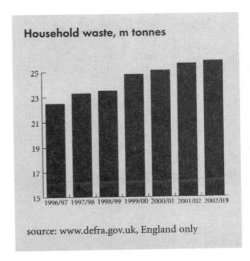

Household waste, m tonnes

source: www.defra.gov.uk, England only

The average household spends a sixth of its food budget on packaging

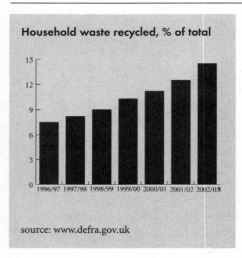

Household waste recycled, % of total

source: www.defra.gov.uk

Households in the south east recycle 4.8 kg per week, compared to 1.6 kg per week in the north east

51% of households have paper and card collected for recycling and one-third have no materials at all collected

2002/03" publication. The summary results can be found on their website www.cipfastats.net. The analysis is based on responses from 70% of authorities in England and Wales. The figures show that the overall recycling rates for England and Wales rose by 1½% to 12½% in 2002/03 – a lower rate but showing a similar trend to the government figures. Cipfa collects this data as it requires more detail than found in the government figures. The official government figures from Defra are for England only as the devolved assemblies collect their own data (Defra publishes the figures in association with

What is Cipfa?

The Chartered Institute of Public Finance is a leading professional accountancy body in the UK and the only one which specialises in the public services. Cipfa's Statistical Information Service (SIS) was established as a partnership between individual authorities and CIPFA and has been undertaking annual surveys of local authority operations since 1885. Their figures are generally thought to be impartial and offer a comprehensive account of the extent and achievements of each individual council helping to underpin the accountability of local authority services. It publishes many surveys each year, covering all the main activities of local government such as environmental health, homelessness, housing, libraries and many other locally delivered services. Few of their figures are quoted in this book as most are not freely and readily available.

GLA so that London is included in the England figures).

Britain's rate of recycling is lower than most other EU countries and is failing to hit domestic targets. For England and Wales, the government (Defra and the National Assembly) set targets for recycling or composting 25% of household waste by 2005, 30% by 2010 and 33% by 2015 (source: "Waste strategy for England and Wales, 2000, www.defra.gov.uk). These were set alongside statutory Best Value Performance Indicator targets for local authorities in 2003/04 and 2005/06 which equated to national figures of 17% and 25% respectively. (The targets are higher still in Wales and European rules foresee an even larger proportionate fall in the amount going to landfill by the middle of the next decade.)

Of the amount recycled, 3.7 million tonnes was collected from homes,

How surveys can be hit by privatisation

After the local government reorganisation of 1974, two surveys were set up to measure waste collection (by government and Cipfa) and disposal (by Cipfa alone). By the late 1980s response rates had fallen and the surveys were discontinued. The explanation for the fall was the introduction of compulsory competitive tendering for many services including waste collection. Authorities were concerned about the sensitivity of the data given they were now in a competitive environment. The surveys were relaunched in the mid-90s with a greater focus on EU regulations and environmental protection.

1.3 million tonnes from kerbside schemes and 2.5 million tonnes at civic amenity sites. Regional household waste recycling rates vary from a high of nearly 20% in the east and south east to 7% in the north east. The amount collected at civic amenity sites fell in the latest year – thought to be attributed to efforts councils are taking to stop trade waste from being taken there (by, for example, imposing height restrictions on vehicles entering).

Just over a half of local authorities provide wheeled bins for waste collection, a quarter supply plastic sacks and one in five provide nothing. Areas where wheeled bins are predominantely used generate more waste and recycle less. The higher amount of waste is thought to reflect the nature of the areas with bins which are more frequently the norm in areas of detached and semi-detached housing generally occupied by larger households.

Home composting is becoming more popular as two-thirds of local authorities distribute bins for use at home – though only one in ten do so free of charge. Authorities have now distributed around 1¾ million bins to homes and 40% have carried out promotional visits to homes.

Less data is published about non-household waste. Sewage is a major waste and most of it is treated, leaving sewage sludge. Because dumping sewage sludge at sea was banned in 1998, it has been applied to farmland, incinerated and land filled. Recycling sewage sludge to soil can provide valuable nutrients and organic matter but the Environment Agency regulates the process to ensure that pathogens do not enter the food chain and to avoid the build up of harmful substances in soils.

17 billion plastic bags are handed out annually by the major supermarket chains, enough to cover Sussex and Surrey

Fridge mountain

In the wake of the European environment laws that came into force in 2002, it became illegal to dump fridges and 2½ million are disposed of each year in the UK in landfill sites unless CFCs, harmful to the ozone layer, were removed first. The government signed up to the regulation before facilities were in place to recycle or burn the fridges, leading to the stockpiles, known as "fridge mountains" springing up across the country. The scale of the problem meant the Environment Agency allowed the private companies which took the old fridges to operate without site licences. (Source: www.environment-agency.gov.uk) It is thought there were over 1 million old fridges in storage at the peak. As is often the case for issues that arise without warning, no official figures are available.

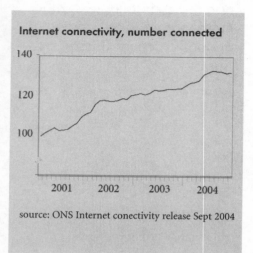

Internet connectivity, number connected

source: ONS Internet conectivity release Sept 2004

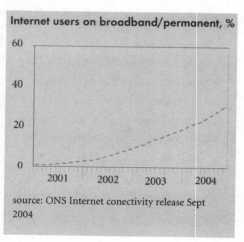

Internet users on broadband/permanent, %

source: ONS Internet conectivity release Sept 2004

Section 78 • **Internet age**

E-enablement, the digital age, and the knowledge economy, are among the descriptions for one of the hottest topics of the last few years. Yet there are next to no data available from the official sources to judge how great a change this revolution represents. The lack might reflect partly the difficulty in pinning down what is meant by this particular revolution and partly its newness (statisticians are rarely quick to get new surveys up and running), nonetheless little information is available.

The ONS started a survey of access to the internet but there is little else. Another ONS survey measures the value of e-commerce but it presents only annual results. (source: www.statistics.gov.uk) The latter showed that £23 billion of sales, just 1.2% of total sales, were made online in 2002. About one-quarter of that was to households.

The annual report from the government's e-envoy (a job created in 1999 to drive a programme of work "to make the UK a leading knowledge economy") contains facts drawn from a variety of sources but little in the way of hard data in time series form. (source: "UK online, annual report, 2003, Cabinet Office) Indeed, that report was the last from the e-envoy, who signed off, saying the job was done, and that opportunities to access the internet are "now available to all".

Subsequent data from the ONS suggests that there is more work to do. It showed there has been barely any increase in the number of companies with a website or using the internet in 2003 – and four out of ten businesses are still not hooked up. There was a large jump in the number businesses – to 29% in 2003, up from 13% in 2002 – that bought goods and services over the internet, although much of the activity was limited to stationery and computer software purchases. But only 5% of businesses used the internet for sales in 2003, up fractionally in the year.

The divergent trend between companies' use for buying and selling is partly explained by some suppliers requiring their wholesaling or retailing customers to use the net. The new experimental statistics, from the annual e-commerce survey, published in November, revealed the extent of the gap between large and small businesses with the former having much greater information and communication technologies (ICT) usage. It also reported that three out of ten businesses did not have access to a personal computer in 2003, though they were mostly smaller businesses with fewer than 50 employees.

The percentage of businesses with internet access increased from 59% in 2002 to 62% in 2003. Almost all large businesses had access but more than two out of five small businesses still did not. One in four businesses used broadband as the primary method of internet connection at the end of 2003, a rise from one in seven in 2002. Some 52% of firms had email. The number of people with access to the internet at work rose to 7.1 million at the end of 2003 – just over one-third of workers – from 6.5 million at the end of 2002. 31% of businesses reported having a website in 2003, compared to 29% in 2002. The survey which questioned 12,000 firms covered businesses classified to the non-financial sector. (source: www.statistics.gov.uk)

The Oxford Internet Institute has conducted a survey that gives a fuller picture of the progress being made in bringing the new technology to the people. It found that the average person has access to the internet in at least two out of four places: home, work, school or at a public library. Only four percent of the British population lacks ready access to a place where they could sign on to the internet. The lack of a computer at home is not a major obstacle, since the average internet user goes on line away from home as well as at home. Nor is having a computer at home a sufficient reason for using the internet. (source: Oxford Internet Survey, Oxford Internet Institute, 2003, www.oii.ox.ac.uk, this periodic survey is expected to be repeated in 2005)

Among Britons age 14 and over, 59% used the internet in 2003. The biggest difference between users and non-users is age. Among those still in school, 98% are users and among people of working age, 67%. By contrast, only 22% of retirees use the internet. Educational differences are less important. All youngsters, whether or not they are numerate or literate, appear able to click on the internet.

Once on line, the average person finds multiple uses for the internet. The most popular are to get information, browsing, email, and shopping and youths tend to make more use of the web for studies than for music or entertainment. Between a tenth and a fifth of users employ the net to get news, banking or public services.

> One third of workers have internet access at work

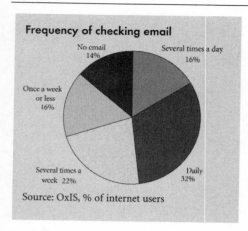

Frequency of checking email

Source: OxIS, % of internet users

The survey showed that among the two-fifths who are not users, it is not fear or dislike of using electronic technology that holds them back, rather they don't see how it will help them in their everyday affairs. Half of the non-users are informed but indifferent about the internet – they know someone who could send an email or get information for them but have not bothered to ask for this to be done. An additional one in fifteen are proxy users, who have asked for a friend to sign on the internet on their behalf. One in seven are excluded because they do not know anyone who could send get on on their behalf, and this group divides equally into those who are anti-technology and those who are apathetic.

The survey concluded that, "Government and commerce will have to wait a generation or more before nine-tenths of Britons regularly use the internet" suggesting that the government still needs to do some promotional work.

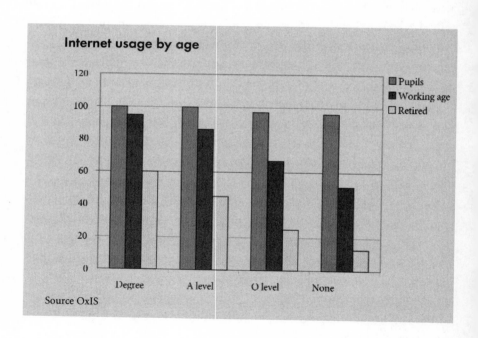

Source OxIS

Glossary

Accrual accounting – records flows when the economic value is created or exchanged, irrespective of when cash is paid or received.

Artefact – an artificial result, in particular a mistaken or biased result produced by the measuring instruments rather than by the phenomenon being studied, or something the researcher created by the way he or she gathered or analysed the data.

Ascending order – data arranged so that each item in the series is higher than the previous items.

Average – see mean.

Balance of payments – a statement that summarises the economic transactions of an economy with the rest of the world.

Bar chart or bar graph – a way of depicting a frequency distribution for nominal or discrete variables, such as religious affiliation or place of residence. Rectangles are drawn with lengths proportionate to the magnitudes concerned.

Base year – the time period from which relative levels are measured and which is usually allocated the value of 100 in an index.

Basis points – in some fields, such as finance, where very small percentage changes are significant, measurement might be in basis points. A basis point is 100th of 1%. An interest rate increase of ¼% might be described as being of 25 basis points.

Bivariate – relating to two variables only.

Census – a survey of an entire population – in contrast to a survey of a sample.

Chain linking – a method of constructing one index series from two or more index series of different base periods or different weights.

COFOG – classification of the functions of government.

COICOP – classification of individual consumption by purpose.

Compound growth – a series of numbers where the difference between them is found by multiplying the preceding number by a fixed amount. For example, if 100 grows as a compound rate of 5% per annum, it would value 121.55 after four years.

Confidence interval – a range of values of a sample statistic that is likely, at a given level of probability, called confidence level, to contain a population parameter. For example, if you weighed a sample of children from a school, you might be able to say that you were 95% confident that the average weight of children in the school was between 22 and 24 kilograms.

Constant prices – constant prices refer to volume measures whose values are derived by applying to current quantities, prices pertaining to a specific base period. They allow figures to be represented so that the effects of inflation are removed. The values for each time period are expressed in terms of the prices in some base period, such as 2000.

Current prices – Current prices are the actual or estimated recorded monetary value over a defined period for, for example, a group of industries or products. They show the value for each item expressed in terms of the prices of that period.

Data – information collected by a researcher normally thought of as statistical or quantitative.

Dataset – a collection of related items, such as the answers given by respondents to the questions in a survey.

Decile – one of the points that divides a frequency distribution into ten equal parts – for example, 10% of cases fall below the first decile and 20% below the second.

Deflator – A price index used to produce a set of volume measures from a set of current values.

Demography – the statistical study of the characteristics of human communities and their populations, such as size, growth, density and distribution.

Denominator – the part of the fraction that is below the line.

Devisor – another term for denominator.

ECB – European Central Bank

EEA – The European Economic Area came into being in 1994 following an agreement between EFTA and the EU, to allow EFTA countries to participate in the European single market without having to join the EU.

EFTA – European Free Trade Association – established in 1960 as an alternative for European states that did not wish to join the European Union. Original membership was the UK, Denmark, Norway, Sweden, Austria, Switzerland and Portugal, with Finland, Iceland and Liechtenstein subsequently joining. Current membership is Iceland, Norway,

Switzerland and Liechtenstein.

ESA – European System of National and Regional Accounts – an integrated system of economic accounts. The UK National Accounts have been based on the European System of National Accounts 1995 (ESA 95) since September 1998. Prior to this they were based on ESA79 which is still in use for compiling the Gross National Product.

EU-15 – Austria, Belgium, Denmark, Finland, France, Germany, Greece, Ireland, Italy, Luxembourg, the Netherlands, Portugal, Spain, Sweden, and the UK. The EU increased from 10 members to 12 in 1986 when Portugal and Spain acceded, and grew to 15 in 1995 with the addition of Austria, Finland and Sweden.

EU-25 – the EU-15 plus the ten countries which joined in May 2004 – Cyprus, Czech Republic, Estonia, Hungary, Latvia, Lithuania, Malta, Poland, Slovakia and Slovenia.

Euro area – the area comprising the 12 EU member states which adopted the Euro. Sometimes called the Eurozone or Euroland.

Eurostat – the statistical office of the EU.

Factor cost – output less the value of any taxes less subsidies.

Frequency distribution – a tally of the number of times each score occurs in a group of scores or a way of presenting data that shows the number of cases having each of the attributes of a particular variable.

G7/G8 – the "Group of seven" is a coalition of the major industrial democracies – the UK, France, Germany, Italy, Japan, the US and Canada. The G7 was in part superseded by the addition of Russia in 1998 to create the G8.

Geometric mean – the nth root of the product of the distribution. This average is used to measure changes in the rate of growth. If there are three items, it is the third root (cubed root) of the items multiplied together.

Graph – a diagram showing the relationship between two variables. It can be in many forms, such as line chart, bar graph or histogram.

Gross – before any deductions. For example, gross income is income before deducting tax.

Gross domestic product – the sum of all the values added of all resident units engaged in production.

Growth rate – if output increases by 5% between year one and year two, it is said to have a growth rate of 5%. It is important to distinguish between different growth rates, including: the change during a year (from December of one year to December in the next year), the change between successive calendar or financial years, the change over any specified 12 months or four quarters, or annualised change (the change over a month or quarter grossed up to cover the year).

Hedonics – a method used to estimate the effects of quality change on prices, based on the idea that products can be trated as bundles of characteristics to which prices can be attached.

ILO – International Labour Organisation, a UN agency promoting social justice and internationally recognised human and labour rights.

Index numbers – values expressed in relation to a single base figure, often set at 100, and designed to show changes over a period of time. The indices may be of prices, quantities or values. For example, if the industrial output of an economy rose by 5% in one year, output in the second year can be said to be 105% of the base year. In index terms, output in the two years is 100 and 105.

Law of averages – the principle that random errors in measurement will tend to balance one another out, suggesting that the average is the best estimate of the true value.

Law of large numbers – the larger the sample, the more likely, other things being equal, it is to represent the population from which it was drawn – specifically the more likely it is the sample mean will equal the population mean.

Mean – the arithmetic mean, or the average, is the sum of all the items divided by the number of them. An average is useful as it can summarise a group of figures, smoothing out abnormalities to help comparison. While the mean can provide a simple mental picture of the distribution it represents, it can also conceal important facts. Averages provide the first stage of investigation but not all the information required for many purposes. One disadvantage of the mean is that it may not correspond to an actual value, making the figure looked unrealistic. For example, the mean number of legs possessed by the population of the country is 1.99 – nearly everyone has two legs but a few people have one or none bringing down the average and leading to a clearly meaningless statistic. The word "average" is often used very loosely in daily conversation.

Measurement errors – when the response differs from the "true" value. Can be due to the respondent, interviewer, questionnaire etc. Can be random or biased.

Median – the middle score in a set of ranked scores. It is a preferable measure to the mean when there are a few items of very high of very low value that could make the mean unrepresentative of the distribution. For example, median income might be more useful than mean income, as a small number of very high earners can distort the mean. When the number of scores is even, there is no single middle score, in which case the median is found by taking an average of the two middle scores. See also mean.

Metadata – information describing and defining data.

Mode – the most common or most frequent score in a set of scores. See also mean. As the mode is an actual value, it often appears to be realistic and sensible to users.

Moving average – a method of smoothing the data. Individual observations are replaced by an average of each observation and the observations on either side of it. For example, if monthly data are very erratic, the series might be presented as a three month moving average.

NACE – Nomenclature generale des activites economiques dans les communates europeennes, the general industrial classification of the EU.

Numerator – the number above the line in a fraction. The number into which the denominator is divided.

OECD – the Organisation for Economic Co-operation and Development is a grouping of 30 developed countries accepting basic principles of democracy and free market economy.

Odds – the ratio of success to failure in probability calculations. For example, the odds of drawing a heart from a deck of cards are 13 to 39, or 1 to 3. By contrast, the probability of drawing a heart is 0.25 or one out of four.

OPEC – Organisation of Petroleum Exporting Countries – a grouping of 11 countries organised for the purpose of negotiating with oil companies on petrol production and prices. Founded in 1960, its members hold roughly three quarters of the world's oil reserves and supply just under half of the world's oil.

Outlier – a unit of analysis that has extreme values of the variable. Outliers are important because they can distort the interpretation of data or make misleading a statistic that summarises values. See the difference between mean, median and mode.

Percent – %, per hundred, one part in 100. Commonly used for describing increases or decreases over time. If the price of an item has increased from £10 to £11, it is said to have risen by 10%.

Percentage point – if the inflation rate increases from 4% to 5%, it is said to have risen by 25% or, more meaningfully, one percentage point.

Pie chart – a circle with areas, or slices, marked to represent the proportion of total units in each category.

Population – a group of persons (or institutions, events, or other subjects) that is being described or studied.

Primary data – data collected by or for the people who are going to make use of it. Primary data is in contrast to secondary data.

Quartiles – while a median divides a distribution into half, the quartiles divide it into four equal parts. The difference between the upper and lower quartile is called the inter-quartile range.

Random sampling – selecting a group of subjects from a larger group so that each individual is chosen entirely by chance. Sometimes called equal probability sampling. Alternative sampling frameworks include probability sampling, cluster sampling, quota sampling and stratified random sampling.

Range – a measure of variability, of the spread or the dispersion of values. In its most crude form, you subtract the lowest value or score from the highest.

Ratio – a combination of two numbers that shows their relative size. The relationship between the numbers can be expressed as a fraction, a decimal, or simply separating them with a colon.

Rounding – fractions and decimals are frequently rounded to the nearest whole number. Sometimes numbers are rounded to the nearest 50 or 100. Different organisations have different conventions for rounding – some will round up or down, rather than to the nearest whole number. Sometimes data are truncated – the final, unwanted digits are omitted. Components may not add to the total when rounded.

Sample – a group of subjects selected from a larger group in the hope that studying the small group will reveal the key features of the larger group. Samples are used because they are cheaper and quicker than a full census of the population, and total accuracy is rarely required.

Scatter plot – also called a scatter diagram and scattergram – is the pattern of points that results from plotting two variables on a graph.

Seasonality – a process of seasonal adjustment can adjust raw data for any seasonal pattern, for example, retail sales are higher around the Christmas period. For some purposes it is useful to conduct analysis without the seasonal pattern affecting the data.

Secondary data – secondary data are used by people other than the people for whom the data were collected. It is important to know as much about the data as possible to reduce the possibility of misinterpretation. Consider, for example: how the data has been collected, processed, its accuracy, and how it has been summarised into categories or tables. Data may come from administrative sources or specially conducted enquiries or surveys.

Significant figures – rounding to a number of significant figures is a process by which the number of digits that are significant are stated and, after that number, zeros replace other digits.

Skewed distribution – a distribution of scores or measures that, when plotted on graph, produce a nonsymmetrical curve.

Spurious accuracy – spurious accuracy is implied when a figure is given in greater detail that can be justified. Annual inflation rates are quoted to one decimal point, for example 2.1%, because it is deemed to be accurate to such detail. To give a figure of 2.164% would be spurious.

Standard deviation – a measure of dispersion which uses all the values in a distribution. It is a more sophisticated measure than the range or the inter-quartile range. It shows the dispersion of values around the arithmetic mean. Therefore, a distribution with an arithmetic mean of ten and a standard deviation of four has a wider dispersion than a similar distribution with a standard deviation of two. In a "normal" distribution, 95% of the observations would be within two standard deviations of the mean and 99% within three.

Survey – the drawing of a sample of subjects from a population to make inferences about the population.

System of National Accounts – an internationally agreed, consistent and comprehensive set of rules relating to macroeconomic accounts.

Time series – a set of measures of a single variable recorded periodically over time, such as the inflation rate in the UK during the 1990s. Time series can be separated into different types of trend: the long-term trend, cyclical fluctuations, seasonal variations, and irregular fluctuations.

Value terms – or current prices, nominal prices or nominal terms. A time series which includes the effects of inflation.

Volume terms – or constant prices or real terms. The volume change in a product is the change in its value divided by the price change, in other words excluding the impact of inflation. From year to year, industrial output generally rises, but some part of that increase is due to increased prices. Extracting the part due to price increases leaves the volume increase in industrial output.

Weighted mean – a procedure for combining the means of two or more groups of different sizes, taking the sizes of the groups into account when computing the overall mean.

X-axis – the horizontal axis on graph.

Y-axis – the vertical axis on graph